CAMBRIDGE STUDIES IN EARLY MODERN HISTORY

Editors

J. H. ELLIOTT   OLWEN HUFTON
H. G. KOENIGSBERGER

Renaissance and Revolt

CAMBRIDGE STUDIES IN EARLY MODERN HISTORY

Edited by Professor J. H. Elliott, The Institute for Advanced Study, Princeton, Professor Olwen Hufton, University of Reading and Professor H. G. Koenigsberger, King's College, London

The idea of an "early modern" period of European history from the fifteenth to the late eighteenth century is now widely accepted among historians. The purpose of the Cambridge Studies in Early Modern History is to publish monographs and studies which will illuminate the character of the period as a whole, and in particular focus attention on a dominant theme within it, the interplay of continuity and change as they are represented by the continuity of medieval ideas and political and social organisation, and by the impact of new ideas, new methods and new demands on the traditional structures.

Renaissance
and
Revolt

Essays in the intellectual and social history of

early modern France

~~~~~~

J. H. M. SALMON

The right of the
University of Cambridge
to print and sell
all manner of books
was granted by
Henry VIII in 1534.
The University has printed
and published continuously
since 1584.

CAMBRIDGE UNIVERSITY PRESS
Cambridge
London   New York   New Rochelle
Melbourne   Sydney

Published by the Press Syndicate of the University of Cambridge
The Pitt Building, Trumpington Street, Cambridge CB2 1RP
32 East 57th Street, New York, NY 10022, USA
10 Stamford Road, Oakleigh, Melbourne 3166, Australia

First published 1987

Printed in the United States of America

Library of Congress Cataloging-in-Publication Data
Salmon, J. H. M. (John Hearsey McMillan), 1925–
Renaissance and revolt.
(Cambridge studies in early modern history)
Includes bibliographies and index.
1. France–Intellectual life–16th century.
2. France–History–16th century. 3. France–Social
conditions. I. Title. II. Series.
DC33.3.S25 1987 944'.028 86-33416
ISBN 0 521 32769 5

For Jan and Ashley

Contents

~~~~~~

Acknowledgements

Ten of the essays in this collection have previously appeared in print and permission to include them in this collection is gratefully acknowledged. Details are as follows:

"Cicero and Tacitus in Sixteenth-Century France," *American Historical Review*, 85 (1980), 307–31.

"Protestant Jurists and Theologians in Early Modern France: The Family of Cappel," *Die Rolle der Juristen bei der Entstehung des modernen Staates*, ed. Roman Schnur (Duncker and Humblot, Berlin, 1986), pp. 357–79.

"French Satire in the Late Sixteenth Century," *Sixteenth Century Journal*, 6 (1975), 57–88.

"Rohan and Interest of State," *Staatsräson*, ed. Roman Schnur (Duncker and Humblot, Berlin, 1975), pp. 121–40.

"Bodin and the Monarchomachs," *Verhandlungen der internationalen Bodin Tagung*, ed. Horst Denzer (C. H. Beck, Munich, 1973), pp. 359–78.

"An Alternative Theory of Popular Resistance: Buchanan, Rossaeus and Locke," *Diritto e potere nella storia europea*, ed. Bruno Paradisi (Leo S. Olschki, Florence, 1982), pp. 823–49.

"Venality of Office and Popular Sedition in Seventeenth-Century France," *Past and Present*, 37 (1967), 21–43.

"Peasant Revolt in Vivarais, 1575–1580," *French Historical Studies*, 11 (1979), 1–28.

"The Paris Sixteen, 1584–1594: The Social Analysis of a Revolutionary Movement," *Journal of Modern History*, 44 (1972), 540–76.

"The Audijos Revolt: Provincial Liberties and Institutional Rivalries under Louis XIV," *European History Quarterly*, 14 (1984), 119–49.

A short version of the paper on Gallicanism and Anglicanism was presented in 1985 at the Folger Library Seminary at the invitation of Donald R. Kelley.

I should like to thank G. R. Elton for encouraging me to publish this volume, and Roland Mousnier for his support over the years. I have benefited greatly from the helpful criticism of my wife, Janet Oppenheim. In the preparation of these papers for publication I am grateful to two graduate students, Adrianna Bakos and Barbara Whitehead. The cost of typing and copying was met by the Madge Miller Fund of Bryn Mawr College.

Introduction

METHODS AND APPROACHES

These papers, written over the past twenty years, are the outcome of an even longer period of preoccupation with the history of early modern France. This involvement began when I arrived at Cambridge University from New Zealand in 1953 with the intention of studying the ideas of Jean Bodin and their impact upon English political thought. The project widened into a comparative study of French and English ideas. Perhaps it was relevant to the theme which emerged from my research that, fresh from what was then a colonial background, I resented certain assumptions, doubtless misperceived, about the nature of the English past, and turned to a French counter-model where discontinuity, social protest, and a vein of rationalist idealism presented alternatives to stability, the acceptance of status, and the much vaunted methods of British empiricism. A growing appreciation of the tolerance and respect for academic values that prevailed among my mentors eventually tempered my brashness. An argument appeared: that the ideas generated in the French wars of religion were taken up on a massive scale by English controversialists in the subsequent age and applied to a parallel set of conflicts across the Channel. In consequence English liberalism was much less the product of native experience than it was reputed to be.[1] While this hypothesis, like many revisionist interpretations, was partly the unconscious result of my own conditioning, the evidence for it seemed then, and seems still, entirely to justify the conclusion. It resulted, however, in the subordination of ideas to contingent political events, and owed far more to the methods then in vogue at Cambridge than I realised at the time.

Many of these essays have tried to restore the balance. They have been written in the belief that intellectual and social history should complement each other, if not actually be conjoined in an endeavour to reach a more general understanding. Ideas can be a stimulus to action as well as a means of legitimating the outcome of events. They do not always follow a logical sequence, for no

[1] J. H. M. Salmon, *The French Religious Wars in English Political Thought* (Oxford, 1959).

I

theory of political obligation or social change is immune to the vagaries of human fears and ambitions when it is applied to, or arises from, actual problems of human conflict. In times of stability there are always voices of protest to mobilise discontents and to identify contradictory elements in reigning orthodoxies. In times of revolutionary change the defenders of the status quo invariably discover inconsistent aspects in the attitudes of their opponents. It is not surprising that the temptations of expediency and the desire to invoke tradition sometimes produce paradoxes and appeal as much to mystiques as to reason. The sixteenth and seventeenth centuries were times of flux and conflict in France, and it is in the most intense crises that previously unconscious assumptions rise to the surface to expose forces of change in what outwardly seem the most durable of structures. I have not tried to represent ideas as the determinants of historical process, but rather to see them as both signposts and accelerators of shifts in the pattern of society. Each problem, whether it concerns a new direction in the intellectual habits of the élite or a revolt by the unprivileged masses, has been treated within its own context, and the evidence has determined the priorities in its interpretation.

Before the triumph of the school of historians associated with the journal now known as *Annales: Économies, sociétés, civilisations,* attempts to connect social and intellectual history tended either to see theory and belief about politics and society as the reflection of mechanisms of change dependent upon material forces, or to give religion and ideology a positive role in transforming human institutions. Montesquieu identified two kinds of underlying causes in history, the physical and the moral, and those who sheltered under the Marxist umbrella of economic determinism were heirs to the former, just as those who sociologised in the Weberian mode assumed the mantle of the latter. On the other hand, the tradition in the history of ideas prevailing in the English-speaking world, and also in French academic circles, was suspicious of grand theory and had no wish to integrate the subdisciplines of history. It detached ideas from their social context and investigated them analytically in order to discern patterns of influence, to trace intellectual pedigrees, to establish climates of opinion, and to explain intrinsic meaning.[2] The result was often a Whiggish kind of history where modern concerns dictated the material chosen and the conclusions reached.[3] Its practitioners made vague contact with legal and constitutional history, but incurred the contempt of political and diplomatic historians, who tended to regard professed principles as smokescreens to conceal the pursuit of real interests.

It was against narrow professionalism and a preoccupation with discrete

[2] E.g. Carl L. Becker, *The Heavenly City of the Eighteenth-Century Philosophers* (New Haven, Conn., 1932); J. N. Figgis, *From Gerson to Grotius, 1414–1625* (Cambridge, 1907); Alan Lovejoy, *The Great Chain of Being* (Cambridge, Mass., 1936); Pierre Mesnard, *L'Essor de la philosophie politique au XVIe siècle* (Paris, 1936).

[3] E.g. C. H. McIlwain, *Constitutionalism and the Changing World* (Cambridge, Mass., 1939); Karl Popper, *The Open Society and Its Enemies* (4th ed., 2 vols., Princeton, 1963).

events on the part of political and diplomatic historians that Lucien Febvre and Marc Bloch, the founders of the *Annales* movement, reacted. They turned to social history and associated with it the study of mental habits and attitudes to life and death. When they wrote upon ideas they did not link them with political events, but preferred to investigate such problems as whether atheism could exist in the sixteenth century, or how it was that people could believe in the magical healing power of kings.[4] The next generation expressed an outright hostility to history as event, partly from distaste for diplomatic and military history in the aftermath of the Second World War, and partly under the spell of those atemporal social scientists with whom the first generation had been linked. *L'histoire événementielle* came to be denounced by Fernand Braudel as an abnegation of the historian's true responsibility. It was not only that the minutiae of individual actions seemed to trivialise the past; it was also that the kind of evidence consulted by the political historians, despite their archival expertise, inhibited certain and meaningful generalisation. Furthermore, history as the realm of the political fact and the personal decision appeared to some within the movement as the expression of liberal bourgeois ideology.

Hence the *annalistes* looked towards a time frame that transcended the actions of individuals and subordinated personality to collective mentality. In the vast perspective of the *longue durée* problems of objectivity disappeared, and so, too, did the unsatisfying relativism that caused history to be constantly rewritten as the criteria of what was important in the past varied from one generation to the next. This, as Thucydides had once boasted, was indeed history for all time, and yet time, it seemed, had all but vanished from consideration. Even within the shorter span of *conjoncture* acknowledged by the *annalistes*, change was slow and continuity the norm. Concepts imported from geography and anthropology gave a static air to explanation. Quantitative history affirmed the slow pulsation of demographic shifts and revealed an alternation of times of dearth and times of plenty. Emmanuel Le Roy Ladurie declared that "history which is not quantifiable cannot claim to be scientific," and extolled "present-day historiography with its preference for the quantifiable, the statistical and the structural."[5] His own work on peasant society in Languedoc took its place beside Braudel's study of the Mediterranean basin, Pierre Goubert's analysis of Beauvais, and Pierre Chaunu's serial accounting of Atlantic shipping – all of them cast in the early modern period.[6] What was achieved in terms of certitude, and

[4]Marc Bloch, *Les Caractères originaux de l'histoire rurale française* (Oslo, 1931), and *Les Rois thaumaturges: étude sur le caractère surnaturel de la puissance royale* (Paris, 1923); Lucien Febvre, *Philippe II et la Franche-Comté* (Paris, 1912), and *Le Problème de l'incroyance au XVIe siècle: la religion de Rabelais* (Paris, 1942).

[5]*The Territory of the Historian*, tr. Ben Reynolds and Sian Reynolds (Chicago, 1979 [1973]), pp. 15, 111. The quotations come from papers first published in 1968 and 1972 respectively.

[6]Emmanuel Le Roy Ladurie, *Les Paysans de Languedoc* (2 vols., Paris, 1966); Fernand Braudel, *La Méditerranée et le monde méditerranéen à l'époque de Philippe II* (Paris, 1949); Pierre Goubert, *Beauvais et le Beauvaisis: contribution à l'histoire sociale de la France au XVIIe siècle* (2 vols., Paris, 1960); Pierre Chaunu and Huguette Chaunu, *Séville et l'Atlantique* (9 vols., Paris, 1954–9).

it was no small achievement, was described as stability, not as change. In all this, intellectual history had little part to play. The realm of conscious ideas belonged to the passing parade. The historian perceived ultimate reality but the transient individual was always the dupe of his time. Braudel eventually came to justify his approach in terms of grand theory, and cited Werner Sombart's aphorism "No theory, no history."[7] One could reply, "No change, no history."

Febvre and Bloch had perceived collective patterns of belief underlying the particular articulation of ideas that had interested them. Robert Mandrou sought to identify these patterns in an analysis of French sixteenth-century society which he called an "essay in psychological history."[8] It was a part of the series *L'Evolution de l'humanité*, founded by Henri Berr to integrate the social sciences, and it revealed the interdisciplinary ideals that had inspired the movement from the outset. This was a work anticipating the future direction of *Annales* and summarising much that had gone before. After describing the material conditions of life, it reconstructed the emotional and sensational aspects of popular collective mentality under the rubric *l'homme psychique*. It followed Febvre in giving primacy over sight to hearing and touch, and contrasted past with present attitudes to language, space, and time. In his survey of social structures, Mandrou analysed the family, the parish, and the Marxist triptych of nobility, bourgeoisie, and common people. These he named *solidarités fondamentales*, as opposed to *solidarités menacées*, which comprised state, monarchy, and religion. Although he listed the major works of resistance theory and mentioned literate and religious culture, primarily in terms of its secular implications, Mandrou passed quickly over articulate thought and made little attempt to relate it to events. His history was contrived with statuesque immobility. Indeed the structures it depicted appeared to hold humanity in so rigid a grip that Mandrou felt obliged to list those who escaped the system as *évasions*. They included mercenaries, actors, utopians, mystics, satanists, and suicides. When the third generation of *annalistes* made a methodological cult of what they now called *mentalité*, the mental structures that concerned them, like their social counterparts, were still seen to be, in Braudel's words, the "prisons of the *longue durée*."[9]

It was this generation that came to embrace structuralist techniques developed in literary theory and anthropology. Ferdinand de Saussure, the founder of structural linguistics, saw language as an arbitrary code of conventions in which intelligibility depended upon synchronic relations between its components, conveying nothing meaningful about the nature of external reality. His followers mapped these relations both syntagmatically (as sequence) and paradigmatically (as association), with no regard for philological change through time. There were logical problems when Claude Lévi-Strauss applied this approach to primitive culture and the savage mind, and Braudel himself sug-

[7]*Civilisation matérielle et capitalisme* (Paris, 1967), p. 9.
[8]*Introduction à la France moderne: essai de psychologie historique, 1500–1640* (Paris, 1961).
[9]*Ecrits sur l'histoire* (Paris, 1969), p. 51. "Les cadres mentaux aussi sont prisons de longue durée."

gested reservations.[10] Such difficulties were compounded when structuralist concepts invaded *annaliste* history. By definition the historian must think diachronically. The detritus left by the past is his evidence and occupies the status of external referent in whatever he writes. To a linguistic structuralist a work of history is nothing more than a text to be appraised solely in terms of the association of its internal components, but it is a strange historian who denies the reality of the sources he employs, or of the past society that engendered them. Roland Barthes's essay on historical discourse admits that structural linguistics is incompatible with the idea of history, and finds the later *annalistes* more concerned with certainty in the present than with reality in the past.[11]

Another approach derived from literary theory – one sometimes associated with structuralism – is the view that tropes such as synecdoche, metonymy, and metaphor underlie the process whereby language develops from imaginative or poetic consciousness to sophisticated conceptualisation. The application of this to history is at least as old as Vico's *New Science*, and it has value for the understanding of *mentalité* in the decoding of myth and the analysis of popular superstition. It has also been applied to historiography by those who contend that the rhetorical strategy of the historian takes shape unconsciously through a dominant trope before the emergence of the rational constructs it subsequently controls. Hayden White has shown the relevance of this assumption to the interpretation of Romantic historiography, and it is true that French Romantic historians in the first half of the nineteenth century were themselves protagonists of the poetic imagination and conscious practitioners of the art of intuitively conveying the feel of the past. Perhaps this explains the rapport the *annalistes* claim with Michelet, despite the fact that he was writing *l'histoire événementielle*.[12] Imagination is certainly an important element in the understanding of past attitudes – not for the purpose of filling lacunae in the evidence, but rather to lead the historian to testimony he might otherwise have overlooked and to understand it as something different from his own experience.

Past literary fashions are important sources for the historian of ideas, just as modern literary theory may sharpen his insights and add a new dimension to his methods. Recent studies of eighteenth-century historiography have established formal relationships with the structures of fiction and epic poetry.[13] Such associations may support belief in the priority of the literary aspect of history, but equally they may yield valid generalisations about past attitudes. To some,

[10]*Ibid.*, p. 42.
[11]"Historical Discourse," in Michael Lane (ed.), *Introduction to Structuralism* (New York, 1970), pp. 145–55.
[12]Hayden White, *Metahistory: The Historical Imagination in Nineteenth-Century Europe* (Baltimore, 1973); Braudel, *Ecrits*, pp. 38, 47.
[13]On the association of fiction and epic see Harold L. Bond, *The Literary Art of Edward Gibbon* (Oxford, 1960); Leo Braudy, *Narrative Form in History and Fiction* (Princeton, 1970); and Suzanne Gearhart, *The Open Boundary of History and Fiction: A Critical Approach to the Enlightenment* (Princeton, 1984). The last book sets the ideas of modern structuralists and poststructuralists in parallel with selected *philosophes*.

style serves as a primary indicator of the nature of a particular historical endeavour; to others, at second best, it is a mask that must be removed before the
historian's real purpose is discovered.[14] To me the poetics of style may afford
clues to the general modification of literate mentalities. Two papers in this
collection associate a shift in literary genre with a change in moral climate.[15]

The investigation of élite literature in the history of ideas is not, however, the
strategy of the majority of the new *annalistes* and their disciples. *Mentalité* for
them is primarily the study of such phenomena of low-level culture as carnivals
and village fêtes, folklore, popular religion, and rural witchcraft.[16] The distinction between high and low culture is not just another sign of preference for the
deep-rooted and immobile aspects of human mentality; it is also an indication
of the familiar trend to see social and intellectual history in terms of class
antagonism. Conflicts of this type seldom impinged upon the methods of the
second generation of *annalistes*. They were less occupied with the motive forces
for revolution than with stability and rhythmic regularities. They chose the
middle ages and the early modern period to exemplify their methods, leaving
the age of revolutions as the domain of historians with a Marxist bent. Many
annalistes in the new wave, however, have linked the modern age with preceding
periods, and brought Marxist sympathies to the investigation of *mentalité* in
every epoch. Retaining their interest in mechanisms of social change, they have
reintroduced the historical event and used it as a fulcrum in discussion of social
conflicts and popular attitudes.[17]

The concept of *mentalité* has become looser and more mobile in the hands of
Marxist scholars already influenced by structuralism. Michel Vovelle, for example, has probed the relationship between ideology and *mentalité* and concluded
that the former has been absorbed by the latter. Ideology was conceived as the
realm of *la pensée claire*, as a systematic vision of the world that enables the
individual either to come to terms with it or to work to change it. *Mentalité* has
now been widened to include both articulated thought and the collective unconscious. In the process ideology has lost its revolutionary aspect and become a kind
of systematic illusion. To understand *mentalité* is to stand outside the historical
process and see the falsity of ideology. One of the most influential of neo-Marxist

[14]Peter Gay, *Style in History* (New York, 1974).

[15]See below, pp. 27–53, 73–97.

[16]Some representative studies of this kind (not all of them directly associated with *Annales*) are:
Peter Burke, *Popular Culture in Early Modern Europe* (New York, 1978); Natalie Z. Davis, *Society
and Culture in Early Modern France* (Stanford, Calif., 1975); A. N. Galpern, *The Religion of the
People in Champagne* (Cambridge, 1976); Robert Muchembled, *Culture populaire et culture des élites
dans la France moderne, XVe–XVIIIe siècles* (Paris, 1978). Mandrou's *Introduction* (note 8) is in many
respects a model. His *Magistrats et sorciers en France au XVIIe siècle* (Paris, 1968) attributes the
ending of witchcraft trials to growing rationalism in élite culture.

[17]A remarkable example where social analysis and the elucidation of collective attitudes are brought
to a focus by an event is Le Roy Ladurie's *Le Carnaval de Romans* (Paris, 1979). That *Annales* may
operate at several levels simultaneously is demonstrated by Denis Richet, "Aspects socio-
culturels des conflits religieux à Paris dans la seconde moitié du XVIe siècle," *Annales: Economies,
sociétés, civilisations*, 32 (1977), 764–89.

historians, Louis Althusser, redefined ideology as "the imaginary relationship of individuals to the actual conditions of their existence."[18] To the neo-Marxist, the structuralist, and the Braudelian, the historically situated individual has a spurious view of reality, and to think otherwise is to share the misconceptions of liberal empiricists who reject grand theory and take refuge in the evanescent procession of events and conscious ideas. Thus in the outcome the *annaliste* viewpoint has triumphed over the intellectual baggage its new acolytes have brought to the cult of *mentalité*. Yet the cult has become somewhat vaguer in the process. François Furet, who, like Vovelle, is a historian of revolution but, unlike him, has renounced his Marxist affiliations, is sceptical of its continued value. He has remarked astutely that the marriage of Marxism with structuralism has transformed Marxist ideological commitment. To use his neologism, what has resulted is "la désidéologisation structuraliste du marxisme."[19]

It has been necessary to sketch the methodological development of the *annalistes*, and to trace their association with structuralism, because they represent the dominant mode of linking social with intellectual history and because they have contributed so much new knowledge about society in early modern France. Their general approach, however, has devalued the objectives I have pursued in these papers, which have used events as a focus for the investigation of social tensions and have preferred the articulate expression of ideas to the manifestation of unconscious attitudes. I have resisted the reduction of history to immobility and facelessness, and have felt no enthusiasm for the view, implicit in the application of structural linguistics to human behaviour, that the course of human affairs is arbitrary and ultimately inexplicable. But what they have actually written on France in the centuries before the Revolution has often been far less stereotyped than this critique of their methods may imply. Le Roy Ladurie, for example, has adapted *annaliste* techniques to fit the particular historical problems his vivid imagination has defined. To reread what I have written on popular revolts is to realise how much I have benefited from the insights many specific *annaliste* works afford, if not from the methods they so stridently maintain. There are, however, other important ways of treating ideas in their social context that are more relevant to my purpose.

These essays share some common ground with Donald Kelley's *Beginning of Ideology*. This remarkable book blends generalisations about collective rational and emotional states of mind with an appreciation of historical circumstance. Unlike the *Annales* school, it gives ideology a privileged position over *mentalité*, and uses events and personalities in sixteenth-century France as inseparable parts of its analysis. Kelley seeks "a way of relating the study of society, whether in terms of institutional or class structure or set of cultural forms, to particular human thought and testimony," and he directs attention to "that pivotal and

[18]Cited by Michel Vovelle, *Idéologies et mentalités* (Paris, 1982), p. 6.
[19]*L'Atelier de l'histoire* (Paris, 1982), p. 51.

almost inaccessible juncture between society and consciousness."[20] The Reformation in France is treated as an intellectual revolution, and its impact is to
be understood as much in changing institutional structures as in formulated
ideas. An essential confrontation is assumed between Protestant transcendence
and Catholic immanence, while the infusion of religious enthusiasm into existing political and social tensions produces, by way of reaction, a secularised
pattern of modern ideology in embryo. The development of political theory is
conveyed through a series of impressionistic sketches, or "soundings," from the
first outbursts of heterodox opinion through the effects of conversion and its
formalisation upon the family, the congregation, the university, the legal profession, the mode of propaganda, and the political party.

It is not surprising that there are some themes here comparable with Kelley's,
given our parallel interests and mutual criticism over the years. There are also
important differences. *The Beginning of Ideology* adopts a bolder and more imaginative method, and is more indebted to insights from modern anthropology and
sociology, than the present collection. These essays give greater weight to the
adaptation of institutions and secular ideas to meet political needs than they do
to the moulding force of religion. They seek to be more specific and precise
within a more limited terrain. They take a different view of the social crisis of
the sixteenth century, locating it towards the end of the religious wars rather
than in their early stages. They dispute the logical priority accorded to Protestantism, and discern a radical spirit in French Catholicism. They stress a
secular resemblance between the two, based on their common roots in earlier
patterns of thought rather than on a metaphysical contrast, and they find more
significance in a general shift in public and private morality.

Another point of departure in these papers from Kelley's method is that they
are rather less preoccupied with the issue of modernity, a disposition which, by
definition, raises the relevance of the past to present concerns and subtly
contradicts the most resolute endeavour to understand the past in its own
terms. To see ideas in the context in which they were formulated, and to
evaluate them with sensitivity to the vocabulary and the general literature of
their day, are approaches endorsed by J. G. A. Pocock and Quentin Skinner.[21] I
have attempted to follow these injunctions, with the reservation that one cannot
escape entirely from one's own mental conditioning, nor communicate one's
findings without using words bearing anachronistic implications. Historicism,
the term in current use for scholarly objectivity, or seeing the past for its own
sake, is itself loaded with ambiguity. Karl Popper employed it with a quite
antithetical meaning to describe the practice of speculative history, of endowing
historical process with metaphysical purpose.[22] Current usage is rather nar-

[20]Donald R. Kelley, *The Beginning of Ideology: Consciousness and Society in the French Reformation*
(Cambridge, 1981), pp. 3, 4.
[21]J. G. A. Pocock, *Politics, Language and Time* (New York, 1971); Quentin Skinner, "Meaning and
Understanding in the History of Ideas," *History and Theory*, 8 (1969), 3–53.
[22]*The Poverty of Historicism* (London, 1957).

rower than what Meinecke meant by *Historismus*, which included the ability to see human institutions discretely rather than holistically, and to understand their development as a matter of circumstance rather than as the teleological unfolding of a predetermined form.[23]

The natural science model of governing general laws continues to assert a mental blockage in history and the social sciences, and it is, of course, from this kind of positivism that structural linguistics has sought an escape. The conviction that there must be one true explanatory model for the physical universe for long impeded a historicist approach to the history of science. Only those past explanatory theories which led in linear fashion to modern science seemed worthy of study, and those which were digressions or dead ends by this mode of thinking were consigned to oblivion. Such an approach prevented understanding of the context in which an alternative general theory or paradigm could gather strength until it could challenge and replace accepted orthodoxy.[24] The elaboration of this insight by Thomas Kuhn has encouraged a relativist approach to the history of thought in general, but there are always some who find it difficult to compare one paradigm with another without reference to some ultimate paradigm which, as the repository of truth, provides criteria to evaluate the others.

The modern historicist encounters paradoxes in Renaissance thought. The age which discovered the meaning of anachronism in history through humanist philology was also that which sought to emulate the superior achievements of the ancients. Moreover, despite the persistence of Aristotelian teleology in political and social thought, many saw change as a process of corruption, and desired to reform and purify by return to pristine models. Thus Protestantism, and even some strands in Catholic thought, desired a return to the primitive church; Machiavelli sought to restore the Italian city state by reversion to the conditions of its foundation; and François Hotman called for the reestablishment of the principles upon which the original constitution of Francogallia had been created. Even among that extraordinary group of French historians in the late sixteenth and early seventeenth centuries who are credited with a historicist outlook there was a tendency to look back to antiquity for principles to guide the present. In this way Etienne Pasquier insisted upon associating the parlement with remote Frankish assemblies to justify its constitutional role in his own time.

Present-mindedness reveals itself unexpectedly whenever the historian of ideas pursues a particular insight over an extended period. By seeking the foundations of *modern* political thought in the late middle ages and the Renaissance, Quentin Skinner appears at times to undermine his own contextual and

[23]Zachary Sayre Schiffman, "Renaissance Historicism Reconsidered," *History and Theory*, 24 (1985), 170–82. Schiffman uses Meinecke's analysis to criticise J. G. A. Pocock, Julian H. Franklin, Donald R. Kelley, and George Huppert for misusing the term, and Orest Ranum and me for adopting their usage.
[24]Thomas S. Kuhn, *The Structure of Scientific Revolutions* (Chicago, 1962; 2d enlarged ed., 1970).

relativist method. By granting privileged treatment to past historicist percep-
tions when identifying the foundations of *modern* historical scholarship, Donald
Kelley steps back from the canon of historicism at large.[25] In neither case does
the paradox seriously detract from the author's achievement in communicating
the sense of past attitudes to the present, and it may be that a retreat from
relativism is justified when a particular insight, a Pocockian "Machiavellian
moment," is given atemporal status.

It is, of course, a complicating element in the historicist approach that literary
texts may survive the audience for which they were intended and receive the
attention of subsequent generations in very different circumstances. A method
of literary interpretation amenable to the historical treatment of ideas is the
technique developed in the 1970s by the Constance school of *Rezep-
tionsgeschichte und Rezeptionsästhetik*. Its votaries deny synchronic value and
meaning to a literary work, and proceed relativistically to place it in dialectical
relationship with the chain of similar works before and after it, as well as with
the interpretations of successive generations of readers.[26] The extent to which a
work alters the threshold of the reader's expectation from one age to the next
provides the criterion of literary value. In the conjunction within French humanism of stylistic and ideological change the insights of the Constance school
find a particular use. Here it is necessary to take account of the Renaissance
debate on imitating the works of classical antiquity. Those who offered Ciceronian style as an absolute standard defended their model with such intensity that
it provoked a reaction in which the image of Cicero as a political sage was
altered to fit new moral criteria. Generic literary changes seem likely to occur in
periods of social or political stress, and also in their aftermath, when analytic
thought achieves historical understanding and rhetoric becomes formalised.[27]
This conclusion seems to fit Athens in the ages of Pericles and Demosthenes
and Rome in the last throes of republicanism. It has also been effectively
applied to Florentine humanism in the quattrocento.[28]

A few of these essays were written before some of the particular approaches
just outlined received formal definition, and occasionally they anticipate the
methods in question. Many of the papers in the collection have been influenced
in positive or negative fashion by new hermeneutic techniques. Others are
avowedly traditional. It needs to be repeated, however, that the methods employed arise primarily from the subject matter, and that all the papers stress
discontinuity and change. This is because later sixteenth-century France expe-

---

[25]Quentin Skinner, *The Foundations of Modern Political Thought* (2 vols., Cambridge, 1979); Donald
R. Kelley, *The Foundations of Modern Historical Scholarship* (New York, 1970).
[26]Hans Robert Jauss, *Kleine Apologie der ästhetischen Erfahrung* (Constance, 1972), and *Liter-
aturgeschichte als Provokation* (Frankfurt am Main, 1974).
[27]See below, pp. 27–53.
[28]Nancy S. Struever, *The Language of History in the Renaissance: Rhetoric and Historical Consciousness
in Florentine Humanism* (Princeton, 1970).

rienced not only religious and political conflicts but violent popular movements and conscious social antagonisms. Seventeenth-century France also endured massive disorders, but these, like the early religious wars, tended to cut vertically through the society of orders, and not to threaten the social fabric by the horizontal alignment of one estate against another. Memories of the time of the League continued to haunt a society in which hierarchical distinctions were more rigidly fixed, corporate privilege more vigorously defended, and an increasingly bureaucratised and autocratic government held off a recurrence of social anarchy. While many of the essays in this volume turn upon the ideas of a classically educated élite, others examine the actual processes of popular revolt, and in so doing reveal occasional instances of the way popular discontents were verbalised. At the same time the satires and polemics of the later religious wars, although directed primarily by one upper-class faction against another, vividly express fears felt by the higher orders at the revolt of the lower. This was the situation that fostered the growth of the Bourbon state, which, while rigidifying social barriers, in turn opened new fissures in the social edifice and experienced a concomitant change in moral values.

In this way it is possible to suggest points of junction between intellectual and social history. For an age of social turmoil and shifting ways of legitimating authority and justifying personal action, it has seemed appropriate to concentrate upon the indicators of flux and instability. The actual process of social change cannot, of course, be fully explained by the testimony of political ideas at any level. For this it is also necessary to look at different evidence concerning such large-scale events as the expansion of the royal fisc, the institutionalising of venal office, the employment of the intendants, the reactions of the traditional nobility, and the revolt of the masses. A section of this volume consists of investigations into some of these topics, but even here use has been made of dissenting voices to supplement the archives of officialdom. Very often the cracks in the system allow the most revealing insights into the structures themselves. A petition to Henri III from the *peuple orphelin* of the Vivarais peasantry, a Leaguer protest against social oppression, a declaration of provincial liberties addressed to Louis XIV by the estates of Béarn – these are as important in this collection as treatises on sovereignty, the divine right of kings, or reason of state.

PARTICULAR THEMES

The preceding remarks about methodological concerns have already introduced the general theme of the relationship between ideas and social tensions at points of crisis in the history of early modern France. It remains to explain the particular themes under which the papers have been grouped, and to comment on relevant studies published subsequent to their composition.

Renaissance and revolt

Humanism, stoicism, and interest of state

A broad change in moral climate can be traced throughout French history in the sixteenth and seventeenth centuries. After the active and participatory humanism of the reign of François 1er a shift towards neostoicism occurred during the religious wars, and this in turn was transformed into the justification of self-interest and reason of state in the time of Richelieu. This alteration is associated with the political conflicts and social tensions of the time, but it is illustrated through the evolution of Renaissance literary fashions and their relationship to political theory. The paper on the reputations of Cicero and Tacitus discusses the debate within French humanism about Latin style, and traces the subsequent role of Cicero in prudential morality. With the rise of neostoicism in the later religious wars, Tacitus and Seneca become the accepted models, changes in classical stylistic preferences running parallel with the spread of rationalism, scepticism, and a philosophy of withdrawal.

These trends are further exemplified by the history of the Cappel family in the same period. As its members rose through the law they applied their humanist learning in the service of the monarchy. Their subsequent Protestantism checked their careers but they retained contacts with the judicial bureaucracy and most of them shared its politique attitudes. The family also remained in close touch with literary and philosophical circles in the later sixteenth century. It provided religious enthusiasts on both sides of the religious conflicts, who happened also to be translators of Machiavelli, Tacitus, and Seneca. As if to compensate for their decline in social status, later generations included scholars with European reputations. In the Renaissance they helped to formulate Gallican arguments, and in the seventeenth century their English contacts reinforce the conclusions of the essay on Gallicanism and Anglicanism in the next section.

Like the paper on Cicero and Tacitus, the study of sixteenth-century French satire traces the fortunes of a literary genre and connects it with the politics and social upheavals of the League. During the religious wars the models of Horace, Juvenal, and Persius were rejected in favour of another classical source of satirical inspiration, the so-called Menippean mode. This was adapted to fit popular French traditions and employed in a wide range of personal and political polemics. Religious hypocrisy, moral criticism of the higher orders, and fear of social anarchy were common themes. The vogue casts some doubt on the current belief in the unbridgeable gulf between high and low culture in the early modern period. After the civil wars, it is true, Casaubon, Vauquelin de la Fresnaye, and Mathurin Régnier return to the purer models admired by the Pléiade, but Régnier retained his links with free-form popular satire, and expressed a scepticism reflecting the contemporary mood of disillusionment.

The last paper in this section analyses the writings of Henri de Rohan during the regency of Marie de Médicis and the regime of Richelieu. Rohan seems to bear three personae as exemplar of the self-interest of the high nobility, idealist leader of the Huguenot cause in the 1620s, and spokesman for the amoral pursuit of reason of state. His pose as Huguenot leader is shown to be a mask, and his thought serves to illustrate the interplay between theories of private and public interest.

Several studies published after the composition of these papers intersect with their themes. The essays on neostoicism which Gerhard Oestreich had revised before his death contain an important reassessment of the main figure in the movement, Justus Lipsius. Oestreich treats the editor of Tacitus and Seneca as a moderate absolutist who is alleged to have influenced the statecraft of the princes of Orange-Nassau, Henri IV, Oldenbarneveldt, Richelieu, Gustavus Adolphus, and others. He contends that "around 1600, especially in the France of Henri IV and the Netherlands, stoicism became the ideology, almost the religion, of educated men."[29] Lipsius is represented here, as he is also in my paper on the fortunes of Cicero and Tacitus, as the master of prudential politics, but Oestreich emphasises his moral influence upon the state, whereas I have seen him as offering comfort to the victims of religious enthusiasm and arbitrary rule, an ideology of resignation for the disappointed, and an exercise in survival for the courtier. It is true that some of the readers of Lipsius took stoicism as a creed applicable to participation in public life rather than as a doctrine of withdrawal and self-sufficiency. Guillaume du Vair, who published an imitation of Lipsius's *De Constantia*, is mentioned in this respect in my paper. There is, however, a negative private side to Lipsius's teaching which balances the positive role Oestreich has given him in public policy.

Another book which expands the argument of the first of these essays is Marc Fumaroli's study of the revival of Ciceronian rhetoric in the first half of the seventeenth century.[30] Fumaroli covers much the same ground as I have in the preliminary part of his work, and reaches similar conclusions, although with more stress upon style and less upon changes in moral climate. It would seem that I buried Cicero the rhetorician rather too early, but at least I have not been mistaken in asserting the survival of the prudential interpretation of his political thought. In the context of classical scholarship at the turn of the sixteenth century, I should mention the first volume of Anthony Grafton's study of Joseph Scaliger, which contains a vast amount of information about the learning of Scaliger's precursors and contemporaries.[31]

Nannerl Keohane's survey of French political ideas from the Renaissance to the Enlightenment touches on many themes germane to this collection.[32] Per-

[29]*Neostoicism and the Early Modern State* (Cambridge, 1982), p. 37.
[30]*L'Age de l'éloquence: rhétorique et "res literaria" de la Renaissance au seuil de l'époque classique* (Geneva, 1980).
[31]*Joseph Scaliger, a Study in the History of Classical Scholarship*, vol 1: *Textual Criticism and Exegesis* (Oxford, 1983).
[32]Nannerl O. Keohane, *Philosophy and the State in France: The Renaissance to the Enlightenment* (Princeton, 1980).

haps the most persuasively argued is the one that traces the parallel development of theories of private and public interest in the seventeenth century. Although preoccupied with those strands that point towards Montesquieu and Rousseau in the prerevolutionary age, Keohane treats ideas in their social and political context, and sees the roots of French individualism in Montaigne, Lipsius, and Charron against the background of the religious wars.

Sovereignty, resistance, and Christian obedience

To historians more concerned with the evolution of modern theories of the state than with the meaning of ideas in the context of their own time, the doctrines of absolutist and popular sovereignty have long been recognised as the most significant ideological contribution to emerge in the course of the French wars of religion. From the first, however, these ideas were beset with paradox. The desire to rely upon historical tradition and to seek solutions in custom and precedent ran counter to the concept that a community, through the will of its ruler or of its representatives, could break with the past and legislate in the present whatever best promoted its welfare. The idea of fundamental law was a means of meeting this dilemma, and yet it diminished the force of both historical constitutionalism and the logic of sovereignty. To argue that the laws made at the origin of the state bound its governors for all time detracted, on the one hand, from the idea of the evolution of constitutional forms, and, on the other, from the power of the sovereign to do what he willed. These judgments are the result of hindsight. Few thinkers of the time could untangle the paradox, and to have done so would have weakened the ability of their argument to appeal to both reason and history.

Concepts of sovereignty, custom, and fundamental law were not, of course, religious ideas. There was another authority: that of revelation. It is probably true that doctrines of obedience and rebellion, justified in scriptural terms, appealed to a wider audience than did their secular counterparts. Even in the last phases of the civil wars, when an increasingly secular tone was manifest in the works of the magistrates and antiquaries, the intensity of religious belief within sections of the League was answered by an equally uncompromising royalist dogma, the divine right of kings. The appearance of a Protestant claimant to the throne and the intervention of the papacy in the Leaguer cause divided the Gallican Church, and made relations between church and state a key issue in the polemics of the day. At the same time it is misleading to imagine that sixteenth-century minds carefully distinguished between the religious and the secular aspects of political debate, any more than they separated normative argument from historical demonstration. It is to these problems that the three papers in this section are devoted.

The essay on Bodin goes back to a time when Julian Franklin, Ralph Giesey, Donald Kelley, and I were all working on Jean Bodin and François Hotman, and in many ways it is the fruit of exchanges between us in preparation for the 1970 conference on Bodin held in Munich.[33] To see Bodin's concept of sovereignty in its own time is to realise that he had moved abruptly from a more constitutionalist position, and that the impulsion to do so came, as he himself declared, from the anarchy of the current wars and the need to answer the doctrine of popular sovereignty in Huguenot resistance theory. This is demonstrated in the paper through covert references to the works of Hotman, Beza, and others in the text of Bodin's *Commonwealth*, and through the juxtaposition of certain key passages there with corresponding sections of his earlier *Method for the Easy Comprehension of History*. Bodin is a supreme instance of the need for the historian of ideas to accept, at times, the existence of contradictions in the text he is investigating, and to seek their explanation in the circumstances of the work's composition rather than resolving them by speculation. Bodin's subsequent influence in the United Provinces, Germany, and England supports, as the paper shows, a variety of political positions because of ambiguity in his premises.

The next essay is an example of a more traditional approach. It concentrates on resistance theory, showing that Buchanan, William Reynolds ("Rossaeus"), and Locke represent a variant from the usual exposition of popular sovereignty, which contends that the whole community is superior to the ruler and, through its representatives, may discipline and depose him. With their concept of a presocial state of nature, their neglect of the doctrine of contract between community and ruler, and their stress upon a continuing popular, or constituent, authority, these three theorists have much common ground. Reynolds, whose radical ideas were advanced in support of the Catholic League, did not hesitate to adapt secular theories from the Calvinist Buchanan. Writing a century later, Locke admits no debt to either Buchanan or Reynolds, and his natural law viewpoint differs in certain important respects from theirs. Nevertheless, there is enough similarity between the three, and sufficient common points of departure from the Calvinist, Leaguer, and Whig doctrines of resistance prevailing in their own times, to justify their treatment as a variant group. The roots of the tradition to which they belong, as well as those of the more orthodox view, can be found in Conciliarist theory.

The transformation of Huguenot thought from the justification of resistance to support for the dynastic rights of their leader when Henri de Navarre became heir to the Valois crown suggests how deeply political ideas in the religious wars could be at the mercy of unexpected events. So too does the manner in which the evolution of the resistance theory of the League followed the same course as that of its most bitter opponent, the Protestant faction. Yet to balance the

---

[33]Julian H. Franklin, *Constitutionalism and Resistance in the Sixteenth Century* (New York, 1969), and *Jean Bodin and the Rise of Absolutist Theory* (Cambridge, 1973); Ralph E. Giesey and J. H. M. Salmon (eds.), *"Francogallia" by François Hotman* (Cambridge, 1972); Donald R. Kelley, *François Hotman, a Revolutionary's Ordeal* (Princeton, 1973). See also respective contributions in Horst Denzer (ed.), *Verhandlungen der internationalen Bodin Tagung* (Munich, 1973).

cynicism that these situations might provoke, the third paper in this section shows how, in the debate between Gallican and Anglican spokesmen on the one side and the defenders of ultramontanism on the other, the parties concerned frequently adhered to their stated positions when circumstances no longer made them appropriate. In particular, *parlementaire* mentality remained entrapped by the web of historical myths it had woven round the past of the national church. The issues involved in the relationship between church and state were fundamentally similar in France and England, despite theological differences. Both secular governments achieved substantial control of clerical administration, but the manner in which this was justified was usually a response to the initiatives of the Counter-Reformation papacy and its agents. In both countries the role of the Jesuits and the assertion of the papal right to excommunicate and depose temporal rulers were the principal points in the series of exchanges beginning at the time of the final session of the Council of Trent and the Elizabethan religious settlement, rising to crescendo at the time of the Armada and the League, and continuing through the first two decades of the seventeenth century.

These debates are analysed in the context of each of their phases, and what initially was a question of parallel development is shown to have become a matter of reciprocal influence and even of association. In the time of the League a large body of Gallican propaganda appeared in English translation, some of it advancing the theory of the divine right of kings in conjunction with the Bodinian view of sovereignty. In the next century the stream of influence reversed itself. After the coincidence of the papal interdict against Venice and the Gunpowder Plot, the oath of allegiance controversy, involving once again the respective rights of church and state, spread throughout Europe and continued for a decade. At this time it was James I who led the antipapal cause. In these controversies detached observers noted the curious circumstance that the ultramontane defence of the pope's absolute authority within and beyond the church was accompanied by the defence of the right of the secular community to discipline a king; whereas, in the other camp, the claim that the pope could be controlled by the council of the church was advanced in conjunction with the assertion of the divine and unchallengeable rights of the temporal ruler. Bizarre as it might seem, absolutism and constitutionalism walked hand in hand on both sides of the debate.

Among recent studies of the concept of sovereignty, one of the most interesting, although not perhaps the best organised, is London Fell's *Origins of Legislative Sovereignty*.[34] Fell revises orthodox interpretation of sixteenth-century French jurisprudence by examining the contemporary genre, or "art," of explaining the internal articulation and external relationships of different kinds of law. In the course of this he blurs the line between the Bartolists, or rational

[34]A. London Fell, *The Origins of Legislative Sovereignty and the Legislative State* (2 vols., Cambridge, Mass., 1983).

systematisers, and the legal humanists, whose historical view of the provenance of law contributed generally to historicist attitudes. He also argues that the modern idea of sovereignty emerged from dialectical application of Aristotle's four causes to the systematising of law, and maintains that in this respect Bodin was anticipated by Jean de Coras, who is better known in our time as the magistrate concerned in the trial of Martin Guerre. It will be noted that Fell's approach is a strictly intellectual one.

Other studies of Bodin have stressed the constitutional, rather than the absolutist, aspect of his thought. Keohane, whose *Philosophy and the State in France* is organised around the concepts of absolutism, constitutionalism, and individualism, distinguishes all three currents in Bodin, arguing that reconciliation may have been achieved through the inclusion of the words "droit gouvernement" in his definition of the commonwealth.[35] David Parker's ingenious article on the subject, which touches on the social side of Bodin's thought, points out that absolutism and constitutionalism could coexist in his mind because of his distinction between the form of the state and the method of its administration.[36] This distinction, incidentally, was taken up by Bodin's much neglected disciple, Pierre Grégoire, whence it entered Gallican political thought.[37] Finally, mention should be made of the important study of Bodin's complex religious attitudes by Paul Lawrence Rose, a study which helps to illuminate Bodin's political thought. Rose is also the author of a paper elucidating Bodin's relationship with Leaguer thought, and the editor of some of Bodin's lesser-known writings.[38]

Structures and fissures

The structures in which the articulation of society is conceptualised are as much subject to change as more ephemeral phenomena, but, of course, the tempo of change is usually much slower. In his later years Michelet used the phrase "l'allure du temps" to describe what seemed to him a quickening in the pace of historical process. Daniel Halévy's essay on acceleration in history began from this suggestion, and speculated about the way the rapid flux of the historian's own age made it difficult to appreciate past attitudes to time.[39] This need not result in reducing past epochs to the near immobility that the structural study of demographic and unconscious mental phenomena may encourage. Rates of structural change are variable, and there are times of revolutionary

[35] *Philosophy and the State*, pp. 67–82.
[36] "Law, Society and the State in the Thought of Jean Bodin," *History of Political Thought*, 2 (1981), 253–85.
[37] See below, p. 178.
[38] *Bodin and the Great God of Nature: The Moral and Religious Universe of a Judaiser* (Geneva, 1980); "Bodin and the Bourbon Succession to the French Throne, 1583–1594," *Sixteenth Century Journal*, 9 (1978), 75–98; *Jean Bodin: Selected Writings on Philosophy, Religion, and Politics* (Geneva, 1980).
[39] *Essai sur l'accélération de l'histoire* (Paris, 1961), p. 17.

change when shifts in social articulation momentarily march in step with political events. The kind of social history I have preferred is one closely in touch with politics, one that appreciates an alteration in "l'allure du temps." It accepts the fact that a society like early modern France had structures, such as relations in agricultural production and relations between corporative groups, that altered more slowly than others, and because they did so, encountered blockages, when inbuilt tensions burst out into political action. It is at such moments that the ideas in which human fears, frustrations, and aspirations are expressed afford the best insights into the structures which are imperilled. For this reason the essays in the final section of this collection are devoted to popular revolts and the reactions of the higher orders to them.

The first paper is concerned with the historical debate on the nature of popular revolt in early modern France and its relationship to institutional changes in government and society, notably the system of venal judicial offices and nonvenal intendancies. By one view the lower orders were in revolt against their social superiors, some of whom were sufficiently alienated by the political regime to side temporarily with the rebels. By another, provincial society in general was so opposed to the extension of the centralising powers of the royal fisc that the higher orders sympathised with, and at times supported, the revolts. The debate provides a general perspective on the structures of the Old Regime and the tensions within them. It is argued that, while the form of seventeenth-century revolt often followed a tradition established in the sixteenth century, social antagonism was much more evident in the later religious wars than it was in the time of Richelieu and Mazarin. The causes of the earlier revolts are substantially different from those of the later. These conclusions are tested by the particular study of a revolt in Vivarais in the reign of Henri III. It becomes evident that local conditions must be taken into account, and that wide-ranging generalisations on this issue are often suspect.

The analysis of the revolutionary group within the Parisian League known as the Sixteen provides many examples of social conflict, although not in the form suggested by the classic Marxian model. The Sixteen have usually been seen as a static organisation, whereas their membership and ideas underwent in reality considerable variation. The decade from the formation of the clandestine radical party in Paris to the recovery of the capital by Henri IV (1584–94) was one of violent political fluctuation, suggesting superficial comparison with the phases of the French Revolution. The analysis provided here complements the essay on satire in this period, and includes an appendix describing the provenance of one of the most remarkable political documents of the time, *Le Dialogue d'entre le Maheustre et le Manant*. While this tract reflects the tendency found at all levels of sixteenth-century society to see present problems in terms of an idealised past, it also contains direct statements of a radical popular sovereignty and a proposal to abolish the hereditary nobility.

The concluding essay in this section investigates a revolt in southwest France

Introduction

in the early years of the personal reign of Louis XIV. Here again historical orthodoxies are questioned, and overlarge generalisations are revised in the light of particular circumstances. The revolt of Audijos and his followers involves the structures and tensions discussed in the paper on venality of office and popular revolt. Local society sympathised with Audijos, and resented the imposition of the *gabelle*, the methods of the intendant, and the presence of royal troops, but rivalries divided the local estates from the local parlement and personal jealousies reversed expected alignments. The governor used his influence at court to oppose the intendant, and systems of clientage within robe and sword cut across group interests. This was a situation in which the king preferred manipulation and compromise to the imposition of his supposedly absolute authority. Apart from revealing the strains within the system and the way in which the antagonists conceived them, the essay demonstrates the gap between absolutist theory and practice.

Most of the studies of popular uprisings published after the composition of the first paper are discussed in the essays on the Vivarais and Audijos revolts. A number of important recent works touch directly or indirectly on the issues raised in the paper on the Sixteen. Peter Ascoli has edited a variorum text of *Le Dialogue d'entre le Maheustre et le Manant* and appended, where he could, short biographical notes on the 236 names (many of them, of course, not members of the Sixteen) which appear in that remarkable tract.[40] Barbara Diefendorf has made expert use of archives to analyse the professional and social background of Paris city councillors, and has traced the patterns of their marriages and property holding.[41] Although her study stops short of the period of the League, it is now possible to understand more fully the nature of the oligarchy that the Sixteen challenged but did not overthrow. Philip Benedict's book on Rouen in the period successfully relates events to social structures. It employs statistics to compare Protestants with Catholics in terms of status and background, and reveals how the established orders in the city retained power under the League.[42] Robert Harding's comparative study of the League in Angers, Rennes, and Nantes reaches conclusions similar to Benedict's, and suggests that the experience of the Sixteen in Paris was untypical.[43] Both these studies refute the view that republican separatism was a general trend in Leaguer towns.

Two major books about the Sixteen have appeared which acknowledge the essay included here as the pioneering analysis.[44] Their conclusions do not vary

---

[40]Peter M. Ascoli (ed.), *François Cromé: Dialogue d'entre le Maheustre et le Manant* (Geneva, 1977).
[41]*Paris City Councillors in the Sixteenth Century: The Politics of Patrimony* (Princeton, 1983).
[42]*Rouen during the Wars of Religion* (Cambridge, 1981).
[43]"Revolution and Reform in the Holy League: Angers, Rennes, Nantes," *Journal of Modern History*, 53 (1981), 379–416.
[44]Elie Barnavi, *Le Parti de Dieu* (Louvain, 1980); Robert Descimon, *Qui étaient les seize? Mythes et réalités de la Ligue parisienne* (Paris, 1983).

much from my own, although Elie Barnavi criticises my failure to rank the clergy higher in the social hierarchy (a point rectified in the present version). He also has reservations about my concentration upon the professions of the revolutionaries rather than upon the titles of address they bore, but the outcome, in terms of the social composition of the Sixteen, appears to be unaltered. Barnavi's study is at times distorted by his attempt to show the Sixteen as the ancestors of revolutionary totalitarian parties.[45] The book by Robert Descimon has the opposite kind of bias, for he sees the group as a backward-looking reenactment of a medieval sense of community. These views belong to the speculative part of his study, and are only tenuously connected with its major achievement, an extremely detailed prosopography of 225 members of the movement. Finally in regard to the Sixteen, one may note a recent important paper by Jacqueline Boucher analysing pamphlet literature leading up to the fall of Henri III, and seeking to establish the respective attitudes of the urban notables and the lower orders. What emerges, not unexpectedly, is the deep fear of the latter felt by the élite and the readiness of the populace to be manipulated by their social superiors.[46]

The large-scale questions about the nature of absolutism and its relationship with French society in the early modern period have been the subject of much revisionism since Roland Mousnier and Boris Porshnev clashed about venality of office and popular revolt in the age of Richelieu and Mazarin. Mousnier himself has continued to defend his view that changes within the state apparatus, particularly the institutionalising of venal office and the consequent need to strengthen the central power by introducing intendants and *commissaires,* brought new social tensions. He has also continued to insist that these tensions took the political form of resistance to centralisation and fiscal pressure on the part of both privileged and unprivileged elements in local society. He still prefers to see this society in its own terms as grouped in orders and estates, and denies horizontal class antagonisms, stressing the vertical ties of clientage as obstacles to such confrontation. It is also still his contention that the two nobilities of sword and robe represented two separate ways of life without any significant measure of assimilation between them. In his recent overview of French political and social institutions he has made few concessions to his critics, but in his observations on developments in the eighteenth century he has noted the appearance of a new kind of official, the *fonctionnaire,* and he has charted the signs suggesting the coming of a class society to replace the old hierarchy of orders.[47] Neither alterations in ideology nor economic shifts are

[45]In this respect see his article "La Ligue parisienne (1585–94); ancêtre des partis totalitaires modernes," *French Historical Studies,* 11 (1979), 29–57.

[46]"Culture des notables et mentalités populaires dans la propagande qui entraîna la chute de Henri III," in Jean Nicolas (ed.), *Mouvements populaires et conscience sociale, XVIᵉ–XIXᵉ siècles* (Paris, 1985), pp. 339–50.

[47]Roland Mousnier, *Les institutions de la France sous la monarchie absolue,* vol. 1: *Société et état* (Paris, 1974); vol. 2: *Les organes de l'état et la société* (Paris, 1980).

for Mousnier such potent forces for change as human tensions within institutions themselves, and in this he has received further general support from historians such as Yves Bercé, Yves Durand, and Madeleine Foisil, who followed his initial explanation of the popular uprisings.[48]

Among criticisms of Mousnier's view of the polarity of robe and sword are studies by Jonathan Dewald, Albert N. Hamscher, Robert R. Harding, and James B. Wood.[49] However, these works freely admit evidence of a non-statistical kind for continuing animosity, even though they come close to saying at times that there was only one nobility, not two. Mousnier, too, uses figures, but his case for endogamy is based upon the main stems of the *parlementaire* families and takes more account of the parlement of Paris than of the provincial robe. The revisionists cast their nets more widely, and Hamscher shows that even in Paris greater assimilation occurred in the reign of Louis XIV. It is clear that statistics of intermarriage do not provide the final answer to the way in which the old and the new nobility regarded each other. No one can deny the contempt with which the duc de Saint-Simon and many others at the top of the social hierarchy referred to the men of the robe, particularly those who served in an executive rather than a judicial capacity.

That venality of office was in itself a restriction upon the authority of the king has been a common element in discussion of the constitutional nature of absolutism. Hamscher demonstrates that, even in the period when Louis XIV issued his fiats to put the parlements in their place, the magistrates held on to their judicial authority and their propertied interest in the apparatus of state. The venal apparatus had increased to such dimensions at this point, and was so entwined in its own laborious processes, that it was less the judicial review of royal enactment than the sheer dead weight of bureaucratic procedure which limited the freedom of the crown. This is one of the points made by J. S. Morrill in his survey of the recent trend to see the practice of French absolutism in terms quite antithetical to the overriding powers it claimed in theory.[50] It is certainly true that Louis XIV represented the culmination of a long trend towards autocratic rule, and that he controlled and employed military force unheard of by his ancestors. No one can deny that the cult of king-worship

---

[48]See the tributes to Mousnier in Yves Durand (ed.), *Hommage à Roland Mousnier: Clientèles et fidélités en Europe à l'époque moderne* (Paris, 1981).

[49]Jonathan Dewald, *The Formation of a Provincial Nobility: The Magistrates of the Parlement of Rouen, 1499–1610* (Princeton, 1980); Albert N. Hamscher, *The Parlement of Paris after the Fronde, 1653–1673* (Pittsburgh, 1976); Robert R. Harding, *Anatomy of a Power Elite: The Provincial Governors of Early Modern France* (New Haven, 1978); James B. Wood, *The Nobility of the Election of Bayeux, 1463–1666: Continuity through Change* (Princeton, 1980). On the views expressed by these authors see my review article "Storm over the Noblesse," *Journal of Modern History*, 53 (1981), 242–57. Other works discussed in this article are: Richard Bonney, *Political Change in France under Richelieu and Mazarin* (Oxford, 1978); George Huppert, *Les Bourgeois Gentilshommes* (Chicago, 1977); Sharon Kettering, *Judicial Politics and Urban Revolt in Seventeenth-Century France: The Parlement of Aix, 1629–1659* (Princeton, 1978); J. Russell Major, *Representative Institutions in Early Modern France* (New Haven, Conn., 1980); and Mousnier, *Institutions*.

[50]"French Absolutism as Limited Monarchy," *Historical Journal*, 21 (1978), 961–72.

achieved unprecedented proportions in his reign, and that his attempt to alter the fundamental law of the succession justifies the description of his brand of absolutism as different in kind from the dynastic and the constitutional varieties that had preceded him.[51]

Mousnier depicts the regime of the Sun King as a radical break in continuity, and a blow to the harmony of the society of orders. On the other hand, the complexity of privilege, both at Versailles and in centres of provincial administration, was so great that it offered enormous obstacles to the imposition of a uniform and centralised system. Roger Mettam may have gone too far in claiming that the endeavour to force such a system upon the provinces had encountered so many problems that it was abandoned before the end of Colbert's ministry.[52] Nevertheless, the absolutism of Louis XIV was not administratively what it pretended to be. The lines of clientage might now all ascend to the royal ministers under the king, but there was sufficient rivalry within the council to permit the adjustment of interests in a way not directly consonant with the personal will of the sovereign. Looked at from the opposite point of view, rivalries and contending interests between and within provincial institutions allowed the king to manipulate affairs to his own advantage. It is in this vein that David Parker has approached the nature of absolutism,[53] and this is the pragmatic conclusion of the paper included here on the Audijos revolt.

Yet another line of reasoning to deny that absolutism actually involved the exercise of absolute power has been adopted by the German sociologist Norbert Elias.[54] *The Court Society* is a highly schematic and abstract revision of the view that the monarchy deprived the nobility of its independence of action by duping them with status and etiquette at Versailles. Elias describes the king as transforming aristocratic culture while becoming its prisoner. He is both the oppressor and the preserver of the aristocracy, and is dependent upon it as an actor is dependent upon the reactions of his audience. In this argument the role of the king as manipulator as well as autocrat complements the approach employed in more genuinely historical investigation.

Much of the discussion so far has concerned the institutional structure of

---

[51] This categorisation is used by Sarah Hanley in her study of the evolution of the *lit de justice* ceremony. Her book is based upon the symbolic significance of ritual as well as upon contemporary justification for the role of the parlement: *The Lit de Justice of the Kings of France: Constitutional Ideology in Legend, Ritual and Discourse* (Princeton, 1983). Another recent viewpoint, based mainly on constitutional and ideological changes in the sixteenth century, maintains that it is the concept of the state, rather than of the monarchy, that is significant: Howell A. Lloyd, *The State, France, and the Sixteenth Century* (London, 1983).

[52] *Government and Society in Louis XIV's France* (London, 1977), p. xi.

[53] *The Making of French Absolutism* (London, 1983).

[54] *The Court Society*, tr. Edmund Jephcott (Oxford, 1983). Elias derives from nineteenth-century historiography the view that historians, being concerned only with unique and discrete events, should not generalise. Unfortunately, the secondary sources from which he builds his "figurations" are of similar antiquity. It is also a pity that the generalisations reserved for the realm of sociology are cast in such language as "the sociogenesis of aristocratic romanticism in the process of courtization" (p. 214).

Introduction

absolutism and its mode of operation, rather than the relationship of absolutism to society. Elias, of course, is involved with this relationship, and so, too, are those who approach the problems of robe and sword and the genesis of the popular revolts. Most of the historians who take a stand upon these issues broadly agree with Mousnier in giving their social history an institutional emphasis, even if they demur from all his conclusions.

A challenge to this approach is presented by the historical sociologist Perry Anderson, who has adopted a proto-Marxist view of class antagonism to explain absolutism. Porshnev and some other Marxist scholars who studied French absolutism were prepared to see the state as in some measure escaping from the control of the dominant class (the feudal nobility), and as holding the balance between the aristocracy and the bourgeoisie. Not so Anderson, whose *Lineages of the Absolutist State* sees absolutism as a special type of feudalism, a means of extracting surplus wealth produced by the labouring classes through "extra-economic coercion." To Anderson even the towns were an integral part of feudalism, and their importance as a source for taxation was a factor that encouraged the nobility to institute a more centralised government structure. In short, Bourbon absolutism was "a redeployed and recharged apparatus of feudal domination."[55] This interpretation has recently been restated by William Beik as the theoretical framework for his book on seventeenth-century Languedoc. To Beik "absolutism was the political manifestation of a system of domination protecting the interests of a privileged class of officers and landed lords."[56] Beik rejects Mousnier's society of orders except as a means of distributing authority, and finds hostility implicit in the relations between the élite and the common people. The disruption of the religious wars, he argues, created a need to strengthen the state, but until Louis XIV the necessary restructuring was mismanaged and provoked opposition. The idea of the king's success as a manipulator of the system has much in common with the institutional interpretations already mentioned, but it differs from them dramatically by making the forces of production the determining, although not the only, agent of change. Beik's conclusion is that Louis XIV's absolutism reinforced hierarchical class rule. "Languedocian society," he says, "was shored up, not levelled."[57]

This account of recent interpretations of the issues raised by the third section of this collection shows the breadth and vigour of a field that attracted far less attention when I first became interested in the problems of early modern French history. It also reveals that *annaliste* approaches are by no means the only ones in fashion. Social conflicts are the distinguishing characteristic of French experience in the sixteenth and seventeenth centuries, and the forces of

[55](London, 1974), p. 17.
[56]*Absolutism and Society in Seventeenth-Century France: State Power and Provincial Aristocracy in Languedoc* (Cambridge, 1985), p. 335.
[57]*Ibid.*, p. 334.

23

change ought to be a vital consideration for historians of the period. These conflicts contain elements of large-scale antagonism between social groups, and, if they are not groups that can be described as classes in the modern sense, they often represent alignments differing from the corporate structure recognised by law in their own age. It is a mistake, however, to see the forces of change as always economically determined. In any case, the ideas expressed at moments of crisis are by no means irrelevant to the interpretation of historical process. When seen in their social context they attest to the powerful but unpredictable ways in which human volition has shaped the past.

PART I

Humanism, stoicism, and interest of state

Cicero and Tacitus
in sixteenth-century France

In early sixteenth-century France Cicero seemed a perfect model to humanists who challenged scholasticism through a rhetoric embodying both philosophy and history. Admiration for Ciceronian style was accompanied by a moralising civic humanism and a respect for Cicero, the philosopher, as the purveyor of Greek wisdom. At the end of the century Tacitus had become a more important linguistic influence, while the ideal of the active citizen and virtuous orator had been replaced by one of Stoic fortitude and withdrawal. Tacitus, the historian of the corruption of liberty, emerged as the exemplar of private and public prudence, and a reinterpreted Cicero was relegated to the role of a minor precursor in prudential morality. This parallel shift in linguistic structures and moral ideologies did not simply result from the stresses of the religious wars in the last third of the century. It was also, in part, a long-term consequence of the earlier importation from Italy of a debate about the extent to which Cicero should be imitated – a debate that attained a new dimension in the context of the Reformation. Other elements that contributed to the demise of Ciceronian humanism were not only the relativist implications in the new historical approach to law but also the logic of Peter Ramus, who, while pleading for the union of eloquence and philosophy, effectively disjoined rhetoric from its component parts. As the neostoic movement developed in reaction to rival religious enthusiasms, the literary models of Tacitus and Seneca invaded Latinity and left their mark upon the vernacular.[1] In the new climate of absolutism Cicero, *pater eloquentiae,* yielded place to Tacitus, *pater prudentiae.*

This exercise in counterpoint is not intended to explain more than a limited number of elements in an exceedingly complex movement of modes and ideas.[2] Yet in these terms the juxtaposition of Cicero and Tacitus seems more sug-

---

[1] There is no easy way to find logical connections between the aesthetics of style and the shifting ideological assumptions of the French Renaissance. For some comments on the methods employed here, see above, p. 10.

[2] Attempts to capture this complexity in full may be self-defeating; see, for example, Jean Jehasse, *La Renaissance de la critique: L'Essor de l'humanisme érudit de 1560 à 1614* (Lyon, 1976).

gestive than the many separate studies that have related Cicero to French humanism in the first two-thirds of the century and have traced connections between Tacitism and *raison d'etat* after the religious wars.[3] In particular, the use that is made of both Latin authors in the interval between these two periods is important for an understanding of the shift in emphasis from one to the other. It may also be that preoccupation with particular disciplines has impeded a grasp of the broader significance of the changing Renaissance view of the classical world. Concern with the role of Cicero in humanist scholarship has been more obvious in studies of Renaissance rhetoric and philosophy than it has been in surveys of attitudes to history and politics. The reverse has been true of modern works on the influence of Tacitus, where his relationship to various strands of Machiavellism has seemed of primary importance. Moreover, it is easy to find in Livy a historical counterpart to Ciceronianism and in Seneca a philosophical counterpart to Tacitism. The apparent connections between the stylistic revolution and neostoicism have been tentatively explored,[4] and several scholars have examined the relative popularity of Livy, Polybius, Tacitus, and other classical historians during the Renaissance.[5] What is attempted here is, on the one hand, more ambitious in its scope and, on the other, more eclectic in its exemplification.

Misconceptions born from the desire to simplify readily invade discussion of literary mode. Cicero's style is by no means as monolithic as the *Ciceronianus* debate might at times suggest. The easy discursiveness of the *Epistolae ad Familiares* contrasts markedly with the balanced rhythms of *De Oratore*. Within the speeches themselves one should distinguish between the rich Asianism of *Pro Milone*, the middle style of Attic antithesis in *Pro Caelio*, and the "lean and energetic" vigour of the *Philippics*.[6] Like Cicero, Tacitus knew that the style he adopted for history was quite unsuited to rhetoric. In the sixteenth century some Tacitean scholars refused to accept Tacitus as the author of *Dialogus de*

---

[3]André Stegmann, "Un thème majeur du second humanisme français, 1540–1570: L'Orateur et le citoyen," in Peter Sharratt, ed., *French Renaissance Studies, 1540–1570: Humanism and the Encyclopedia* (Edinburgh, 1976), pp. 213–33. On Tacitism, see Else-Lilly Etter, *Tacitus in der Geistesgeschichte des 16. und 17. Jahrhunderts* (Basel, 1966); Jürgen von Stackelberg, *Tacitus in der Romania* (Tübingen, 1960); André Stegmann, "Le Tacitisme," in his *Machiavellismo e Antimachiavellici nel Cinquecento* (Florence, 1969), pp. 117–30; Etienne Thuau, *Raison d'etat et pensée politique à l'époque de Richelieu* (Paris, 1966), pp. 32–54; and Giuseppe Toffanin, *Machiavelli e il "Tacitismo"* (Padua, 1921). For a recent survey, wider in period than its title suggests, see Kenneth C. Schellhase, *Tacitus in Renaissance Political Thought* (Chicago, 1976).

[4]Morris W. Croll, *Style, Rhetoric, and Rhythm*, ed. J. Max Patrick and Robert O. Evans (Princeton, 1966).

[5]Peter Burke, "A Survey of the Popularity of Ancient Historians, 1450–1700," *History and Theory*, 2 (1966), 135–52; Arnaldo Momigliano, "Polybius' Reappearance in Western Europe," in Olivier Reverdin, ed., *Polybe* (Geneva, 1974), pp. 347–72; and J. H. Whitfield, "Livy > Tacitus," in R. R. Bolgar, ed., *Classical Influences on European Culture, A.D. 1500–1700* (Cambridge, 1976), pp. 281–93.

[6]R. G. M. Nisbet, "The Speeches," in T. A. Dorey, ed., *Cicero* (London, 1965), pp. 47–9.

Oratoribus because it seemed so out of character with the Tacitus they knew.[7] Trained as an orator in his youth, Tacitus was just as concerned about the decay of eloquence since Cicero's age as he was about the decline of history in the sycophantic climate of imperial authority. Yet Tacitus, in his view of both oratory and history, alternated between indignation against the process of corruption and decay and acceptance of change for its own sake: Aper, one of the characters in the *Dialogus*, criticises Cicero and argues also that all things are relative and each generation has its own fashions.[8]

Cicero's opinions on history were even better known than those of Tacitus on rhetoric. In *De Oratore* he called upon the historian to tell the truth, the whole truth, and nothing but the truth. No one was better qualified than the orator to light the lamp of the past as a guide through present darkness, and yet the style of history was not that of rhetoric.[9] In *Brutus*, his history of Roman oratory, Cicero praised the simplicity of Caesar's *Commentaries:* "They are bare, simple and straightforward, and devoid of all ornament. But, while Caesar wished to preserve the materials from which others might write history, he did a service for those clumsy writers who burn holes in them by trying to twist them into new shapes with curling tongs. So great is his achievement that it deterred men of good sense from writing, for there is nothing in history more agreeable than pure and shining brevity."[10] Although Jean Bodin and Montaigne cited this passage, they took less account of Cicero's description of how other kinds of history should be written, notably the dramatic account of a single event like Sallust's *Conspiracy of Catiline* and the high-flown Asianism of later annalist technique, a form that Livy perfected. Together with Lucian's *De Scribenda Historia* and the appraisal of Thucydides by Dionysius of Halicarnassus, Cicero's remarks on history in his three mature works on rhetoric formed the *loci classici* for Renaissance scholars who sought the views of the ancients on history and its style.[11] Cicero wrote no history, but few were ignorant of the privileged place he ascribed to it. Without history, men would remain forever children.

Three paradoxes within the Ciceronian corpus were transmitted unrealised to the humanism of the Renaissance. First, although prudence was itself a traditional virtue, tempering the ideal to the practical demands of circumstances and advocating the expedient, as Cicero did in the second book of *De Officiis*,[12]

[7]Tacitus, *Dialogue des orateurs: Dialogus de oratoribus*, ed. Henri Goelzer (Paris, 1947), p. 4.
[8]*Ibid.*, p. xvii.
[9]Cicero, *De Oratore libri tres*, ed. Augustus S. Wilkins (Amsterdam, 1962), 2: 36 (p. 245), 62 (p. 258). Also see Pierre Boyancé, *Etudes sur l'humanisme cicéronien* (Brussels, 1970), p. 136.
[10]Cicero, *M. Tulli Ciceronis Brutus*, ed. A. E. Douglas (Oxford, 1966), 262, 75.
[11]Michel Montaigne, *Essais*, ed. Maurice Rat (Paris, 1962), vol. 1, p. 458; and Bodin, *Method for the Easy Comprehension of History*, trans. Beatrice Reynolds (New York, 1969), p. 56; and Claude-Gilbert Dubois, *La Conception de l'histoire en France au XVIᵉ siècle* (Paris, 1977), p. 72.
[12]In the third book of *De Officiis* Cicero attempted to reconcile *utile* with *honestum*. Most modern commentators have assumed that Cicero subordinated *utile* to the common good, which is in itself

weakened the morality of the common good. Second, behind the active role that Cicero for the most part commended to the citizen lay the alternative concept of the contemplative life, which pervaded his philosophical works at the end of his career and also appeared in the Stoic elements of *De Officiis*, written in the same period. Third, history could not simply teach virtue if it also maintained the standards of objective truth that Cicero recommended. To later historians it was apparent from his letters to Atticus that Cicero had himself at times allowed ambition to bend the path of duty. The methods of the legal humanists involved historical relativism, and they valued Cicero's speeches and letters as sources for the science of philology and the understanding of Roman law in the particular society in which it had reached maturity. Even so, it seldom occurred to them that this society had not always lived up to Cicero's ideals.

There was a fourth area in which vision was restricted. Although, as philologists, the legal humanists were sensitive to neologisms and changes in grammatical structure, they often judged them by fixed standards of eloquence. Thus Lorenzo Valla, at once the progenitor of legal humanist method and the severest critic of Latinity, was more indignant at the barbarisms in the language of Bartolus than he was at the great commentator's lack of historicity. Yet Valla, no slavish admirer of Cicero, preferred Quintilian in matters of style, although Quintilian was himself generous in Cicero's praise. The wide popularity in France of Valla's *Elegantiae Linguae Latinae* contributed to the controversy aroused by the *Ciceronianus* of Erasmus.[13] Valla felt no attraction to the style of Tacitus, who in any event was little known in the fifteenth century.

The first legal humanist to refer favourably to Tacitus in this respect was Andrea Alciato, and even he once described the historian's prose as "a thicket of thorns." Alciato published his edition of Tacitus's works in 1517, declaring him to be the best of Roman historians. Moreover, he saw in Tacitus a guide to conduct in the face of evil princes, advocating a private prudence that complemented the concept of prudence Guillaume Budé found in Cicero. For all this, it is doubtful whether Alciato, when he began to teach at Bourges in 1529, brought with him any enthusiasm for Tacitus except as an important source for the history of Roman law, and even there he made far greater use of Cicero. Alciato's mentor, Budé, who embodied all the paradoxes of civic humanism in its French guise, had no time at all for Tacitus, calling him "omnium scriptorum perditissimus" in the light of his denunciation by the Church Fathers,

---

a moral concept. A recent interpretation, however, reverses these priorities. Whether or not this was Cicero's intention, it was certainly seen this way by some Renaissance writers. See Maria L. Colish, "Cicero's *De Officiis* and Machiavelli's *Prince*," *Sixteenth-Century Journal*, 9 (1978) 81–93; and pages 44–5, below.

[13]Donald R. Kelley, *Foundations of Modern Historical Scholarship* (New York, 1970), p. 26. Many of the Paris editions of *Elegantiae* were produced by Budé's publisher, Josse Bade. On the role of Valla's textbook in the *Ciceronianus* debate, see Augustin Renaudet, *Erasme et l'Italie* (Geneva, 1954), p. 203.

Orosius and Tertullian.[14] Budé admired Cicero without imitating his style and felt that, in introducing Greek philosophy to the Romans, Cicero had anticipated his own vocation in respect of the French. Budé filled his *Commentarii Linguae Graecae* with Ciceronian citations.

In his *Institution du Prince*, addressed to François 1er, Budé used Cicero to associate rhetoric and history, observing that "the father of Latin eloquence" had described history as the "witness of time, light of truth, mistress of human life, and messenger of antiquity." Budé recommended that the king make history his "great mistress."[15] It was a mirror in which the present reflected the past:

By its consideration men can greatly acquire prudence and better deal with affairs at hand in the counsels of princes, as we see happening every day. There is nothing more important for men of discretion than to understand the state of the world and condition of human nature and to foresee what may come to pass and how to provide for it or forestall it. This is what historians teach. Prudence is acquired in this way by the man of good judgment in reading and reflecting about the past and present government of the world and how all kingdoms and great monarchies have met their end and by what shortcomings they have fallen into difficulty or by what means they have long been preserved and maintained in power and prosperity. . . . Prudence comes for the most part from experience and from observing those examples in the past for which history serves as register.[16]

In the preceding passage Budé had explained how rhetoric required knowledge of history, together with "a style graceful through nature and ready invention, and the discretion and prudence to adapt what is said to the audience and the circumstances of the occasion."[17] Prudence in rhetoric was the ability to take account of the particular, and prudence in history was to understand the particularity of events and to apply to them general rules of human behaviour in the interest of the public weal. It was this aspect of Cicero that was seized upon and distorted later in the century, when Ciceronian style went out of fashion and the Tacitean mode gained ascendancy. Budé represented the type of early French humanism that accepted authority in the prince and preached virtue in the citizen. Rhetoric, philosophy, and history were associated means to this end, and the works of Cicero seemed its perfect instrument. Tacitus, on the other hand, was distrusted and little known in France at this time.

The publication of Erasmus's satirical dialogue, *Ciceronianus*, in 1528 exposed the tensions within the French version of civic humanism. It was not, of course,

[14]Peter Burke, "Tacitism," in T. A. Dorey, ed., *Tacitus* (London, 1969), p. 149; and Schellhase, *Tacitus in Renaissance Political Thought*, p. 87.
[15]Budé, *Institution du Prince* (1524), ed. Claude Bontems, *Le Prince dans la France des XVIe et XVIIe siècles* (Paris, 1965), p. 87. This passage is a direct translation of Cicero; see his *De Oratore*, 2: 36 (p. 245) – see note 9, above.
[16]Budé, *Institution du Prince*, pp. 90–1.
[17]*Ibid.*, p. 89.

the initiation of a new controversy. Following Valla's reservations about Cicero in fifteenth-century Italy and his exchanges on that subject with Poggio Bracciolini, Poliziano had advised the reader to choose from many models, whereas his critic, Cortesi, insisted upon the stylistic pre-eminence of Cicero. Then Giovanni Pico della Mirandola had taken a stand similar to Poliziano's, while Barbaro had followed Cortesi. In the next generation the younger Pico, Gianfrancesco, supported his uncle, and Bembo earned a reputation as the archetypal Ciceronian.[18] In these debates, form and content received different priorities, and rhetoric drew apart from philosophy. The *Ciceronianus* transferred the quarrel to France at a time of religious crisis. Perhaps Erasmus, after his editing of Jerome, recalled the dream in which the saint found his Christianity at odds with his worship of Cicero.[19] In his preface Erasmus turned a northern knife in an open wound. "What a loss to scholarship," he wrote, "if one began by saying that Cicero alone should be imitated. I suspect that under cover of his name another matter is at issue: I mean, to make us forget Christ and lead us back to paganism. But, for my part, no task is more necessary than to consecrate good letters to the glory of Christ, our Lord and Master." This was the same evangelism that had moved Erasmus to declare in his *Paraclesis* that the eloquence of Cicero was far less to be preferred than that of the gospel.[20]

It seemed a gratuitous insult to couple this accusation in the preface with a slight upon the pious master of French humanism, Guillaume Budé, who twelve years earlier had extravagantly praised Erasmus's Greek New Testament to which the *Paraclesis* served as introduction. Erasmus's last letter to Budé in 1528 was a sad piece, denying any intended slur upon French learning. He wrote also to Louis de Berquin, the translator of Luther, to explain that, when the text of *Ciceronianus* had ranked the Parisian publisher, Josse Bade, before his patron Budé, the speaker had been the ridiculous arch-Ciceronian, Nosoponus, not Bulephorus, who represented Erasmus's own opinions in the dialogue.[21] Circumstances destroyed the point of this apology. A few months later, in April 1529, the bigots of the parlement finally accomplished the execution of Berquin for heresy, and not long after that Budé issued his *Commentarii Linguae Graecae*, where Cicero, Greek philosophy, and Christian humanism were mingled without overt incongruity.

Erasmus, the editor of *De Officiis* in 1507 and *Tusculanae Disputationes* in

[18]Remigio Sabbadini, *Storia del Ciceronianismo* (Turin, 1885), pp. 25–50; Eduard Norden, *Die antike Kunstprosa vom VI Jahrhundert V. Chr. bis in die Zeit der Renaissance* (Leipzig, 1898), vol. 2, pp. 773–9; and Izora Scott, *Controversies over the Imitation of Cicero as a Model for Style* (New York, 1910), pp. 10–22.
[19]M. L. Clarke, "Non Hominis Nomen sed Eloquentiae," in Dorey, *Cicero*, p. 87.
[20]Erasmus, *De recta Latini Graecique sermonis pronuntiatione: Dialogus Ciceronianus* (Lyon, 1531), p. 150; and Emile V. Telle, *L'Erasmianus sive Ciceronianus d'Etienne Dolet* (Geneva, 1974), p. 32.
[21]Erasmus, *La Correspondance d'Erasme et de Guillaume Budé*, ed. Marie-Madeleine de la Garanderie (Paris, 1967), pp. 263–4. For the links between Erasmus and Berquin, see Margaret Mann, *Erasme et les débuts de la Réforme française* (Paris, 1934), pp. 113–49.

1523, did not intend to denigrate Cicero but merely to ridicule those fanatical worshippers who allowed no other standard of Latinity. While he was being denounced in France, Erasmus continued his amiable correspondence with the Italian Ciceronians, Bembo and Sadoleto, and dedicated his 1532 edition of St. Basil to the latter.[22] The most vicious of his French critics was a then obscure Agenais physician named Jules-César Scaliger, whose two invectives against Erasmus, published in 1531 and 1537,[23] launched him upon his career as a scholar of international reputation. More important to the present theme was the attack of Etienne Dolet, whose burning ambition and nonconformist temperament involved him in one feud after another. Tainted with accusations of heresy, Dolet fled from Toulouse in 1534 after a brush with the judges of the parlement, whom he labelled indiscriminately as "robed vultures" and "superstitious Turks."[24] At Lyon he was welcomed under the sign of the phoenix and winged orb of the bookseller-printer Sébastien Gryphe, who published Dolet's two discourses against the magistrates. Gryphe had issued a new edition of the *Ciceronianus* corrected by Erasmus in 1531 and, in his anxiety to stir the profitable pot of controversy, had just printed *Cicero Relegatus, Cicero Revocatus,* two dialogues by Ortensio Landi, an Italian exile in France. Dolet had in his possession the manuscript of his *Commentarii Linguae Latinae,* a Ciceronian Latin counterpart to Budé's introduction to Greek letters. While Dolet went to Paris to obtain a privilege for his masterpiece (arriving there in the midst of the storm created by the posting of extremist Protestant placards), Gryphe began to set up the text of a new reply to Erasmus adapted from several entries in the *Commentarii.* It appeared in 1535 as *Dialogus de imitatione Ciceroniana adversus Desiderium Erasmum Roterodamum pro Christophoro Longolio.*[25]

Longolius, or Longueil, was a Ciceronian protégé of Bembo much revered by Dolet. A new and posthumous edition of his works in 1526 may have provoked Erasmus to compose the *Ciceronianus.* His published letters had accused the sage of Rotterdam of Lutheranism and compared his scholarship unfavourably with that of Budé. Assuming Longueil to be the model for Nosoponus, Dolet inserted into his own dialogue Longueil's friend and Dolet's master at Padua, Simon de Neufville. Through the mouths of Villanovanus (Neufville) and his foil Morus (a deliberate travesty of Erasmus's friend, Sir Thomas More, then awaiting execution in the Tower of London), Dolet vilified the character and works of Erasmus. After the latter's death Dolet also responded to an Italian defender of the *Ciceronianus,* Floridus Sabinus, who, oddly enough, had been secretary to Alberto Pio, prince of Carpi, the anti-Erasmian. There was little but personal abuse in this polemic coupled with

[22]Renaudet, *Erasme et l'Italie,* p. 218.
[23]Scaliger, *Oratio pro M. Tullio Cicerone contra Erasmum Roterodamum* (Paris [1531]), and *Adversus Des. Erasmi . . . dialogum Ciceronianum oratio secunda* (Paris, 1537).
[24]Marc Chassaigne, *Etienne Dolet* (Paris, 1930), p. 56.
[25]Telle, *L'Erasmianus sive Ciceronianus d'Etienne Dolet,* pp. 40–2.

praise of Budé and Poliziano and a note of respect for the shade of Erasmus.[26]

Dolet published his reply to Sabinus on the press he had recently established at Lyon, and in the following year, 1541, he issued his own edition of Valla's *Elegantiae*. It was almost as if Dolet, beset by foes among humanists of both camps as well as defenders of scholastic method, was trying to shelter beneath past authority. Scaliger pursued him with implacable hatred. Led by Jean Visagier and Gilbert Ducher, the circle of Latin poets also united against him, including Hubert Sussannée, the author of a Ciceronian dictionary, and Antonio de Gouvea, who later opposed the Ciceronianism of Ramus. Nor did Dolet find support from the legal humanists, with whom in his early years he had shown an affiliation. Jean de Boyssoné, the disciple of Budé and friend of Alciato who had been expelled from his chair of Roman law because of accusations of heresy, was probably his protector at Toulouse. In his letters to Boyssoné, Dolet had denounced the Bartolists, and he had once written to Budé expressing the hope that he could study under Alciato.[27] But Alciato came to profess impatience with Valla's literary preoccupations, and Dolet in his last years sided with Valla, symbolising the growing divorce between literary and legal humanism. While Alciato became more concerned with history than with philology and used literary texts purely to exemplify aspects of Roman society, Dolet turned into a grammarian who subordinated historical truth to literary excellence and Christian to pagan inspiration.

Dolet's device on the title page of the works he published as a printer in Lyon consisted of a hand holding an axe to trim the branches of a fallen tree. The punning motto read, "Scabra et impolita adamussim Dolo atque perpolio" ("accurately, do I hack and level rough and unpolished pieces"). His axe sought to lop off French humanism from its evangelical stem. Among the many classical works that issued from his press were Cicero's *Tusculans* and *Rhetorica*. As stories circulated about his unbelief, he put tongue in cheek and supported his vigorous denials by printing a book as bizarre as *Cato Christianus*, an attempt, dedicated to Sadoleto, to explain Christian doctrine with the aid of an arch-pagan moral reformer. Dolet also began to translate into French Cicero's *Epistolae ad Familiares*, a task that, when completed by the historian Belleforest in 1565, was accompanied by the latter's warning to the reader that his predecessor had been "un imitateur trop sévère." Dolet's French edition of *Tusculans* contains a preface to François 1er pleading that his fellow printers in Lyon were falsely accusing him of heresy in order to eliminate a successful competitor. Nonetheless, Dolet's version of the text in which Cicero questioned the immortality of the soul in this same volume contains added ambiguity. Here, too, are

---

[26]*Ibid.*, pp. 35–6; and Dolet, *Stephani Doleti Galli Aurelli liber de imitatione Ciceroniana adversus Floridum Sabinum* (Lyon, 1540), pp. 7, 54. Dolet apologised for calling Erasmus "delirans senex batavus."

[27]Lucien Febvre, *Le Problème de l'incroyance au XVIᵉ siècle: La Religion de Rabelais* (1942; Paris, 1968), pp. 51–61; and Chassaigne, *Etienne Dolet*, pp. 23–9.

remarks about Roman use of prudence in government and Greek association of prudence and rhetoric.[28] Dolet's attitude to Cicero suggests that Erasmus's reproach of paganism was not entirely wide of its mark. His involvement in the *Ciceronianus* debate reveals the tensions within the French humanism of the time. Erratic, perverse, and eternally enigmatic, Dolet met his cruel death in the Place Maubert in 1546, but it is not only for his martyrdom that he deserves to be remembered.

The year of Dolet's execution was a turning point in Ciceronian scholarship for another reason. In 1546 Pierre de la Ramée (Ramus) published *De Studiis philosophiae et eloquentiae conjugendis*, his commentary on *Brutus* (*Brutinae Quaestiones*), and *Dialecticae Institutiones*, which bears the name on the title page of Omer Talon, Ramus's acolyte.[29] Ramus was in search of a single logical method that he hoped to apply to all of the disciplines of the liberal arts. Some of his inspiration was derived from Rodolphus Agricola's *De Inventione Dialectica*, a fifteenth-century treatise on the logic of disputation aimed at scholasticism. But, ultimately, Ramus's system probably stemmed from Cicero's remarks in *Brutus* on the traditional division of rhetoric into five parts: *inventio* (discovery of material or general arguments), *dispositio* (arrangement), *elocutio* (style), *pronuntiatio* or *actio* (delivery), and *memoria* (memory).[30]

The new method consisted essentially in transferring the first two elements to logic and using them as a means of proceeding from the general to the specific by way of bifurcatory analysis. Only style and delivery remained to rhetoric, while recollection or narration dropped from consideration. Although Ramus might pretend to conjoin philosophy and rhetoric, and rhetoric appeared to be his starting point, he advanced to a position in which dialectical logic became the queen of the sciences and rhetoric was reduced to a matter of technique. Moving logic and dialectic back to philosophy thus recreated an essential element in the attitudes of the schoolmen. These changes reversed the priorities that the Ciceronian humanists held dear – for rhetoric was no longer the dominant discipline that could gather others beneath its roof – and Ramus accomplished it all in Cicero's name. In so doing, he changed the entire concept of the union of citizen and orator. As Ramus gradually refined his method, he altered his stance from edition to edition of his works until the dialectical system came to consist of four parts: invention, disposition, distribution, and definition (or reconstruction). So fixed in its final form did this structure be-

---

[28]Cicero, *Les Epistres familières de Marc Tulle Ciceron père d'éloquence . . . traduites de Latin en François . . .*, trans. Dolet and F. de Belleforest (Paris, 1566), unpaginated *advertisement au lecteur*, and *Les Questions tusculanes de M. T. Ciceron: Oeuvre très utile et necessaire pour résister à toute vitieuse passion d'esprit, et parvenir au mespris et contemnement de la mort* (Lyon, 1543), pp. 2–20.

[29]Walter J. Ong, *Ramus – Method and the Decay of Dialogue: From the Art of Discourse to the Art of Reason* (Cambridge, Mass., 1958), p. 30.

[30]Ramus, *Brutinae Quaestiones*, in his *Petri Rami praelectiones in Ciceronis orationes octo consulares*, ed. Freigius (Basel, 1575), p. 472. For a list of Cicero's references to the five divisions in *Brutus*, see Douglas, Introduction to *Brutus*, p. xxxi.

come that in his lecture *De Logicae Definitione* Ramus declared that, whatever the part of the world in which men dwelt, whatever their customs and governments, and whatever the divisions of knowledge they chose to admit (*grammatici, rhetores, poetae, historici, arithmetici, geometrici, musici, astrologi, physici, ethici*), all were obliged to follow "the one law and reason postulated in the dialectic."[31]

Ramus's dramatic flair and arrogant single-mindedness provoked intense opposition from fellow Ciceronians and all of the followers of Aristotle, whom Ramus had denounced. The resistance within the Ciceronian movement to Dolet's attempt to isolate letters from other humane studies was carried over into the struggle to prevent Ramus from imposing upon them a method supposedly derived from Ciceronian premises. Antonio de Gouvea, one of Dolet's critics, played the major part in the commission that resulted in the royal edict of March 1544, which censured Ramus for "témérité, arrogance, et impudence." While officially suspended from public teaching in the years that followed, Ramus continued to compose works on Cicero and Quintilian that exemplified his system, including many commentaries on Cicero's speeches and philosophical treatises. After the advent of Henri II in 1547, the suspension was lifted, and Ramus, with strong support in the royal entourage, made new converts in the parlement and the university. His appointment as joint professor of eloquence and philosophy at the Collège Royal in 1551 enabled him to initiate institutional reforms of the liberal arts and provoked new waves of opposition. Pierre Galland, the conservative rector of the university and an early critic of the *Brutinae Quaestiones*, led the outcry, describing Ramus as "a harpy that fouls all that he touches" and "a viper vomiting forth floods of poison."[32] Galland was followed by Ramus's most relentless enemy, Jacques Charpentier, who, together with his friend, Marc-Antoine Muret, criticised the *Dialecticae Institutiones* and resisted the union of rhetoric and philosophy.

Unlike Dolet, Ramus was careful not to mix religious speculation with his commentaries on Cicero's philosophical works. When he lectured on the *Somnium Scipionis* and hinted, darkly enough, that the rest of Cicero's *Republic* was doubtless kept well hidden by superstitious men, he used the occasion not to discuss problems of the afterlife but to apply his practical method to physical science. The very nomenclature used in astronomy, he said, was the product of the scholastic mind and suited only for "altercationes scholasticae." But Ramus's colleague, Adrien Turnèbe, did not object to metaphysical speculation in his criticism of the distortions involved in the application of Ramus's interpretative system. In this context Turnèbe branded Ramus with the epithet

[31]Ramus, *Scholae in liberales artes* (1569), ed. Walter J. Ong (Hildesheim, 1970), p. 30.

[32]Charles Waddington, *Ramus (Pierre de la Ramée): Sa vie, ses écrits, et ses opinions* (Paris, 1885), pp. 50–2, 94. For a list of Ramus's commentaries, see Walter J. Ong, *Ramus and Talon Inventory* (Cambridge, Mass., 1958), p. 38. Several of these commentaries, together with *Brutinae Quaestiones* and *De Studiis philosophiae et eloquentiae conjugendis*, were published in 1575 in the posthumous collection edited by Freigius, Ramus's discipline at Fribourg; see note 30, above.

usuarius, meaning that he had exploited Cicero to illustrate his method and had no proprietary claim to the Ciceronian canon. Ramus seemed close to asserting such a demand. After rereading the *Brutus* on famous orators, he published in 1557 a number of his lectures under the title *Ciceronianus*. Here he identified himself with the father of eloquence and was so contemptuous of earlier controversies and commentaries that he labelled them "patchwork quilts of rags" (*panniculorum centones*).[33]

In the religious wars of the 1560s Ramus, a declared if irregular Calvinist, fled from Paris, leaving the field to his enemies. Meanwhile, Denis Lambin, successor to Turnèbe as professor of Greek at the Collège Royal in 1566, proceeded with his edition of Cicero's *Opera Omnia* in unyielding opposition to Ramist influence. Henri Estienne, whose revised version of the Ciceronian lexicon composed by his father, Robert, was completed by Lambin's index in 1568, returned to the tradition of Poliziano and Erasmus and satirised Mario Nizzoli, the leader of the old-style Italian Ciceronians. Estienne also drew attention to the rising star of Justus Lipsius, who with Marc-Antoine Muret, Charpentier's friend, inaugurated the age of Tacitean scholarship. Even Ramus, for whom Estienne had no sympathy, anticipated Lipsius in some respects. His angular Latin style resembled that of the great antiquarian, and his view of the virtue of prudence in the orator touched, as Budé had formerly done, upon a theme that Lipsius later expanded.[34] Ramus met his death in the massacre of St. Bartholomew's Day – legend has it by Charpentier's conniving – while Estienne continued a stylistic debate that became increasingly irrelevant. In the religious wars the burden of intellectual debate shifted from rhetoric and philosophy to politics and history, and Tacitus suddenly assumed a new dimension.

The new tone was explicit in Jean Bodin's *Methodus ad facilem cognitionem historiarum* in 1566: "It is true that on account of his unpolished manner of speaking Tacitus is usually repudiated by those who prefer the lighter trifles of grammarians to the more serious accounts of those who have spent the whole of their lives in public affairs." Bodin reproached Alciato for quibbling about the style of Tacitus and remarked that those who criticised Tacitus for plain writing were like Christians attacking Jerome for being a Ciceronian. In contrast to Ammianus Marcellinus, Tacitus had "maintained the dignity of Roman

---

[33]Ramus, *Somnium Scipionis ex sexto libro de republica M. Tullii Ciceronis Petri Rami Veromandae praelectionibus explicatum* (Paris, 1546), p. 26v, *Ad Turnebi disputatio ad librum Ciceronis de fato adversus quemdam qui non solum logicus esse, verumetiam dialecticus haberi vult* (Paris, 1554), p. 27, and *P. Rami regii eloquentiae et philosophiae professoris Ciceronianus ad Carolum Lotharingum Cardinalem* (Paris, 1557), unpaginated dedication. For an account of the exchanges between Turnèbe and Ramus, see Ong, *Ramus and Talon Inventory*, pp. 289–94.

[34]Jchasse, *La Renaissance de la critique*, pp. 189–90, 330; Dubois, *Conception de l'histoire en France*, p. 250; and Ong, *Ramus – Method and the Decay of Dialogue*, p. 246. Henri Estienne's *Pseudo-Cicero* appeared in 1577, and his *Nizoliodidasculus* in 1578; see Scott, *Controversies over the Imitation of Cicero*, p. 105.

speech." He ranked with the great historians of antiquity – Polybius, Thucydides, Xenophon, and Caesar – for like them he revealed "the causes of things, the origins, the progress, the inclinations, all the plans of everyone, the sayings and the deeds at their just weight." Influenced by Ramus and disillusioned with legal humanist attitudes, Bodin set out in his *Methodus* to deduce the principles of government from a comparativist approach to history. If he differed from Budé in this respect, he repeated Budé's observation that for men of affairs history was the essential means of acquiring political prudence. Cicero, however, did not appeal to Bodin. He accused Cicero of being digressive, refuted his belief in a government of mixed forms, and decried the republican and democratic values he discerned in Cicero's political thinking. "Cicero's definition of the state," he wrote, "as a group of men associated for the sake of living well indicates the best objective indeed, but it does not indicate the power and nature of the institution." He also assailed another Ciceronian account of the commonwealth as "the union of several associations under an approved law for a common advantage." Bodin's preference for strong monarchy led him to distort Tacitus's acceptance of the principate as the necessary consequence of the decay of republican virtue, and to see the historian as approving undivided authority by preference: "It is not only salutary, as Tacitus wrote, but also necessary in the administration of great affairs that power should rest entirely with one man."[35]

Another admirer of Tacitus, and one who described him as "a good author, and as serious and reliable as any,"[36] was Montaigne's friend Etienne de la Boëtie. His *Discours de la servitude volontaire* was completed about 1550 on the model of a classical indictment of tyranny, but it was not published until after the St. Bartholomew's Day Massacre, when it was pressed into the service of Huguenot propaganda against the monarchy.[37] Although he esteemed Tacitus as much as Bodin, La Boëtie interpreted him quite differently and cited him in condemnation of the many crimes of the Julio-Claudian dynasty. Interestingly enough, the passage where he particularly praised the merits of the historian was as scathing of the *plebs sordida* as it was of Nero, who had so corrupted them that they mourned his death. A more celebrated work that used Tacitus against monarchical absolutism was François Hotman's *Francogallia*, composed largely in the late 1560s and first published in 1573. Yet among the greatest achievements of Hotman's early career were his massive textual commentaries on the orations and letters of Cicero. His major collection of observations upon Cicero's forensic pleadings had appeared as early as 1554. The stature of his scholarship in this respect may be judged from the pride of place given his

[35]Bodin, *Method for the Easy Comprehension of History*, pp. 70, 83, 73, 17, 158, 272.
[36]La Boëtie, *Discours de la servitude volontaire* (1574), ed. Paul Bonnefon (Paris, 1922), p. 83.
[37]The *Discours* first appeared in the second of the *Dialogi ab Eusebio Philadelphio* (or *Reveille-Matin*) in 1574 and was reprinted in the various editions of Simon Goulart's *Mémoires de l'estat de France sous Charles Neufiesme* (1576–79).

comments in the Cologne compendium of Cicero's speeches in 1685 and his remarks on the *Epistolae ad Brutum et ad Quintum fratrem* in the composite edition of Gronovius in 1725.[38] Consciously or unconsciously, the political demands of the civil wars bent the objectivity of scholars. Hotman made selective use of both Cicero and Tacitus as allies in his cause.

The French situation resembled that in Germany at the beginning of the century, when humanists such as Conrad Celtis and Ulrich von Hutten enlisted Tacitus's *Germania* in the cause of patriotism and resurrected Arminius from the darkness of the Teutoberger Wald. The Alsatian humanist Beatus Rhenanus had imposed a more scholarly view with his edition of Tacitus's works in 1532, which surpassed even Alciato's in accuracy.[39] Now the French began to examine Tacitus for the light he might shed upon the political practices of their ancestors, the Franks, and such relevance as they might have for the sixteenth-century constitution. Although Hotman had made his name as a historian of Roman law, he came to see the tribal customs of the Germanic Franks as more important to Frenchmen than Roman jurisprudence. When Bodin was writing his *Methodus* in the interval between the civil wars of the 1560s, Hotman was preparing both his *Anti-Tribonian* and, with the help of the Beatus edition of Tacitus, his early outline of the history of the Francogallic constitution. The *Germania* was used by other historians and polemicists writing in this period, such as Etienne Pasquier and Jean du Tillet, although their views of French government were very different from Hotman's.[40] Their arguments were complicated by a debate about whether the Franks had been Teutons or migrant Celts and about the relative merits of Gaulois and Frankish customs. When these controversies were initiated in the previous decade Ramus had been a leading Gallicist and Charles du Moulin an early advocate of Germanism.[41] Bodin and Hotman, respectively, continued these opposing traditions.

When the *Francogallia* appeared in 1573 and went through massive revision and expansion in subsequent editions, the scholarly intentions of the draft begun in the 1560s took second place to the political needs of the later period. Tacitus and Cicero were invoked in tandem: the first to reveal the primitive Franks as the authors of liberty who elected their kings *ex nobilitate* and chose their war chiefs *ex virtute;* the second to extol the merits of mixed government and repeatedly to stress the doctrine *salus populi suprema lex esto*, taken by Cicero from the Twelve Tables and described in *De Legibus*.[42] For all his Ciceronian

---

[38]Hotman, *Francogallia by Francois Hotman* (1573), ed. Ralph E. Giesey and J. H. M. Salmon (Cambridge, 1972), pp. 38–52; and Cicero, *Marci Tullii Ciceronis orationum commentaria selecta* (Cologne, 1685), and *M. Tullii Ciceronis epistolarum ad Quintum fratrem et ad Brutum* (The Hague, 1725).

[39]Schellhase, *Tacitus in Renaissance Political Thought*, pp. 37–47, 61–5.

[40]Hotman, *Francogallia*, p. 22.

[41]*Ibid.*, p. 13; and Ramus, *Liber de moribus veterum Gallorum* (Paris, 1559).

[42]Hotman, *Francogallia*, pp. 208, 294, 296, 300, 342, 414, 450.

scholarship, Hotman overlooked a vital reference that would have helped his case, the mention in *Epistolae ad Atticum* of the German Francones. The antiquarian Claude Fauchet took pride in pointing this out. He agreed with Hotman on the possible identification of the Franks with the Sicambrians of Batavia, but, more sympathetic to monarchical authority, he held the references of Tacitus to Germanic tribal kingship to be less restrictive on royal power than Hotman had claimed.[43]

Other Huguenot theorists of resistance made less use of Tacitus than did Hotman, but they frequently cited Cicero. In *Du droit des magistrats* Théodore de Bèze referred to a passage that Seneca had quoted from the missing books of *De Republica* to the effect that even under the early Roman kings final appeals could be made to popular assemblies. Similar use of this example was made in *Francogallia*.[44] Bèze drew the attention of his readers to a section describing tyranny in Cicero's *De Officiis*, where it was held that in the last resort it was the duty of a son to accuse a father who threatened the safety of the state through tyranny. The author of *Vindiciae contra Tyrannos* cited *De Officiis* on many occasions to demonstrate that those in authority had to protect true religion, respect the law, and act for the welfare of the people who had placed them in office. As in *Du droit des magistrats* Cicero was invoked to greatest effect in defining the nature of tyranny. Rulers who betrayed their trust or broke their contract with those who had created them to govern became enemies of the people, committed treason against the commonwealth, and ought to be punished.[45] The *Discours politiques des diverses puissances*, a Huguenot tract rather less known than *Francogallia*, *Du droit des magistrats*, or *Vindiciae contra Tyrannos*, seems to have been inspired by Ciceronian concepts in its attempt to adapt principles of civic humanism to secular resistance theory. Once again, *De Officiis* was the work most often cited in the text.[46]

Apart from Hotman, Huguenot writers generally confined their use of Tacitus to historical exemplification.[47] Cicero seemed an appropriate source for the definition of tyranny and Tacitus for its illustration. Those of moderate persuasion, who supported both royal authority and religious toleration, were even

---

[43]Fauchet, *Oeuvres* (Paris, 1590), vol. 1, pp. 29v, 30r.

[44]Bèze, *Du droit des magistrats* (1574), ed. Robert M. Kingdon (Geneva, 1971), p. 25; and Hotman, *Francogallia*, p. 300.

[45]Bèze, *Du droit des magistrats*, pp. 47–8; and Cicero, *De Officiis*, ed. H. A. Holden (Cambridge, 1899), 3: 23, 90 (p. 127). And [Mornay] *Vindiciae contra Tyrannos . . . Stephano Iunio Bruto Celta Auctore* (n.p., 1580), pp. 28–9, 75, 105, 109, 121–2, 156, 179, 212, 215–16. Only one Ciceronian allusion in the *Vindiciae contra Tyrannos* was not drawn from *De Officiis* but came from Cicero's *Paradoxa Stoicorum* instead; *ibid.*, p. 179.

[46]*Discours politiques des diverses puissance establies de Dieu au monde* (1574) in Goulart's *Mémoires de l'estat de France sous Charles Neufiesme* ("Meidelbourg," 1579), vol. 3, pp. 147v, 213r. For some definitions of tyranny from Cicero often employed in resistance theory, see *ibid.*, pp. 165r, 167r (references to *Second Philippics*), p. 168v (*De Officiis*, 1: 8, 26 [p. 12]), p. 177v (the passage from *De Officiis* that Bèze cited in *Du droit des magistrats*; see *De Officiis*, 3: 23, 90 [p. 127]; and note 45, above). The author also referred to Tacitus. I am indebted to Sarah Hanley for drawing my attention to the Ciceronian tenor of this important and neglected tract.

[47]For example, see [Mornay] *Vindiciae contra tyrannos*, p. 141; and *Discours politiques*, pp. 165r, 182v.

more inclined to see Tacitus's *Annales* and *Historiae* as useful sourcebooks, especially when they found themselves opposing alleged flatterers and Machiavellians around the throne. Such was the case with the Protestant magistrate Innocent Gentillet, who, while he was no monarchomach, shared the xenophobic Huguenot view that the crown had been corrupted by Italian influence in general and Machiavelli in particular. Gentillet's *Discours contre Machiavel* made much of flattery, deceit, and treason under Tiberius from Tacitus's *Annales*. He quoted Tacitus's version of the speech of the jurist Gaius Ateius Capito that the emperor should not pardon the technical treason of Lucius Ennius because the "laws desire that in such crimes of treason the least suspicion and appearance suffice to convict the accused, and it is in the great interest and utility of the state that one who has attempted anything, however slight, against the ruler should be rigorously punished."[48] Capito's words came close to genuinely Machiavellian reasoning, but Gentillet, who was so accustomed to distorting Machiavelli's precepts that he could not recognise a true instance of *raison d'état* when he saw it, was concerned only to criticise a piece of hypocritical flattery. Gentillet never accused Tacitus of being a precursor of Machiavelli. The Roman historian could still be seen in La Boétie's image of the exposer of tyrants, not the exponent of tyranny.

Jean Bodin, as we have seen, was an admirer of Tacitus not merely as a historian of causes and motives but also as an advocate of royal authority. His *Six livres de la République*, published in the same year as the *Discours contre Machiavel*, was also critical of Machiavellians and was aimed, besides, at the Huguenot theorists of resistance who themselves condemned the Florentine. At the beginning of his new book Bodin defined the commonwealth as "a lawful government of several families and what they hold in common, together with sovereign power." This sounded reminiscent of the definitions cited from Cicero in the *Methodus*, but the addition of sovereignty made all the difference in the world. With sovereignty described as absolute, with perpetual and indivisible law-making power located in the French crown, Bodin went one better than the monarchomach collective sovereignty of the people, exercised negatively to restrain or discipline the king.[49] Like Gentillet, Bodin saw no resemblance between Tacitus and Machiavelli, and he, too, used passages from the *Annales* without recognising an affiliation with *The Prince*. Tiberius was the subject of several critical references in *Six livres de la République*, while Bodin alluded to Sejanus as an example of the useful royal technique of diverting discontent towards a tyrannical minister.[50] In this passage Bodin did not hesitate to call Tiberius himself a tyrant, but he went on to cite Cicero, first, on the

---

[48]Gentillet, *Discours contre Machiavel* (1576), ed. A. d'Andrea and P. D. Stewart (Florence, 1974), p. 77; and Tacitus, *Annales*, 3: 70. For other relevant allusions to Tacitus, see Gentillet, *Discours contre Machiavel*, pp. 98, 101, 102, 163, 197.

[49]See below, pp. 119–35.

[50]Bodin, *Les Six livres de la République* (Geneva, 1577), 2: 5 (p. 392). In another passage Bodin did not hesitate to follow Tacitus in observing that Tiberius took away from the people "l'ombre de la liberté"; *ibid.*, 1: 6 (p. 83).

futility of abolishing the good with the bad in attempting to erase a tyrant's memory after his death and, second, on the dilemma confronting a member of a tyrant's council during the consideration of some profitable law. Tacitus was also called in on many occasions in *Six livres de la République* to sustain erudite references to such miscellaneous issues as Roman paternal authority, the chastity of the ancient Germans, and the Parthian custom of swearing alliances in blood. Except for a new rebuttal of the theory of mixed forms of government, Cicero was also employed more as a source of historical illustration than of evaluative judgment. His letters and speeches, together with *De Officiis* and *De Finibus*, were cited over thirty times on matters such as the family, citizenship, usury, and the role of magistrates.[51] Bodin was too conscious of his own originality to require authorities to buttress his theoretical viewpoint. The architect of politique absolutism used Cicero and Tacitus indiscriminately as a grab-bag of information.

Bodin chose to write *Six livres de la République* in French, although he turned it into Latin in 1586, and the issues of Latin eloquence and literary style were irrelevant to his treatise. As more emphasis in political dialogue was placed upon the vernacular, a number of French translations of Tacitus and Cicero began to appear. Mode could still be important, however, to a translator. In 1575 Blaise de Vigenère published a composite volume in French containing part of Tacitus's *Germania*, the sixth book of Caesar's *Commentaries*, and Cicero's *De Oratore*.[52] His declared purpose in placing these three works between one set of covers was to show how a diversity of Latin styles could be faithfully represented in French. Vigenère, who had studied under Turnèbe and Dorat, also translated Livy and the dialogues on friendship of Plato, Cicero, and Lucian. Claude Guillemot published a complete French version of *Germania* in 1580, but it had evidently been prepared at the beginning of the Gaulois–Germanist controversy, for its dedication was dated 1551. The *Agricola* was translated in 1574 by the Huguenot lawyer Ange Cappel, who also rendered several of Seneca's works into French.[53] In 1582 Fauchet, the antiquarian, issued a complete translation of the works of Tacitus, incorporating parts of the *Annales* that Etienne de la Planche had already turned into French.[54] Among the more remarkable translators of Cicero at this

---

[51]For Tacitus, see Bodin, *Six livres de la République*, 1: 4 (p. 47), 8 (p. 174), 5: 1 (p. 776); and, for Cicero, see *ibid.*, 1: 4 (p. 47), 2: 1 (pp. 338–9), 5: 2 (p. 802), 3: 5 (pp. 522–7).

[52]Vigenère, comp., *Le Traicté de Cicéron de la meilleure forme d'orateurs, le sixième livre des commentaires de Caesar . . . , et la Germanie de Cornelius Tacitus* (Paris, 1575). After serving the duke of Nevers, Vigenère was employed in the French embassy in Rome and then in the office of one of the secretaries of state. He was a prolific author, and among his more curious works are treatises on comets, alchemy, and writing in cipher. Also see his translations of Plato *et al.*, *Trois dialogues de l'amitié: Le Lysis de Platon – le Laelius de Cicéron – et le Toxaris de Lucian* (Paris, 1579), and of Livy, *Les Décades*, 2 vols. (Paris, 1583).

[53]Tacitus, *Discours excellent auquel est contenu l'assiete de toute l'Alemaigne, les moeurs, coustumes, et façon de faire les habitans en icelle*, trans. Claude Guillemot (Paris, 1580), and *La Vie de Jules Agricola*, trans. Ange Cappel (n.p., n.d. [dedication dated 1574]). See below, pp. 65–6.

[54]Tacitus, *Les Oeuvres de C. Cornelius Tacitus*, trans. Claude Fauchet (Paris, 1582). *Le Dialogue des orateurs* was added to the edition of 1584–5. A third edition was published in 1594. Tacitus's *Annales* also entered France through Guicciardini's *Storia d'Italia*, which was deeply influenced

time was the strange figure of Guy le Fèvre de la Boderie, remembered for his
Syriac New Testament, his Chaldean grammar, his refutation of Islam, and his
translations of Ficino and Giovanni Pico. Not surprisingly, he chose to publish
Cicero's *De Natura Deorum* in French in 1581.[55]

While Tacitus was increasing in popularity among French readers and while
the theorists of resistance, together with their critics, managed to set him beside
Cicero in support of their contentions, the two greatest Taciteans of the century
– Marc-Antoine Muret and Joost Lips, Muretus and Lipsius – were laying the
foundations for the triumph of their idol. Both were concerned with elegance
and accuracy in Latin style; both began as Ciceronians and, after changing the
focus of their attention to Tacitus, returned to Cicero with new insight; and
both found the times in which Tacitus had lived a better analogue for the
troubles the monarchies of Europe were experiencing in their own day than was
the age of Cicero. It was in part because of their joint perception that a new
literary mode was to be accompanied by a shift in the mode of political discourse.

As a youth Muret was an admirer of Erasmus's critic Jules-César Scaliger.
His erudition and the brilliance of his own Latin style secured him lectureships
at several French universities, including Paris, where he was a member of
Charpentier's anti-Ramist group, and Bordeaux, where he may have tutored
Montaigne. Charges of heresy and sodomy caused him to take refuge in Italy.
At Venice in 1557 he dedicated to the doge a commentary on Cicero's speeches
against Catiline, and adopted so ultra-Ciceronian a stance that he addressed
Mocenigo, "It is extraordinary to see how these men, who in our own and our
father's memory wanted to be called Ciceronians, could come out with so many
barbarous expressions and defective constructions taken from the corrupt texts
they consulted."[56] Typical of Muret's academic showmanship was his laying a
trap for his rivals when they attended his lectures in the hope he would utter a
phrase not in Cicero's canon. He put careful stress on a number of words that
he knew to be contained in Cicero's works but that had been inadvertently
omitted from the great lexicon prepared by Nizzoli. Muret was a professor in
Rome for twenty-one years, until shortly before his death in 1585. When he
began his series of lectures on Tacitus in 1580 his enthusiasm for his subject
was so great that he declared history to be the queen of the humanities.[57] He

---

by them. French editions of Guicciardini's history were published in 1568 and 1577; see Vin-
cenzo Luciani, *Francesco Guicciardini e la fortuna dell'opera sua* (Florence, 1949), pp. 32, 398.
Guicciardini's *Ricordi*, containing allusions to Tacitus, appeared in French in 1576; see Guicciardini, *Plusieurs advis et conseils de François Guicciardin tant pour les affaires d'estat que privées* (Paris,
1576). I am indebted to Lionel A. McKenzie for this point.
[55] Cicero, *De la nature des dieux*, trans. Guy le Fèvre de la Boderie (Paris, 1581). In his Oriental
interests and his religious syncretism La Boderie was a follower of Guillaume Postel.
[56] Muret, *M. Antonii Mureti ad Leonardum Mocenicum Patricium Venetum, orationum Ciceronis in
Catalinam explicatio* (Venice, 1557), p. iii.
[57] Muret, *M. Antonii Mureti opera omnia* (Leyden, 1789), vol. 1, p. iii. For Muret's showmanship,
also see J. E. Sandys, *A History of Classical Scholarship* (Cambridge, 1908), p. 150.

had a utilitarian history in mind, and Tacitus was its high priest. The lessons that Tacitus taught applied to the current age. While Muret was cautious enough to declare that Europe had no contemporary tyrants to compare with Tiberius, Caligula, and Nero as described in the *Annales*, he believed "it profitable for us to know how good and prudent men managed their lives under them, how and how far they tolerated and dissimulated their vices. . . . Those who do not know how to connive at such things not only bring themselves into danger but often make the very princes worse."[58] When the lectures on Tacitus had been completed, Muret turned back to Cicero and used *Epistolae ad Atticum* as his text. The Cicero that now emerged from the confidences imparted to his closest friend was a devious statesman in whom ambition vied with prudence. The only use for eloquence in modern times, Muret concluded, was in the writing of letters.[59]

There is no space here to follow in detail the academic peregrinations of Lipsius from Jena to Leyden to Louvain or his religious apostasies among Lutheranism, Calvinism, and Catholicism. He was first known not only as a Ciceronian scholar but also as a supreme Ciceronian stylist. In later years he recalled his youthful enthusiasm and continuing, if modified, affection for Cicero in a piece of Latin that is almost a parody of the Tacitean mode: "Ciceronem amo. Olim etiam imitatus sum: alius mihi sensus nunc viro. Asianae dapes non ad meum gustum, Atticae dapes."[60] But, if Lipsius altered his estimate of Cicero's style, he remained consistent in his belief that Cicero's principal merit in politics was the advocacy of prudence. This was the virtue he commended when dedicating his first lectures on Cicero to Cardinal Granvelle before setting out for Rome in 1567.[61] In Rome he met Muret and began his career of Tacitean scholarship, in which the concept of prudence developed into a kind of short-hand for political necessity, guarded by the moral reservations of the individual.

The two aspects of prudence, the private and the public, and the two fields of its exemplification, history and rhetoric, had been left disjoined by Budé. Now public and private prudence were directly associated, and politics replaced rhetoric as the second area in which prudence could be learned and applied.

---

[58]Croll, *Style, Rhetoric, and Rhythm*, p. 152.

[59]Muret, *Mureti opera omnia*, oratio XVI, pp. 318–25. Despite his new view of Cicero and his contempt for ultra-Ciceronians, Muret paid tribute to Sadoleto, Bembo, and Longueil in this lecture.

[60]"I love Cicero. Formerly I even imitated him. Now as a man I have other tastes. Asian feasts are not to my liking. Attic ones are." Lipsius, as quoted in Clarke, "Non Hominis Nomen sed Eloquentiae," p. 95. For brief outlines of Lipsius's life, together with comments upon his ideas, see V. A. Nordman, "Justus Lipsius als Geschichtsforscher und Geschichtslehrer," *Suomalainen tiedeakatemia Toimituksia (Annales Academiae Fennicae)*, ser. B, 28 (1932), 1–101; Jason Lewis Saunders, *Justus Lipsius: The Philosophy of Renaissance Stoicism* (New York, 1955); and Knud Banning, *Justus Lipsius* (Copenhagen, 1975).

[61]Jehasse, *La Renaissance de la critique*, p. 208. Lipsius cited Cicero and Tacitus together on prudence; see Lipsius, *Politicorum sive civilis doctrinae libri sex* (Leyden, 1589), p. 212.

The connections had already been implicit in Cicero and the Stoic context of the orator's thought. The intellectual climate of the religious wars in France and the Netherlands had at first encouraged the application of Ciceronian rhetoric to political debate, but as the wars intensified the Ciceronian emphasis upon the active participation of the citizen no longer seemed appropriate. The helplessness of the individual in face of forces he could not control suggested resignation or withdrawal, and the tenets of Senecan neostoicism provided the moral fortitude that enabled him to preserve his dignity and integrity. In this way neostoicism conjoined the two kinds of prudence, encouraged the politics of necessity, and elevated history as the record of pragmatic realism and the source of individual consolation. The transformed Cicero still had a role to play in this new structure, but among classical authors Tacitus now occupied the centre of the stage. Lipsius personified this intellectual shift and popularised the change in literary mode through which it was expressed. In France he had his counterparts or disciples in Montaigne, Guillaume du Vair, and Pierre Charron.

Despite his desire for scholarly withdrawal, Lipsius could not ignore the blood-bath in his own country and across the borders to the south. When he lectured on Tacitus at Jena in the year of the St. Bartholomew's Day Massacre, he compared the Duke of Alba to Tiberius.[62] Three years later appeared the first version of his masterly edition of the works of Tacitus, which he refined and improved in subsequent editions until his death in 1606. Also published in 1575, Lipsius's *Antiquae Lectiones* confirmed the revision of his view of Cicero, although here he turned to Plautus and Seneca, rather than to Tacitus, for literary models. In the next decade came his neostoic *De Constantia* (1584) and his political handbook based extensively upon Tacitus, *Politicorum Libri Sex* (1589). A statement of expediency in the latter work – that the toleration of two religions inside one state was inconceivable and that one of them must be exterminated *ense et igne* – caused indignation at Leyden but was evidently ignored by Calvinists at La Rochelle, who printed a French translation there in 1590.[63] Lipsius continued to publish studies of Roman antiquities and earned equal rank with Isaac Casaubon and Joseph Scaliger in the scholarly "triumvirate" of the age, though Casaubon and Scaliger did not see eye to eye with Lipsius in his role of *Sospitator Taciti*. Casaubon denounced Tacitus as a spe-

---

[62]Arnaldo Momigliano, "The First Political Commentary on Tacitus," in his *Essays in Ancient and Modern Historiography* (Oxford, 1977), pp. 222–4; this essay was first published in the *Journal of Roman Studies*, 37 (1947) 91–101. The later version includes as an appendix a reprint of Momigliano's review of Jose Ruysschaert, *Juste Lipse et les Annales de Tacite* (Louvain, 1949), itself a valuable work on the editorial methods of Lipsius. In the review Momigliano discussed whether the oration in question was actually delivered by Lipsius at Jena in 1572 and pointed out that Lipsius also remarked in the oration that Tacitus was more relevant to his own times than were Sallust and Livy. Also see Jehasse, *La Renaissance de la critique*, p. 213.

[63]Lipsius, *Les six livres des politiques, ou Doctrine civile de Iustus Lipsius*, trans. Charles le Ber sieur de Malassis (La Rochelle, 1590).

cialist in shame and slighted his commentator by saying that anyone who thought Tacitus a guide to practical politics was either accusing kings of being tyrants or teaching them how to become so. Scaliger, with an acerbity reminiscent of his father, wrote that "Lipsius is the cause that many have now little respect for Cicero, whose style he esteems about as much as I do his own." Yet in literary matters Lipsius became something of a relativist. One of his most readable pieces was a satire, published in 1581, in which he described a dream where he witnessed the Roman senate prosecuting a group of audacious philologists who sought to correct ancient texts by their own standards.[64]

Before the new current had become firmly established in France a curious echo of that phase of Huguenot resistance theory that had enrolled Cicero and Tacitus together under its banners sounded in the propaganda of the Catholic League. The most weighty ideological opponent of the last Valois and the first Bourbon kings was Jean Boucher, doctor of the Sorbonne and associate of the revolutionary group of the Sixteen. His *De justa Henrici Tertii abdicatione* appeared in 1589, just after the monarch it sought to depose had been assassinated by a Leaguer fanatic. To illustrate the nature of tyranny Boucher cited Tacitus's judgment of Sejanus together with some of the extracts from *De Officiis, Pro Milone, Ad Brutum,* and *Tusculanae Disputationes* that formed the corpus of humanist sources on the subject. From *De Amicitia* he repeated Cicero's words on the climate of tyranny: "Under it there can be no trust, no love, no kind of enduring good will: suspicion and unease lurk everywhere, and there is no place for friendship."[65] This, Boucher maintained, was precisely that atmosphere surrounding Henri de Valois and his would-be successor, Henri de Navarre. Boucher's pseudonymous colleague, "Gulielmus Rossaeus," published a better reasoned and less personal treatise to the same effect: *De justa Reipublicae Christianae in reges impios et haereticos* (1590). Rossaeus cited one of Cicero's letters to Atticus and, a little later, the second book of *De Officiis,* to establish the difference between a king and a tyrant. Each reference to Cicero was associated with a quotation from Tacitus on the reign of Tiberius.[66] Another enemy of Navarre was the Leaguer publicist and *parlementaire* Louis Dorléans, whose humanist inclinations had been shaped by

[64]Jehasse, *La Renaissance de la critique,* pp. 394–6; Saunders, *Justus Lipsius,* p. 65; and J. Ijsewijn, "Neo-Latin Satire: *Sermo* and *Satyra Menippea,*" in Bolgar, *Classical Influences on European Culture, A.D. 1500–1700,* p. 49.

[65][Jean Boucher] *De justa Henrici Tertii abdicatione e Francorum regno* (1589; Lyon, 1591), p. 258 (mispaginated as 266).

[66]Rossaeus, *De justa reipub. Christianae in reges impios et haereticos authoritate* (Paris, 1590), pp. 17r, 18v, 22r, 22v. The use by Rossaeus of Cicero's *De Officiis* is very like that of the French monarchomachs; see page 40, above. He is probably directly indebted, however, to the Scottish monarchomach George Buchanan, to whom he referred on several occasions with surprising respect. Rossaeus's citation from *De Officiis* is the same as Buchanan's: Buchanan, *De Jure Regni apud Scotos* (n.p., 1680 [1579]), p. 28. And see Cicero, *De Officiis,* 2: 12, 41 (p. 75). On Rossaeus (William Reynolds) and his relationship with Buchanan, see below, pp. 144–47.

Dorat and whose first polemics for the League were written in the guise of "the Catholic Englishman." Like Boucher, Dorléans fled to the Netherlands when Henri IV recovered Paris in 1594. He returned in later years after making his submission, and he eventually issued his *Novae Cogitationes in libros Annalium Taciti.* Here Tacitus was represented not as the critic of imperial tyranny but as the ultimate guide to prudent kingship. During his exile Dorléans had evidently become a disciple of Lipsius. Formerly, he argued, it was customary "to praise the declamation of Cicero, but Tacitus is more deserving in our age." To Dorléans Tacitus had become "a flower among authors and a prince among historians."[67]

The first separate political commentary on Tacitus was published in Paris in 1581, three years before Navarre had become the next heir to the French throne and the League had been revived to oppose his claim. It was issued with the text of the first four books of the *Annales,* and its author was a Piedmontese, Carlo Pasquale.[68] He was a protégé of the statesman and man of letters, Guy du Faur de Pibrac, a widely respected populariser of Seneca. Pasquale turned to Seneca in his preface to the reader when he wished to commend those who, as Tacitus had shown, knew how to respond to unexpected adversity and even to death. He used Seneca, too, to defend the enigmatic brevity of the historian's style, remarking that language responded to changes in public attitudes.[69] Lipsius was popularising gnomic political utterances on the Tacitean model, and when Pasquale republished his commentary in 1600 he chose to retitle it *Gnomae seu axiomata politica ex Tacito.*[70]

No single writer better illustrates the shift in moral attitudes, the new mode of discourse that displaced humanist rhetoric, and the altered relationship between Cicero and Tacitus than does Montaigne in the first two books of his *Essais,* which were published in 1580, and then in their revised form, together with the third book, in 1588. Montaigne developed his own early Stoicism through Seneca and Plutarch quite independently of Lipsius, and only after Lipsius praised his essays in 1583 did they begin to correspond. Indeed, apart from two mentions of Lipsius in the third book, Montaigne's acknowledged and unacknowledged debts to *Sospitator Taciti* were included only in the revisions of the essays made after 1588.[71] By his own account Montaigne first paid close

---

[67]Dorléans, *Novae cogitatrones in libros Annalium Cornelii Tacti qui extant* (Paris, 1622), unpaginated dedication.

[68]Momigliano, "The First Political Commentary on Tacitus," pp. 205–29.

[69]Pasquale, "Genus dicendi, ut ait Seneca, imitatur publicos mores," in Tacitus, *C. Cornelii Taciti Equitis Romani ab excessu Divi Augusti Annalium libri quatuor priores et in hos observationes Caroli Paschali cuneatis* (Paris, 1581), unpaginated preface to the reader.

[70]See Lipsius's own collection of Tacitean and other political axioms, *Iusti Lipsii monita et exempla politica libri duo, qui virtutes et vitia principum spectant* (Paris, 1605). Once again, *civilis prudentia* is represented as the governing concept in this volume.

[71]The section that follows is heavily dependent on Pierre Villey's *Sources et l'évolution des Essais de Montaigne,* vol. 1: *Les Sources et la chronologie des essais* (Paris, 1908), pp. 224–6 (Tacitus), 98–103 (Cicero), 214–16 (Seneca), 198–9 (Plutarch), 161–2 (Lipsius).

attention to Tacitus soon after the time that Bodin praised the historian in the *Methodus*. Nevertheless, most of the references to Tacitus in the essays of 1580, including even the passage on the death of Seneca, were indirectly acquired through Bodin's work and other sources. Montaigne was in Rome when Muret lectured on Tacitus in the winter of 1580–1. He reread Tacitus when composing the third book, and he offered his most important judgments upon him in "De l'art de conférer." He noted how Tacitus revealed the effects that the cruelty of the emperors produced upon their subjects, and declared that this kind of material offered more insights than standard accounts of battles and high matters of state: "This type of history is by far the most useful: public affairs depend more upon the whim of fortune, private ones upon our own conduct." Montaigne found more precepts and judgments than narration in Tacitus: "It is a seed-bed of ethical and political discourses for the use and ornament of those who have status in the management of the world."[72] As Bodin and Muret had done, the essayist defended Tacitus for his adherence to the state religion. Like Lipsius, Montaigne held it to be the duty of a citizen to follow the religion established by law, and, while he was more tolerant towards the individual conscience than was the scholar of Leyden, he agreed with Lipsius that lack of religious uniformity was an invitation to civil strife.

Montaigne developed a strong interest in the personality of Tacitus, and offered a few criticisms, largely in the revisions for the 1595 posthumous edition of the essays. Tacitus was said to conceal himself too much from the reader and even from himself. His judgment of individuals was occasionally at fault, and there were times when he wrongly preferred the rules of civility to frankness and truth. Nevertheless, he was "a great personage, upright and courageous, endowed not with a superstitious nature but philosophical and generous." The value of his history was never in doubt. No one else had managed to blend consideration of manners, attitudes, and particular motives with a record of public events. His opinions were sound, and he had taken the right side in Roman politics. His role had been "proper in a sick and troubled state, as ours is in the present age."[73]

As it might be expected from Montaigne's humanist background, the essays abounded in references to Cicero, but, on nearly every occasion where Montaigne offered personal judgments in the versions of 1580 and 1588, they were of a negative sort. Montaigne admitted that Cicero deserved his reputation for eloquence, but that was not the author's concern in the essays. His main interest lay in moral ideas, and Cicero's were not to his taste. He made considerable use of such works as *De Amicitia*, *De Senectute*, and *De Finibus*, but he apparently did not study Cicero's speeches or his treatises on rhetoric; Montaigne's references to such works were stock ones borrowed from other sources,

[72]Montaigne, *Essais*, vol. 2, pp. 377–8 (3: 8). (Book and chapter numbers in these and subsequent references to Montaigne appear in parentheses.)
[73]*Ibid.*, pp. 380, 378 (3: 8).

including the *Dialogus de Oratoribus* of Tacitus. As a man, Montaigne found Cicero vain and untrustworthy. His harshest comments, however, were reserved for Cicero's style, which he described as "lasche et ennuyeuse."[74] Cicero's work was filled with prefaces, definitions, and digressions without reaching the substance of his discourse. One could read him for an hour and come up with no more than a bag of wind. Montaigne despised both the subtleties of the grammarians and the logic-chopping of the Aristotelians. Cicero, he declared, might be suitable for the schoolroom or the bar – or, indeed, to the kind of sermon where one could go to sleep for fifteen minutes and awake to find the same thread of argument. Cicero's artifice negated the point he wished to make. If Montaigne wanted to hear a speech on love of liberty, he preferred Brutus to Cicero, and, if he wished to cultivate disdain for death, he read Seneca before Cicero.[75]

After 1588, however, Montaigne's view of Cicero changed in the last respect. His developing interest in metaphysical questions led him to see Seneca and Cicero as complementary, and he made considerable use of Cicero's philosophical works, especially *Quaestiones Academicae, Tusculanae Disputationes, De Natura Deorum, De Divinatione, De Officiis,* and *De Finibus.* Much of the scepticism shown in *Apologie de Raymond Sebond* had dropped away, and Montaigne renewed his earlier interest in the tempered and resigned Stoicism of Seneca. There were aspects of Cicero, especially in *De Finibus,* which could easily be reconciled with this stance, but Montaigne never varied his view of Cicero's rhetoric. Like Pasquale, he remembered what Seneca had written on the adaptation of linguistic structure to the concerns and moral conventions of the age. His own opinions resembled the moral and political attitudes of Seneca and Tacitus, and his mode of discourse in the vernacular was the counterpart of the new Latinity of Lipsius.

Guillaume du Vair shared the attitudes of Montaigne and Lipsius on the inefficacy of the individual to affect the capricious twists of fortune, on the need for a resolute demeanour in personal conduct, and on the disastrous political consequences of religious innovation. He served in the parlement of the Catholic League, where his patriotism and his dislike of the revolutionary element in the Catholic faction moved him to oppose the suggestion that the Spanish Infanta should become queen of France. Du Vair composed his treatise on constancy during Henri IV's siege of Paris in 1590 and published it when the king finally entered his capital four years later. His work was inspired by Seneca and, more immediately, by Lipsius. Du Vair had written on Epictetus and on Stoic moral philosophy in general, but he was also an admirer of Cicero, whom he adapted to fit the neostoic mood. The future keeper of the seals was the author of *De l'éloquence française,* where he provided Cicero's *Pro Milone* as an

---

[74]*Ibid.,* vol. 1, p. 454 (2: 10). (The 1595 version omits *lasche.*)
[75]*Ibid.,* vol. 1, p. 455 (2: 10), vol. 2, p. 121 (2: 31).

example for emulation, and explained the decay of French rhetoric in terms of the loss of the old Ciceronian ideal of the union of the orator and the citizen. Despite his lament about present evils and the powerlessness of the individual to hold back the tide, Du Vair continued to plead for the active life. In this vein he wrote *Exhortation à la vie civile*, which became attached to his tract on constancy. Moreover, he was an advocate of political prudence who despised a priori political theorists: "They want to reduce political government, which depends upon particular prudence, to the general rules of some universal science, and in applying rules in this way where they ought to be applying exceptions they have distorted judgment in everything."[76]

Editions of Cicero were still being produced and read, based upon the Aldine versions, especially that of Paulus Manutius, and those of French scholars such as Charles Estienne and Denis Lambin.[77] Yet even in the editorial process a change was evident. In 1588 the jurist Denis Godefroy published at Lyon a revised text of Cicero's *Opera Omnia* as prepared by Lambin. In his preface Godefroy criticised his predecessor for being too concerned with trivialities of language at the expense not only of philosophical issues but also of practical matters of politics and individual conduct. "I have always thought," he wrote, "that we should rather pay attention to what concerns the *mores* of our own country, family life, and government, than wear away childishly this fleeting, brief, and miserable life in wrestling with the forms of letters: it is more important to live well and wisely than to learn to speak too scrupulously and exactly." In consequence, Godefroy omitted many of Lambin's philological notes. Godefroy had been trained at Louvain as a Ramist and had later become a Calvinist. Immediately after editing Cicero, in his Genevan place of exile, he set to work on the textual emendation of Seneca's philosophical works, not by the comparison of manuscripts but rather by conjecture. Like his edition of the *Corpus juris civilis*, his edition of Cicero went through many reprintings in later generations. It was dedicated to Frederick IV, Elector Palatine, who became Godefroy's patron. He was invited by the jurist to pay less attention to examples of Cicero's elegance than to Cicero's practical precepts, which should be applied to government and the reformation of public morals.[78]

Times were indeed changing. Montaigne and Pasquier both remarked that Ciceronian eloquence could only apply where the vulgar had power: it was irrelevant in France. The *Satyre Ménippée*, the politique riposte to the quasi-

---

[76]Du Vair, *Traité de la constance et consolation es calamitez publiques*, ed. Jacques Flach and F. Funck-Bretano (Paris, 1915), p. 201. The other works mentioned are Du Vair's *De l'éloquence française* (Paris, 1590) and *La Saincte philosophie, la philosophie des Stoiques, manuel d'Epictete, civile conversation, et plusieurs autres traictez de pieté* (Lyon, 1600). On Du Vair in general, see R. Radouant, *Guillaume du Vair: L'Homme et l'orateur* (Paris, 1909); and L. Zanta, *La Renaissance du Stoicisme au XVIᵉ siècle* (Paris, 1914).

[77]Villey, *Sources et l'évolution des Essais de Montaigne*, pp. 102–3.

[78]Cicero, *M. Tullii Ciceronis opera omnia, praeter hactenus vulgatam Dionysii Lambini editionem, accesserunt D. Gothofredi* (Lyon, 1588) vol. 1, unpaginated dedication and preface to the reader.

democratic propaganda of the league, had its most serious spokesman, Daubray, refer to a page of Tacitean history and to Tacitus himself as "an evangelist to some."[79] There was a hint here that Tacitus could be a source of amoral counsel, which was also the view of Giovanni Botero, a Savoyard diplomat who had visited Paris in 1585. Botero's *Della Ragion di Stato* (1589) was the first work directly to associate Tacitus with Machiavelli, and it was published in French translation in 1599.[80] Such an opinion long remained uncommon in France. The Huguenot poet and historian, Théodore-Agrippe d'Aubigné, who upheld an intensely moral position in his later years, described Tacitus as *mon maître*.[81] Scipione Ammirato invoked Tacitus to refute Machiavelli's republicanism and composed his *Discorsi sopra Cornelio Tacito* (1594) as a counter to Machiavelli's *Discourses on Livy*. Ammirato saw Tacitus as the supreme advocate of political prudence. Jean Baudouin, who provided a new French version of the works of Tacitus, also translated Ammirato's *Discorsi*. Evidently he did not expect his readers to be shocked by the Italian's personal explanation: "If I gave here precepts and lessons on how to dissimulate, it is sufficient for me to record the words of holy scripture where it is said that even God dissimulates the sins of men so that they may be converted."[82]

Even if Machiavelli was still regarded with some suspicion in France, political prudence, soon to be linked with reason of state,[83] was becoming an accepted part of the ideology of monarchical absolutism. Pierre Charron, the disciple of Montaigne, represents the completion of the shift in moral philosophy. The third book of Charron's *De la sagesse* discussed "the four moral virtues of prudence, justice, strength, and temperance." Strength (*force*) had been substituted for the traditional fortitude, and prudence had replaced wisdom. Prudence, indeed, had become "the general queen, superintendent, and guide of all the other virtues," and Cicero was cited as the interpreter of the two complementary kinds, private and public.[84] In actuality Tacitus and Seneca dictated the manner in which Charron interpreted Cicero. They were cited together to demonstrate that sovereignty required equity in its exercise and should not be confused with a tyranny in which the prince was above the law. Yet the world

[79]*Menippée*, (Ratisbon, 1726), vol. 1, pp. 146–7. On the background of the *Satyre Ménippée*, see below, pp. 84–8.
[80]Schellhase, *Tacitus in Renaissance Political Thought*, p. 124.
[81]Thuau, *Raison d'état et pensée politique à l'époque de Richelieu*, p. 35; and Tacitus, *Les Oeuvres de C. Corn. Tacitus . . . avec des discours politiques* by Ammirato, ed. and trans. Jean Baudouin (Paris, 1628), *Discours* (separately paginated), p. 10. On Ammirato, see Schellhase, *Tacitus in Renaissance Political Thought*, pp. 142–5.
[82]Botero, *Raison et gouvernement d'état* (Paris, 1599).
[83]On the affiliation between such terms as prudence, interest, and reason of state, see Anna Maria Battista, "Morale 'privée' et utilitarisme politique en France au XVIIe siècle," in Roman Schnur, ed., *Staatsräson: Studien zur Geschichte eines politischen Begriffs* (Berlin, 1975), pp. 87–119.
[84]Charron, *De la sagesse: Trois livres* (Paris, 1604 [1601]), pp. 477–8, 482. On Charron in general, see J. B. Sabrié, *Pierre Charron: De l'humanisme au rationalisme* (Paris, 1913); and H. Busson, *Le Rationalisme dans la littérature française de la Renaissance, 1533–1601* (Paris, 1957).

was full of malicious men whose treachery was wont to subvert the state unless the prince mixed prudence with justice and composed his cloak of both the pelt of the fox and the skin of the lion. It was in this context that one acted for the public welfare and cited the Ciceronian maxim *salus populi suprema lex esto*.[85]

Cicero had counselled the statesman to be watchful, to believe nothing and guard against all eventualities, and Seneca had taught the necessity of dissembling. As Tacitus had indicated in *Agricola*, the prince must keep himself informed of all that happened, must never relax, and must constantly employ dissimulation. Many references of this kind played fast and loose with the texts they purported to cite, and the names of Tacitus, Seneca, and Cicero in the margins of Charron's book did not necessarily imply a just reflection of what these authors had actually written. Tiberius and Vespasian joined the ranks of "great princes and wise statesmen" with Augustus, Trajan, Hadrian, and the Antonines. Tacitus had taught that evil princes were the instrument of God's justice and must be suffered, and when Cicero had cited Greek opinions about tyrants he had referred to those who had usurped authority, not to legitimate princes. Seneca, for his part, had instructed the counsellor of rulers to trim his sails to fit the wind, while Tacitus had taught him discretion not to pry into royal secrets that should be kept hidden.[86] Piety, honour, and equity were words that Charron employed at intervals, but they, like everything else, were twisted to conform with the new linguistic mode in which wisdom had become the slave of prudence.

It would be easy to assume that the linguistic and ideological shift evident in the alternating fortunes of Cicero and Tacitus was merely the by-product of the religious strife and social dislocation experienced in sixteenth-century France. Certainly, the personal lives of those whose allusions to Cicero and Tacitus have been traced in these pages were profoundly affected by persecution and civil war. Dolet and Ramus met violent deaths. Muret and Lipsius accommodated their outward creed to the places in which they found refuge. Among the opponents of absolutism, Hotman and Bèze were intimately concerned with the conduct of the Protestant cause, and Boucher and Dorléans with that of the Catholic League. Those whose opinions were in some sense politique – Gentillet, Bodin, Du Vair, and even Montaigne – were to a greater or lesser degree involved in negotiations or administrative responsibilities in time of civil faction and religious conflict. Undeniably, the emergence of Tacitean prudence and the reinterpretation of Cicero owed much to the triumph of politique compromise and the mutual exhaustion of Catholic and Protestant enthusiasts.

Yet the wave of humanist culture in the early part of the century and the

---

[85]Charron, *De la sagesse*, pp. 488–9. The image of the lion and the fox was not necessarily from Machiavelli: Charron could have found it in *De Officiis;* see Cicero, *De Officiis*, 1: 13, 41 (p. 17).
[86]Charron, *De la sagesse*, pp. 497, 526, 504.

determination of its epigoni to give it practical expression in the higher levels of the royal administration contained undercurrents of intellectual change, whatever the political environment. Ciceronian rhetoric embraced too many disciplines. The debates among the philologists, the dialecticians, and the defenders of eloquence for its own sake destroyed the unity of humanist endeavour and fostered the advance of new theories of politics and history. This was the malaise after the reign of François Ier, which Bodin recalled as "the bitterest sense of grief that those brilliant flashes of talent which shone throughout all France have been extinguished in desolation and want."[87] Ultimately for this reason Montaigne came to profess his contempt for the grammarians and the logicians. It was also true that war and fanaticism had caused the humanists either to appear irrelevant or to adapt their moral and political ideas to inappropriate ends. Disillusionment resulted in the triumph of the least virtuous of the virtues. Prudence, the art of particularity and dissimulation, emerged in both its public and its private aspects, the one to shield the arcana of the absolutist state, the other to shelter the citizen in the fortress of the individual mind. Attitudes to Cicero and Tacitus in sixteenth-century France reflected the destruction of that humanist ideal whereby a highly educated élite might participate in an enlightened administration. State and society stood in antithesis to one another, and the French variety of Renaissance humanism disappeared from intellectual life.

[87]Bodin, *Method for the Easy Comprehension of History*, p. 7.

2

Protestant jurists and theologians in early modern France: the family of Cappel

The institutional development of early modern France owes almost everything to the robe. The men of the law did not merely build the state; in a sense, they were the state. They did not, however, share an undivided view of the nature of the state. The particular structure of the Ancien Régime grew out of three centuries of rivalry between the executive aspect of government, centred in the men of the robe in the royal council, and the judicial aspect, represented primarily by the magistrates of the sovereign courts.[1] Social conflicts had little to do with this process. While tension between the nobility of the sword and that of the robe may have contributed from time to time to political crises, the struggle between the executive and the judiciary had no social base. This was because the same dynasties of the robe provided both *parlementaires* and intendants. In recent years their familial ramifications have been studied in great detail, and so, too, have the ideological assumptions involved in relations between *officiers* and *commissaires* and between robe and sword in general.[2] A dimension missing from these studies has been the effect of Protestantism upon the early manifestations of these rivalries. Nor do any of the modern works on the family structures of the robe and the ideas of its protagonists make mention of an important family of Protestant jurists and theologians who exemplify the intellectual milieu in which the state apparatus of sixteenth- and seventeenth-century France was constructed. This is the family of Cappel, to whom this paper is devoted.

Admittedly, the Cappel cannot be compared with such Catholic dynasties as the Lamoignon, the Séguier, and the Phélypeaux-Vrillière; nor did they produce a theorist of the stature of Bodin, Loyseau, Domat, or Montesquieu. The

---

[1] This is the theme of the second volume of Roland Mousnier's *Les Institutions de la France sous la monarchie absolue* (Paris, 1980). It was the chancellor Maupeou who spoke of the three-hundred-year conflict when he reproached Louis XVI for recalling the parlement after its suspension in 1771.

[2] E.g. Roland Mousnier et al., *Le Conseil du Roi de Louis XII à la Révolution* (Paris, 1960); François Bluche, *L'Origine des magistrats du Parlement de Paris, 1715–1771* (Paris, 1956); and Jean Egret, *Louis XV et l'opposition parlementaire* (Paris, 1970).

most distinguished office held by a member of the line was that of *avocat-général* in the parlement of Paris under François Ier. During the wars of religion the Protestant affiliations of the Cappel interrupted their ascent through venal office-holding and fostered the development of the family tradition in theology. One of them became a confidant of Sully in the opening rounds of the conflict between the executive and the office-holders, but he failed to make his mark because of his eccentric scheme to reform the judicial process. In the early seventeenth century, when more orthodox robe families were securing a permanent role in government, the two best-known Cappel brothers were professors of Hebrew and theology at Saumur and Sedan. They were the third generation of the Cappel to leave behind them an impressive corpus of published works. It is mainly in this respect that the family deserves to be remembered. From the age of humanism to the era of *raison d'état* their writings constitute a remarkable cross-section of new ideas in letters, politics, and religion.

The earliest Cappel of whom there is any record was a certain Denis, who was buried in the cemetery of the Innocents in 1472. That he was a man of solid bourgeois means and status is attested by the sum he left for the recital of masses for his soul, and by his widow's status of *honorable femme*. The inscriptions on the tombstones were copied in 1612 by his descendant Ange Cappel (the client of Sully already mentioned), and later repeated by Ange's nephew Louis Cappel II in his short history of the family.[3] One of the sons of Denis, Guillaume Cappel Ier, became dean of the Paris faculty of theology. In 1491 Guillaume, then rector of the university, led the opposition to a papal *décime*, and thus inaugurated the family tradition of resistance to ultramontane pretensions. There was another son, Gervase, but Ange did not record any tombstone for him in the Innocents. He found, however, the grave of his own father, Jacques Cappel Ier, who was probably Gervase's son and had died in 1541.

It was this first Jacques Cappel who became the defender of the king's rights as *avocat-général*. Like the great scholar and master of requests Guillaume Budé, Cappel won advancement through recognition of his humanist erudition. A doctor of both civil and canon law (*utriusque juris*), he dedicated his first published work, a collection of extracts from classical authors with commentaries, to his uncle the dean of theology.[4] The *Fragmenta* were intended for candidates in humane letters, but most of their themes concerned occult pagan religious practices, treated with a liberal and urbane rationality. In the preface Cappel suggested that the religions of remote antiquity formed a continuous chain of arcane wisdom and that mankind came gradually to understand them as leading to true faith, as a child left in a cave gropes its way towards the light.

[3]Ange Cappel, *Extraict de chose merveilleuse mais véritable que l'on peut veoir gravée au cimitière des Saints-Innocents* (n.p., n.d. [Paris, 1612]); Louis Cappel II, *De Cappellorum Gente*, in *Commentarii et notae criticae in Vetus Testamentum* (Amsterdam, 1689). Most of the biographical details subsequently given come from *De Cappellorum Gente*.
[4]*Jacobi Cappelli Parrhisiensis fragmenta ex variis authoribus pressim concinnata, humannarum literarum candidatis, dicere ausim, ediscenda* (Paris, 1517).

Citing Cicero's *De Oratore*, the editor demanded that all things should be reduced to logical principles, since philosophy was the mistress of learning. His extracts, which defied such reduction, were grouped under titles like "diverse opinions as to God among philosophers" (this from Cicero's *De Natura Deorum*), "what victims were sacrificed to which gods," "various oracles of the gods," and "examples of the secret religion." While topics such as the Eleusinian mysteries and esoteric Egyptian cults received particular attention, there were a few more prosaic subjects in the miscellany, varying from performing elephants to ancient war machines. With this textbook to his credit, Jacques Cappel began to practise law at the bar of the *sénéchaussée* court at Poitiers. It was there that he composed an oration in praise of Paris dedicated to a president of the parlement.[5] This self-conscious piece of Ciceronian oratory apparently had the desired effect. Cardinal Guillaume du Bellay became his patron, and he was appointed first to the court of the *prévôté* in the capital, and then, in 1534, as *conseiller d'état* and *avocat-général* in the parlement itself. President Poyet, the future chancellor, gave him a generous welcome, and he began to acquire a formidable reputation for forensic eloquence. Two matters to which his rhetorical gifts were applied were of fundamental importance in the definition of the French monarchy.

The first was an adaptation of the principles of vassalage to the territorial needs of the nation state. In 1537 Jacques Cappel delivered an oration in parlement before the king calling for the integration of Flanders, Artois, and Charolais into the royal domain. The argument was under two heads. On the one hand, the ruler of these territories, the Habsburg emperor Charles V, was declared a rebel and consequently in forfeiture of fiefs held from François Ier. On the other, the citizens of certain towns, such as Arras, Tournai, Tornesis, Mortaigne, and Saint-Amand, were described as direct subjects of the king, since they inhabited parts of crown patrimony inalienable under fundamental law.[6] There was also an elaborate historical analysis of different kinds of homage rendered in these lands since the time of Charlemagne. The speech was carefully contrived on the Ciceronian model, and included copious references to Caesar, Livy, and Plutarch. This was the kind of practical humanism advocated by Budé in his *Institution du Prince*, which advised the king to combine history and philosophy in the framework of formal rhetoric, and to apply wisdom to political reality through Ciceronian prudence.[7] Indeed, Cappel's attitude was precisely that of Budé, accepting the king as the sole source of authority and commending his service to the active and virtuous citizen. The pragmatic patriotism of the *avocat-général* even cut across the legality of the

[5]*Jacobi Cappelli Parrhisiensis in Parrhisiensum laudem oratio Pictavis habita* (n.p., n.d.).

[6]*Plaidoyez de feu maistre Jacques Cappel, advocat du Roy, en la cour de Parlement à Paris* (Paris, 1561), p. 9r. In his account of this occasion Sleidan noted that the *avocat-général* refused to credit Charles V with his imperial title. Jean Sleidan, *Commentaires . . . touchant l'estat de la religion et république sous l'Empereur Charles V* (Geneva, 1566), p. 80.

[7]Guillaume Budé, *Institution du Prince* (1524), ed. Claude Bontems, *Le Prince dans la France des XVIe et XVIIe siècles* (Paris, 1965), p. 87. See above, p. 31.

royal cause, for he admitted that in time of war legal precedent took second place to military necessity. "Silent leges inter arma," he quoted from Cicero's *Pro Milone*.[8] It may have been this speech that inspired the concluding lines of the epitaph composed for the king's advocate, claiming that he incarnated all the "brilliance, subtlety, wisdom, knowledge, and eloquence" to be found among the men of his time.[9]

The second issue was the king's relations with Rome. Like his uncle Guillaume, the first Jacques Cappel was an outspoken defender of Gallicanism. It was the corollary of the king's secular sovereignty that clerical administration should fall within his purview. Although François 1er's concordat with Leo X had given the crown general rights of nomination to clerical benefices, there was contention over certain exceptions and friction over the payment to Rome of the fees necessary for canonical institution. Cappel's *Mémoires dressez pour le Roy tres-Chrestien et l'Eglise gallicane*[10] was written some time before Henri II's clash with Rome over the "Edict of the Little Dates,"[11] and served as a model for a long line of Gallican treatises. The first part was designed to show royal rights to be based on the premise that the king was emperor in his own kingdom, holding his crown immediately from God and recognising, as patron and principal founder of the churches of France, no other temporal superior.[12] Beside Cappel's battery of authorities from Roman and canon law were an exhaustive list of historical precedents, pragmatic sanctions (including the dubious one attributed to Saint Louis), and royal ordinances. The second part provided examples of measures that might be taken when the papacy refused to accept the king's *règlements*, varying from the arrest of Boniface VIII to the appeal of the University of Paris led by Guillaume Cappel. The parlement was depicted as the primary defence against ultramontane influence, and the author did not hesitate to repeat the pious sentiment that when the court issued an ecclesiastical *arrêt* the Holy Ghost came to reside in the Palais de Justice.[13] The third and fourth parts suggested means of preventing the constant efflux of French money to Rome. Cappel marshalled his exposition into seventy-three numbered points, even advancing answers to possible objections that might be raised. However prejudiced against Rome, his statement was thorough, well documented, and more practical in its thrust than the lists of regalian rights

---

[8] Jacques Cappel Ier, *Plaidoyez*, p. 17v.
[9] *De Cappellorum Gente* (unpaginated):
> Quanto ingenii splendore, quanta argutia,
> Sapientia, scientia, eloquentia,
> Quam magno animo, quam libero, integro,
> Quotquot fuerunt temporibus omnes suis,
> Si non superavit, continuit certe pares.

[10] In Pierre Dupuy (ed.), *Traitez des droits et libertez de l'Eglise gallicane* (2 vols., n.p., 1731), vol. 1, pp. 13–33.
[11] See below, pp. 158–60. See also Donald R. Kelley, *The Foundations of Modern Historical Scholarship* (New York, 1970), pp. 165–6.
[12] Jacques Cappel Ier, *Mémoires dressez pour le Roy tres-Chrestien et l'Eglise gallicane*, in Dupuy (ed.), *Traitez*, vol. 1, p. 14.
[13] *Ibid.*, p. 23.

composed by contemporary legists such as Grassaille, Ferrault, and Chasseneuz.[14]

Not only did the first Jacques Cappel deserve his reputation as an advocate of royal causes, he also seemed the likely founder of a new *parlementaire* dynasty in the age when venality of office was first expanding overtly throughout the judiciary. He married the daughter of an *avocat* who was descended on her mother's side from the distinguished robe family of Boucher, allied with the De Thou. The *avocat-général* acquired the seigneuries of Vaudoy and Le Tilloy in Brie. Nine children were born of the marriage, four of whom died in infancy. One daughter married a minor nobleman of the sword, the *bailli* Christophe de Varin de Semerville. The alliance was not untypical of the time. Although the eldest sons of the high robe married within their own group and expected to inherit their father's office, some of their daughters had dowries that attracted husbands from the lesser ranks of the traditional aristocracy. The four surviving Cappel sons themselves became landed seigneurs, three of them being educated in law in the expectation of office and one in medicine. This was the generation that experienced the bitter fruits of religious division and sought new solutions to vastly more complex problems of church and state than had existed in the past. Some of the law schools were seedbeds of Protestantism. Calvin, Théodore de Bèze, and François Hotman all encountered heterodox ideas there. The sons of Guillaume Budé and of the future chancellor Michel de l'Hôpital were attracted to the reformed faith. Budé, although he approved of the Catholic procession that responded to the Protestant affair of the placards in 1534, may have had some sympathy for the reform, and L'Hôpital was later to seek a tolerant solution. This may also have been the attitude of the first Jacques Cappel. Among his first duties as *avocat-général* was to propose to the royal council a modification of the system of censorship designed to stop Protestant publications.[15] But, with one or two notable exceptions, the magistrates of the high robe resisted the new opinions and turned their instruments of repression against the neophytes of the next generation. The three Cappel brothers who studied law all became Protestants, while the fourth brother eventually moved to the other extreme and joined the Catholic League. If the family hopes of advancement through judicial office were disappointed, each of the brothers made his particular contribution to the intellectual and political life of the new age.

The eldest son, Jacques Cappel II, sieur du Tilloy (1529–86), could expect high office through his father's connections, but he had no assurance of it. His father died before the son was old enough to assume responsibility, and, in any case, the office of *avocat-général* was not one that could be inherited. When he had completed his studies in the law, he travelled in Italy and Germany. In Italy he may have taken an interest in the continuing literary debate, initiated in the

[14]See Julian H. Franklin, *Jean Bodin and the Rise of Absolutist Theory* (Cambridge, 1976), pp. 6–8.
[15]*Bulletin de la Société de l'histoire du protestantisme français* (henceforth *B.S.H.P.F.*), 53 (1904), p. 134.

previous century, between those who saw Cicero alone as the model of Latinity and those who maintained that there were many stylists among Latin authors from whom to choose. Valla belonged to the relativist camp, but he had extended his criticism to the medieval civilians not only in terms of their lack of historicity but also because of their bad Latin. The literary debate had infiltrated the teaching of Roman law, and opposed legal humanists such as Budé and Alciato, who saw bodies of ancient law historically in the context of the societies that produced them, to the Bartolists, who sought to educe principles of eternal justice by the comparative method, regardless of the provenance of their texts. It is likely, of course, that the young Jacques Cappel II first acquired an interest in these academic disputes in France itself, where differences between the grammarians had been excited by Erasmus's *Ciceronianus* in 1528, and where the historicist school of legal erudition had been introduced into some of the law schools by Alciato and his followers.[16] Whenever it was that Cappel began to interest himself in these debates, it is difficult to believe his claim that his own contribution was entirely the result of a chance encounter with Valla's *Elegantiae Linguae Latinae*. Late in 1575 he completed a book defending "the old jurisconsults" against Valla's criticism.[17]

In the first place, there was a paradoxical element in Valla's absolute standards of correct Latin usage and his relativist approach to legal history. Cappel accentuated this paradox. He was not really concerned to defend the glossators and Bartolists: His interest lay in the original Roman jurists. While extolling the glories of Cicero and Virgil, he defended the right of Tribonian, together with his colleagues and predecessors, to invent neologisms and to adapt the past meaning of words to the juristic needs of the moment. He attacked his fellow Protestant, the jurist and polemicist François Hotman, for accusing Tribonian of wilful barbarism and ignorance in codifying the law of previous centuries.[18] In this way Cappel was outdoing the legal humanists at their own game. There was nothing illogical about his admiration for the golden age of Latin literature and his acceptance of change in the legal terminology of later centuries. By retaining his father's Ciceronianism and indulging his own genuine interest in etymology, Cappel bridged the gap between the disputes of the grammarians on the one hand and the conflicts between the *mos italicus* and the *mos gallicus* on the other. Literary idealism walked hand in hand with historical relativism. Cappel's *Defensio* does not deserve the oblivion into which it has lapsed, for it reveals the limitations of those who were restricted either to the literary or to the legal aspects of these controversies.

[16]On the background to these debates see above, pp. 31–4.
[17]Jacques Cappell II, *Veterum Iureconsultorum* [sic] *adversus Laurentii Vallae reprehensiones defensio* (Paris, 1583). The date of completion is given at the end of the text, p. 80r.
[18]*Ibid.*, p. 4v. On Hotman in this respect see Ralph E. Giesey and J. H. M. Salmon (eds.), *"Francogallia" by François Hotman* (Cambridge, 1972), pp. 26–38. Hotman differed fundamentally from Cappel in claiming that Roman law had no relevance to French public law. It is unlikely that Cappel knew Hotman's *Anti-Tribonian*, which remained in manuscript until 1603. There were, however, some early published works by Hotman criticising Tribonian, notably his life of Justinian.

If Italy revived the humanist past of the Cappel for Jacques II, Germany led him to initiate a new family tradition through his conversion to Protestantism. It is probable that he and his younger brother Louis were concerned in the promulgation of a reformed catechism, consisting of one hundred and one questions with scriptural answers, which is alleged to have justified the presentation of the reformed confession to the young king, François II, in the aftermath of the disastrous Huguenot plot at Amboise in March 1560.[19] It may even be conjectured that the two brothers had a hand in its composition, but there is no certain proof in the matter. In any event the catechism reveals the kind of Calvinism with which the Cappel were associated. The catechism is firmly prelapsarian, stating unequivocally that God willed both the fall and the salvation of the elect through Christ "devant la fondation du monde."[20] The last three sets of questions and answers are devoted to political issues. Calvin would have nothing to do with the conspiracy of Amboise in the form in which it was finally organised, but in the penultimate paragraph of the fourth book of his *Institution* he had allowed constitutional resistance to tyrants by rightfully appointed magistrates. After Amboise there were some Huguenot theorists who elaborated parallel doctrines. Yet the catechism preached unvarying obedience to the prince in terms of the standard text in Romans 13:1. Under Romans 13:4 it defended the right of the magistrate to use the sword with the words "Beware if you do wrong, for as the servant of God the magistrate does not wield the sword without cause." To the question "Should we pay them *tailles?*" the catechism responded with the expected passage from Matthew 12:2 on rendering Caesar his due, and on the issue of whether a subject could attack his sovereign it declared with Samuel that the ruler was the anointed of God.[21] While Bèze, Hotman, and others developed increasingly radical theories in later years, the Protestant Cappel adhered to the doctrines of nonresistance stated in their catechism. In the next generation, when they accepted a more liberal view of grace, it is not surprising to find them in close contact with English Arminian clergy.

François Hotman reacted against his father's stern Catholicism by abandoning his family's assured future in the parlement of Paris and making his mark first as an eminent professor of Roman law, and then as an effective propagandist in the Huguenot cause. Jacques Cappel II, on the other hand, struggled to emulate his father's career despite his religion. In 1565 he married the daughter of Nicolas Duval, a *conseiller* in the Paris parlement who was much

[19]*Chatéchisme [sic] confirmant par l'Escriture la confession de Foy présentée par les églises de France au Roy François II* (n.p., n.d. [Sedan, 1613]). A manuscript note in the Bibliothèque Nationale copy (D² 14328) states, "après l'édit d'Amboise mars 1560, pâques échéant le 14 d'avril." Jacques Cappel III, the son of Jacques II, appears to have edited this edition. At the end of the text a note indicates which parts of the catechism were taken from the confession of faith, and mentions certain editions allegedly approved by Catholic censors. On the activities of Louis Cappel at this time, see below, p. 64.
[20]*Chatéchisme*, p. 12.
[21]*Ibid.*, pp. 30–1.

respected as a jurist for his treatise on dubious points of law[22] and who had accepted office in the new parlement of Rennes created in 1554. Duval made his son-in-law the heir to his Breton office, and for four years after the marriage the second Jacques Cappel intermittently exercised his functions as a *conseiller*. Anti-Protestant feeling was intense at Rennes during the two civil wars fought in this period. A document from the Conciergerie in Paris shows that, despite his judicial rank, Jacques Cappel was brought there in March 1569 as a prisoner, "because the said Cappel, being of the new opinion, has not obeyed the edicts of the king and the parlement."[23] Among his fellow prisoners were Jacques Budé and Jean Bodin. The *conseiller* was eventually released, and in January 1570 was obliged to resign his post. He returned to his estates in Brie, whence he had to flee to Sedan at the time of the massacre of St. Bartholomew. At the return of peace he went back to Le Tilloy, and it was at this time that he completed his refutation of Lorenzo Valla. The new peace treaty of 1576 provided for the establishment of *chambres mi-parties* in the parlements to adjudicate disputes between litigants of different religions. Jacques Cappel was named as a *conseiller* in the chambre at Paris, but he was never permitted to assume his new office. He remained at Le Tilloy until 1585, when the Catholic League was revived and the wars recommenced. With his young children and his pregnant wife, Cappel fled once more to Sedan. He was to die in the following year.

Louise Duval left her eldest son, Jacques Cappel III, to continue his studies in Sedan, and took the three younger children back to Brie, where she converted to Catholicism to avoid the confiscation of the family's lands. The Protestant tradition is that remorse at this act caused her death, and it is true that she died within a few months of her abjuration.[24] It was then the turn of the eldest of her husband's three surviving brothers to play the wicked uncle. Guillaume Cappel II, sieur de Preigny (1530–86), was widely known in medicine for his work on nutrition and his editing of texts on how to avoid the plague and on general medical diagnosis.[25] A member of the Catholic League, he was determined not only to bring up his brother's children in the Catholic faith but also to exploit Le Tilloy to his own profit. However, in 1586 he was killed in an affray with the enemies of the League. His sister Marie, widow of the *bailli* de Semerville, then arrived at Le Tilloy to seize her share of the spoils. Her endeavours were frustrated by Matthieu Bochart, sieur du Ménillet and an *avocat* before the parlement of Paris, who took the necessary measures to protect the property rights of the children. Bochart was a member of a celebrated robe dynasty that had proved rather more successful than the Cappel in retaining office despite

---

[22]*Nicolai Vallae . . . de rebus dubiis et quaestionibus in jure controversiis tractatus XX* (Paris, 1571).
[23]*B.S.H.P.F.*, 72 (1922), p. 88.
[24]Eugène Haag and Emile Haag, *La France protestante* (Geneva, 1966), vol. 3, p. 199.
[25]*Cautiones ad praevisionem pestis ex rogatu procerum politicorum hiisdem a decano medicorum oblatae* (by N. Le Gros and J. Haultin), *item consilium pro valetudine conservanda civium parisiensum in re alimentaria* (by Guillaume Cappel, Paris, 1581); *Consiliorum medicinalium liber* (by Jean Fernel, ed. Guillaume Cappel, Paris, 1582).

Protestant affiliations.[26] One of his sisters married Pierre Berger, a *conseiller* in the parlement, and the daughter of this alliance was to wed Jacques Cappel III.

Family divisions of the kind that occurred at Le Tilloy were customary during the religious wars, but it is not because of his part in them, nor even because of his Catholic enthusiasm and his medical reputation, that Guillaume Cappel deserves attention. In 1553, at the age of twenty-three, he published a French translation of Machiavelli's *Prince*, dedicating it to a powerful patron, the *garde des sceaux* Jean Bertrand. Appended to the book were poems praising Machiavelli, and Cappel as his French interpreter, by Marc-Antoine Muret and Rémy Belleau, and other verses about the relative merits of French and Italian princes by Etienne Jodelle. Guillaume Cappel clearly mixed in the foremost literary circles of the time. He claimed to be a student of politics, as well as of medicine and letters, and in his dedication to Bertrand, which he modelled on Machiavelli's own prefatory letter to Lorenzo de' Medici, he expressed an admiration for Machiavelli that knew no bounds. Politics, he remarked, constituted the highest branch of philosophy, itself the queen of the "sciences." Other political writers were sophists producing utopias, but Machiavelli wrote of government as it really was. Cappel went on to argue in his preface that men were more ungrateful towards their ruler than any animal towards its master. The exercise of power was shaped by necessity, not by virtuous intentions, and only those who understood this could govern successfully. For his part, the ruler necessarily pursued two aims, to keep his authority intact and to extend his dominions. According to Cappel, Machiavelli had boldly analysed the faults committed by princes in the past, had shown how problems could be dealt with in the future, and had brilliantly explained the causes of political upheavals.[27]

Guillaume Cappel's translation of *The Prince* was the first of three to be published in France before the massacre of St. Bartholomew, when the black legend of Machiavelli became dominant.[28] The version of Gaspard d'Auvergne, for whom Marc-Antoine Muret also wrote some laudatory verses, was apparently commenced in 1547 and perhaps completed in 1553, although it was not published for another decade.[29] That by Jacques Gohory, who also

[26]Matthieu Bochart's grandfather, the contemporary of Jacques Cappel Ier, was an *avocat* before the parlement. His father was *avocat-général* in the *chambre des comptes* and then *conseiller* in the parlement. Apart from his sister Marie, other sisters married into the robe families of Gayant and Luillier. Matthieu's brother, René, was a pastor at Rouen, who married the sister of Pierre du Moulin, a member of a family that also achieved distinction in the law before turning to Protestantism. René's son, Simon Bochart, was himself a pastor who became one of the greatest philologists of the seventeenth century. Haag and Haag, *La France Protestante*, vol. 2, pp. 319–23.

[27]*Le Prince de Nicolas de Machiavelle secretaire et citoien de Florence traduit de l'italien en françoys par Guillaume Cappel* (Paris, 1553), unpaginated dedication.

[28]Donald R. Kelley, "Murd'rous Machiavel in France: A Post Mortem," *Political Science Quarterly*, 85 (1970), 545–59.

[29]*Le Prince de Nicolas de Macchiavelli [sic] secretaire et citoien de Florence traduit d'italien en françois* (Poitiers, 1563). The privilege at the end of the book is dated 1547, followed by the words "achevé d'imprimer le 12 avril 1563." The dedication is to James Hamilton, second earl of Arran, who is described as governor of Scotland and duc de Châtellerault. Arran acquired the latter dignity in 1553 and lost the governorship in 1554.

translated Machiavelli's *Discorsi*, was issued in 1571.[30] Gaspard d'Auvergne was aware of his subject's propensity to shock, and his dedication carefully apologised that "his words seem to be a little too licentious," and also that Machiavelli had not always "adopted the most virtuous way of endorsing what in places has the appearance of vice."[31] His translation blunted the impact of Machiavelli's prose. Gohory, on the other hand, spoke of the Florentine as "the gentlest spirit we have seen in the world in recent centuries."[32] He was a Ciceronian himself and he chose, quite erroneously, to see Machiavelli in the same light, partly because his primary concern was with the *Discorsi* and it was perhaps possible to think the *virtus* of Livy and Cicero was identical with Machiavelli's *virtù*. Thus it was that Guillaume Cappel was not only the first French translator of *The Prince* but also the one most in sympathy with Machiavelli himself. He scornfully refuted those who accused his author "de façonner un prince trop rigoureux." A good doctor, said Cappel in his dedication, did not worry whether his patient disliked the remedy he prescribed, but merely whether the cure would work. Cappel refused to take up the rumour that Machiavelli was an atheist, because, he claimed, there was nothing he had written that could support or deny the charge. In one respect Guillaume Cappel did mitigate his praise a little. It seemed overbold to tell his patron how to exercise his authority by way of Machiavelli, and so the translator hastily added that, whatever the Florentine had said, the French monarchy was the best kind of government imaginable, and, under Bertrand's supervision, the best administered. Cappel's translation was sharper, and truer to the original that Gaspard d'Auvergne's or Gohory's. For instance, the celebrated sentence in the eighteenth chapter as to whether a prince should keep faith was rendered by Cappel: "Il est souvent contraint pour maintenir ses estatz de se gouverner contre la foy, contre la charité, contre l'humanité, et contre la religion."[33] The young Guillaume Cappel was, at this time at least, a true Machiavellian.

Guillaume's younger brother, Louis Cappel Ier, sieur de Montgembert[34] (1534–86), could never have professed such amorality. By curious coincidence he died in the same year as his elder brother, leaving behind him a will later to be published as a model of piety and good sense: "I leave to my children as my legacy the fear of God, a good nurture, a domestic example to follow in whatever is good – and I shall never be put out if they do better – and not much property, but enough if they be gentlefolk and too much if they be otherwise, which God forfend."[35] After making his mark at the collège Cardinal Le Moine in Paris, Louis went to Bordeaux to study law, and was there attracted by the

---

[30]*Le Prince de Nic. Machiavel . . . avec la vie de l'auteur mesme par Jac. Gohory* (Paris, 1571).
[31]*Le Prince*, tr. Gaspard d'Auvergne, unpaginated dedication.
[32]*Les discours de Nic. Machiavel . . . sur la première decade de Tite Live . . .* , tr. Jacques Gohory (Paris, 1571), unpaginated dedication.
[33]*Le Prince*, tr. Cappel, p. 95. Cf. the bowdlerised versions by Gaspard d'Auvergne (p. 61v) and Gohory (p. 40v).
[34]This is the preferred spelling among several variants: *B.S.H.P.F.*, 71 (1921), p. 94.
[35]*Testament de Louis Cappel, Sedan, le 30 juillet 1585* (B.N. F26848).

reformed doctrine. He visited Geneva and returned to Paris to become one of the most fearless activists for the Huguenot cause in the capital. He was concerned, as we have seen, with the promulgation of the confession of faith and its justificatory catechism after the Amboise plot in the spring of 1560. Later in the same year he dared to propose the adoption of reform at an assembly in the Paris hôtel de ville preparatory to the meeting of the estates general at Orléans. He became a pastor, serving several congregations successively including one in Antwerp, and at least on one occasion acted as secretary to provincial synods. Like his brother Jacques, he escaped to Sedan after St. Bartholomew's Day 1572. There he took part in a formal debate about dogma with the celebrated Jesuit theologian and rationalist friend of Montaigne, Juan Maldonado.[36] Louis Cappel went on diplomatic missions to Germany and acted as almoner with the army of John Casimir of the Palatinate when the latter invaded France in 1576.

The best-remembered incident concerning Louis Cappel occurred in the preceding year when he was appointed a foundation professor at the new university of Leyden, and delivered the university's inaugural address. Apart from this oration, no published works appear to have survived to attest to the erudition of this Huguenot man of affairs. His rhetoric certainly shows that he could rise to an academic occasion in the style of his father's forensic pleading. He put particular stress upon the practical role the new university could play in times of peace. Not only would the arts be brought to perfection but future statesmen and men of religion would be trained in the prudent government of church and state.[37] Prudence was the theme stressed in the speech, as the virtue that should guide the university. Prudence applied wisdom to practical matters, and to Louis Cappel it by no means implied the debasement of academic values. A man could act prudently, he argued, only if he attained a full understanding of truth. In fact Cappel moved easily between politics, the pulpit, and the academy. He left his chair at Leyden to accompany Casimir, and then went back to Sedan as professor of theology.

The fourth surviving son of the *avocat-général* was a gifted yet bizarre figure. Ange Cappel, sieur du Luat (1537–1623), was trained in the law, like Jacques and Louis before him. He adopted the reformed faith in 1557, and in the 1560s followed with growing interest the reforms of the legal structure promoted by the chancellor, Michel de l'Hôpital. He was to pursue one particular reform, proposed at this time but never adopted, with a single-minded energy that

[36]Maldonado (or Maldonat) includes his own account of this occasion in his compilation *Disputationum ac controversiarum decisiarum et circa septem Ecclesiae romanae sacramenta inter Catholicos praesertim et calvinistas . . . agitari solitarum* (2 vols., Lyon, 1614). On his rationalism and link with Montaigne see Henri Buisson, *Le Rationalisme dans la littérature française de la Renaissance, 1533–1601* (Paris, 1957), p. 432.

[37]"Etiam summum pacis et togae decus adiecisse, institutionem Academiae, in qua excolarentur artes, et instituta omnia, quae faciunt ad ecclesiae et reipublicae prudentem guvernationem et felicem conservationem." *Ioannis Meursii Athenae Batavae sive de urbe Leidensi, et academia virisque claris* (Leyden, 1625), unpaginated preface *Oratio inauguralis academiae Lugduno-Batavae habita a Ludovico Capello*.

bordered on the eccentric. Ange had his share of the pragmatism that seemed to infect this generation of the family. Jacques II had cut through the quarrels of grammarians and legal humanists to insist that there were times when one could use a word to mean exactly what one meant it to mean. Guillaume II had interpreted Machiavelli as a political nominalist and depicted the acceptance of the way men actuallv behaved as the key to the science of politics. Louis Ier had been an activist and a pastor, a diplomat and a theologian, and as a professor had stressed prudential practicality in university education. Ange became the translator of Tacitus and Seneca, thereby contributing to a movement that came to replace the Ciceronian humanism of the past. Jean Bodin had praised Tacitus as the realistic historian of causes and motives in *Methodus ad facilem cognitionem historiarum* (1566). Marc-Antoine Muret, who had commended in verse two translations of Machiavelli's *Prince*, turned from Cicero to Tacitus in the late 1570s. Justus Lipsius, who arrived at Leyden from Louvain four years after Louis Cappel, began his career as the greatest Tacitean scholar of the age with his edition of the historian's works published in 1575, the year of the University of Leyden's foundation. As well as being the publicist for Tacitean political prudence, Lipsius was the prophet of neostoic withdrawal and private prudence through the philosophy of Seneca. Montaigne himself exemplified the new spirit in his use of Seneca and Tacitus in the *Essays*.[38]

In 1574 Ange Cappel dedicated his translation of Tacitus's *Agricola* to Elizabeth of England, reminding the queen of Tacitus's allusions to her illustrious precursor Boudicca. His praise of the Roman historian in this dedication was unbounded:

Tacitus wrote only for the great and those who handle great affairs. His judgment was admirable. He was so skilled in knowledge of what actually happens in the world that one could call his book an education in affairs of state, enhanced by an unforgettable kind of history. He was one of the most judicious, shrewd, and wise courtiers that ever were.[39]

Ange ended his book with an engraved medallion of a personified Prudence, carrying the device: "Nullum numen abest, si sic prudentia." Not only did he recommend *Agricola* as a handbook of prudential politics, but he also discerned how useful the survival techniques which Tacitus and his father-in-law had practised under tyrannical regimes might be in his own time. That Seneca was the guiding spirit of Ange Cappel's own conduct is clear from four essays published together, which cited the philosopher extensively and touched upon such themes as the virtues necessary to a good life and the remedies for unexpected misfortunes.[40] The dedication of this collection to the duc de Joyeuse, that favourite of Henri III who had close ties with the League, shows

[38]See above, pp. 43–9.
[39]*La Vie de Jules Agricola descripte à la vérité par Cornelius Tacitus son gendre* (n.p., n.d.), pp. 2–3.
[40]*Discours touchant les quatre vertus ou bien un formulaire de l'honneste vie; Recueil des bonnes moeurs extrait de divers passages de Sénecque; Des Sciences libérales; Des remèdes des choses fortuites* (Paris, 1582).

that the Protestant sieur du Luat practised what he preached. Moreover, Cappel balanced this appeal for patronage by dedicating his translation of Seneca's *De Ira* to Joyeuse's main rival, the duc d'Epernon, and his version of Seneca's *De Clementia* to Henri III himself.[41] The writings of both Leaguers and Huguenots discovered all the traits of the tyrant in this uncertain monarch, but Ange Cappel chose to forget his hints about tyranny in the preface he had composed to Tacitus's *Agricola*. In this new royal dedication he preferred to stress the king's "douceur et incroyable bonté."

Quite evidently, Ange Cappel was in desperate need of a patron similar to those his father had found in Guillaume du Bellay, Guillaume Cappel in Jean Bertrand, and his two other brothers in the duc de Bouillon. Nevertheless, he published in 1586 what purported to be an objective analysis of the civil wars as a struggle between two self-interested political parties. He traced the origins of the conflict back to the factions of noble favourites which had flourished under Henri II, and he did not hesitate to show how these factions had exploited religious differences. A touch of robe prejudice coloured his opinion that the mass of the lesser *noblesse d'épée* had continued the wars for material profit at the expense of the third estate, and also to pay off old scores against enemies within their own order. Another argument boldly stated by the author – and one that showed he no longer sought the favour of the *archimignons* Joyeuse and Epernon – was that royal government had been reduced to a nullity by the excesses and inadequacies of the king's favourites. Ange Cappel condemned the League as the refuge "de tous les turbulens, ambitieux et usurpateurs," and praised leaders of moderate politique or Protestant opinion, such as Navarre, Damville, and Montpensier.[42] The youngest Cappel inclined to the Protestant–politique position. He knew neutrality to be impossible in current circumstances and quoted an appropriate line from *Agricola:* "Dum singuli pugnant, universi vincantur." The horrors of the French situation were illustrated by parallels with events described in the *Annales* and the *Historiae* of Tacitus.

Ange Cappel eventually found his patron, one whose political opinions were very like those expressed in his *Discours sur la comparaison,* Sully. In 1596 the future chief minister of Henri IV took Cappel with him in his forays in the Loire valley to confiscate royal revenues amassed by local fiscal officers and deliver them personally to the king. In the next century the gossip-monger Tallemant des Réaux told the story that the future *surintendant des finances* simply could not handle figures and took Ange Cappel with him as an accounting expert. Tallemant described Cappel as "une espèce de fou de belles-lettres," remarking that he tried to flatter Sully with a pamphlet entitled *Le Confident* and that he gave "des avis très-pernicieux" on restoring the finances by a system of fines.[43]

[41]*Les Trois Livres de Séneque de la colère* (Paris, 1585 [privilege dated 1582]); *De la clémence* (Lyon, 1595). Another translation of one of Seneca's works by Ange Cappel is *De la pauvreté* (n.p., n.d.).
[42]*Discours sur la comparaison et ellection des deux partis qui sont pour le iourd'huy en ce royaume* (Montauban, 1586), pp. 20, 27, 34, 50.
[43]Tallemant des Réaux, *Historiettes*, ed. Antoine Adam (Paris, 1960), vol. 1, p. 46. In his notes M.

Little in Tallemant's comments can be taken at face value, but it is clear at least that Ange had won Sully's confidence. He became a *secrétaire de la chambre du roi*, but it seems unlikely that the minister gave him any support in the special reform project ridiculed by Tallemant and others. Ange Cappel had pursued his plan from the time of L'Hôpital, who, he claimed, had given it personal support. In 1597 he submitted it to the assembly of notables at Rouen. A decade later he persuaded the royal council to set up a commission to investigate the proposal, but no recommendation eventuated. Cappel published several descriptions and justifications of the scheme, and included rebuttals of his critics and even details of the history of his family later included in *De Cappellorum Gente*, by his nephew Louis Cappel II.[44]

The 1607 version of the reform began with a long encomium to Henri IV, praising the prudent policies of the king in tolerating two religions and healing the wounds of civil war.[45] The proposal itself was relatively simple. The profits of justice were part of the revenues of the royal domain. In early times, Cappel asserted, a domanial right existed to fine a litigant who lost his suit in the royal courts, and this right should be reclaimed. It was just that an unsuccessful pleader should be punished, for, if he lost, he must have been trying to deceive royal justice. An ancient maxim, according to Cappel, had existed in the time of Charlemagne "que le battu paye l'amende."[46] Such was the current flood of litigation, especially in taxatory matters, that the reassertion of this right by the crown would prove a panacea for all the kingdom's ills. Revenues from such fines would enable the king to pay his private as well as his public debts; they would restore the government *rentes* operated through municipal councils; they would repurchase the alienated parts of the domain; and they would check venality of office by buying out the holders of unnecessary offices. Ange Cappel doubtless expected some personal financial reward if his scheme were adopted. Had he been more modest in his estimate of the results, he might have persuaded some members of the council. But while he was asserting, on the one hand, that his project would solve all the fiscal problems of the crown, he was

---

Adam has clarified the allusions to Ange Cappel (*ibid.*, pp. 722–3). It is the diarist Pierre de l'Estoile who describes how Cappel's little book, *Discours de la confidence* (Paris, 1599), offended the constable Montmorency-Damville and led to the brief incarceration of Ange by the Châtelet until the parlement suspended the sentence. Tallemant's account is based upon comments on the *Oeconomies royales* of Sully written by Marbault, secretary to Duplessis-Mornay.

[44] *Advis et mémoires presentez au Roy sur l'abbréviation des proces par le restablissement de l'ancien droict domanial des defaux et amendes* (Paris, 1607; B.N. F28613); *L'Advis donné au Roy sur l'abreviation des procès par le restablissement de l'ancien droict domanial des deffaulx et amendes* (n.p.. n.d., ms. title page, a later edition than the preceding one; B.N. Rés. F 278). This edition is bound with six supporting broadsides and the memoir on the Cappel tombs in the Innocents entitled *Extraict de chose merveilleuse* (see note 3 above). A third version is *Maxime, preuves, articles, replique et ofres présentées par le sieur du Luat Ange Cappel* (n.p., n.d.; B.N. Rés. F 277). This includes a record of the *lit de justice* held at Rouen to register the majority of Charles IX (pp. 99–122) with the text of L'Hôpital's speech on judicial reform. The last known edition of Ange Cappel's scheme is dated 1622 (B.N. Rés. F 914).

[45] *Advis et mémoires*, pp. 5–7.
[46] *Ibid.*, p. 59.

also arguing, on the other, that the system of the *amende* would abbreviate the judicial process by reducing the amount of litigation – an argument which, if true, would run counter to the enormous profits he had predicted.

Ange Cappel went on publicising his scheme in the regency of Marie de Médicis and even in the early years of the personal reign of Louis XIII. It was not only his refusal to admit failure but also the bad verses and personal posturing with which he adorned his pamphlets that gave him an eccentric reputation. Some editions of his proposal contain an engraving of Henri IV cutting the Gordian knot of corrupted justice with, beside him, the remains of a hydra whose heads of civil discord lie severed on the floor. A facing page in these editions shows a portrait of Ange Cappel with grizzled hair and beard and an incongruous set of angelic wings. The figure holds a cornucopia of plenty and a bound text of the reform.[47] As if this were not bad enough, consider such accompanying lines as these:

> Quel spectacle nouveau! quelle figure estrange!
> Est-ce Ange, homme ou Demon qui paroist à mes yeux?
> Si je luy voy le dos je pense voire un Ange;
> Mais les Anges n'ont point le visage si vieux.
> Cette barbe et ce front plus à l'homme ressemblent,
> Mais quoy, ces ailes d'or monstrent qu'il n'est pas tel:
> Donc c'est quelque Demon ou tous les deux s'assemblent,
> Demon participiant de l'Ange et du mortel.[48]

One can understand why Tallemant called him "une espèce de fou de belles-lettres." Ange Cappel's serious purpose and political insight had degenerated into a senile obstinacy. His last years also cost him the respect of his family, for in 1617, six years before his death, he abjured the reformed faith.

Ange Cappel appears to have taken little interest in the orphaned children of his eldest brother. There were four of them: Jacques III, Olivier, Marie, and Louis II. After the intervention of Matthieu Bochart at Le Tilloy, it was Jacques who took charge of his younger sister and brothers. He arranged for the adoption of Marie and her subsequent marriage to a pastor named Sigisbert Alpée, sieur de Saint-Maurice. Olivier, who was sent to Montpellier to study medicine, went blind and died in adolescence. Louis, like Jacques, studied theology and oriental languages. This generation renounced the family's aspirations for judicial office. In the spring of 1596 Jacques III was trying to rebuild the congregation at Vaudoy. He was evidently well known to the widow of François de La Noue, the iron-armed Huguenot paladin, for at this time she wrote to the ageing Beza, describing the work of the young pastor of Le Tilloy and Vaudoy: "His youth makes him full of good cheer and he has a great deal of doctrine. He has married Bourdet whom you have seen in my retinue."[49] The bride of

[47]*L'Advis donné au Roy*, pp. 19–20.
[48]*Ibid.*, p. 13.
[49]*B.S.H.P.F.*, 65 (1916), p. 112.

Jacques III was a poor noblewoman and governess. They did not stay in Brie. Selling the family seigneuries, he withdrew again to Sedan, where he became professor of Hebrew under the patronage of the new duc de Bouillon, the former vicomte de Turenne. When his wife and five-year-old son died in 1601, Jacques Cappel III married Charlotte Berger, the daughter of a *conseiller* in the Paris parlement who had somehow managed to retain both his office and his Protestant sympathies. Marie, the daughter of this second marriage, was wed to Jean de Brion, seigneur de Chenevelle. In this period, when many of the Huguenot *noblesse d'épée* were turning to Catholicism, there were more alliances between Protestant families of the lesser robe and sword.

There was a trend, too, for intermarriage between the children of pastors. Louis Cappel II, who had been born adventurously during the flight of his father and mother to Sedan in 1585, married the daughter of Benjamin Launay, sieur du Graviers and pastor at Chilleurs. Louis became one of the greatest biblical scholars of the age, and as a professor at Saumur helped John Cameron and Moïse Amyraut to fashion a more liberal variety of French Calvinism that was in contact with Dutch and English Arminianism. The two professorial brothers at Sedan and Saumur had Bouillon and other members of the high Protestant *noblesse* as their patrons. Louis II published the elegant verses he composed on the death of Bouillon's daughter, the young princess Louise de la Tour, in 1607.[50] Jacques III dedicated his polemical anti-Roman tract *Les Livrées de Babel* to Bouillon, and his attack upon the Jesuit Gonthier to Madame de la Trémoille, duchesse de Thouars.[51]

By his death in 1624 Jacques Cappel III had published more than a score of works of scriptural commentary, biblical and early Christian history, ancient Roman antiquities, and anti-Catholic polemic.[52] Louis II, who lived on until 1658, was even more prolific and also acquired a better scholarly reputation. Casaubon, Grotius, and Vossius praised his erudition and consoled him when he was attacked by Calvinist theologians of less learning and narrower conviction. Jacques III was the more vigorous polemicist. His ripostes to Jesuit writers such as Gonthier, Rosweyd, and Eudaemon-Johannes[53] formed part of a European controversy on the respective powers of popes and kings. It began in France and England with the excommunications of Henri de Navarre and Elizabeth, was resumed in England in the early years of James I with the

---

[50]*Sur la douleureuse et non iamais assez regrettée mort de très-illustre et vertueuse princesse mademoiselle Louise de la Tour* (Sedan, 1608).

[51]*Les Livrées de Babel ou l'histoire du siège romain* (Sedan, 1616); *Les Trophées de P. Gonteri Iesuite avec un catéchisme pour son instruction* (Sedan, 1613). The catechism, which was also published separately with a letter to Mme. de la Trémoille, was that promoted by Jacques Cappel II and Louis Cappel Ier in 1560 (see note 19).

[52]See the list in Haag and Haag, *La France protestante*, vol. 2, pp. 200–1.

[53]Other works in this context by Jacques Cappel III, apart from those mentioned in note 51, are: *Vindiciae pro Isaaco Casaubono* (Frankfort, 1619, dedicated to James I); *Assertio bonae fidei adversus praecipuas Heriberti Rosweydi Iesuitae strophas* (Sedan, 1619); *Artes Romanae Sedis* (Sedan, 1619); *Apologie pour les églises réformées contre les blasmes de L. Lessius, P. Coton et autres* (Sedan, 1611). For general accounts of these controversies see below, pp. 184–8.

Gunpowder Plot and the oath of allegiance, and returned to France after the assassination of Henri IV and the debates in the estates general of 1614–15. Jacques Cappel was well acquainted with the Anglican thesis that there was little difference between Calvinist resistance theories and ultramontane Catholic doctrines of church and state. Although he knew well the attack upon Catholic and Huguenot monarchomachs *De Regno et regali potestate* (1600), by William Barclay, the would-be protégé of James VI and I,[54] he chose to ignore the tradition of Beza, Hotman, and the *Vindiciae contra Tyrannos*, and to concentrate upon his Jesuit antagonists. To Cappel the correct Calvinist attitude to the relations of church and state was the doctrine of nonresistance stated in the catechism of 1560. He was equally indebted to those Gallican ideas developed by his grandfather, the *avocat-général*, denying the pope either direct or indirect power to infringe the sovereignty of the king of France.

In the sphere of Hebraic erudition and biblical commentary Louis II was without rival. His interest descended to two of his three surviving sons by his marriage with Suzanne Launay. Jean, the eldest, edited his father's study of Old Testament textual variants,[55] but abandoned the family's Protestant tradition by his abjuration in 1656. Louis Cappel III, who did not possess the same penchant for biblical scholarship, also converted to Catholicism. However, in the youngest surviving son, Jacques Cappel IV, four generations of the family found their last scholarly representative. Jacques IV followed his father as professor of Hebrew at Saumur, and took refuge in England at the time of the revocation of the edict of Nantes. The Cappel had close ties with Stuart divine right Anglicanism. From the days when James I had employed the elder Pierre du Moulin and Isaac Casaubon in his *guerre académique*, through the period when Moise Amyraut condemned the Long Parliament and Claude de Saumaise denounced the regicide, to the time when the younger Pierre du Moulin defended the later Stuart kings, there were many links between English and French Arminians.[56] Louis Cappel II received a special testimonial from the leading theologians of Oxford in 1612. He dedicated two of his works to Archbishop Usher of Armagh, and was much admired by the erudite satirist and theologian Joseph Hall, bishop of Norwich.

[54]Cappel cites Barclay in *Les Livrées de Babel*, pp. 88, 351ff.

[55]*Ludovici Cappelli critica sacra sive de variis quae in sacris Veteris Testamenti libris occurrunt lectionibus libri sex . . . edita in lucem studio et opera Joannis Cappelli* (Paris, 1650).

[56]The two Pierre du Moulin belonged to a different branch of the family from the great jurisconsult, Gallican polemicist, and Protestant independent Charles du Moulin. The elder Pierre du Moulin (1568–1658) studied at Sedan and Cambridge, and became professor of philosophy at Leyden at the age of twenty-four. He was for twenty-one years thereafter a pastor at Charenton, refusing academic preferment. He came to England under the protection of James I to work on church reunification, and ended by writing pamphlets in the king's cause against Cardinal du Perron and others. The younger Pierre du Moulin (1600–84) was made chaplain to Charles II at the Restoration. His brother, Louis, supported Cromwell and the Puritan cause. See in general G. H. Dodge, *The Political Theory of the Huguenots of the Dispersion* (New York, 1947); and Elizabeth Israels Perry, *From Theology to History: French Religious Controversy and the Revocation of the Edict of Nantes* (The Hague, 1973).

When Jacques Cappel IV arrived in England he did not take part in political controversy. Under the joint impact of the revocation of the edict of Nantes and the English Revolution of 1688, many Huguenot exiles such as Pierre Allix and Jacques Abbadie followed the lead given by Pierre Jurieu in resurrecting the Huguenot resistance theory of the sixteenth century and adapting it to the new circumstances.[57] But Jacques IV devoted his energy to editing the scriptural commentaries of his uncle and his father. The large folio volume of their works (principally those of Louis II) which appeared in Amsterdam in 1689 was dedicated to William Sancroft, the nonjuring Archbishop of Canterbury.[58] Since Sancroft was suspended in that year and deprived in 1690, it is likely that, by the dedication, Jacques IV was deliberately following the path of nonresistance defended by his elders. The book includes Louis II's history of the family (*De Cappellorum Gente*), some sternly moral letters written by Jacques II in Le Tilloy to Jacques III in Sedan in the years 1582–5, the testimonial awarded Louis II at Oxford, a list of the works of Louis II and Jacques III, and, finally, a treatise on the secret of ancient Hebrew accents and punctuation based on the work of the learned Erpenius. This last item recalls the kind of pure erudition encountered in Jacques Ier's *Fragmenta* and the refutation of Valla by Jacques II. There is even a section reminiscent of Jacques Ier's adaptation of Cicero's *De Natura Deorum*, although its title is provided with a far more Christian tailpiece: *ΝΕΚΡΩΝ ΒΙΟΣ sive de hominum post mortem statu, usque ad ultimum judicii diem.*[59] But there had also been an element of pragmatism in the Cappel, especially among the sons of the *avocat-général*. This final text contains a quotation from Saint Augustine that epitomises their attitudes towards religion and the law: "Melius est dubitare de occultis quam litigare de incertis."[60]

Through two centuries the writings of the Cappel provide a tracery of intellectual patterns in French humanism, in neostoic morality, in politique political theory, and in Protestant theology. They began as a remarkably talented family whose future seemed assured in a rapidly expanding judiciary. As with the families of Budé, Bochart, Du Moulin, and Hotman, the path of ascension through the law was blocked for those of the Cappel who adopted heterodox religious opinions. Their marriage alliances and patronage connections held to the general pattern for some time after their association with the reformed faith, but eventually their familial links were restricted to a narrower Protestant circle, and their protectors were drawn solely from the diminishing band of Huguenot grandees. It is almost as if their failure to hold their footing within the state apparatus stimulated them to express their talents in the field of scholarship.

---

[57] J. H. M. Salmon, *The French Religious Wars in English Political Thought* (Oxford, 1959), pp. 148–53.
[58] *Ludovici Cappelli . . . commentarii et notae criticae in Vetus Testamentum accessere Jacobi Cappelli. . . . observationes in eosdem libros, item Ludovici Cappelli arcanum punctationis auctius et emendatius, eiusque vindiciae hactenus ineditae. Editionem procuravit Jacobus Cappellus . . .* (Amsterdam, 1689).
[59] *Ibid.*, pp. 243–58. "Life in Death, or the State of Men after Death until the Last Judgment."
[60] *Ibid.*, p. 257. "It is better to doubt secret things than to dispute about uncertain things."

Certainly, their contribution to the building of the French state was by no means a negative one. They continued to support royal absolutism, even when the Catholic state that had accorded them a brief century of formal toleration decided to expel them from its borders or to force them to abandon their faith.

APPENDIX: THE CAPPEL

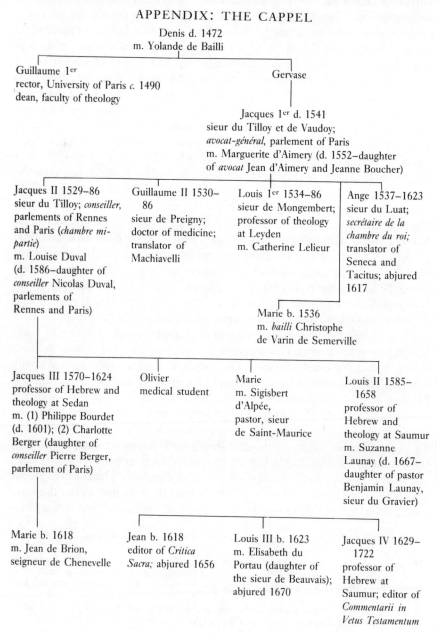

Denis d. 1472
m. Yolande de Bailli

Guillaume 1ᵉʳ
rector, University of Paris *c.* 1490
dean, faculty of theology

Gervase

Jacques 1ᵉʳ d. 1541
sieur du Tilloy et de Vaudoy;
avocat-général, parlement of Paris
m. Marguerite d'Aimery (d. 1552–daughter
of *avocat* Jean d'Aimery and Jeanne Boucher)

Jacques II 1529–86
sieur du Tilloy; *conseiller,*
parlements of Rennes
and Paris (*chambre mi-partie*)
m. Louise Duval
(d. 1586–daughter of
conseiller Nicolas Duval,
parlements of
Rennes and Paris)

Guillaume II 1530–86
sieur de Preigny;
doctor of medicine;
translator of
Machiavelli

Louis 1ᵉʳ 1534–86
sieur de Mongembert;
professor of theology
at Leyden
m. Catherine Lelieur

Ange 1537–1623
sieur du Luat;
*secrétaire de la
chambre du roi;*
translator of
Seneca and
Tacitus; abjured
1617

Marie b. 1536
m. *bailli* Christophe
de Varin de Semerville

Jacques III 1570–1624
professor of Hebrew and
theology at Sedan
m. (1) Philippe Bourdet
(d. 1601); (2) Charlotte
Berger (daughter of
conseiller Pierre Berger,
parlement of Paris)

Olivier
medical student

Marie
m. Sigisbert
d'Alpée,
pastor, sieur
de Saint-Maurice

Louis II 1585–
1658
professor of
Hebrew and
theology at Saumur
m. Suzanne
Launay (d. 1667–
daughter of pastor
Benjamin Launay,
sieur du Gravier)

Marie b. 1618
m. Jean de Brion,
seigneur de Chenevelle

Jean b. 1618
editor of *Critica
Sacra;* abjured 1656

Louis III b. 1623
m. Elisabeth du
Portau (daughter of
the sieur de Beauvais);
abjured 1670

Jacques IV 1629–
1722
professor of
Hebrew at
Saumur; editor of
*Commentarii in
Vetus Testamentum*

3

French satire in the late sixteenth century

My intention is to select some examples of political satire in the time of the French Catholic League, and to draw some inferences about their place in the development of the satiric genre. Any discussion of satire is perplexed by problems of definition. If one talks generally of a satiric temper it is difficult to know where to draw the line. Charles Lenient, the author of the standard nineteenth-century work on the subject,[1] invented a variety of ingenious categories – *satire philosophique, satire religieuse, satire politique, satire littéraire* and the like – so that almost anything with a vaguely satiric flavor could be tucked neatly away in his *omnium gatherum*. At the other extreme, a critic concerned with the particularity of genre is likely to find satire a slippery fish to net. In a recent work on classical and contemporary Italian influence on French sixteenth-century satire, Olga Trtnik-Rossettini found it necessary to confine her material to "poems called satires, and isometric pieces in decasyllables or alexandrines in rhymed couplets which are also satiric in character."[2]

There is also a tradition linking definition with etymology.[3] An early instance in sixteenth-century humanism was the elder Scaliger, who insisted upon the Greek origin of the genre and associated it with the word Σαꞇτυρος (satyr). At the beginning of the seventeenth century Isaac Casaubon strenuously asserted the counter-position that, while satiric elements might be discerned in Greek poetry, the classical genre was specifically Roman, and was named from *satura lanx*, the Latin for a dish of mixed foods.[4] Dryden, who referred to these

---

[1] *La Satire en France, ou la littérature militante au XVIe siècle* (2 vols., Paris, 1877).
[2] *Les influences anciennes et italiennes sur la satire en France au XVIe siècle* (Florence: Institut français de Florence, 1958), p. 3.
[3] J. W. Jolliffe, "Satyre: Satura: ΣΑΤΥΡΟΣ – a study in confusion," *Bibliothèque d'Humanisme et Renaissance*, 18 (1956), 84–5.
[4] Casaubon's opinion was expressed in *De Satyrica Graecorum poesi et Romanorum satira libri duo* (Paris, 1605), and the title in itself conveys the theme. Casaubon had made known his views several years before they appeared in print. On September 3, 1601, he sent an abstract of his argument – perhaps the whole manuscript of *De Satyrica* – to his friend, the jurist Scipio Gentile. His accompanying letter explained that he had set down the issues in simple terms because he intended to convince the general public. The edition of the satires of Persius that he was preparing had the same purpose. A manuscript of this letter is held in the Haverford College Roberts

opinions in his *Discourse concerning the Origin and Progress of Satire,* also cited the definition of Joseph Scaliger's pupil, the Dutch philologist, Daniel Heinsius, who had modified Casaubon's conclusion: "Satire is a kind of poetry, without a series of action, invented for the purging of our minds; in which human vices, ignorances and errors . . . are severely reprehended . . . partly dramatically, partly simply, . . . partly also in a facetious and civil way of jesting, by which either hatred or laughter or indignation was moved."[5] The author of *Absalom and Achitophel* was not entirely happy with this definition because to him it seemed to favour Horace at the expense of Persius and Juvenal. But the truth is that Dryden regarded the entire Roman trilogy as the supreme exemplars of the genre.

It seems unquestionable that Horace, Persius and Juvenal did in fact constitute a classical core of satiric inspiration, possessing in common a certain inbuilt poetic formalism and an ancestry in Lucilius. Literary circles in Renaissance France certainly anticipated the establishment of the satiric canon by a Heinsius, a Dryden or a Boileau. Of the various French translations of the three Roman satirists that were published in the 1540s the rendering of Horace's *Ars poetica* by Jacques Peletier du Mans was perhaps the most important. While Peletier inspired the general idea of poetic reform in Du Bellay and Ronsard, he also arrived at a specific definition of the rules for French satire based on the Horatian model. These were set out in *L'Art poétique français* in 1555, ten years after his translation of Horace's own rules. Joachim du Bellay was among the first deliberately to follow Horace. The satiric elements in his *Regrets* of 1558 closely resemble Ariosto's satires, which were also set in Rome and were equally redolent of Horace. Du Bellay did not imitate Ariosto. It was his purpose to evoke Rome as it had been in the days of the Augustan poets,[6] and the similarity to Ariosto was due to their common source. Yet, as Rossettini and others have shown, many in the generation of the *Pléiade* were influenced by Italian satirists, especially by the insipid pleasantries of Berni and his followers. Whether through Italian influence or direct from the Latin sources, the poetic genre of the French satire was already firmly established in the middle decades of the century. Ronsard himself explained how the poet should employ satire to expose the vices of the time in his *Royal Grove* (*Bocage royal*), which contained verses described as a combination of Juvenal's first satire with Horace's fourth.[7] Early in the religious wars Ronsard's *Discourse on the Miseries of this Time* was another important example of the genre.

Collection (ms. 170), and a slightly different version of it appears as the first of four letters by Casaubon on satire appended to the 1699 Leiden edition of his *De Satyrica.* In his dedication of the latter work to Jean de Rieux in 1605 he further discussed the issue of Greek or Roman primacy.
[5] *Essays of John Dryden,* ed. W. P. Ker (Oxford, 1926), vol. 2, p. 100.
[6] M. A. Screech, introduction to Joachim du Bellay, *Les Regrets et autres oeuvres poëtiques,* ed. J. Jolliffe (Geneva, 1966), p. 24.
[7] Joseph Vianey, *Mathurin Régnier* (Paris, 1896), p. 66.

In satire the *Pléiade* was striving to replace the native traditions that had produced the *fabliaux*, the plays of the *basoche*, the second part of the *Roman de la Rose*, Villon's *Testament* and the *coq-à-l'âne*. It is usually assumed that, as the civil wars intensified, satire escaped the influence of Du Bellay and Ronsard and reverted to native *gauloiseries*. Then, when peace was established at the end of the century, French satire returned to the Lucilian genre with Vauquelin de la Fresnaye and Mathurin Régnier. But the truth is more complex than this. It seems to have gone almost unnoticed that there was an alternative classical satiric tradition possessing remarkable vitality in sixteenth-century France. This was the Menippean variety, involving a miscellany of dialogue, poetry and prose, and associated with Menippus of Gadara, Varro and Lucian. It dealt with persons as well as abstract vices, and its moralising implications were tempered, if not subverted, by a scepticism borrowed from its originator, whose reputation as a Cynic philosopher survived the loss of his writings. Although it had nothing to do with satyrs, it was principally Greek in inspiration. Nevertheless, in form it was close to the Roman idea of *satura lanx*, and Ennius was composing his *saturae* in Latin early in the second century B.C., not long after Menippus. In the early sixteenth century it was probably the Greek editions of Lucian's satires prepared by Erasmus and More that introduced the learned to this alternative mode. Rabelais, whose Greek humanism mingled with French satiric realism, was deeply indebted to Lucian, and popularised Menippean concepts among a wider audience.[8] The Menippean form was less constricted than the purely poetic Lucilian genre, and, instead of appearing as a reaction against the native tradition, it became assimilated with it.

This was the mould in which the younger Henri Estienne cast his satire of the Catholic church and contemporary lay society, *Apology for Herodotus* (1566). Like Rabelais, whose moral laxism he despised, Estienne drew upon the medieval French as well as the classical heritage. The historical anecdote and the fictional narrative alternated in his prose. Among his recent sources were the *Colloquies* of Erasmus, the verse of Marot, and the *Heptaméron* of Marguerite d'Angoulême. As a Calvinist he accused Lucian, reborn in Rabelais, of mocking religion,[9] but as a satirist he adapted Lucian's method to attack the corruption of his own times. Estienne's *Apology* remained popular and influential for more than a generation, but it was not until the time when its thirteenth edition appeared in 1592 that the Menippean mode began to come fully and con-

[8]Dorothy Gabe Coleman, *Rabelais: a Critical Study in Prose Fiction* (Cambridge, 1971), pp. 84–9. Alone among works of modern criticism, this study recognises the conscious recovery of the Menippean mode in the sixteenth century. Voltaire, it might be noted, recognised the affiliation between Lucian, Erasmus and Rabelais, who constitute the *personae* of one of his *Entretiens*, and end their conversation to dine with Swift. *Oeuvres complètes de Voltaire* (Paris, 1879), vol. 25, pp. 339–41.
[9]"Qui est donc celuy qui ne sçait que nostre siècle a faict revivre un Lucian en un François Rabelais en matière d'escrit brocardans toute sorte de religion?" *Apologie pour Hérodote*, ed. P. Ristelhuber (Paris, 1879), vol. 1, pp. 189–90.

sciously into its own. With its contempt for poetic formalism and its ready applicability to the political issues of the day, it was far better suited to the climate of the civil wars of the League than the Horatian model. When the wars ended, and order and stability briefly returned, the Lucilian brand of satire was reestablished as the canon of literary taste. Yet something of the spirit, if not of the form, of the Menippean mode permeated the satires of Régnier.

Literary forms are not always responsive to climates of political opinion, and yet the last phrases of the League constituted so intense a social crisis that literature was, for once at least, enslaved by historical circumstance. This is a topic in which the historian and the critic must come to terms. On the one hand, no one preoccupied by literary form will make much of the satires of the League unless he is familiar with the intricacies of the political and social history of the period. These satires do not concern abstract vice or folly personified, but real persons and real events. On the other hand, any historian who seeks evidence from literary satire to illustrate some political or social generalisation, and lacks awareness of the extent to which his sources are based upon classical models, is heading for egregious error. For instance, there is a vogue in sixteenth-century French writing to suggest that the essence of nobility is not race but virtue. How tempting to see such statements as evidence of class struggles or conflict between the old warrior aristocracy and the new legal nobility of the gown! But some of these opinions are merely a reflection from Juvenal's eighth satire, which begins "*Stemmata quid faciunt?*" (What good are pedigrees?), attacks pride of ancestry, and enunciates the counter-principle of virtue. Of course, it is possible for Juvenal to be adapted to what is in fact an expression of sixteenth-century social change.

During the first two decades of the religious wars, when the Huguenots were the principal opponents of the crown, satirical elements may occasionally be distinguished in the flood of propaganda from the Calvinist presses. In the 1560s there were several *ad hominem* tracts denouncing, with satiric overtones, the house of Guise in general and the cardinal of Lorraine in particular.[10] After the massacre of St. Bartholomew in 1572 several works added a flavour of satire to the *ad feminam* argument directed against Catherine de Médicis.[11] Yet the

[10]The best known example of the vogue, François Hotman's *Epistre envoiée au tigre de la France* [1560] ed. Charles Read (Paris, 1875), is modelled upon Cicero's denunciation of Catiline, and can scarcely be termed satire. A true satire, however, is Louis Régnier de la Planche's *Le livre des marchands, ou du grand et loyal devoir, fidélité et obéissance de messieurs de Paris envers le roy et couronne de France* [1565] (ed. J. A. C. Buchon, *Choix de chroniques et mémoires sur l'histoire de France*, Paris, 1836, vol. 2, pp. 422–70). La Planche provides an imaginary conversation between a number of worthy Parisian bourgeois about the cardinal of Lorraine. An example from this period of a non-satirical expository pamphlet which developed the dialogue form later so important in Menippean satire is the anonymous *Discours par dialogue sur l'édict de la révocation de la paix, publié à Paris le vingthuictieme jour de Septembre, l'an mil cinq cens soixante huict* (n.p., 1569).
[11]Examples are *Le Reveille-Matin des françois et de leurs voisins, composé par Eusebe Philadelphe Cosmopolite en forme de dialogues* ("Edimbourg," 1574), and *Discours merveilleux de la vie, actions et déportemens de Catherine de Médicis* (attributed to Henri Estienne, n.p., 1575). The latter bears interesting comparison to André de Rossant's denunciation of Henri III, which also contains

tone of this Huguenot literature was often too plainly expository and declamatory to admit its classification as satire. Henri Estienne's *Two Dialogues of the Italianised French Tongue* (1578) constitutes an important exception, but that was essentially a literary exercise. While it frequently used the dialogue form and grossly exaggerated the failings of its adversaries, Huguenot propaganda seldom invoked the covert pose, the bite of ridicule, and the ironic inversion of values that mark off satire from mere polemic or justification. Nevertheless, the satirists of the later sixteenth century doubtless learned from the touches of satiric inspiration that illuminated early Huguenot prose, just as the later Catholic theorists of resistance adapted the ideas of their Calvinist precursors.

There are two phases in the satire of the time of the League. The first is set in the court of the last Valois king, Henri III; the second in the Paris defended by the ultra-Catholic faction against his Protestant successor, the Bourbon Henri de Navarre. The League was formed initially in 1576 to restrain the crown from granting the Huguenots an advantageous peace, a policy supported by the moderate Catholics, or politiques, who put political expediency before religious uniformity. In its second phase, dating from 1584, the League revived in more militant form to exclude the relapsed heretic, Navarre, from the succession. From an aristocratic association led by the house of Guise, it widened its base to include elements from the lower clergy and the urban middle classes. In 1588 Henri de Guise defied the royal ban against his entering Paris, and a popular insurrection followed in which the king was expelled from the city and a revolutionary commune was installed. Henri III struck back by arresting the leading Leaguer deputies to the estates general and murdering Guise and his brother, the cardinal. The League then declared the Valois tyrant deposed and established a rival national government controlled by Mayenne, another brother of the martyred Guise. Ultra-Catholic fanaticism accomplished the assassination of Henri III in 1589, and Navarre began his long struggle for the throne against the combined forces of the League, Spain and Rome.

By the end of 1592 he was still far from establishing the new dynasty, but deep divisions had appeared in the ranks of his adversaries. Among the princes of the League there were several Catholic candidates for the crown. Thirty years of massacre and rapine during the civil wars had induced a certain lassitude, and there was a growing repugnance within segments of the League against dependence upon Spain. In their different ways the upper bourgeois and the radical lower-class elements in the League became disenchanted with aristocratic leadership and began to accuse their social superiors of waging war for private advantage. But the critics of the *noblesse* were more antagonistic to

satirical elements: *Les meurs, humeurs et comportemens de Henry de Valois* (Paris, 1589). The *Reveille-Matin* was cast in the form of dialogue. Another important example of this genre after the massacre was *Dialogue de l'authorité des princes et de la liberté des peuples* (also known as *Archon et Politie*), which appeared in *Mémoires de l'estat de France sous Charles Neufiesme* (Meidelbourg, 1577), vol. 2, pp. 89–150.

each other than they were towards the military commanders. In Leaguer Paris politique sympathies grew among merchants and magistrates, while the fanatics among the lower clergy exhorted the masses and encouraged acts of terrorism against suspected traitors. The popular terrorists and revolutionaries were known as the Sixteen. In the last years of Henri III this conspiratorial group had included zealous Leaguers from the entire spectrum of Parisian society, but, after the triumphs over the Valois, the more respectable elements cooperated with the conservative Mayenne, while the lesser lawyers, clerks, sergeants and artisans moved further to the left. Mayenne needed the Sixteen to counter-balance loss of enthusiasm for the League within the parlement, but in November 1591 they went too far and murdered the first president of the sovereign court and two senior magistrates. The League's lieutenant-general hanged four of the terrorists and temporarily suppressed their organization, but, as his support among the high bourgeoisie diminished, he was obliged to allow the survivors to recommence their activities. Military necessity, and the hope of securing the crown for himself or his son, had caused Mayenne to postpone the calling of the estates general to choose a Leaguer king. By January 1593 delay and indecision so threatened the unity of his party that Mayenne allowed the deputies to assemble in Paris.

Such in outline is the social and political setting for the satires of the time of the League. In their first phase they are directed at the vices of Henri III's court, and they represent both Catholic and Protestant indignation. The most celebrated example to be set in the early period is the second book of Agrippa d'Aubigné's *Les Tragiques*, which reflects the Huguenot poet's own experiences at court in the years 1573–76 but includes references to the later duels and scandals of the *mignons*. A few lines from *Les Princes* establish the tone and the theme:[12]

> Fortunate Romans, for your tyrant race
> Loved all the arts and bore a martial face:
> Unlucky he who lives his slavish span
> 'Neath manlike woman and a female man.
> A suspect mother, pander to her brood,
> Caused one to roam the woods in savage mood,
> And claim his conquest, where the deed was least,
> In triumph at the blood of some poor beast.

. . . .

[12]*Les Tragiques*, ed. A. Garnier and J. Plattard (Paris, 1932), vol. 2, pp. 53–4 (lines 757–64 and 773–6):

> Bien heureux les Romains qui avoyent les Cesars
> Pour tyrans, amateurs des armes et des arts:
> Mais mal-heureux celui qui vit esclave infame
> Sous une femme hommace et sous un homme femme!
> Une mere douteuse, apres avoir esté
> Macquerelle à ses fils, en a l'un arresté
> Sauvage dans les bois, et, pour belle conqueste,
> Le faisoit triompher du sang de quelque beste.

. . . .

The other learnt the niceties of dress
Of whores at court: in feminine excess
He'd shave his chin, put powder on his cheeks,
And eye the vice Sardanapalus seeks.

The *femme hommace*, the manlike woman, is Catherine de Médicis. The frenetic huntsman is her unstable son, Charles IX, who reputedly shot down his Protestant subjects from a window in the Louvre during the massacre in which d'Aubigné himself so nearly became a victim. The *homme femme*, the female man, is Henri III, whose appearance, with his slashed Spanish doublet, his headdress bedecked with pearls and his layered sleeves descending to the floor, caused the poet to liken him to the Assyrian voluptuary who disguised himself as one of his own concubines:

> And thus tricked out, he wore throughout the day
> This monstrous garb that matched his lover's way,
> And at first glance no person could decide
> If woman-king or man-queen he descried.[13]

As his invective reaches crescendo d'Aubigné calls the last Valois *une putain fardée* and compares him with the androgynous Nero. His theme is that this is the last, albeit the most distasteful, example of a degenerate brood, and he invokes the shade of that pet aversion of Huguenot propaganda, Machiavelli, who had advised his prince to exhibit the qualities of both the lion and the fox:

> The crafty fox our princes emulate,
> But with the lion's strength they n'er debate.[14]

Yet, since all this constitutes an unconcealed tirade of righteous indignation, one may well ask whether the tradition that names *Les Princes* a satire within a poem of tragic and epic proportions is really correct. If it is correct, then the main problem discussed by James Sutherland in his Clark Lectures on satire – how to distinguish satire from comedy[15] – is complicated by an additional need to differentiate it from tragedy. True, d'Aubigné writes in alexandrines that form the vital criterion for Mme. Rossettini. He has the exaggeration, the gross distortion, the *saeva indignatio* necessary to satire. But another essential element

---

L'autre fut mieux instruit à juger des atours
Des putains de sa cour, et, plus propre aux amours,
Avoir ras le menton, garder la face pasle,
Le geste effeminé, l'oeil d'un Sardanapale.

[13]*Ibid.*, pp. 55–6 (lines 793–6):
Pour nouveau parement il porta tout ce jour
Cet habit monstrueux, pareil à son amour:
Si qu'au premier abord chacun estoit en peine
S'il voyoit un Roy femme ou bien un homme Reyne.

[14]*Ibid.*, p. 65 (lines 907–8):
Nos princes des renards envient la finesse,
Et ne debattent point aux lions de prouësse.

[15]*English Satire* (Cambridge, 1967), p. 2.

is missing. While he is very much concerned with the disguises assumed by the Valois kings and their courtiers,[16] he does not attempt to disguise the standpoint of the author. There is nothing of the allegory, the imagined situation, the fictional veneer that serve to emphasise the greater sin or the greater absurdity of the real object of attack.

Certainly the next book of *Les Tragiques*, *La Chambre dorée*, meets this criterion. Here justice, panting and distraught, bursts into the rainbow arc of heaven, scatters the gambolling angels, and pleads before the glorious throne of the Almighty. Piety intervenes on her behalf, and the Lord of Hosts visits the earth to conduct his own inquiry. He hovers over the many-towered palace, and then the golden room of the administrators of the law, and sees injustice usurping the judgment seat. The judges are of the kind who are gentle with murderers, and murderers of the gentle. They favor liars, thieves, pimps and adulterers, and put up for sale truth, reason and authority. A variety of particular judicial vices assume personal form as the inquiry proceeds – ambition, anger, avarice, envy, hypocrisy, vanity, and the like. Besides using this traditional device of the satirist, d'Aubigné refers to real persons who were the perpetrators or victims of actual injustices. These lines were clearly composed in the 1590s because among the magistrates of the parlement specifically excluded from the general reproach are Jacques Gillot, one of the circle who created the *Satyre Ménippée* in 1593, and the three judges butchered by the terrorists in 1591. The Parisian *curés* who supported the terrorists are depicted as having assumed additional functions and as performing a multiple role as sergeant, judge, confessor and executioner.[17]

In sentiment, if not in form, d'Aubigné was writing in an established vein. Before the climax of the Menippean mode in the 1590s there were many satires in the preceding decade that anticipated the style and sometimes the targets of the last years of the League. The most difficult to classify among these earlier works is *The Cabinet of the King of France containing Three Precious Pearls*, published anonymously by the Huguenot Nicolas Barnaud in 1581.[18] It consists of a curious medley of anti-Catholic vituperation and statistical reckoning, expressed in a prose broken by occasional satiric verses. The pearls are the scriptural word of God, the true virtue of the nobility, and the loyalty of the third estate. Their brilliance is concealed by the corruption of Catholic prelates and false nobles, who have arrogated to themselves the wealth of the kingdom, who ruin and exploit the common people, and who prevent effective government by the crown and the representative estates general. Clerical riches, acquired to the ignominy of kings and the desolation of the poor, are alleged to

[16]Imbrie Buffum, *Agrippa d'Aubigné's "Les Tragiques"* (New Haven, 1951), p. 117.
[17]*Les Tragiques*, vol. 3, pp. 150 and 163.
[18]*Le Cabinet du Roy de France, dans lequel il y a trois perles precieuses d'inestimable valeur: par les moyens desquelles Sa Majesté s'en va le premier monarque du monde et ses suiets du tout soulagez* (n.p., 1581). To Barnaud is also attributed the authorship of *Le Secret des finances* or *La Poligamie sacrée*, which was published under the pseudonym of Nicolas Froumenteau and is often cited in *Le Cabinet*.

support "all the brothels of Christendom." The figures that support this claim are rivalled by a list of sexual vices and material crimes that render the church "a sewer full of ordure" under the patronage of "the Great Whore of Babylon."[19] The *mignons* in the retinue of Henri III are subjected to abuse more explicit than that accorded them by d'Aubigné. Their unnatural habits in the manner of "shameless Ganymede" are described in two sets of verses entitled "Indignities at Court" and "The Court's Escutcheon."[20] For that matter, the greater part of the nobility are said to prostitute their honour in every kind of depravity. They share in the loathsome practices of the Catholic church and block the king from resuming clerical property after the example of the Tudors. Some are "werewolves, enemies of peace and the public good," and worst of all are those "recently ennobled by theft, brigandage, cruelty, forgery and assassination."[21] At the same time, those who call loudest for their dignity *as noblesse de sang* are the last to respect the true *noblesse de vertu*, the second pearl that must be plucked from its shell and exposed to light.[22]

In his essay on sixteenth-century satire, Fernand Fleuret deplores Lenient's summary dismissal of *The Three Precious Pearls*, asserting that the critic's surfeit of delicacy prevents him from a just appraisal of its Rabelaisian aspects.[23] The same accusation is levelled at Lenient's discussion of *The Island of the Hermaphrodites*, a satire attributed to Artus Thomas, sieur d'Embry, and composed apparently in the 1580s, although not published until 1605. In fact, however, Lenient bestows a singular accolade upon the *Hermaphrodites*, comparing it with *Gulliver's Travels*.[24]

Although Laputa is a floating isle, like its Hermaphroditic counterpart, it is improbable that Dean Swift would have let Gulliver visit Embry's creation. A shipwrecked traveller is cast upon this unstable land and finds his way to a magnificent palace. He proceeds to the chambers of the lord of the Hermaphrodites and watches the sybaritic mysteries of the royal toilet. He listens to conversations about love and friendship in which affectation and hypocrisy mock the vogue of Platonic academies. Then the traveller wanders down a long corridor and finds a guide, who leads him to a room where four statues are enthroned. One represents Ganymede, another a being part male and part female, and the other two Sardanapalus and Heliogabalus. The traveller inspects books and papers consisting of "pasquinades, satires and other kinds of poetry," together with extracts from the Hermaphroditic laws. The author of these is entitled: "Imperator varius, Heliogabalus, Hermaphroditicus, Gomorricus, Eunuchus, semper impudicissimus."[25] Later the narrator encounters a

[19]*Ibid.*, pp. 203, 207.
[20]*Ibid.*, pp. 301–6.
[21]*Ibid.*, p. 295.
[22]*Ibid.*, pp. 287, 369.
[23]"La satire française au XVIe siècle," *De Ronsard à Baudelaire* (Paris, 1935), p. 26.
[24]Lenient, vol. 2, p. 56.
[25]*L'Isle des Hermaphrodites nouvellement descouvert* (n.p., n.d.), pp. 44–5.

chaotic scene of *grande bouffe*, in which the gluttony of the participants is tempered only by the babble of voices demanding royal favours. Aghast at such customs, the narrator breaks into verse denouncing the whole Hermaphroditic cult.[26]

The *Three Precious Pearls* and the *Hermaphrodites* lack the lightness of touch and comic inspiration to be found in the popular satires collected by the diarist, Pierre de l'Estoile, in the years 1585–1587. Many of these are lampoons and *coq-à-l'âne*'s owing little or nothing to classical models. Here, for example, is *Le tout de l'an 1586*, a year in which everything was attempted and nothing achieved:

> The Leaguers ask for everything,
> The king grants them everything,
> The Guisard deprives him of everything,
> The soldier pillages everything,
> The poor people bear everything,
> The queen-mother arranges everything,
> The chancellor seals everything,
> The duc d'Epernon spoils everything,
> Religion covers everything,
> The pope pardons everything,
> The devil in the end will take the lot.[27]

In the following year L'Estoile added several gems to his collection. One of them was a mock Latin letter, ostensibly written by the duc de Guise to the Paris hôtel de ville. It began: "My lords the Parisians, the duc de Guise writes you this brief epistle so that in future you will feel confident and lack any doubt in your task of keeping the *fleurs de lis* safe for him. Whatever the Huguenots may say of it, it is we who are the nearest heir to the crown. The king of Navarre, staying down there by the seaside [at la Rochelle], is too far away."[28]

Next to this piece is *The Manifesto of the Ladies of the Court*, in which the queen-mother, a variety of princesses and their ladies of honor, confess to a bewildering number of crimes and vices, including converting the court into a brothel and sleeping with "kings, princes, cardinals, gentlemen, bishops, ab-

---

[26]*Ibid.*, pp. 178–81.
[27]*Journal de l'Estoile pour le règne de Henri III*, ed. L.-R. Lefévre (Paris, 1943), p. 478:
> Les ligueurs demandent tout,
> Le roi leur accorde tout,
> Le guisard lui vole tout,
> Le soldat ravage tout,
> Le pauvre peuple porte tout,
> La reine-mère conduit tout,
> Le chancellier scelle tout,
> Le parlement passe tout,
> Le duc d'Epernon gâte tout,
> La religion couvre tout,
> Le Pape pardonne tout,
> Le diable enfin portera tout.

[28]*Ibid.*, p. 530 (*Epître de Mgr le duc de Guise aux seigneurs de la ville de Paris*).

bots, priors, poets, muleteers, valets, pages and lackeys."[29] There follows the prize satire of the collection, *The Library of Madame de Montpensier,* an imitation of Rabelais's library of Saint-Victor. It is not pedantry that is under attack on this occasion but the scandals of the great and the religious enthusiasm of the Catholic League. Madame de Montpensier, the sister of the Guises, who was said to direct the sermonising of the radical Parisian *curés,* had already been libelled in *The Manifesto of the Ladies of the Court.* She was now depicted as the owner of such remarkable books as:

An epitome of the affectations of Father Commolet, Jesuit, carefully set in musical notation by two devout ladies from Amiens;

A singular treatise on the realignment of the brain, the causes and effects of the same, and from whence it proceeds. Dedicated to M. Rose, bishop of Senlis;

The grand chronicle of cuckolds, dedicated to the king of Navarre, with the observations of the sieur de Champvalon [Champvalon was the lover of Navarre's wife, Marguerite de Valois];

New secrets for the painless extraction of money from the people, by Zamet, dedicated to M. le duc d'Epernon, with royal privilege [Sebastiano Zametti was a banker and tax-farmer, while the king's favourite, Epernon, played a prominent rôle in some of his schemes];

The perfect slanderer, by Louis Dorléans, barrister at the parlement, printed at Paris and for sale at the sign of the Catholic Englishman.[30]

The last of these fictitious titles refers to *The Warning from English to French Catholics,* composed by the Leaguer polemicist Dorléans in 1586.[31] Insofar as the adoption of a feigned position qualified an author as a satirist, Dorléans met the mark, for he took the pose of an English Catholic persecuted by the Jezebel Elizabeth of England and foretold similar tribulations for Catholic Frenchmen if the Protestant Navarre were to be acknowledged heir to the Valois. The partially concealed elaboration of a supposed historical parallel may also involve satirical elements. Such was the case with *The Tragic and Memorable History of Gaveston, a Gascon Gentleman, formerly the Mignon of Edward II of England* (1588). This thinly disguised attack upon the *archimignon* Epernon, to whom it was ironically dedicated, is generally attributed to Jean Boucher, doctor of the Sorbonne, who later composed an interminable tirade justifying the deposition of Henri III and, later still, a set of sermons on the so-called simulated conversion to Catholicism of his successor, Henri IV.[32] But neither *The Catholic*

[29]*Ibid.,* pp. 532–4 (*Le manifeste des dames de la cour*).
[30]*Ibid.,* pp. 534–8.
[31]*L'Advertissement des catholiques anglois aux françois catholiques du danger où ils sont de perdre leur religion, et d'expérimenter, comme en Angleterre, la cruauté des ministres s'ils reçoivent à la couronne un roy qui soit hérétique* (n.p., 1586).
[32]*Histoire tragique et memorable de Gaverston, gentilhomme gascon, jadis mignon d'Edouard II, roi d'Angleterre, tirée des chroniques de Th. Valsingham et tournée de latin en français, dédiée à monseigneur le duc d'Epernon* (n.p., 1588); *De Justa abidicatione Henrici tertii* (Paris, 1589); *Sermons de la simulée*

83

Englishman nor *The History of Gaveston* really constitutes sustained satire since the two authors frequently abandon their pose and substitute direct denunciation of their enemies.

The satires concerned with the League and the court of Henri III in the 1580s mark a clear departure from contrived literary satire and the direct imitation of Horace and Juvenal found earlier in the century. They also represent a distinct advance upon the occasional satiric techniques of the Huguenot polemicists during the reign of Charles IX. In the 1590s the freeform expression of the genre reached its culmination through deliberate association with the Menippean tradition. The year 1593 was distinguished by the composition of two outstanding satires, the *Satyre Ménippée* and the *Banquet of the Comte d'Arète*, and of a third work, *Le Dialogue d'entre le Maheustre et le Manant*, which, in the light of its curious history and the mystery surrounding its author's purpose, deserves consideration under the same rubric.

While the deputies of the League estates were assembling in Paris in the first weeks of 1593, a group of politique sympathisers were meeting secretly in the house of Jacques Gillot, the magistrate from the parlement mentioned in d'Aubigné's *Chambre dorée*. One of their number, Pierre Le Roy, a chaplain to the younger cardinal of Bourbon, conceived the idea of the composite work later entitled the *Satyre Ménippée*. Other contributors were Jean Passerat, a professor at the Collège-Royal; Nicolas Rapin, a Poitevin poet in the school of Ronsard; Florent Chrestien, a former tutor to Navarre; the antiquary Pierre Pithou; and Gilles Durant, a writer of facetious verse. Soon after the official opening of the estates in February copies of a manuscript began to circulate under the title *Epitome and Essence of the Estates (Abbregé et l'Ame des Estatz convoquez à Paris en l'an 1593, le 10 de febvrier)*. This was the first draft of the *Satyre Ménippée*, less than one-third the length of the first published edition, which appeared in the spring of 1594 as *The Virtue of the Catholicon of Spain with an Epitome of the Holding of the Estates of Paris (La Vertu du Catholicon d'Espagne avec un abregé de la tenue des Estats de Paris)*. The first edition included a mock preliminary discourse, ostensibly written by the printer, and the second edition, which took the title by which the work is remembered, added a second such discourse.[33] In explaining the new title this second discourse carefully identifies the Menippean tradition.

---

conversion et nullité de la prétendue absolution de Henri de Bourbon, prince de Navarre, à Saint-Denis en France, le dimanche 25 juillet 1593 (Paris, 1594).

[33]The problems associated with the provenance of the *Satyre Ménippée* were finally elucidated by Charles Read in the introduction to his text of the first edition of 1594: *La Satyre Ménippée ou la vertu du Catholicon* (Paris, 1876). The notes prepared for the editions of 1664 and 1677 by the royal archivist Pierre Dupuy contain a great deal of explanatory material. These were incorporated and extended in the eighteenth-century Ratisbon editions, of which the 1726 three-volume version is the most common. This version, edited by Prosper Marchand, included further comments by Le Duchat and Godefroy. All three texts are based upon later variants of the work and include additions drawn from editions subsequent to the first in the late sixteenth century. The use of a false date, 1593, in some of the early printed versions for long caused confusion. Read

The first printer's discourse provides a burlesque account of the supposed author, a Florentine who had been in Paris during the estates, and whose servant had stolen his horse on the way to Flanders with the manuscript in the saddlebag. The second discourse corrects this story and named the Seigneur Agnoste (Unknown) from the town of Eleuthere (Liberty) in the land of Alethie (Truth). Seigneur Agnoste has initiated the writer into the mystery of the Spanish talisman *Higuiero [higuera] del Infierno* (the infernal fig-tree) described in the satire. The leaf of the fig-tree had been used to cover the "shameful parts" (*parties vergogneuses*) of Adam and Eve after their sin, and was consequently a perfect symbol for the crimes and deceits of the Spaniards. Apart from providing such further illustrations of the Menippean spirit, the writer of the second printer's discourse explains in all seriousness the origins and nature of the tradition he shares. The author may have been Passerat, who had composed a lost commentary on Rabelais and had introduced the flavour of Pantagruel into the satire on several occasions.[34] It may equally well have been the learned Pithou, who was described in his time as "the Varro of France," and who edited works of Juvenal, Persius and Petronius.[35]

The printer's discourse on Menippean satire distinguishes it from the purely poetic form used by Lucilius, Horace, Juvenal and Persius to refer to general or particular vices. The Menippean tradition involved a mixture of literary forms on a variety of topics and arguments, wherein prose and verse were mingled as "salt-beef tongues between dishes." With the concept of *satura lanx* in mind, the author recalls Varro's statement that the word had once described a concoction of meats and vegetables. In his own view, however, it is specifically Greek in origin, and is derived from the practice of acting the part of satyrs and using the disguise to lampoon any subject or individual whatever. The Romans had banned the mode from their theatres, whereupon its spirit had been translated to literature, and in this sense it survived among Parisians who would rather lose "un bon amy qu'un bon mot." This kind of prose satire would wound the conscience of those who felt themselves to be its object but would amuse the fancy of the innocent. As for "Menippean," Varro had used the word to describe his satires, and Macrobius had explained that it was derived from the Cynic Menippus, who had employed "salted squibs" (*brocards salés*) and "spicy scoffings" (*gausseries saulpoudrées*) to laugh the wicked out of court. Petronius, Lucian and Apuleius had used the technique, and in present times "the good Rabelais" had been its most striking exemplar. Recently the term had been

---

consulted a surviving manuscript of the draft circulated in the spring of 1593. The rôle of Le Roy is authenticated by Jacques-Auguste de Thou, *Historarium sui temporis continuatio, pars quarta* (Frankfurt, 1621), book 105, p. 1206. Identification of the contributors was established by Dupuy.

[34]M. Girard, "Passerat et la *Satire Ménippée*," *Revue des Questions historiques* 39 (1885), 340–56. See also Dorothy Coleman, *Rabelais*, p. 85.

[35]Donald R. Kelley, *Foundations of Modern Historical Scholarship: Language, Law and History in the French Renaissance* (New York, 1970), pp. 56–9.

employed "by a learned Flemish antiquary."[36] Passerat was here referring to the *Satyra Menippea* published at Antwerp in 1581 by Justus Lipsius. His whole exegesis was an attempt to link hands with the alternate classical tradition of satire, with a clear preference, like that of Estienne, for Greek before Roman origins. Confused as much of this was, it represented, nevertheless, a definition of literary genre with its roots in antiquity.

As one might expect from a work of group composition in which each author accepted a separate assignment, the *Satyre Ménippée* consists of a number of loosely related sections which bear no resemblance to what actually happened in the Leaguer estates.[37] The first describes the sale of a patent medicine, "Catholicon" or "Higuiero d'Infierno," by two charlatans, who set up their stalls in the Louvre to greet the incoming deputies to the estates. One of the charlatans is a richly dressed Spaniard, who advertises his brand of catholicon as infinitely more efficacious than the Romish variety: the other a poor Lorrainer – a reference to the claims to the crown of the penurious duke of Lorraine – whose jar of unguent is frankly labelled "fin galamatias" or "well-ground rubbish." The Spaniard puffs his product as "elaborated, calcinated, sublimated at the Jesuit college of Toledo: a sovereign electuary surpassing the philosopher's stone." With it come assurances for the buyer that it will enable him to rob and pillage at will. It opens the gates of fortresses, procures the assassination of enemy princes, and stirs up popular sedition. Moreover, it enables the user to become a prince of the church, for a touch applied to the hat turns the article red and transmutes the wearer into an incestuous and ambitious prelate.[38]

The next section describes the comic procession of the League before the meeting of the estates. When Paris was under siege by Henri IV in 1590, there were many such processions and on one occasion a contingent of armed clerics was alleged to have fired a salute in honor of the legate and to have shot one of his retinue.[39] In the corresponding part of the satire in 1593 the legate hastily forbids any salutes. The rest of the procession, with its priests and friars in a curious mixture of armour and clerical garb, is depicted in terms rather like those used by L'Estoile to record the original event. The terrorists of the Sixteen are there – or what Mayenne has left of them – and so are the Leaguer aristocracy, including Mme. de Montpensier carrying a soiled cloth for one of her lovers, and Mayenne himself flanked by two mace-bearers furred in ermine and preceded by two Walloon guards carrying an emblem of Phaeton, who had tried to drive the chariot of Phoebus and so threatened heaven and earth with conflagration that Jupiter had been obliged to strike him down with a thunderbolt.[40]

---

[36]*Satyre Ménippée* (ed. Read), pp. 11–14.
[37]Cf. *Procès-verbaux des états généraux de 1593*, ed. Auguste Bernard (Paris, 1842).
[38]*Satyre Ménippée*, pp. 31–42.
[39]Palma Cayet, *Chronologie novenaire* (London and Paris, 1790), vol. 1, p. 386. The incident is not, however, mentioned by L'Estoile in his account of the original procession.
[40]*Satyre Ménippée*, pp. 43–50.

There follows a preliminary viewing of the twelve tapestries hung in the great hall where the deputies are about to take their places. Some of these reflect the distaste of the upper classes for the demagoguery of the League and the popular uprisings that had occurred under its banners. One, for instance, shows a fallen giant with vipers and monsters springing from the corpse and labelled Gautiers, Lipans and Châteaux-verts, the names of insurgent peasant groups. Another shows Spartacus haranguing his slave army. There are tableaux showing the Jacquerie, the Maillotins and the barricades of May 1588. There is an apotheosis of the so-called saints, the four revolutionaries of the Sixteen hanged by Mayenne. A tapestry of the golden calf shows Henri III as Moses, the elder cardinal de Bourbon as Aaron, and the people worshipping an image whose head is that of Henri de Guise.[41]

Then the herald summons the deputies to take their places and the speeches are delivered – a process distorted by a great deal of noise, horse-play and elemental coughing, sweating, spitting and farting. Moreover, the orators are seized by a strange compulsion to reveal their true motives instead of their ostensible ones. Thus Mayenne begins: "My lords, all of you will bear witness that since I have taken arms for the Holy League, my own preservation has been foremost in my mind: so much so that with all my heart I have preferred my own self-interest to the cause of God, who knows very well how to look after himself without me."[42] Thus the Spanish ambassador tells all Frenchmen to continue fighting among themselves, for it is all to the advantage of the king of Spain. Rieux, the spokesman for the nobility, says: "*Vive la guerre!* We must have it, whencever it comes. I have nothing but contempt for those who talk of preserving religion and the state. . . . As for me, I don't give a damn for all that, so long as I can levy *tailles* and get a pension for my entourage. Why should I care what becomes of the pope and his wife?"[43] One of the most entertaining of the mock speeches is that of Bishop Rose, who describes the new régime of the League in the university of Paris. In fact the university had been used to accommodate peasants from outlying areas and their livestock. Rapin, the author of Rose's oration, makes the most of this situation. Instead of students and professors there were now dairymen from Vannes, pimps from Montrouge and Vaugirard, vignerons from Saint-Cloud and tile-layers from Ville-Juive. These were all natural philosophers. They learned from life and nature – not from books. Plato had said that the happiest commonwealths were those where philosophers were kings. Therefore, argued Rose, we should elect a village cowman for our king, for he has meditated philosophy among his cows in our great university.[44]

The last and by far the longest of these orations was written by Pierre Pithou and was put into the mouth of Claude Daubray, a respectable bourgeois member of the League and former mayor of Paris, who in real life defied the radical

[41]*Ibid.*, pp. 51–65.
[42]*Ibid.*, p. 71.
[43]*Ibid.*, p. 162.
[44]*Ibid.*, pp. 136–59.

Sixteen and made no secret of his politique inclinations. No device or pretence is attempted in Daubray's speech. It is a direct denunciation of the Legaue and of the disasters its policies have entailed:

It has to be admitted that we have become more like serfs and slaves than free men. We are like Christians in Turkey or Jews in Avignon. . . . Our privileges and ancient franchises have gone down the drain (*à vau l'eau*): our hôtel de ville, once the assured source of aid to our kings in time of crisis, has become a butchery: our court of parlement is a nullity: our Sorbonne is a brothel: our university is a wilderness . . . Paris is Paris no more, but a lair of wild beasts, a citadel of Spaniards, Walloons and Neapolitans, a refuge and safe retreat for thieves and assassins . . . Do you never wish to cure yourselves of this madness that, in place of a legitimate and gracious king, has engendered fifty kinglets and fifty tyrants to oppress you?[45]

This long and eloquent harangue is the climax of the *Satyre Ménippée*. After the oration the farcical note is briefly resumed with a maze of absurd constitutional proposals. Finally, there are a number of oddments in verse, some in epigrammatic form and others as quatrains and sonnets. Among the supplements and tailpieces associated with later editions of the *Satyre Ménippée* in 1594 and 1595, the best in verse is a lengthy lament on the passing of a donkey, said to embody more virtues than Apuleius' golden ass, which had to be killed and sold for the sustenance of the legate during the siege of Paris in 1590. The prose additions include the second "Printer's Discourse" already mentioned, a "History of the Monkeries of the League," and "News from the Countries of the Moon." The last has been described as a conflation of Lucian's *Icaromenippus* with Rabelais's account of the voyage to the land of the Holy Bottle in the fifth book of *Pantagruel*.[46] These supplements continue in the Menippean mode, and maintain the mixture of mockery, burlesque and abuse that characterises the first edition of the *Satyre*.

While the Spanish were presenting their credentials to the estates in April 1593, arrangements were being made for discussions between Catholic royalists led by the archbishop of Bourges and moderate Leaguers under the archbishop of Lyon. A local truce followed, and then the king announced his intention to be instructed in the Catholic faith. The move was timed to disrupt the endeavours of the League to elect a substitute. The Spanish responded by suggesting the election of the Infanta, and when this proposal met with opposition, they put forward the name of the Habsburg archduke Ernest. Finally they called for the enthronement of a Guisard prince, offering Philip II's daughter as the future consort of the successful candidate. But patriotic sentiment was

---

[45]*Ibid.*, pp. 175–6. In the second "Discours de l'imprimeur," Passerat thought it necessary to defend the inclusion of Daubray's long and serious harangue when the rest were "toutes courtes et burlesques." He explained that Daubray was just as prolix in real life, and that he alone deserved to have the truth attributed to him. Daubray's speech, it may be noted, contains verse as well as prose.

[46]Charles Labitte. In the introduction to his edition of *Satyre Ménippée* (Paris, 1883), p. vi.

growing within the League, and the drift towards Henri IV had already begun. On July 25 the king's conversion was completed. A general truce was accepted, and the estates quietly muttered themselves into dissolution. The Leaguer captains began to sell the cities they commanded to the king. Mayenne had to resume the war, and in March 1594 the Bourbon entered the capital he had deemed worth the price of a mass. However, another eighteen months elapsed before the papacy would grant Navarre absolution, and in this last phase of resistance the hard core of the League constantly reiterated that the abjuration was an act of arch-hypocrisy.

This is the note sounded by the *Banquet of the comte d'Arète*, which was composed in the summer of 1593, although, as with the *Satyre Ménippée*, a few references to later events were added to the manuscript before publication in March of the following year.[47] Were it not for his name upon the title page, it would be difficult to believe that the author of this antidote to the *Satyre Ménippée* was in fact the Louis Dorléans, whose ponderous historical arguments in the *Catholic Englishman* had been ridiculed by Passerat and his collaborators. Yet Dorléans was a man of many parts. He had studied in his youth under Jean Dorat, the humanist professor at the Collège-Royal who, with Jacques Peletier du Mans, inspired the classicism of the *Pléiade*. Dorléans composed Latin verse, and there is reason to believe that he was the author of an earlier Leaguer satire, *La Description du politicque de nostre temps*, first published in 1588. Certainly he did not hesitate to pillage the verses from this work and to insert them in the *Banquet*.[48] As a simple barrister Dorléans had been a member of the original Parisian conspiracy against Henri III; but he was a conservative by inclination, and the appearance of radicalism in his earlier polemics had been due to his belief that the catholicity of the French crown was a fundamental law more important than the dynastic laws of succession. He came to deplore the terrorism of his colleagues in the Sixteen, and as an attorney-general in the Leaguer parlement he aligned himself with the respectable Mayennistes. This did not deter him from continuing to attack the character of Henri IV in terms as personal and venomous as those employed by Jean Boucher in his *Sermons on the Simulated Conversion*. Not surprisingly, he fled from Paris at the time of its surrender. Years later, when the king permitted his return, he expressed his thanks with nauseating sycophancy.

[47]This is explained in a note added by the printer: *Le Banquet et apresdinée du conte [sic] d'Arete, où il se traicte de la dissimulation du Roy de Navarre, et les moeurs de ses partisans, par M. Dorléans advocat du Roy au Parlement de Paris* (Paris, 1594), p. 262. An entry in L'Estoile's diary suggests that there may have been an earlier published version of the *Banquet*. Cf. L'Estoile, *Mémoires-Journaux; Journal de Henri IV*, ed. Brunet *et al.* (Paris, 1888), vol. 6, p. 132 (December, 1593).

[48]At the end of the 1590 Toulouse edition of Dorléans' *Premier et second advertissement des catholiques anglois aux françois catholiques* the brief *Description du politicque* is printed with the ascription "du mesme autheur." Most of the text of the original *Description* (Paris, 1588) appears on pp. 21–9 of the *Banquet*. This identification was made by Robert Gould of Bryn Mawr College, who has kindly allowed me to cite it.

After the rantings of the Parisian pulpits the *Banquet* may seem a curious piece for the League. It smells of preciosity. This is because it, too, is deliberately set in the Menippean tradition of Varro and Lucian and interweaves verse and prose with a host of classical allusions. The discussion begins at the luncheon table of the count, who is said to be as well versed in letters as he is in martial pursuits – a paragon of virtue as his Greek title ('Ἀρετή) indicates. Among the guests he and his countess welcome to the table are two erudite and charming ladies, a poet, a magistrate from the parlement who has recently helped the count to win a case, a bishop, and the abbé d'Epistème ('Ἐπιστήμη), "who because of his vast learning was commonly called the father of knowledge."[49] The conversation turns to the problem of distinguishing appearance from reality in human motives, especially in those governing Navarre's conversion. Navarre, or the "Béarnais" as his detractors call him, can betray God and deceive man because human understanding is limited and fallible. Barn owls and moles have eyes that can see in the dark but not in the sunlight. The abbé begins to monopolise the discussion, extolling the principles of the ancient constitution, which, he says, has existed for eleven hundred years.[50] A true politique would love God and the law without contradiction, but the present so-called politiques see the crown as based on irreligion, impiety and vice. The abbé breaks into borrowed verse at this point and the countess pleads with him to continue in this delphic mode, elegant as his prose style may be. He obliges by reciting a poem attacking the late chancellor, Michel de l'Hôpital, whom he holds responsible for the growth of corrupt politique opinion.

> The politique has humours like the fox;
> His eye incessantly on princes locks,
> Agrees with them in all, denies the Lord
> And looks in ev'ry place he can afford
> In search of gain. He'll do it, come what may,
> For, rain or shine, he'll bear his loot away.[51]

The luncheon over, the company strolls along a gallery, strewn with statuary far less explicit than that to be found on the isle of Hermaphrodites. Here, for instance, is an alabaster nymph, so exquisitely formed, and yet so jealous of her virginity that, according to the count, Apollo had tired of chasing her and irritably converted her into a statue. At this point two new guests arrive – the marquis de Saint-Eugénie, who typifies the supposed virtues of the old nobility

---

[49]*Banquet*, p. 12.
[50]*Ibid.*, p. 20.
[51]*Ibid.*, p. 28. These are some of the verses lifted from the *Description du politicque* (note 48):
> L'humeur du Politique est un humeur renarde,
> Son oeil incessamment sur les Princes regarde,
> Et leur agree en tout, et fust ce contre Dieu,
> Mais s'il a reconeu et la place et le lieu
> De faire son proffit il y entre de sorte
> Que soit froid ou soit chaud la piece il emporte.

with his truthfulness and honour, and a lady named Euphrosyne, whom he has rescued from one of Navarre's generals after experiences that reveal the perfidy of the Bourbon entourage. The rest of the afternoon then settles down into a competition to determine the worst of the appalling atrocities of which Navarre has been guilty, not forgetting the sins of his ancestors, of his Huguenot auxiliaries, and of the self-styled Catholics who assisted his false conversion. The king is described as an incestuous adulterer, a despoiler of churches, a seducer of nuns and a killer of priests. Sometimes he is depicted more as a vicious buffoon than as a satanic figure. The magistrate, Symuol, says that he is better fitted for a part in a comedy by Terence (he suggests Dorus in "The Eunuch") than one in a tragedy by Euripides. Being unable to violate the church in the habit of a Huguenot, he was trying to corrupt it under the chaste cloak of Catholicism.[52] There are numerous comic confusions in the dialogue, such as a discussion at cross-purposes in which one of the ladies mistakes a reference to Gabrielle d'Estrées, Navarre's mistress, for the angel Gabriel.[53]

Heretics, says Epistème with a nod to St. Bernard, are like foxes in thought and wolves in action. Those who follow the example of the Béarnais are like the foxes in Aesop's fable whose leader, having lost his tail by misadventure, persuaded his fellows that it was more convenient to be without one. The sudden conversion is treated as a mock miracle, "when the deaf heard, the dumb spoke, and the lame walked – straight to Saint-Denis." It was not the holy dove that had visited Navarre, but rather the pigeons from the church of René Benoist (a former radical *curé* who had assisted the conversion), and, far from approving of the occasion, they had made known their displeasure in the manner pigeons will. The conversion is shown to be an expedient response to affairs in the estates, especially to the offers of the Spanish, and the problems encountered by the deputies are blamed not upon Mayenne and the ambitions of his rivals but upon the agents of Navarre who subtly performed a series of "dirty tricks" (to use the current term) during the elections.[54]

The question of choosing a king was a serious one. A candidate should have the probity of Philip Augustus, the chastity of Louis VIII, the saintliness of Louis IX, and the benignity of Louis XII. Clemency could be a fault, remarks the abbé, because Charles IX's failure to ensure the complete extermination of heretics on St. Bartholomew's Day had caused untold suffering to true Catholic Frenchmen. In selecting a king one should take at least the care the Romans had done in buying a slave, and, lest such an analogy seemed damaging to royalty, it should be remembered that kings are the first servants of the people. Nor does anyone question the assumption that the monarch is elective although the bishop later rehabilitates the prestige of royal office a little by calling it "the vital spirit and true radical humour of our state." It is not the principle of

[52]*Ibid.*, p. 45.
[53]*Ibid.*, p. 111.
[54]*Ibid.*, pp. 97–100, 114.

monarchy that is assailed so much as the vices of the nobility of both sides who, Epistème declaims, "beat, strike, kill, ransom and run upon our poor peasants and their cattle and set themselves up like Pisistratus in our Athens or Dionysius in our Syracuse – who turn our towns into nests of tyrants, deny their God, and devour the people to their very bones."[55] It is, indeed, the Catholic peasantry who receive the greatest praise in the discussion, and the ladies recount several stories to show how the common people have the purity of heart that enables them to see through the wicked dissimulation of the Béarnais.

The theme of the deliberate continuation of civil war by the nobility as a means of exploiting the lower orders had already appeared in Rieux's speech in the *Satyre Ménippée*. It received its most eloquent exposition in the third of the satires composed in 1593, the *Dialogue of the Courtier and the Commoner (Le Maheustre et le Manant)*. The theme reflected the contemporary situation in which the complex social hierarchy had broken down into two divisions, the oppressors and the oppressed, and vast peasant armies were about to form in Limousin and Périgord in the revolt of the original *Croquants*. The claims of *Le Maheustre et le Manant* to be considered as satire are rather more complex than those of its rivals. At first glance it might seem that it has no greater case for inclusion than earlier polemics in dialogue form. One of James Sutherland's judgments in his Clark lectures is that it is fatal to satire if something is said on both sides,[56] and yet dialogue is an essential ingredient in the Menippean tradition. The *Satyre Ménippée* overcomes the problem with a mixture of burlesque and direct declamation, while the *Banquet of the comte d'Arète* does so by having the conversation proceed through a series of comic misunderstandings, and the confessed technique of the *advocatus diaboli*, rather than by reasoned defence of the contrary view. But the puzzle encountered by readers of *Le Maheustre et le Manant* is to determine the standpoint of the writer.

One major element of confusion in this matter has now been laid to rest.[57] The version of the *Dialogue* known to posterity is that published as a tailpiece to the 1726 edition of the *Satyre Ménippée*. This is not the original text. It is reprinted from a cleverly doctored version, edited by a supporter of Henri IV and first published at the time when both the *Banquet of the comte d'Arète* and the *Satyre Ménippée* first appeared in print, that is, in the spring of 1594. The original *Dialogue* was the work of a radical member of the Sixteen, probably Louis (also known as François) Morin de Cromé, who was as critical of Mayenne and the leaders of the League establishment as he was of the Bourbon party. Like Dorléans' *Banquet*, the piece was composed in the weeks following the conversion of Henri IV on July 25, 1593, although the opening pages (about one-tenth of the whole) may have been written before that event. When this original version was printed in December, it was promptly suppressed by Mayenne and censured in a semi-official Leaguer reply.

[55]*Ibid.*, pp. 59–62, 257, 48.
[56]Sutherland, *English Satire*, p. 16.
[57]See below, pp. 264–6.

The Maheustre of Cromé's *Dialogue* is a politique opportunist, who is frequently convinced by his opponent's arguments and dubious of the sincerity of the conversion. He is used by Cromé to denounce the betrayal of Leaguer principles by Mayenne and his followers, and serves as a foil for the unshakeable religious sincerity of the simple Manant. From time to time the Manant is used to expose "the bloodsucking nobility" of both sides, who have waged war merely to exploit the poor and unprivileged. The Manant does not suggest that there should be no nobility: he distinguishes between those in whom virtue predominates and those in whom it does not. He states that the experience of the past thirty or forty years has convinced him that few of the hereditary nobility deserve a place in the former category, and he proposes that nobility should be based upon virtue, not race. Since Cromé's Manant is the spokesman for the small radical wing of the Sixteen, whose revolutionary terrorism against the higher orders has led to their being disowned by their colleagues from the upper strata of Parisian society, this statement represents something more than another instance of the vogue inspired by Juvenal's satire preferring virtue to pedigree. The editor of the 1594 doctored version certainly read the Manant in this light, and for this reason he had the Manant's part stand virtually unchanged, assuming that those who subscribed to traditional values would read it with a fascinated abhorrence. However, he made substantial changes in the part of the Maheustre, who forgets his doubts and his apprehensions and becomes an eloquent defender of divine right dynastic monarchy.

If the confusion caused by the two versions of the *Dialogue* have been dispelled, a new set of problems related to its author's purpose have arisen in a recent analysis of the work.[58] In this study Peter Ascoli maintains that Cromé sought to persuade those Parisian "bourgeois who were wavering in their support of the League and the Sixteen" by devising a form of dialogue more subtle than that previously employed. According to this view, Cromé deliberately appealed to the sophisticated by saying something on both sides, and this calculated ambiguity created "an example of a new type of political dialogue." Further, Ascoli depicts Cromé as writing partly to discover the explanation for the apparent failure of the League, and partly to appeal from the heart "to the people of Paris," whose sympathy and sense of moral outrage he seeks to arouse. All these theories cannot be true. If Cromé were engaged upon an objective piece of retrospection, he could hardly assume it could also be slanted to persuade the uncommitted. Moreover, this interpretation is marred by factual errors and by a misunderstanding of the history of the Sixteen and the context in which the surviving radicals operated in 1594.[59] The *Dialogue* is

---

[58] Peter M. Ascoli, "A Radical Pamphlet of Late Sixteenth Century France: Le Dialogue D'Entre Le Maheustre Et Le Manant," *Sixteenth Century Journal*, 5 (1974), 3–22.

[59] The Sixteen were active during the meeting of the Leaguer estates as well as in the period December 1593–March 1594 (Ascoli, p. 11). This is revealed in the contemporary manuscript account of the estates: Bibliothéque Nationale ms. fr. 16265, ff. 62r, 149v, 150v, 155r. The argument about the nobility of virtue (Ascoli, p. 19) was used by Jean de Caumont, *De la vertu de noblesse* (Paris, 1585). Far from being extremely rare, denunciations of the nobility were common

indeed a *cri de coeur*, a *cri de coeur* for the common people exploited by their social superiors in the camps of both Mayenne and Navarre. Cromé has not deliberately introduced ambiguity but, rather, dramatic tension. He has done so because he is writing satire and is using his conceits to attack his enemies. The royalist editor makes an equally skilful use of satiric techniques, for he has succeeded in borrowing a satire from the most unyielding core of opposition to Henri IV and turning it round to satirise both the popular aspect of the League and its Mayenniste leadership.

Of the three major satires concerned with the crisis of 1593, one was written to discredit the League, another the politiques, and the third, originally aimed at the nobility in both camps, was adapted to serve the cause of Henri IV. Despite their differing viewpoints, they offer a common social criticism. It may be that they played some rôle in the abandonment of faction and self-interest on the part of the established classes and the rallying to the Bourbon crown. The Menippean vogue continued through the late 1590s with the additions to the *Satyre Ménippée*, and even found a convert in d'Aubigné. But the Huguenot poet could stomach a change of literary mode more easily than he could a religious conversion. His *Confession de Sancy*[60] was composed before the turn of the century to satirise those Protestants who, like Dorléans' foxes, had imitated the fashion set by their king and, having converted to Catholicism, magnified their fault by publicly defending their action.

In the last years of Henri IV a political climate existed very different from that of the crisis of the League. Formalism and stability came increasingly to be reflected in literary tastes as they were in the political order, and the art of satire began to divorce itself from the real social needs and political pressures of the time. In 1605 L'Estoile collected a copy of the newly published *Island of the Hermaphrodites* and complained that it was so sought after that it cost twelve times as much as it should.[61] Like 1593, this year was something of an *annus mirabilis* for French satire, but it witnessed a strong reaction against the Menippean mode. In this year Casaubon finally published his conclusions on the

---

during the crisis of the League. Many examples, including *Le Maheustre et le Manant*, are listed by Myriam Yardeni, *La Conscience nationale en France pendant les guerres de religion* (Paris, 1971), pp. 243–61 ("Le débat sur l'ordre social"). It should also be pointed out, despite Professor Ascoli's observations on the matter, that many Mayenniste nobles who lived by banditry were attacked in peasant risings. Two notorious examples were Guy Eder de la Fontenelle in Brittany and the baron de Gimel in Limousin. Among other errors in Ascoli's paper is the claim that the Sixteen were "largely in control of Paris in 1591" (p. 9). Had they been so, they would not have been obliged to make their unsuccessful attempts to win election to the hôtel de ville in the summer of that year. Their *coup* in November was the result of their failure and was in no sense an attempt "to consolidate their power." (See below, pp. 253–6).

[60] *Confession Catholique de sieur de Sancy, et Declaration des causes, tant d'Estat que de Religion, qui l'ont meu à se remettre au giron de l'Eglise romaine* (composed in 1599, retouched in 1604, but not published until 1660). See *Oeuvres complètes de Théodore Agrippa d'Aubigné*, ed. Réaume and Caussade (Paris, 1877), vol. 2, pp. 235–373.

[61] *Journal de l'Estoile, 1601–1609*, ed. André Martin (Paris, 1958), p. 164.

primacy of the Roman school and buttressed his opinion with the edition of Persius' satires that was later to serve Dryden in making his English version.[62] At the same time the Norman magistrate, Vauquelin de la Fresnaye, issued his *Art poétique* to reaffirm the tastes of the *Pléiade*. He knew the work of the man he called "learned Peletier," and repeated the latter's *dicta* on the satiric canon.[63] The views set forth in these uninspired verses were repeated with greater vigour in the prose preface he added to his own satires, which were also published in 1605.[64] Despite Casaubon, Vauquelin included the old story that the word itself came from the representation of horned satyrs in primitive Greek comedy. But he insisted that Lucilius was the founder of the only respectable kind of poetic satire. After him Horace was the master, Juvenal and Persius the disciples, while in recent times Ariosto was the guide for modern satirists. Satire should be a pleasant and profitable exercise in its French guise, "provided that one refrains from defaming particular persons and one is not moved by vengeance or other motives to compose verses crammed with slanders, insults and lies after the manner of the *Cocqs à l'Asne*." Vauquelin was prepared to give some credit to older French satiric forms, and he thought that Marot had moderated the violence of the *coq-à-l'âne*. His invective was aimed at the satirists of the previous decade – "those rhymsters who, like so many monkeys, wrote, and still write, cocks to the ass and asses to the cock in insulting and defamatory verses that deserve to be burnt with their progenitors rather than being seen by any man of honour."[65] As might be expected, Vauquelin's own *Satyres françoises* kept to the rules he defined, and generally were pallid and innocuous productions. Internal evidence in these poems reveals that many of them were written during the last years of the civil wars[66] – a signal exception to generalisations about the concurrence of satiric intensity and social crisis. At times, it is true, Vauquelin's lines assume a note of sincere indignation, especially when he writes of the disruption of family life, of the corruption of the church, or of the treason and brigandage of the time. When he directs his scorn against the *mignons* of Henri III he achieves something close to the power of d'Aubigné.[67] Yet, despite such occasional passages, the rules of the genre seem more important to Vauquelin than the evils he wants to expose. Satire, he said, should be modest and courteous, full of *douce gravité*. The pleasure it conveys must be appropriately clothed in moral exhortation. Vauquelin found that *ser-*

---

[62]*Persii satirarum liber* (Paris, 1605). See also note 4 above.

[63]*L'Art poétique de Vauquelin de la Fresnaye*, ed. George Pellissier (Paris, 1885), pp. 99–107 (book II, lines 679–820), and p. 144 (book III, line 314). It was also in 1605 that John Barclay began publication of *Euphormionis Lusinini Satyricon*, a comic novel modelled on Petronius and regarded by the author as Menippean satire.

[64]"Discours pour servir de préface sur le sujet de la Satyre," *Les diverses poésies de Jean Vauquelin, sieur de la Fresnaie*, ed. Julien Travers (Caen, 1869), vol. 1, pp. 123–33.

[65]*Ibid.*, p. 130.

[66]A. P. Lemercier, *Etude littéraire et morale sur les poésies de Jean Vauquelin de la Fresnaye* (Nancy, 1887), pp. 269–76.

[67]*Diverses poésies*, vol. 1, pp. 294–5. Cf. Lemercier, p. 210.

mones was the word used by Horace to describe both his satires and his epistles, and it seemed to epitomise the spirit of the genre.

In 1605 Mathurin Régnier, the nephew of Desportes, left his patron, the cardinal de Joyeuse, and settled in Paris, where Malherbe arrived a few months later. This was the time when Régnier composed most of the satires he was to publish in 1608. Although he has been given an equal place beside Vauquelin for returning to the formal poetic mode in satire, his genius was wholly unlike Vauquelin's mediocre inspiration. Régnier certainly paid his tribute to Horace, but he preferred Juvenal and was suspicious of too much moralising.[68] He cited Juvenal at the end of the royal dedication to his first book of satires: "Difficile est satyram non scribere." The idea of a morality was itself the subject of ridicule. His was the sceptic note lurking within the whole satiric tradition and now rendered explicit. Goodness was no intrinsic quality in things but depended upon the subjective mood of the observer. A custom deemed moral in one country was immoral in another, and all one could do was to affirm a relativism in which good and evil depended upon personal taste.[69] All knowledge was uncertain. Reason and the senses were alike deceptive, and in his ignorance the poet could laugh at himself and the universe, and fashion a satire from his passing humour.[70] Identity itself was in doubt; for time changed all things, and the rake who laughed at the admonitions of his father would come at length to lecture his own sons and see them laugh and shake their heads at him:

> Moods, tastes and pleasures change from day to night,
> And, like our skins, our lusts all turn to white.[71]

[68]*Oeuvres complètes*, ed. Gabriel Raibaud (Paris, 1958), pp. 15–16 (satire II, lines 13–18):
> Mais c'est trop sermoné de vice et de vertue:
> Il faut suivre un sentier qui soit moins rebatu,
> Et conduit d'Apollon recognoistre la trace
> Du libre Juvenal; trop discret est Horace
> Pour un homme piqué, joint que la passion
> Comme sans jugement est sans discretion.

[69]*Ibid.*, p. 49 (satire V, lines 41–6):
> Ainsi c'est la nature et l'humeur des personnes
> Et non la qualité, qui rend les choses bonnes.
> Charnellement se joindre avecq' sa paranté,
> En France c'est inceste, en Perse charité,
> Tellement qu'à tout prendre, en ce monde où nous sommes,
> Et le bien et le mal depend du goust des hommes.

[70]*Ibid.*, p. 102 (satire IX, lines 159–63):
> Dechifrez les secrets de Nature et des cieux,
> Vostre raison vous trompe, aussi bien que vos yeux.
> Or, ignorant de tout, de tout je me veus rire,
> Faire de mon humeur moy-mesme une satyre,
> N'estimer rien de vray qu'au goust il ne soit tel,

[71]*Ibid.*, p. 52 (satire V, lines 113–20):
> Toute chose en vivant avecq' l'age s'altere;
> Le debauché se rit des sermons de son pere,
> Et dans vingt et cinq ans, venant à se changer,
> Retenu, vigilant, soigneux et mesnager,
> De ces mesmes discours ses fils il admoneste

Scepticism, of course, was as much the product of the religious wars as were the new theories of royal absolutism. Régnier had endorsed the form of the Horatian satire, but the spirit behind his poems had more in common with Varro in one of his *Satirae Menippeae*, when he ridiculed the schools of the philosophers, or with Lucian, when he sent his fictional Menippus to Tiresias to resolve the contradictions in his thought, and decided that the best advice was to cultivate one's own garden with a smiling face. Like Vauquelin, Régnier closely imitated the Italian satirists at times, and his verse was replete with allusions to the three major satiric poets of the classical age. But he was also in tune with French satiric traditions, and the shades of Rabelais and Montaigne appeared often in his lines.[72] Moreover, he had contacts with some of the group who had composed the *Satyre Ménippée*, and wrote verses in memory of Nicolas Rapin and Jean Passerat. If something of Menippean inspiration lived on through Régnier, vestiges of the Menippean form itself survived in the satires of lesser writers, such as Sigogne, Motin, Berthelot and Touvant. Three years after Régnier's death in 1613, some of these pieces appeared beside his own work in a volume entitled *Satyres et autres oeuvres folastres du sieur Régnier*.[73] Nor is it difficult to discern Menippean influence in the collection published in 1618 as *Le Cabinet satyrique*. At this time, too, d'Aubigné was writing the early books of his almost unreadable Gascon burlesque, *The Adventures of the Baron de Fæneste*, which continued the Menippean tradition and invested its braggart hero and his host, Enay, with Greek titles.[74] In a later age something of this spirit was manifest in the burlesque playwright, Paul Scarron, who was the husband of d'Aubigné's granddaughter, Madame de Maintenon. In the middle of the century the *Mazarinades* constituted a virtual explosion of free-form satire. For all this, the battle between the satiric genres of Lucilius and Lucian had already been decided in the age of Vauquelin and Régnier. It merely required the fiat of Boileau to turn the victory into a Roman peace. It is perhaps unfortunate that all traces of the Menippean mode were obliterated in the process.

> Qui ne font que s'en rire et qu'en hocher la teste.
> Chaque age a ses humeurs, son goust et ses plaisirs
> Et comme nostre poil blanchissent noz désirs.

[72] See "Tableau des imitations et ressemblances" provided by Raibaud, *Oeuvres complètes*, pp. 281–9.

[73] *Ibid.*, pp. xxiii–xxiv (Raibaud's introduction).

[74] *Oeuvres complètes*, vol. 2, pp. 377–651. The first two books of *Fæneste* were published in 1617, the third in 1619, and the fourth in 1630.

4

~~~~~~

Rohan and interest of state

There is a persuasive simplicity about the opening lines of Rohan's *De l'Interest des Princes et des Estats de la Chrestienté:*

Princes command peoples, and interest commands princes. Knowing this interest is infinitely superior to knowing about the actions of princes, which in themselves are far above the deeds of ordinary people. The prince can be deceived, his council can be corrupted, but interest itself can never fail. Depending on whether it is well or badly understood, it preserves or ruins states. It always has expansion as its aim or, at the very least, the preservation of the state, and to succeed in its purpose it has to change with the times. Therefore to consider properly the interest of princes it is not necessary to go back very far, but merely to turn one's eyes to present affairs.[1]

When Meinecke referred to these sentences he remarked how they made the heart of the modern reader beat faster. In that part of *Die Idee der Staatsräson* where he analyses Rohan's work,[2] Meinecke restates the central theme of his own book in its most powerful form. Rohan is said to reveal that reason which is immanent in the state itself (*die dem Staate selbst immanente Vernunft*). He is assumed to articulate the principles that guided Richelieu's statecraft, and together the two express the ultimate vision of the statesman (*der Schwung staatsmännischen Denkens*). The statesman who has this insight into true interest of state loses the freedom of personal choice and becomes a soldier in the service of the Idea (*ein Soldat im Dienste der Idee*). According to Meinecke,

---

[1] *De l'Interest des Princes et des Estats de la Chrestienté* (Paris, 1639), p. 1. For information on the first (1634) version of *De l'Interest* and on later variants and imitations, see below (notes 43, 45). The original of this key passage reads: "Les Princes commandent aux peuples, et l'interest commande aux Princes. La conaissance de cet interest, est d'autant plus relevée par dessus celle des actions des Princes, qu'eux-mesmes le sont par dessus les peuples. Le Prince se peut tromper, son Conseil peut estre corrompu; mais l'interest seul ne peut jamais manquer, selon qu'il est bien ou mal entendu, il conserve ou ruine les Estats. Et comme il a tousjours pour but l'accroissement, ou pour le moins la conservation; aussi pour y parvenir faut-il, qu'il se change selon le temps. De sorte que pour bien considerer l'interest des Princes d'aujourd'hui, il n'est pas besoin de remonter fort haut: Mais seulement de jetter les yeux sur les affaires présentes."
[2] *Die Idee der Staatsräson in der neueren Geschichte* (Munich and Berlin, 1929), pp. 204–45. Cf. *Machiavellism*, trans. Douglas Scott (New York, 1965), pp. 163–86.

Rohan and interest of state

Rohan has also discerned the essence of modern historical understanding, the primacy of foreign policy over internal politics (*der Primat der auswärtigen Politik über die innere Politik*). His is *der eherene Klang* of experience, beside which the theoretical writing of other apostles of reason of state are but mutterings in the dark.

It is not intended here to follow Meinecke into discussion either of idealist views of the state or of the historical determinism which his identification of the task of the statesman with that of the historian seems to imply. On the other hand, it may be worth pursuing his suggestion that Rohan's political experience is closely related to what he says about interest of state, particularly since Meinecke was at pains to reconcile Rohan's Calvinist morality, his role as the aristocratic leader of a faction, and his function as the interpreter of Richelieu's *raison d'état*. A recent book on Richelieu's statecraft within the context of the political thought of his time has effectively challenged Meinecke's ascription of Rohan's ideas to the cardinal, and at the same time has criticised Meinecke's reconciliation of the three *personae* of Rohan.[3] Meinecke's argument in this respect depends upon Rohan's changed situation after the final defeat of the Huguenot cause in 1629, and upon Richelieu's identification with the foreign policy of Henri IV, of which Rohan, reverting to the early phase of his career, could entirely approve. There is much truth in his explanation, but it fails to take account of the consistency of Rohan's view of interest throughout his life. It has gone unnoticed that Rohan has as much to say about private interest as he has about interest of state. It is proposed to examine both *De l'Interest* and Rohan's earlier writings in order to determine the relationship between the two kinds of interest within the structure of his thought.

The historical Rohan, no less than the author of *De l'Interest*, has traditionally been misunderstood. Sainte-Beuve typed him as a belated representative of the sixteenth-century school *de bons capitaines et d'écrivains d'épée* – after the model, presumably, of Blaise de Monluc or François de la Noue.[4] Michelet called him "âpre, austère, indomptable, héroique, amoureux des causes perdues."[5] A recent writer on the relationship between Richelieu and Rohan described the latter as "un caractère vraiment héroique, toujours constant dans l'adversité, capitaine illustre, ignorant la défaite."[6] The legend of the proud and heroic idealist seems to fit Rohan's ancestry, for he and Henri IV possessed common great-grandparents in Catherine de Foix and Jean d'Albret. Henri IV bestowed great favour upon him, although his mother, who detested the king, complained at his advancement to the dignity of *duc et pair* by citing the family motto: "Roy je ne puis, duc je ne daigne; Rohan je suis."[7] From the first, however, Rohan

[3]William F. Church, *Richelieu and Reason of State* (Princeton, 1972), pp. 352–5.
[4]*Causeries du Lundi* (Paris, n.d.), vol. 12, p. 298.
[5]*Histoire de France* (Paris, n.d.), vol. 5, p. 1796.
[6]Edouard Rott, "Rohan et Richelieu (1629–1638)," *Revue d'Histoire diplomatique*, 27 (1913), 203.
[7]Auguste Laugel, *Henry de Rohan: son rôle politique et militaire sous Louis XIII (1579–1638)* (Paris, 1889), p. 32.

was a realist. Near the turn of the century, at the age of twenty-one he kept a diary of his tour of Europe in which he noted down details of fortifications and remarks about commerce and politics.[8] He first saw military action with Henri IV at the siege of Amiens in 1597. He served briefly with Maurice of Nassau against the Spanish in 1606, and in 1610, after the assassination of his royal patron, he took part in the campaign against Jülich, where Maurice was also in arms against the Habsburg interest.

In the next decade Rohan's rapid changes of front suggest, to say the least, that idealism was not his dominant motive.[9] In 1611 he joined his father-in-law, Sully, in a struggle with the opportunist duc de Bouillon for the leadership of the Huguenots at the assembly of Saumur. In 1612 he defied the regent, Marie de Médicis, by effecting an armed coup in Saint-Jean-d'Angély. In 1614 he refused to support the prince de Condé against the pro-Habsburg policy of the regent because his enemy, Bouillon, was involved in the faction of the princes. This inspired no confidence in Rohan on the part of the court, where his ambition and propensity for intrigue had earned him the soubriquet of "Catiline."[10] In 1615, however, he did join Condé in a revolt intended to block Louis XIII's marriage to Anne of Austria. In the following year Rohan abruptly changed tack, became a supporter of the regent, and refused to aid the rebellion of the princes when Condé was arrested. In the spring of 1617 he joined Lesdiguières, the Huguenot governor of Dauphiné, in the latter's private war against Spain in Savoy. This was the year in which Louis XIII overthrew his mother's regency, sanctioned the murder of her Italian favourite, Concini, and imprisoned Marie de Médicis at Blois. Rohan resented the advent of the king's favourite, Luynes, whose government he was later to describe in his memoirs as "violent et absolu" and marked by "trahisons et desloyautez."[11] When the former regent escaped from Blois and raised the standard of revolt, Rohan prudently refused her overtures. However, two years later he and his brother, Soubise, joined her faction shortly before the defeat of her forces at Pont-de-Cé. In 1621 Rohan accepted command of the Huguenots, and steadfastly led their resistance to the king in the three subsequent religious wars.

During the anarchic decade before the Huguenot wars Rohan acted in the turbulent fashion that distinguished the entire group of princes and magnates to which he belonged. But he excelled them all in the skill with which he justified

[8]*Voyage du duc de Rohan, faict en l'an 1600, en Italie, Allemaigne, Pays-bas unis, Angleterre et Escosse* (Amsterdam, 1646).
[9]One study of his life in this period concludes that Rohan was dominated by ambition and the spirit of intrigue, and that his role was that of a *chef de parti*, not of a hero. Cf. Denys d'Aussy, "Henri de Rohan et le siège de Saint-Jean d'Angély, 1611–1621," *Revue des Questions historiques*, 32 (1882) 98–146. This is also the judgment of Voltaire, *Essai sur les mœurs* (Paris, 1963), vol. 2, pp. 581 and 594.
[10]Laugel, p. 64.
[11]*Mémoires du duc de Rohan sur les choses advenues en France depuis la mort de Henry le Grand jusques à la paix faite avec les Reformez au mois de Juin 1629* (Amsterdam, 1646), pp. 114 and 120.

his conduct in a series of contemporary discourses and manifestos. Many of these statements include the ideas he later developed in *De l'Interest*. For example, his *Discours sur la mort de Henry le Grand* (1610)[12] argued that religion was the pretext, and not the cause, of the divisions between the factions in the civil wars of the sixteenth century. His speech to the deputies at Saumur (1611)[13] argued the necessity of private interest. Every great lord who sought to become the protector of the Protestant churches did so with private ends in view. In this sense there could be no real protector save the king, but the churches, no less than the great, must act in their own interest and maintain the means of self-defence. The concept, if not the phrase, "interest of state" also appears in this address: "La Loy des Estats change selon les temps: on n'y peut donner de Maximes certaines. Ce qui est utile à un Roy est domageable à un autre." In his next discourse, *Sur l'Estat de la France durant les persecutions de Sainct Jean* (1612),[14] Rohan anticipates the central argument of *De l'Interest*. Henri IV had perceived that Europe was balanced by the rivalry between Spain and France. Since Spanish ambition was furthered by a zeal for Catholicism, France was the natural ally and protector of Protestant states and princes. Rohan analysed the individual interest of each of the main powers to demonstrate this conclusion. Spain had convinced the regent that she could only maintain her authority against the princes of the blood by deserting her husband's policies and seeking a Habsburg alliance. Since the interest of the Huguenots coincided with the true interest of the French state, the princes of the blood should form a common front with the churches, and assert their legitimate rights against a government controlled by "usurpers."

Rohan's opportunism clearly emerges in his *Discours sur le voyage du Roy en Juillet 1615*.[15] After advising the queen mother to yield to Condé's demands, he suggests that, if the regent wishes to defeat the princes, she should adopt the policy of Louis XI towards the League of the Public Weal and exploit their selfish interests in order to divide them from each other. This is also the tenor of his paper *Sur le gouvernement de la Reyne Mère*,[16] composed early in 1617 when he was enjoying a measure of favour. The more eloquent the claims of the magnates to be opposing the regency in terms of the public interest, the more self-interested their real intentions. He asks the reader to remember "that there had never been a war made in France under the pretext of the common good without those who began it having a particular interest as their real object." Soon after this Rohan composed his *Libre discours sur le temps present*,[17]

---

[12]*Discours politiques du duc de Rohan faits en divers temps sur les affaires qui se passoient* (Amsterdam, 1646), pp. 3–12.
[13]*Ibid.*, pp. 12–22.
[14]*Ibid.*, pp. 22–42.
[15]*Ibid.*, pp. 43–50.
[16]*Ibid.*, pp. 51–61.
[17]*Ibid.*, pp. 62–75.

in which he combines his explanation of state interest as pro-Protestant foreign policy with his advice to frustrate the grandees by exposing the true motives of some, and satisfying others whose ambitions did not endanger the security of France. This discourse follows the lines of its counterpart in 1612. "The strength of a kingdom," Rohan declares, "consists in a king and his alliances – alliances not of blood but of interest. France and Spain are the two powers under whom all the others preserve themselves by preventing one or the other achieving complete superiority." It is in the interest of the Huguenots to uphold the greatness of France; it is the interest of the king not to persecute the Huguenots, and to align himself with Protestant princes abroad to offset the power of Spain. Rohan's final piece in this phase of life was a *Discours sur le sujet des divisions en Hollande* (1618).[18] Here he advanced another view that he was later to incorporate in *De l'Interest*. He believes the controversy between Arminians and Gomarists to have been artfully contrived by Spain in order to weaken and divide the Dutch. This discourse concludes with the observation that ecclesiastical assemblies should be prevented from meddling in political matters, and that it is the task of the secular magistrate to see that they confine themselves to purely religious issues.

There was nothing particularly original in Rohan's contention that France and Spain were natural enemies, and that a pro-Protestant foreign policy, in which the Huguenot interest coincided, was the most advantageous course to follow. Coligny had advocated it before the massacre of St. Bartholomew,[19] and Sully recorded in his memoirs how Rohan's future rival, Bouillon, had in 1594 presented a carefully reasoned argument to the same effect.[20] Bouillon had said that the French monarchy and the Huguenots were "attached to the same interests by reason of the two great factions formed in Christendom under the titles of the French and the Spanish." Henri IV's precursors had been obliged to ignore the contrary advice of religious zealots "par raison d'Estat et de prudence royalle." Realism and expediency had played almost as large a part in Huguenot thought and action as they had in the tradition of the Catholic politiques from whom Richelieu had descended. Such ideas can even be found in Huguenot thought in the midst of the anti-Machiavel reaction to the massacre. While the first dialogue of the *Reveille-Matin* (1573) denounced Machiavelli, the second dialogue (1574) gave a realistic appraisal of the foreign policy of the powers and even mentioned the name of the Florentine with approval.[21] The re-alignment of Huguenot propaganda when Henri de Na-

[18]*Ibid.*, pp. 75–81.
[19]See the account of the discussions in the royal council on the advisability of war in June 1572 as described by N. M. Sutherland, *The Massacre of St. Bartholomew and the European Conflict, 1559–1572* (London, 1973), pp. 249–59. It is interesting to find that Jean de Morvillier's counter-argument to Coligny was couched just as realistically in terms of the interests of the powers.
[20]*Les Oeconomies royales de Sully*, ed. David Buisseret and Bernard Barbiche (Paris, 1970), vol. 1, pp. 502–8.
[21]*Le Reveille-Matin des François et de leurs voisins composé par Eusebe Philadelphe Cosmopolite en forme de dialogues* ("Edimbourg", 1574), vol. 1, pp. 21, 37, 40, 71, 107, and 141. The favourable

varre became the heir presumptive to the French crown in 1584 is a signal example of such pragmatism.[22] Bouillon's advice was tendered a decade later, after Henri IV's conversion to Catholicism, an act probably approved by Sully and later mentioned with approbation by his son-in-law.[23] Rohan's account of the interest of France was merely a rationalisation of Henri IV's foreign policy, which had involved alliance with England and the Dutch during the war against Spain and an understanding with Maurice and certain German Protestant princes during the Cleves-Jülich succession problem. Elements of the same thinking are to be found in the fragmentary references to the "Grand Design" in Sully's memoirs.

Sully's attribution of the words *intérêt* and *raison d'état* to Bouillon in 1594 may not, of course, be accurate, although Bouillon's speech appears to be verbatim. Sully is thought to have begun the compilation of his memoirs in 1611. The phrase *raison d'état* appears in isolated instances in late sixteenth-century France, not long after Botero and Frachetta had popularised its Italian equivalent.[24] During the regency *intérêt*, the word used by Rohan, was more common in this context. In 1617 the anonymous author of a tract on the best means of evicting the Habsburgs from the imperial dignity observed that "all the princes and commonwealths are guided by their particular interests."[25] His argument about the balance of power in Europe was again based upon the rivalry of France and Spain. Four years later another anonymous pamphlet, advocating French intervention in support of the Elector Palatine, stated that Catholic France should aid Protestantism abroad since *raison d'état*, and not religion, determined French policy.[26] In his *Conseiller d'Etat* (1633) Sully's Catholic younger brother, Philippe de Béthune, claimed that "raison d'état n'est autre chose que raison d'intérêt."[27] During the 1620s *intérêt* was generally preferred to *raison d'état* in the many writings on Rohan's theme. One which used *intérêt*, and in content was closest of all to Rohan's *De l'Interest*, was the *Discours des princes et états de la Chrestienté plus considérables à la France selon les diverses qualitez et conditions* (1624). It was written in support of French intervention in the Valtelline, and, according to Meinecke, may well represent the policy being advocated by Lesdiguières at this time.[28] Rohan in this period

---

mention of Machiavelli in the second dialogue occurs in the Latin but not in the French version: *Dialogi ab Eusebio Philadelpho . . . compositi* ("Edimburgi", 1574), vol. 2, p. 88. I am indebted for these references to Miss Roberta Jacobs of Bryn Mawr College.

[22]Ralph E. Giesey and J. H. M. Salmon (eds.), *"Francogallia" by François Hotman* (Cambridge, 1972), pp. 95–7.

[23]*De l'Interest*, p. 36.

[24]Church, p. 45. R. de Mattei, "Il Problema della 'Ragion di Stato' nei suoi primi affioramenti," *Rivista internazionale di filosofia del diritto*, 41 (1964), 712–32. The latter article ascribes the first use of the term to Della Casa and Guicciardini. The works written by Botero and Frachetta using the phrase in their titles appeared in Venice in 1589 and 1592 respectively.

[25]Etienne Thuau, *Raison d'Etat et pensée politique à l'époque de Richelieu* (Paris, 1966), p. 310.

[26]*Ibid.*

[27]*Ibid.*, p. 312.

[28]For Meinecke's discussion of this pamphlet see *Die Idee der Staatsräson*, pp. 191–203.

wrote little on interest of state but he had much to say about private interest.

It is in the context of his leadership of the Huguenots that Rohan acquired his heroic aura. His retrospective *Apologie sur les derniers troubles de la France à cause de la Religion* (1629) and the memoirs he composed in 1630 are an exercise in the justification of himself and his cause. In the early part of his memoirs, devoted to the years of 1610–1620, he does not disguise his own shifts in position, but his personal role in this period is depicted in counterpoint to his denunciation of the private ambition and public incompetence of such enemies as Bouillon and Luynes. The resistance of the Huguenots in the next decade is defended in terms of their relationship with Henri IV and their contribution to anti-Habsburg foreign policy. Rohan refuses to see that national interest might dictate the reduction of a privileged and independent power within the state, especially when it impeded the conduct of foreign relations. His armed resistance to the crown severely disrupted French measures against the Habsburgs in North Italy and the Valtelline. In 1625, when he sanctioned the armed coup of Soubise that began the second war, he failed to appreciate that it was his own reasoning on French diplomacy that caused the Protestant English and Dutch to lend their ships in the royal operation against La Rochelle. He remained blind to Richelieu's argument that Huguenot rebellion must be crushed if the anti-Habsburg front was to retain the initiative in the conflict with Spain. Nor did he choose to see that Richelieu was better able to contain Catholic *dévot* criticism of his diplomacy through counter-action to French Protestantism. When the English failed his cause in the third war, Rohan turned to Savoy and, ultimately, to Spain, thus contradicting the basic principle of his justification.

In his memoirs Rohan places much of the blame for the outbreak of the first war upon Luynes, who was thought to have persuaded the king to withdraw the privileges of Protestant Béarn. But Rohan also holds the war to have been provoked by the private interests of such Huguenot lords as Favas, Châtillon and La Force, who had prolonged the Huguenot assembly of La Rochelle in defiance of the king in 1620.[29] His own posture at this point is to counsel peace and obedience, and his reaction to the assembly's offer of military command is represented as a reluctant acceptance of that which honour obliged but others had chosen to refuse. After the peace of Montpellier he found it necessary to defend himself against charges that he had failed to continue the war for private advantage. "I shall not bother to refute the charge against me that the need to secure my particular interest made me neglect the general interest, because the whole course of my life, and even this last act of peacemaking, make the contrary clear."[30] Rohan lost his major governments and failed to profit from his negotiations with the crown as Châtillon and Favas had done. He retired to Castres, only to take up arms once more in 1625 in the rising that he claimed was caused by the bad faith of the royal government in failing to honour the

[29]*Mémoires*, p. 118. See also *Discours politiques*, p. 83.
[30]*Discours politiques*, p. 95.

terms of Montpellier. In his *Apologie* he criticises the English and the Dutch for
their intervention in support of Richelieu during the second war, and re-
proaches James I and Savoy for their betrayal in the third.[31] His memoirs
reiterate these charges with rising emphasis. As he surveys the divisions within
the Huguenots during the final stage of the struggle, his bitterness rises to
crescendo:

> During the first two wars divisions appeared among us in some places. In the last war
> they burst out everywhere, there being no locality where corruption did not insinuate
> itself, or where avarice did not assume the cloak of piety. Things were so bad that
> without awaiting the inquiries of our enemies people went and prostituted themselves to
> sell their religion and betray their party. Our fathers would have crushed their children
> in the cradle, had they thought that they would be the instruments of the ruin of the
> churches they had planted in the light of the execution pyres and tended despite the
> tortures of persecution.[32]

Rohan's apologetics on the Huguenot wars need not be taken at face value in
all respects. It is true, of course, that, as the other Protestant magnates deserted
the faction, Rohan came more and more to concentrate military authority in his
own hands and to identify himself with his cause. Nevertheless, he had to
pursue a ruthless and realistic policy to hold his faction together. His proclaimed belief in the legitimacy of Huguenot rights was hardly in accord with
his earlier advice to Marie de Médicis to divide the magnates and make the king
all powerful.[33] In any case, his combination of legalism in terms of privilege and
expediency in terms of the Huguenot contribution to anti-Habsburg state interest was an incongruous one, for each argument weakened the other when
they were placed together. His repeated offers to go into exile or to serve the
king abroad if Huguenot liberties were restored were probably political gestures. Although he did not profit from the situation as flagrantly as La Force
and Lesdiguières, he did acquire a pension and preserve his house from ruin.
His alliances with foreign powers belied his professions of loyalty to the king. In
this respect he knew that, beside the Huguenot tradition of advocating war with
Spain, there had long existed a parallel policy of appeal to England against the
French crown. He invoked this alternate Huguenot interest in his correspondence with James I and Charles I, and it became effective in the early part of the
third religious war.

Perhaps the most "Machiavellian" aspect of Rohan's role as the leader of
Huguenot resistance was his policy towards the peace faction in the movement.
The constitutionalism that pervaded the party established the supremacy of
assemblies, and allowed local town councils to remain neutral if they so decided. Since the *noblesse* were far less significant in the movement than they had

---

[31]*Ibid.*, pp. 103–4.
[32]*Mémoires*, preface (unpaginated).
[33]*Discours politiques*, p. 75.

been, political authority tended to devolve upon bourgeois notables. Rohan negotiated with this group with consummate skill, and at the same time undermined their authority through his agents among the popular classes in the Huguenot towns. In the second war he used this tactic against the pacifically minded consuls of La Rochelle, Nîmes, Uzès, Montauban and Anduze.[34] In the third war he went as far as to arrange armed coups by the popular faction in Mazières, Montauban and Milhaud, and a similar attempt in Castres failed only through the vigilance of the local notables.[35] Rohan had no sympathy for democracy or republicanism. In the first war his difficulty was not to overcome the peace party but rather to convince the bellicose faction to accept the terms he had negotiated with Lesdiguières in August 1622. He called a conference of pastors at Nîmes and denounced those among them who sought to continue the war as seditious republicans.[36] In every respect his conduct of the political aspect of the struggle was as ruthless and hardheaded as his military leadership of the Cévennes peasantry against the armies of Luynes, Montmorency and Condé.

When the religious wars ended in 1629, and Richelieu, having destroyed the political and military independence of the Huguenots, had accorded them religious toleration, Rohan gradually came to accept the situation. His residual bitterness expressed itself in the memoirs he composed during his exile in Venice. He had little respect for royal favourites and suggested that, if they did not exploit government for their own ends, they provided a pretext for others to challenge authority: "The absolute rule of favourites is the ruin of a state. For either they alter it for their own profit or they give cause to the ambitious to do so, and at the very least they are the pretext for all the quarrels that occur in it."[37] He denounced the régimes of Concini and Luynes, and the influence briefly exercised by Schomberg and the first cardinal de Retz after Luynes' death in 1621. He expected powerful ministers to advance their own interest, and noted that in 1624 Richelieu had repaid his obligations to Louis XIII's chief minister, La Vieuville, by toppling him from power. "That is the way all these favourites faithfully repay each other," Rohan scornfully remarks. But the author goes on to express a certain admiration for Richelieu: "The cardinal, finding himself all-powerful, pursued the very same project in foreign affairs begun by his predecessor, and completed what he [La Vieuville] had left unfinished."[38]

Rohan was also putting together his commentaries on Caesar and on warfare

---

[34]Jack Alden Clarke, *Huguenot Warrior: the Life and Times of Henri de Rohan, 1579–1638* (The Hague, 1966), p. 122. Laugel, pp. 180 and 194.
[35]Clarke, pp. 160 and 167: Laugel, pp. 221 and 231.
[36]Clarke, p. 103. Details of Rohan's links with factions within the Huguenot movement are also to be found in Magnus Schybergson, *Le duc de Rohan et la chute du parti protestant en France* (Paris, 1880), and in Henry de la Garde, *Le duc de Rohan et les protestants sous Louis XIII* (Paris, 1884).
[37]*Mémoires*, p. 90.
[38]*Ibid.*, pp. 204–5.

in general, later to be published as *Le Parfait Capitaine*. He observes in this work that healthy states were military and aggressive ones, governed by warriors rather than *gens de lettres*, who sacrificed the national interest to their pacifist ideals and hired mercenaries for fear of the native *gens d'épée*.[39] Rohan was beginning to return to his idea of national interest and its relationship to private interest. He remarks that at the start of the civil war between Pompey and Caesar, the latter made the most of a visit from the tribunes whom the senate had expelled from Rome: "Caesar, profiting from the occasion, made his own cause the public cause, telling his soldiers that he only took arms to free the people from the oppression of the senate."[40] It seems that Rohan now saw Richelieu in a similar way, as one who had identified his private interest with interest of state. Certainly, the cardinal was not one of the *gens de lettres;* nor was he either a foreigner like Concini or an upstart like Luynes. French diplomacy was openly following the path designed by Henri IV, and Rohan, the disciple of the first Bourbon, was anxious to return to favour.

At the end of 1631 Rohan welcomed the opportunity to serve as French envoy and lieutenant general to the Grisons, at Coire, near the Valtelline. All his patience and realism were needed amid the frustrations of the ensuing years. He endured distrust, indecision and lack of financial support from the royal council. Bullion and Père Joseph suspected him, and a second French envoy spied upon him. He lost his post after a year, and then resumed it in July 1633, shorn of his ambassadorial status. He went to court a year later and, after the defeat of Nördlingen, was finally given the chance to exercise his military talents. He defeated Charles of Lorraine in Alsace, re-entered Switzerland and won a remarkable series of victories in 1635. In these years he was constantly negotiating with the Grison leagues and the cantons, and fulfilled his instructions to safeguard the rights of the Catholic peasantry in the Valtelline. In his diplomacy, as in his campaigns against the Austrians and the Spanish, he successfully divided his enemies and exploited local interests. Despite his skill and his prestige, he was discredited in 1637 by a plot among his Grison auxiliaries, and obliged to disband his French troops. Evading the attempt of his old enemy, Condé, to arrest him, Rohan joined the forces of Bernard of Saxe-Weimar, and in 1638 died of wounds received in a skirmish before the battle of Rheinfelden.[41]

While there is a marked change in tone between Rohan's writings from one phase of his career to the next, there is also a consistent set of assumptions underlying his political opinions throughout his entire life, in parallel with a consistent pattern of behaviour. Interest of state and private interest are both defined under Marie de Médicis, although the emphasis is placed on the latter. During the 1620s Rohan is engrossed in a cause in which interest of state

[39]*Le Parfait Capitaine, autrement l'abregé des Commentaires de Cesar* (Paris, 1692 [1636]), p. 126.
[40]*Ibid.*, p. 50.
[41]For Rohan's career in Switzerland see Rott, *passim*.

proves a double-edged weapon of controversy, and private interest is less a subject for detached observation and more a ground for accusations of treachery. With the composition of *De l'Interest* in the 1630s the idea of interest of state is developed in the context of foreign policy, and private interest is discussed as an obstacle to its realisation.

Most of *De l'Interest* seems to have been written when Rohan was at court in 1634, although there is one passage in the text which suggests that the author was engaged on it in 1632.[42] It was first published anonymously in Renaudot's *Mercure françois* in 1634, the year when the 1624 *Discours des Princes et Estats de la Chrestienté*, which it closely resembles, reappeared in print at Geneva in Chastelet's *Mercure d'Estat*.[43] *De l'Interest* was republished, bound up with *Le Parfait Capitaine*, in 1638, and in 1639 it was issued separately. The 1639 version contains a dedication to Richelieu signed by Rohan. Later editions include the preface originally appended to *Le Parfait Capitaine*.[44] Confusion has been caused by editions issued later in the century which are adaptations or imitations, and wholly different from Rohan's text.[45]

Rohan's dedication to Richelieu reveals that the mysterious element in interest of state is not some concept of the state as an organic entity, as Meinecke seems to infer, but rather the difficulty of isolating particular advantage amid the flux of events. A few years earlier a collection of letters by Silhon, Balzac, Faret and others had flattered Richelieu by converting interest of state into the mystique of the all-seeing statesman.[46] Rohan is adulatory enough, and refers to the statesman's need for "supernatural insights to observe the mutations of a thing so difficult to understand."[47] But his is the concrete concern to perceive practical advantage within a maze of competing and fluctuating interests. He goes on to explain that it was for this reason that the most accomplished rulers had confessed at their deathbed that they were but apprentices in the art of

[42]*De l'Interest*, p. 78. Rohan states that it is fourteen years since the election of the king of Bohemia in 1618. This part of the work may have been written late in 1632 or early in 1633, when Rohan had lost his post at Coire.

[43]*Mercure françois* (Paris, 1637), vol. 20 (for 1634–1635), pp. 46–126: *Mercure d'Estat* (Geneva, 1634), pp. 239–400.

[44]The preface, written by J. Silhon or Daniel des Perreaux, is obviously more appropriate to *Le Parfait Capitaine* than to *De l'Interest*, for it moralises about the noble profession of arms. It contains an interesting eulogy of Rohan, asserting that he was unlike those princes who stirred up civil war in pursuit of their private quarrels.

[45]In 1647 a rewritten version, containing an account of events since Rohan's death, was prepared under the title *Traité succinct des vraies maximes des Princes et Estats de l'Europe* (Bibliothèque Nationale, MS Fr. 4253). This served as the basis of *Maximes des Princes et Estats souverains* (Cologne, 1665). This piece, incorporating sections of Rohan's original text, was added to another publication entitled *Intérêts et Maximes des Princes et des Estats souverains* (Cologne, 1666). The first half of this latter work consists of a lengthy historical account of the interests of many European nations together with Turkey, Persia, Abyssinia ("Pretejan"), Armenia, China and the Arabs. The interests discussed are not those of the type conceived by Rohan. They are concerned with the dynastic and legal claims of the powers, extending over many centuries.

[46]*Recueil de lettres nouvelles*. Cf. Church, p. 165.

[47]*De l'Interest*, dedication (unpaginated).

statecraft. As we have seen, Rohan repeats this opinion in the opening lines of the text. In any given situation there is only one correct interest of state. No fixed principles or maxims can determine it, and history is not merely irrelevant but a distinct obstacle to its perception.

After his striking opening passage, Rohan proceeds to an exposé of the particular interests of the powers, based upon two general determinants in European diplomacy. The first is the ambition of Spain to achieve a universal monarchy; the second the corresponding need for France to provide a counter-weight. This is precisely the theme sketched in his discourses of 1612 and 1617, but now the issues are defined and exemplified with greater assurance. Philip II receives unqualified admiration for his perception of Spanish interest, and the craft and dissimulation with which he advanced it. His principal weap-on was an assumed zeal for Catholicism, and he applied it to ruin France by moving the French crown and the papacy to repress the Huguenots while secretly promoting their resistance. As Rohan surveys the Spanish interest in relations with France, Italy, England, Germany, Switzerland and the United Provinces, five principles emerge: Catholicism employed as a political weapon; an excellent system of foreign intelligence; patient, secret and continuing nego-tiation, involving arbitration in the disputes of others to Spanish advantage; military strength concealed behind an apparent desire for peace; and the pres-ervation of national prestige. French interest of state, as discerned by Henri IV, involves a set of counter-principles: exposure of Spanish hypocrisy and ambi-tion, and support of the Protestant powers; a rival intelligence system; involve-ment in every negotiation in which Spain participates; and force to be met by force. Geography is a determining element in all this, for Rohan argues that the size and contiguity of Spain and France show that they are designed by nature to be enemies.[48]

In the same pragmatic and wholly secular terms Rohan defines the interests of the Italian princes, Rome, Venice and Savoy. These interests consist in resistance to Habsburg hegemony in the peninsula, maintaining a balance of power, and avoiding conflict between themselves. The papacy must use the clergy to further its secular designs while protecting them from secular rulers. The sword of excommunication must be wielded infrequently if its edge is to remain sharp, and individual popes should refrain from the nepotism that weakens the Holy See for their successors. Savoy's interest lies in a frequent alternation of alliances to tilt the balance between Spain and France, but, since Spain is the preponderant power in Italy, France is the more profitable ally in the long run. The interests of the German princes lie in checking the imperial expansion of the house of Austria and revealing its political use of religious divisions. In this Poland, Hungary, Denmark and Sweden possess a common interest, for their advantage is inextricably bound to the constitutional balance

[48]*Ibid.*, pp. 1–14.

in the German Empire. The interests of the Swiss and the Dutch, who constitute the two arms of Germany, are dependent upon the geography of their countries. The mountain Swiss sell their bodies as mercenaries to preserve their liberty, and their true interest is in peace; the sea-faring Dutch have won liberty and prosperity through war, and it is their interest to hold firm to France and avoid internal religious divisions. Finally, England constitutes "un petit monde à part." Elizabeth I understood her interest as the support of international Protestantism in response to Spanish exploitation of international Catholicism. Through naval strength and commercial growth England can become a third power in Europe.[49]

The paradox of the first part of *De l'Interest* is that the reader, after being told that there are no fixed principles of interest of state, is immediately confronted with a plethora of them. In the second part, remembering the irrelevance of history, he is presented with a group of historical examples. Rohan discusses seven recent international crises to show how miscalculation or the distortion of reason by passion and "superstition" have prevented rulers and statesmen from acting in accord with true interest. In practice the examples are chosen and interpreted to reinforce the theme of the polarity of European politics. They have the same seeming detachment as the analysis of the interests of particular states in the first part, and at the same time they are influenced by Rohan's original *idée fixe* – the necessity of a pro-Protestant foreign policy for France. However, the examples also serve a purpose that Rohan himself seems only to have contemplated incidentally. They enable the reader to associate public and private interest. This is especially the case with the first crisis, which involves civil war as well as international conflict.

In discussing the revolt of the French Catholic League[50] Rohan is concerned to present the manner in which his hero, Henri de Navarre, appreciated the transformation of personal interest. His rôle as the leader of the Huguenot faction and princes of the blood changed dramatically when he became heir to the crown of Henri III. As Henri IV, he had to discard the part of *chef de parti* and to identify his own interest with interest of state. He preserved something of his earlier *persona* in order to retain the military support of French Protestantism. However, when Philip II attempted to take France in tutelage by elevating the Infanta to the throne, Henri converted to Catholicism and rallied national sentiment by war with Spain. Others did not calculate interest so effectively. Henri III should have remained above faction, but he joined the party of the League against that of Navarre. Finding that Guise, the leader of the League, had subverted his authority, the last Valois again miscalculated his interest, and sought a remedy that completed his ruin. In order to outdo Guise he threw himself into "une devotion affectée et extraordinaire," and incurred

[49]*Ibid.*, pp. 14–24.
[50]*Ibid.*, pp. 31–44.

the distrust and contempt of his subjects. Guise, whom the authors of the *Reveille-Matin* had suggested as a replacement for Charles IX,[51] had always attracted the admiration of his Huguenot enemies. None admired the Catholic *chef de parti* as much as Rohan, who describes him as "bel homme, adroit, courtois, liberal, vaillant." He remarks that Guise knew his own interest so well that he chose to show his Catholic zeal by persecuting the Protestants rather than by haunting cloisters and religious processions after the fashion of Henri III. Yet over-confidence and magnanimity ultimately led Guise to betray his interest. He released the king from his power after he had destroyed royal authority at the day of the barricades, and then lost his life by entrusting it to the man he sought to depose.

Rohan also shows that Philip II came close to realising his interest in the wars of the League, but failed through overreaching himself. He had given the League just enough support to keep it within Spanish control until the point when it became necessary to choose a Leaguer candidate for the French throne. By putting forward his daughter he aroused national sentiment and caused a revulsion which, in his ignorance of the "légèreté" of the French character, he had failed to anticipate. Had he allowed the leaders of the League to divide France between them, he would have gradually acquired the kingdom piecemeal. Instead, he had obstinately pursued the impossible, and facilitated the triumph of Henri IV. Like the first Bourbon, Pope Clement VIII had also undeviatingly followed his true interest. Defying Philip II, he recognised the conversion of Henri IV and absolved him from past heresy. He did so because it was "a maxim of Rome to temper its policy to events so as not to lose the respect and reverence which it tries to preserve everywhere, and without which its authority would not be worth much."[52]

Rohan's second crisis, the Savoy war of 1600, exemplifies his analysis of the interest of Savoy in the first part of *De l'Interest*. He also comments that France had not followed her interest in accepting Bresse in exchange for Saluzzo, the gateway to Italy. Rohan concludes with the more objective remark that, while it was the French interest to share Italy with Spain, the interest of the Italian princes was to exclude all foreigners.[53] The third historical example, the clash between Pope Paul V and Venice in 1605, was also one in which no Protestant interest was involved. According to Rohan, the grandeur and mystique of the papacy had resulted from the concealment of its territorial ambitions, but Paul V allowed his passions to direct his reason, and sought to subordinate Venice to his direct authority. When he encountered the firm but pacific resistance of the Venetians, he took one extreme measure after another which he had subsequently to disavow. Whereas Spain engaged in a number of bellicose and

---

[51] *Le Reveille-Matin*, vol. 1, p. 61, and vol. 2, p. 84.
[52] *De l'Interest*, p. 36.
[53] *Ibid.*, pp. 45–8.

chimerical intrigues, France secured the glory of successful arbitration. However, French policy was complicated at first by a conflict of public and private interest. Rohan alleges that the secretary of state, Villeroy, whose son was ambassador at Rome, sought to please the pope and acquire the dignity of cardinal: "In this way particular interest often prejudices the public interest."[54]

The next issue, the negotiations leading to the twelve-year truce between Spain and the United Provinces in 1609, is seen by Rohan as the triumph of Spanish interest – "a touchstone of Spanish mastery in negotiation."[55] Philip III appreciated that continued war was increasing the power of the Dutch, and sought a truce whereby they might be encouraged to disarm. Henri IV knew that continuation of the war was in the French interest, but, unable to raise French support, he concluded that, if the truce was inevitable, France might as well gain credit through arbitration. James I of England was misled by his pacific inclinations into deserting his country's interest. Rohan was an admirer of the house of Orange, and the challenge presented to Maurice of Nassau by Olden Barneveldt gave him an opportunity to reflect once more on the conflict between public and private interest. The true interest of the United Provinces was the individual liberty of each province and city, and William of Orange had built the resistance of the Dutch to Spain upon this principle. Barneveldt had sought to bend local liberty to his own credit by advancing peace, whereas Maurice's warlike interest in welding together a nation in military discipline coincided with the public interest of the Netherlands state. This was the situation from which the truce had been finally negotiated. It was not totally contrary to French and Dutch interests, for Henri IV had gained the credit as the peacemaker. Moreover, his guarantee of support for the United Provinces, together with the watchfulness of Maurice, had prevented the immediate realisation of the Spanish design. Subsequently, the assassination of Henri IV had given the conduct of French affairs to his widow, and Marie de Médicis put her private interest before that of the state. In order to secure her authority against the magnates she had thrown herself into the arms of Rome and Spain. Moreover, bigotry replaced reason in the mind of the regent, who listened to Spanish counsel that the disunity of the Netherlands prevented the Dutch from supporting the princes of the blood against her. At this time the Spanish fostered religious divisions in the northern Netherlands by means of the Arminian controversy, so that the French ambassadors found themselves in the false position of supporting Barneveldt against Maurice. Rohan had already made some of these points in his discourse of 1618, and in the Huguenot wars he had imitated Maurice's tactic of using the popular faction against the burghers.

The Cleves-Jülich succession question of 1609 served Rohan to illustrate his generalisations about the princes of Germany, and once again to criticise the

[54]*Ibid.*, pp. 48–61.
[55]*Ibid.*, pp. 62–70.

betrayal of French interest by Marie de Médicis. The rulers of Brandenburg, Neuberg, Zweibrücken and Torgau all asserted territorial claims in the name of their wives, the sisters of the late duke. While the princes quarrelled among themselves the Emperor attempted to take Cleves-Jülich under his protection. The Spanish assisted him since Cleves-Jülich lay on the border of the United Provinces. The true interest of the princes was to resist the growth of Habsburg power, while that of France, England and the Dutch was to give them aid. Henri IV's army, which was about to march at the time of his assassination, went on to recover Jülich, but Marie de Médicis preferred her private interest to that of France and refused to press the matter further. Only the Dutch, in the person of Maurice of Nassau, and the Spanish, through their general Spinola, consistently pursued their interest of state in this affair.[56]

With his discussion of the election of Frederick of the Palatinate to the crown of Bohemia, Rohan applies his theories to the early phases of the Thirty Years' War.[57] He seems to deplore the devastation of the war, and ascribes its cause to "the pretext adopted by everyone of defending his religion." James I is criticised for deserting both his interest and his son-in-law, the Elector Palatine. Louis XIII is blamed for remaining neutral – the result of following the private interest of the favourite, Luynes, rather than the interest of state. The magnitude of Habsburg success led Spain to neglect the cardinal principle of concealing aggression under the cloak of religion. The Spanish attack upon Catholic Mantua is described by Rohan as doubly in error. It opened the eyes of Louis XIII to the past neglect of the French interest by his ministers, and it led to a Spanish concentration upon the North Italian theatre at a time when Sweden was tilting the balance in Germany in favour of the Protestant cause. Ultimately, all the powers, save England, returned to the pursuit of their true interest. It is necessity, according to Rohan, that produced this outcome – an observation that seems to run counter to his argument that true interest of state may be constantly obscured. This contradiction is understandable, however, when it is remembered that, as Rohan approaches the moment of writing in his retrospective analysis, he is anxious to demonstrate the correctness of Richelieu's policy.

It is very much in this light that Rohan interprets the last of his examples, the succession to Mantua and Montferrat.[58] It is intriguing that Rohan offers no judgment on his own obstruction of French interest in this affair. In earlier years he sees that Lesdiguières followed the right policy in North Italy, but this was due to the fortuitous coincidence of his private interests with those of France. Rohan mentions dryly that France was impeded in Italy by the intervention of the English and the resistance of La Rochelle in the third Huguenot

[56]*Ibid.*, pp. 71–8.
[57]*Ibid.*, pp. 78–88.
[58]*Ibid.*, pp. 88–96.

war. He praises the resolution of the government in persevering with the siege and in bringing the Languedoc campaign to a successful conclusion. In Languedoc, Rohan remarks, "The Spaniard looked as if he would render aid." Spain recovered from earlier errors of judgment and began to sow divisions within the French council. Referring to the day of dupes, Rohan introduces his only direct reference to Richelieu in the text of *De l'Interest:* "This was the point at which the courage (*vertu*) made itself felt of one against whom all the traps had been set. For at last he emerged from the labyrinth by following the thread of honour."[59] In his conclusion Rohan moves into a kind of triumphant acclamation at Richelieu's success. Casale has been saved from the Spanish, and the French duc de Nevers invested with Mantua by the Emperor. The Valtelline has been secured by the "liberation" of the Grisons. Italy has been preserved from foreigners and a gate left open for the French to provide aid to the Italian princes. It remains the true interest of France to support her neighbours against Spain: "Whence I conclude that the glory of the king, the grandeur of his estate, and the reputation he enjoys will last as long as he holds firm to this resolution."[60]

Commentators on *De l'Interest* have neglected the seven historical examples in the second part. This would occasion no surprise if all the examples included the contradictions and transparent flattery evident in the last. Yet the examples generally offer much insight into the articulation of interest of state. While it may never fail in itself, rulers and statesmen frequently fail to define it, or, having defined it, fail to obey its behest. Among the princes cited in the examples, Henri III fails through miscalculation, Philip II through overreaching himself, Charles Emmanuel of Savoy through caprice, Paul V through passion, James I through congenital weakness, and Philip IV through over-confidence. In no instance, it may be noted, does a ruler fail interest of state because of his private interest. As he indicates in his account of the advent of Henri IV, Rohan evidently assumes that the private interest of the prince is indistinguishable from interest of state. It is true that the princes who disputed the lands of Cleves-Jülich are alleged to be acting counter to the interest of the German Empire, if such interest be construed as an alliance to resist Habsburg imperialism. Yet in so far as they are princes in their own right, they are clearly pursuing their particular advantage. Neither Germany nor the United Provinces quite fit Rohan's criteria. Maurice of Nassau is thought to be following the Dutch interest in his desire for war and his unification of the provinces through military discipline. However, the guiding principle of the Dutch state, as founded by William of Orange, has already been defined as federal liberty. It would appear that Rohan's interest of state is really the interest of an absolute ruler.

[59]*Ibid.*, p. 95.
[60]*Ibid.*, p. 96.

The historical examples also provide instances of the private interest of a regent, a minister or a favourite interfering with interest of state. By her alliance with Spain Marie de Médicis put her own interest in retaining authority before the national interest in opposing the Habsburgs. For similar reasons Luynes prevented France from aiding the Elector Palatine, and turned, instead, to attack the Huguenots. In the same way Villeroy's alleged desire to gain a cardinal's hat at first frustrated the French interest in the conflict between the papacy and Venice. Sometimes, however, a private interest might fortuitously advance interest of state, as when Lesdiguières invaded North Italy. There are also occasions when individuals pursue private aims under pretence of advancing interest of state. This is the case with Johan van Olden Barneveldt, whose advocacy of peace is disguised as the national interest to procure his own advancement. It is also the situation with Henri de Guise, who sought the crown of France while claiming to act for the public welfare. Although Rohan docs not say so explicitly, it is possible for a private interest to disguise itself as the public interest and to attain such success that the individual concerned may end by pursuing the true interest of state. Rohan provides such an example in *Le Parfait Capitaine* when he discusses Caesar and the tribunes. The conclusion of *De l'Interest* elevates Richelieu to such a role.

In his writings under the regency Rohan turns time and again to the dominance of private interest. His apologies and justifications during the religious wars excused the defeat of his faction in such terms. Consistently in every phase of his career as magnate, party leader and royal general Rohan exploited the self-interested aims of his opponents with cynical realism. Self-interest operated at one level with the same inevitability that interest of state commanded the prince at another. By a curious sleight of hand Rohan transmuted the first concept into the second. Since he treated interest of state entirely in terms of foreign policy, the issue of conflict with private interest arose only in respect of a self-serving minister or favourite. All the contradictions in his thought stem from his failure to consider the articulation of authority within the state. If he had chosen to reflect upon the implications of his doctrine for internal government, Rohan would doubtless have agreed with Richelieu that state interest must always take precedence over individual interest.[61] But while he may have been an absolutist at heart, Rohan's own political experience never allowed him to draw such a general conclusion. As a member of the high aristocracy and of a minority religion with entrenched privileges, he was unable to see that the sovereign state he desired to serve must necessarily challenge any authority that denied its ultimate supremacy.

In these circumstances it is misleading to think of Rohan as a precursor of the

---

[61]*Testament politique*, ed. Louis André (Paris, 1947), vol. 2, ch. 3: "On ne saurait s'imaginer le mal qui arrive à un Etat, quand on préfère les intérêts particuliers aux publics, et que ces derniers sont reglés par les autres."

Hegelian state. Interest of state is necessarily an aggressive concept, described in words such as *gloire, grandeur* and *accroissement*. It suggests a view of international politics as a Hobbesian state of nature written large in terms of national entities. Yet Rohan did not intend to endow the state with the same attributes as the individual, who must necessarily pursue private interest at the expense of his fellows. It was the prince, not the state, that he had essentially in mind. Interest of state might never lie, but the princes who tried to discern and apply it were human. They and their ministers might err. It is necessary to read beyond the brazen note sounded in the opening lines of *De l'Interest*. The later parts of the work, taken together with Rohan's other writings, reveal that he was attempting something less than the objectives with which Meinecke credited him.

PART II

Sovereignty, resistance, and Christian obedience

5

<center>~~~~~~</center>

Bodin and the monarchomachs

I. SEVENTEENTH-CENTURY ASSOCIATIONS

For a century after its first publication in 1576 Bodin's *Six Livres de la République* occurred in the marginalia of every notable political controversy. But it was not always cited to the same effect. During the turbulent events in mid-seventeenth century England, for example, Bodin's opinions were marshalled to support such a diverse collection of causes as the sovereignty of the Long Parliament, the prerogative of Stuart monarchy, the rights of the Cromwellian army against the parliament, the execution of Charles I, and the defence of Cromwell against the radical elements that had once supported him. In some instances Bodin's views were palpably distorted, and in many others they were set beside those of the Huguenot critics of absolute monarchy, the so-called monarchomachs, whom Bodin had ostensibly set out to refute.[1]

To find the *République* a bedfellow with Hotman's *Francogallia*, Beza's *De Jure Magistratuum*, and Mornay's *Vindiciae contra Tyrannos* is less surprising than it might seem. Within a decade of Bodin's death in 1596 the great jurist Althusius had turned him upon his head, and assimilated his definition of sovereignty to the opposing doctrine of the sovereignty of the community. If sovereignty were to be supreme and indivisible, as Bodin had argued, then its only possible repository must be the whole community. Althusius quoted the monarchomachs in support of the proposition that the community had agreed upon certain fundamental laws as conditions under which the administration and exercise of the rights of sovereignty were entrusted to the ruler. Althusius could then suggest that, since Bodin had distinguished between the sovereignty of the kingdom and that of the ruler (*inter majestatem regni et regnantis*), and since he had admitted the subordination of the ruler to the fundamental laws, he had meant to show the ruler had no propietary claim to the sovereign rights he exercised. By such subtle inferences Althusius could conclude that Bodin's premises were really those of his opponents.[2]

---

[1] J. H. M. Salmon, *The French Religious Wars in English Political Thought* (Oxford, 1959), pp. 83–106.
[2] *Ibid.*, pp. 40–50.

119

Other jurists within the empire attempted to synthesise the opposing theories that had emerged from the French wars of religion, but their methods and conclusions differed from those of Althusius. The exponents of double sovereignty postulated a balance between *majestas realis*, reposing in the community, and the *majestas personalis* of the ruler. Besoldus of Tübingen cited Althusius and another monarchomach, Lambert Daneau, to demonstrate that the *leges imperii* were the fundamental laws safeguarding a commonwealth against tyranny. Bodin's account of the *leges imperii* as intrinsic to the sovereignty but beyond the reach of the actual sovereign suggested to Besoldus that Bodin had circumscribed the ruler's jurisdiction with a similar purpose in mind. Besoldus, however, was as anxious to defend the rights of the ruler as he was to defend those of the community, while another celebrated jurist, Arnisaeus, believed that Bodin had made too many concessions to the monarchomachs.[3]

How is it possible that the ruler may be *legibus solutus* and yet limited by constitutional law? How can a theory of legislative sovereignty, containing all the implications of interest of state, accept effective moral restraint through principles of natural law? Modern discussion of such issues in Bodin's thought has not always been aware that seventeenth-century commentators attempted to answer their own equivalent of these questions by establishing the relationship between Bodin and the monarchomachs. In the hope that the relationship may offer fresh insight into Bodin's thinking, this paper sets out to discover where precisely he refuted their ideas, and where, if anywhere, he stood with them upon common ground.

II. THE PREFACES TO THE *RÉPUBLIQUE*

Bodin's general purpose in writing the *République,* and his attitude to the theorists of resistance, are set out in the various prefaces to the work. They reveal a marked contrast to the views he had expressed in the sixth chapter of his *Methodus ad facilem historiarum cognitionem,* which served as a preliminary sketch for the *République.* The *Methodus* was first published in 1566, and certain additional remarks in the revised edition of early 1572 displayed Bodin's belief in the stability of the French monarchy during the early phases of the religious wars. Bodin declared that the imposition of peace amid such conflicts demonstrated the splendour and prestige of French institutions and the magnanimity of the race of Valois.[4] The *République* was composed after the massacre of St. Bartholomew and in the course of a new war, where Catholic politiques fought beside the Huguenots against the crown. Bodin's view of the contemporary

---

[3]*Ibid.,* pp. 50–4.
[4]*Methodus ad facilem historiarum cognitionem,* in *Oeuvres philosophiques de Jean Bodin,* ed. P. Mesnard (Paris, 1951), cap. VI, p. 210.

scene was entirely transformed. The first preface in the *République* proclaimed the book an anodyne for anarchy. It declared the impending wreck of the ship of state and suggested that, when the captain and crew were exhausted by the force of the storm, it was time for the passengers to lend a hand. "That is why, for my part," Bodin wrote, "being able to do nothing better, I have undertaken this discourse on the commonwealth."[5]

This preface denounced two kinds of men who had "profaned the sacred mysteries of political philosophy – a practice which has given occasion to disturb and upset some fine states." The first were disciples of Machiavelli who supposedly extolled impiety and injustice. Although the second were critics of the Machiavellians, they constituted a more dangerous threat to the commonwealth. They were men "who under pretence of exemption from burdens and popular liberty make subjects rebel against their natural prince and open the door to a licentious anarchy, which is worse than the greatest tyranny in the world." Bodin unquestionably had the Huguenot libels of the years 1573–1575 in mind when he wrote this passage, for the attack upon the Machiavellian policies of Catherine de Médicis was an established theme in Huguenot literature well before Gentillet published his *Anti-Machiavel* in 1576.[6] Moreover, the phrases "exemption from burdens" and "popular liberty" were apt descriptions of the *De Jure Magistratuum* and the *Francogallia* in the eyes of a hostile critic. Bodin tempered his own asperity by remarking that such authors were moved by ignorance of affairs of state, rather than by malice. The purpose of the *République*, he declared in the preface, was to correct these dangerous errors.

In 1577 the *République* was republished at Geneva without Bodin's authority.[7] The editor, Claude de Juge, added a preface of his own to correct Bodin's errors of fact and interpretation. The first category concerned references to the Genevan constitution, its association with Berne, and the use of excommunication as a political weapon by the consistory.[8] The second kind of supposed error was said to be contained in the chapter of the *République* which discussed the question of resistance to a tyrant. There Bodin had advocated that the penalties stated in the *Lex Julia* for counselling the murder of a magistrate should be applied to those who "by printed books suggest that subjects can justly take arms against their prince when they think him a tyrant, and can put him to death by any means whatsoever."[9] Bodin had claimed that both Calvin and Luther

---

[5]*Les Six Livres de la République* (n.p. [Geneva], 1577), Préface à Monseigneur du Faur, Seigneur de Pibrac, Conseiller du Roy en son privé Conseil (unpaginated).

[6]E.g. *Dialogi ab Eusebio Philadelpho – compositi* ("Edimburgi", 1574 [better known by its French title *Le Reveille-Matin des François*]), Dialogue I, p. 98.

[7]G. Cardascia, "Sur une édition genévoise de la République de Jean Bodin," *Humanisme et Renaissance*, 4 (1937), 212–4; and M. Reulos, "L'édition de 1577 de la République," *Bibliothèque d'humanisme et renaissance*, 13 (1951), 342–54.

[8]*Les Six Livres de la République* (1577), Advertissement au lecteur (unpaginated).

[9]*Ibid.*, II, 5, p. 389. References to *Republique* provide book and chapter numbers.

denied the legality of regicide or rebellion unless there was an indubitable command from God, as in the case of Jehu's divine mission to exterminate Jezebel and the race of Ahab. The author of the Genevan preface called upon Bodin to name the alleged works that counselled armed resistance and tyrannicide by private men. In fact the *Reveille-Matin* had suggested the latter remedy, but the *De Jure Magistratuum* had explicitly forbidden resistance to a tyrant with legitimate title by private citizens, and it had refused to discuss the question of a special divine mandate.[10]

The Genevan preface answered Bodin by quoting in full the celebrated penultimate paragraph in the fourth book of Calvin's *Institutes* where resistance to oppression was allowed through constituted ephoral authority, which, in contemporary terms, Calvin had cautiously designated as residing in "the three estates when they are assembled." Calvin, the author argued, had said in his commentary on St. John XVIII that armed resistance was forbidden except where it was specifically permitted by "the public right and the laws." Hence legitimate opposition to a tyrant need not await Jehu's divine summons. France was listed by Claude de Juge among a number of European states where institutions such as the estates existed for the very purpose of restraining tyrants. Bodin's terminology was vague and evasive. He was mistaken, too, about Luther, for if Bodin had read further in Sleidan's history, whence he had derived his information, he would have seen that Luther later acknowledged the possibility of resistance to the emperor under the provisions of the constitution.[11] The Genevan preface concluded by ridiculing Bodin's astrology, and defending past Huguenot armed action, not as conspiracy, but as an endeavour to deliver the king from those who had usurped his authority. The *République*, in the writer's opinion, consisted of a series of dubious speculations where Bodin had "manipulated historians and jurisconsults to suit his own pleasure."

Here, appended to a pirated edition of Bodin's own work, was a refutation of the very principles which he claimed had impelled him to compose it. Bodin responded with a second preface, published with the 1578 and subsequent editions.[12] His Paris publisher, Jacques du Puy, added a note of his own in which he indignantly assailed the commercial motives and professional antecedents of the Genevan editor.[13] Bodin's reply was far more moderate; indeed, it was wholly defensive. He had praised, he said, the very institutions which his Genevan critic professed to admire. He was amazed that it could be thought he

---

[10]*Dialogi ab Eusebio Philadelpho . . . compositi*, vol. 2, p. 67. *De Jure Magistratuum* (published with the *Vindiciae contra Tyrannos*, n.p., 1580), VI, p. 242. It may be noted that the *Vindiciae*, which, since it was not published until 1579, was not a target for the remarks in *République*, II, 5, was less cautious about a divine mandate (*Vindiciae*, pp. 59–64).

[11]Cf. *République* (1577), II, 5, p. 390.

[12]*République* (Paris, 1578), Io. Bodinus Vido Fabro Curiae Parisiorum Praesidi (second preface to Du Faur – unpaginated).

[13]*Ibid.*, Iacques du Puys, Libraire, au lecteur (unpaginated).

had conceded too much to the authority of a single ruler. He had taken pains to dissociate himself from those who exalted the power of royal prerogative. The authority of kings was subjected in his book to divine and natural law. No king in a royal monarchy could impose taxes without the consent of his subjects, and he was as closely bound by his covenants as they. These, said Bodin, were principles he had always held, and he had made them manifest in his book. What he had opposed were doctrines which would have expelled princes under pretence of tyranny, and which taught that kings held their thrones not by hereditary right but by the choice of the people. These were the voices of anarchy the *République* had been intended to refute.[14] Bodin pointed out that he himself had lost the favour of the king by supporting the constitutional interests of the commonwealth at the Blois estates general of 1576.[15] He made no alteration to the text of *République* II, 5, which the Genevan preface had found objectionable, save to add the precise reference to Calvin's *Institutes* in the margin.[16] The remainder of his second preface was devoted to answering objections of a different kind from Cujas.

When Bodin withdrew to his office in Laon in 1584 he composed a third prefatory letter, which was to be published with the first Latin edition of the *République* in 1586.[17] Here he again referred to the political crisis and the need to dispel ignorance about affairs of state. He did not, however, mention the Protestant monarchomachs, whose ideological role was about to be assumed by the polemicists of the Catholic League. Instead, he concentrated upon the "incurable folly" that had beset the royal policies, and suggested, in apparent despair, that the realm had almost "withered away through its own antiquity." A few years later, when his office and security were threatened by the League's occupation of Laon, he was to sign the notorious statement in which he appeared to reverse all he had said in favour of absolute monarchy and to accept the now-Leaguer doctrine of popular sovereignty.[18]

III. THE ESTATES, THE CORONATION OATH, AND THE ATTRIBUTES OF SOVEREIGNTY

If Bodin's prefaces are taken at face value, it would appear that he discerned in monarchomach thought something novel and subversive, and it was against this, rather than the "Machiavellian" lapses, the weakness and the folly of royal

[14]*Ibid.*, Second Preface.
[15]Bodin also added an account of his role at the Blois estates to the text: *République* (Paris, 1583), III, 7, pp. 485–6.
[16]*Ibid.*, II, 5, p. 305.
[17]*The Six Bookes of a Commonweale*, ed. K. D. McRae (Cambridge, Mass., 1962), p. A 72.
[18]J. Moreau-Riebel, "Bodin et la Ligue d'après des lettres inédites," *Humanisme et Renaissance*, 2 1935), 422–40, and S. Baldwin, "Jean Bodin and the League, *Catholic Historical Review*, 23 (1937/38), 160–84.

policies, that he directed the *République*. Yet the prefaces also reveal extreme caution. His reply to the Genevan attack was cast in the mould of conservative constitutionalism, and he refused the Genevan challenge to cite chapter and verse of the works he claimed to assail. Except for a brief reference to Hotman, who is not quoted in the capacity of the author of the *Francogallia*,[19] no monarchomach author is named throughout the entire text and the substantial marginal apparatus of the *République*. Nevertheless, it is possible to find certain passages and chapters where Bodin appears to answer his professed enemies directly. One such, the chapter on whether resistance to a legitimate tyrant was lawful, was identified by Claude de Juge. Some of the other instances involved a substantial modification, or even a contradiction, of views earlier expressed by Bodin in the sixth chapter of the *Methodus*. These examples have a particular significance, for it is possible to see in them how the novel elements in the *République* are developed in reaction to monarchomach ideas.

The first two examples occur in the chapter on sovereignty (I, 8), and are separated by a remark in which Bodin comes close to citing the title of the *De Jure Magistratuum:* "In this connection those who have written on the duty of magistrates and other such books have deceived themselves when they assert that the estates of the people are greater than the prince – a proposition that makes true subjects revolt from the obedience they owe their sovereign prince."[20] In the *Methodus* Bodin stated, quite unequivocally, not merely that the king was powerless to change fundamental law, but also that he required the consent of the estates to change long established national or provincial custom.[21] In the *République*, where, of course, the inviolability of the *leges imperii* was reaffirmed, Bodin argued that, although it was usual to obtain the consent of the estates for alterations to custom, the king need not do so and might reject the advice of the estates if natural reason and justice suggested such a course.[22]

Bodin's rejection of consent, and his diminution of the role of the estates, were the consequences of his new doctrine of sovereignty. If the king were subjected to the authority of the estates, the form of state was not a monarchy but an aristocracy. The possibility of shared authority was removed by the denial of the mixed form. If an English monarch used parliament, or a French king the court of parlement, to verify their edicts, this was merely to ensure the survival of the legislation after their death. It was the sovereign who convoked and dissolved the estates. They existed merely to provide subjects with an opportunity to present their humble requests. The only active role left to the

[19]*République* (1583), III, 3, p. 402. Bodin cites Hotman's opinion that the Roman censors had *potestas* but not *imperium* as a contradiction in terms. The description of Hotman as "a most skilfull antiquary" in the English version is an addition by the translator, Knolles, and is not to be found in the original text (*The Six Bookes*, p. 304).
[20]*République* (1583), I, 8, pp. 137–8.
[21]*Methodus*, p. 187.
[22]*République* (1583), I, 8, p. 137.

estates (and this only by implication) was to give consent to taxation, and even here the king could dispense with consent in circumstances of necessity.[23] Bodin concluded that the sovereignty of the monarch, far from being diminished by the estates, was exalted by their presence, since it was then that his sovereignty was explicitly recognised.[24] There followed the well-known passage where absolute legislative sovereignty was specifically defined to exclude consent: "Thus one sees that the principal point of sovereign majesty and absolute power lies mainly in giving law to subjects in general without their consent."[25]

In their view of the estates the monarchomach writers began with the ephoral argument of Calvin and depicted the institution in the essentially defensive role of protecting the fundamental laws against tyranny. This was a progression from the "bridles" referred to in Claude de Seyssel's *Grand' Monarchie de France* (1519), where limitations on royal power, exercised through the parlement, turned out in the last resort to depend on the king's acceptance of them. The trend to give the estates a much more active part in government was noticeable in Beza's *De Jure Magistratuum.* He argued that the sovereign was subject to law, and it was the sovereignty, not the sovereign, that obliged inferior magistrates to enforce the law. In the event of manifest tyranny these magistrates should resist by force until the estates, who held supreme authority over the laws and government of the kingdom, should decide what had to be done.[26] The estates were the protectors of the rights of sovereignty. They could hold the sovereign to his duty and correct and punish him, if the need arose.[27] They appointed an administrator in a royal minority. They had the power to elect and depose kings, and, were it not so, Carolingian and Capetian kings must have held the crown unlawfully. The estates had once appointed the chief officers of the commonwealth, and should supervise the king's control of them. They could impose taxes, and all the great affairs of state in peace and war were their concern.[28] The old authority of the estates had gradually been attenuated, and in the time of Louis XI tyranny had supervened.[29]

Beza made explicit the lessons implied in Hotman's historical account of the role of the estates in the *Francogallia.* There the functions of the estates in early times were described as appointing and deposing kings, declaring war and peace, controlling public laws, distributing important offices of the kingdom, assigning appanages to the sons of a deceased king and dowries to his daugh-

---

[23]*Ibid.*, p. 140. Another circumstance when the estates had an active role, according to Bodin, was when the king was a minor, insane, or a captive in a foreign war. This was not included, however, in the 1576 and Genevan editions. It was a point constantly affirmed by the theorists of resistance.
[24]*Ibid.*, p. 141.
[25]*Ibid.*, p. 142.
[26]*De Jure Magistratuum*, pp. 249–50.
[27]*Ibid.*, p. 254.
[28]*Ibid.*, p. 281.
[29]*Ibid.*, p. 283.

ters, and, finally and in general, supervising all major affairs of state.[30] In his violent replies to his critics, Papire Masson and Antoine Matharel, Hotman vigorously repudiated the accusation that the *Francogallia* suggested a return to the election of kings by the estates – a practice which, he admitted, had been replaced by hereditary succession for the past six centuries. At the same time, Hotman clearly believed that the authority of the estates ought to be superior to that of the king, and quoted Seyssel misleadingly to this effect.[31]

If Hotman hid his political opinions under the guise of antiquarianism in the *Francogallia* (though in fact his general reflections upon politics in that work often betrayed him), the *Reveille-Matin* proclaimed his book to be explicit proof of the rightful sovereignty of the estates.[32] *Summa rerum* lay not with the king but in the estates, from which the author of the second dialogue, like Hotman and Seyssel, excluded the clergy. The estates had deposed eight Merovingian and Carolingian kings and ought to depose Charles IX. In comparatively recent times they had been wrongfully deprived of their authority by amibitious ministers on the royal council and venal judges in the parlement. But prescription had no force against the rights of the community, as represented by the estates, and it was upon them that the election and authority of a king depended.[33] It is understandable that Bodin regarded such opinions as an advocacy of elective kingship and popular liberty, for they went far beyond the defensive, constitutionalist position, and, with the *Reveille-Matin* at least, seemed to support the active sovereignty of the estates. Hence Bodin applied his own definition of absolute sovereignty against this body of doctrine and in so doing radically departed from his earlier, constitutionalist attitude.

The same conclusion may be drawn from a second specific change of front between the *Methodus* and the *République*. In the *Methodus* he expressed his admiration for the coronation oath, where the kings of France swore to do justice and thereafter were as closely held by the laws as were private citizens.[34] The monarchomachs repeatedly cited coronation oaths as express formulations of the conditions under which kings held authority. The *Reveille-Matin* recalled the oaths of David and Joshua. The latter's was depicted as a contract made with the people in the presence of God, and similar oaths were said to have been sworn by Christian kings in every age. That for the French monarchy could be found in the Frankish chronicle of Aimoin de Fleury. Should the king break his oath, as had Charles IX in ordering the massacre of his people, the community no longer owed obedience.[35] The *De Jure Magistratuum* quoted the

---

[30]*Francogallia*, ed. Ralph E. Giesey and J. H. M. Salmon (Cambridge, 1972), p. 332.

[31]*Matagonis de Matagonibus . . . Monitoriale* (n.p., 1575), pp. 13, 22, 59. *Strigilis Papirii Massoni* (n.p. 1578 [2d ed.]), p. 19.

[32]*Dialogi ab Eusebio Philadelpho . . . compositi*, vol. 2, pp. 88, 134.

[33]*Ibid.*, pp. 65–6, 91, 135.

[34]*Methodus*, p. 187.

[35]*Dialogi ab Eusebio Philadelpho . . . compositi*, vol. 2, pp. 62–3.

fictitious oath of the kings of Aragon in a passage which stressed the supremacy of the cortes over the king, the conditional nature of royal authority, and the overriding powers of the Justicia. This, Beza stated, was indeed the way kings should be treated, and he went on to cite oaths sworn by the German emperors.[36] The fictitious Aragonese oath was also included in the *Francogallia*, where Hotman regarded it as evidence of the practice of all peoples who lived under legitimate monarchy to hold public councils and to preserve liberty.[37]

The authors of the *De Jure Magistratuum* and the *Francogallia* knew each other's books before either was published. Bodin noted references to coronation oaths, and especially to the Aragonese oath, in at least one of the two, and he seems to have used the French *Du Droit des Magistrats* for the text of the oath of Aragon which he reproduced in the *République*.[38] He cited it, of course, to refute the claim that the oath presupposed the election of kings: "In this he who wrote that the king was then elected by the people was entirely mistaken. Such a thing never happened." In any event he had learnt from "un chevalier Espagnol" that the oath was no longer used.[39]

Bodin proceeded to undermine the monarchomach position, and also to contradict his own opinion in the *Methodus*. In the *De Jure Magistratuum* and the *Reveille-Matin* the oath was associated with a theory of contract. Bodin distinguished between the law of a sovereign prince and the contracts to which he became a party. The laws were his commands, and they could not bind him since they depended upon his will. A contract did bind the king, but if the equity within it, of which the king was the sole interpreter, should lapse, he might reject it, and break his oath or promise. This Bodin illustrated from Aragonese history. Sovereign princes were never advised to swear to uphold the laws of their predecessors, for thereby they renounced sovereignty. A German emperor might so swear, but since the empire was an aristocracy he was not sovereign in any case. Some might advance other examples of royal oaths, such as those sworn by the kings of Epirus: "I say that, notwithstanding all these oaths, the sovereign prince can derogate from the laws, or break and annul them, when they cease to be just. So the oath of our kings, which is the finest and shortest that can be designed, has no bearing on the preservation of the laws and customs either of the provinces or of the king's predecessors." Bodin cited various forms of the French coronation oath to show that kings swore merely to do justice. Moreover, the ancient Hebrew kings had taken no oaths.[40] The argument and the examples chosen constituted a direct reply to the mon-

---

[36]*De Jure Magistratuum*, pp. 276–7.
[37]*Francogallia*, pp. 306–8.   On the use of the fictitious oath by Beza, Hotman and Bodin, see Ralph E. Giesey, *If Not, Not* (Princeton, 1968), pp. 20–4, 220–2.
[38]*Ibid.*, p. 221.
[39]*République* (1583), I, 8, pp. 129–30.
[40]*Ibid.*, pp. 133–6.

archomachs, and, once again, the case which Bodin presented was an application of his new doctrine of sovereignty. It is tempting to think that, when Hotman added to his 1586 Latin edition of the *Francogallia* several pages describing the role of the Aragonese Justicia in support of his view of the oath,[41] he did so to rebut Bodin's remarks on the subject in the *République*.

A third instance of a contradiction between the *Methodus* and the *République* concerns the definition of the attributes of sovereignty. Like the first two examples, the distinction is based upon Bodin's revised concept of sovereignty, but unlike them, there is no specific textual evidence that Bodin was simultaneously refuting the monarchomach ideas. The list which Bodin provided in the *Methodus* of the ways in which supreme authority could be exercised comprised: appointing the high magistrates and defining their office; ordaining and abrogating laws; declaring war and peace; hearing final appeals; and exercising the power of life and death.[42] The first three of these attributes were included in the list provided by Hotman in the 1573 edition of the *Francogallia* as having formerly been included in the powers of the estates.[43] Hotman wished to repose in the estates all, and more than all, the attributes which Bodin in the *Methodus* confided in the king.

In the *République* Bodin referred to the practice of ancient and modern writers (and it would not seem that he here had the monarchomachs in mind) of composing long lists of regalian rights which they believed to be marks of sovereignty. All these writers, Bodin declared, were mistaken. Anything that was communicated by a sovereign prince to a subject was, *ipso facto,* not an attribute of sovereignty. The rights of jurisdiction, the appointment of magistrates, the infliction of penalties, the award of honours, and the taking of counsel – none of these were marks of sovereignty. There was really only one attribute from which all others were derived, the power to make law: "Under this same power of giving and annulling law are comprised all the other rights and marks of sovereignty. So that, properly speaking, one can say that there is only this sole mark of sovereignty, in so far as all the other rights are contained within it."[44] Moreover, law made by the sovereign was superior to custom, which had binding force only in so far as the sovereign was pleased to authorise it.[45]

In their tendency to give supreme authority to the estates, as representing the

---

[41]*Francogallia*, pp. 310–4.
[42]*Methodus*, p. 175.
[43]See note 30.
[44]*République* (1583) I, 10, pp. 223–4. Bodin defines the subordinate attributes as: "to declare war and peace, to be the ultimate seat of appeal against the judgments of inferior magistrates, to impose charges and subsidies on subjects or exempt them from the same, to bestow grace and dispensation against the rigour of the laws, to raise or lower the title, value or constitution of money, to make subjects and liegemen swear to be faithful without exception to anyone to whom such oath is due."
[45]*Ibid.*, p. 222.

superiority of the kingdom as a whole over the king, the theorists of resistance lacked Bodin's precise definition of legislative sovereignty. They respected custom in its own right, and they believed that the exercise of authority ought to be shared. Hence the efficacy of Bodin's argument as a mine to destroy the defences of the monarchomachs. Through the power to make law a sovereign prince was supreme in every aspect of political authority. He could share this power with no one, nor was he obliged to obtain consent, for if he did so he was no longer sovereign, and the commonwealth no longer a monarchy.[46]

But Hotman, for one, remained unpersuaded. Just as he added the passages of Aragonese history to the 1586 version of the *Francogallia*, so, too, he added a new list of constitutional laws which had once limited the French crown. Nor were they all defensive, for the first declared that it was unlawful for the king to determine anything concerning the whole commonwealth without the authority of the estates. He now had reason to include the laws of hereditary succession, which, together with the inalienability of the domain (which he also cited), remained limitations on the sovereign accepted by Bodin. But he also added laws which seemed to answer the subordinate attributes of sovereignty listed in the *République*. These laws included the inability of the king to remit punishment for a capital crime, the irremovability of an officer of the commonwealth without trial by his peers, and the need for the estates to sanction any change in the monetary system.[47]

IV. MIXED MONARCHY, MAGISTRATES, AND ELECTION

Three other major sections of the *République* appear to be aimed at the Huguenot monarchomachs, but none of them represent any notable departure from ideas expressed in the *Methodus*, and only in one (*République* VI, 5, on the superiority of hereditary succession by male primogeniture over election and female inheritance) is it beyond doubt that Bodin was attacking the theorists of resistance.

Bodin denied the existence of the mixed or Polybian form of state in the *Methodus*, but there he found it difficult to show why the marks of sovereignty could not be distributed among different institutions.[48] In *République* II, 1, the new concept of indivisible legislative sovereignty found a dogmatic answer to the problem: "Some have wished to say and publish in print that in this way the state of France also was composed of the three kinds of commonwealth, that the parlement of Paris took an aristocratic form, the three estates a democratic one, while the king represented the royal estate. This is not only an absurd opinion: it is a capital crime, for it is treason to make subjects companions to the

[46]*Ibid.*, p. 221.
[47]*Francogallia*, pp. 458–76. Cf. Bodin's list in note 44.
[48]*Methodus*, pp. 177–81.

sovereign prince."[49] In the 1586 Latin edition Bodin inserted beside this passage a marginal reference to Du Haillan's *De l'estat et succez des affaires de France.*[50]

Bodin may possibly have noticed two approving references to Du Haillan's book in Hotman's reply to Matharel. The second reference associated Du Haillan with Seyssel, and remarked that Du Haillan had discussed the election of kings, the fallibilities of queen mothers and the corruption of the parlement.[51] Hotman provided the most persuasive exposition of mixed monarchy among the monarchomachs. He described the estates as originally a mixture of monarchic, aristocratic and popular elements, in which each tempered the others and the whole rested in harmonious balance. He cited Plato, Aristotle, Polybius, and Cicero on such a form of commonwealth.[52] In the second (1576) version of the *Francogallia* he added a long passage from Seyssel supporting his interpretation.[53]

Bernard de Girard, sieur du Haillan, represented a constitutionalist position with which Bodin and Hotman had some points in common and some of radical divergence. In his *Histoire de France* (1577) he paid tribute to his fellow constitutionalist historians, such as Jean du Tillet and Etienne Pasquier, but he seemed to have Hotman in mind when he denounced those plagiarists who had allowed respect for historical truth to be distorted by political passion: "Their imposture has been revealed in the construction of their works, for, besides their crime of insulting our kings, they have been impudent enough to borrow in the sound part of their edifice the hands and labour of better masons than they."[54] Du Haillan mentioned Bodin with respect in the preface to the second (1580) edition of *De l'estat*, but in the text of his 1594 edition he indignantly repudiated Bodin's assertion that his support of mixed monarchy was a treasonable statement. Later in the text he argued that French kings were accustomed to submit themselves voluntarily to the laws and the magistrates, and to accept limitations. The aristocratic and popular elements in French government did not detract from royal authority. Some audacious writers, remarked Du Haillan, had denied this proposition, and one of them (presumably he meant Bodin) had himself committed treason by joining the Catholic League.[55]

---

[49]*République* (1583), II, 1, pp. 262–3. It may be noted that Bodin's denial of the mixed form was not quite as simple as this. In *République* II, 2, p. 272, Bodin distinguished between the form of the state and the method of its administration. A monarchy could therefore be governed aristocratically or in a popular fashion. Arnisaeus (*De Jure Majestatis* [Strasbourg, 1635], p. 33) was to condemn Bodin for weakening his denial of the mixed state. But Bodin had done no such thing, for he did not admit the sharing of sovereignty, which was the principle underlying the doctrine of mixed monarchy.

[50]*The Six Bookes*, p. A 117 (note to p. 191).

[51]*Matagonis de Matagonibus . . . Monitoriale*, pp. 55, 60.

[52]*Francogallia*, p. 292.

[53]*Ibid.* Cf. Claude de Seyssel, *La Monarchie de France*, ed. Jacques Poujol (Paris, 1961), pp. 127–8.

[54]*L'Histoire de France* (2 vols., Paris, 1577), vol. I, Preface (unpaginated).

[55]*De l'estat et succez des affaires de France* (Paris, 1613, containing the dedications of the 1580 and

Du Haillan quoted Seyssel's views on the estates and on the three "freins" on kingship: *la religion, la justice* and *la police.*[56] Like the *Francogallia,* he saw the public council as controlling important affairs of state under the Merovingian and Carolingian dynasties, but he held all the existing institutions to have been fashioned by the Capetians.[57] Like the monarchomachs, he censured Louis XI for introducing tyranny.[58] A true constitutionalist, he saw the king as absolute within a sphere narrowly defined by law and custom, and voluntarily limited outside that sphere.[59] The paradox of a ruler at once absolute and restrained by law is a paradox only to modern minds, accustomed to the "logic" of legislative sovereignty. The passages in which Du Haillan refers to Hotman and Bodin, and those in which they mention him, indicate that the two extremes had drawn apart in opposing directions from the constitutionalist position.

The role of lesser magistrates to resist a prince who broke the conditions under which authority was entrusted to him, and flagrantly oppressed his subjects, was a major principle of monarchomach theory. Beza declared in the *De Jure Magistratuum* that lesser magistrates shared authority, albeit in an inferior capacity, with the prince. The ruler was not the source of their rights, for upon his death they remained in possession of their offices. The prince could discipline or dismiss a magistrate for failing to administer his office according to the law, and, equally, the magistrate had to resist a prince who acted as a tyrant.[60] Unlike the author of the *Vindiciae contra Tyrannos*[61] Beza did not allow the lesser magistrates to resist an idolatrous prince for religious reasons. He merely permitted resistance to a prince who tyrannically revoked edicts tolerating the exercise of true religion.[62] Like Beza, Hotman distinguished between officers of the king and those of the kingdom, and maintained that the latter had once been appointed by the estates and could not be dismissed without just cause. He did not, however, develop the idea of lesser magistrates as leaders of resistance.[63]

The section on the magistrate (*Quid magistratus*) in *Methodus* VI had dis-

---

1594 editions – the first edition appeared in 1570), Préface au lecteur (unpaginated) and pp. 191r, 191v.

[56]*De l'estat,* pp. 190v, 195v. Cf. *La Monarchie de France,* pp. 113–28.

[57]*Ibid.,* pp. 201r, 190r.

[58]*Ibid.,* pp. 186r–187v.

[59]*Ibid.,* p. 190v. "First there is the king, who is the sovereign and absolute monarch, loved, revered, feared and obeyed; and although he has all power and authority to command and do what he will, yet this great and sovereign liberty is regulated, limited and bridled by good laws and ordinances, and by the multitude and diversity of the officers, who are either close to his person or established in divers places throughout the kingdom. He is not allowed to do all things, but only what is just and reasonable and prescribed by the ordinances and the advice of his council."

[60]*De Jure Magistratuum,* pp. 245–54.

[61]*Vindiciae contra Tyrannos,* pp. 67–8.

[62]*De Jure Magistratuum,* pp. 322–3.

[63]*Francogallia,* p. 404.

cussed the relative meanings of *potestas* and *imperium* in no very conclusive fashion. The old issue of whether *merum imperium* should be possessed by a magistrate, or by the prince alone, had been treated in the following section concerning supreme authority (*Quid summum imperium*).[64] In the *République* the five chapters of the third book (III, 2–6) devoted to officers and magistrates were generally concerned with a more extensive treatment of such topics, without particular reference to the concept of sovereignty. Bodin's statement that office belonged to the commonwealth, and merely its provision to the prince,[65] made his position equivocal, and only in his discussion of the obedience owed by the magistrate to the laws and the prince (*République*, III, 4) is it possible to sense oblique reference to the monarchomach doctrine. Bodin went as far as his professional conscience would permit in denying the right of the magistrate to disobey the command of the sovereign. Although he conceded the right of the parlement to remonstrate against an edict sent to it for registration, he opposed the frequent use of this right, since it encouraged public disobedience and led to rebellion.[66] Nevertheless, he retained from the *Methodus* the example of the fearless president of the parlement, La Vacquerie, who told Louis XI he would rather be put to death than register the king's unjust edicts.[67] Bodin admitted that a magistrate might resign when confronted by an unjust command from his sovereign, but generally he should set an example of submission, for matters of equity were often complex and his own opinion might be in error. The chapter concluded with the remark that conscience and religion should not be alleged by the magistrate as grounds for disobedience.[68] It is possible to construe this as a reference to what he supposed the monarchomach doctrine of the role of lesser magistrates to be, but it does not seem likely that Bodin's other chapters on magistrates were written with this theory in mind.[69]

In his criticism of certain monarchomach doctrines Bodin neither referred to the particular works in which they were expounded nor provided any accurate account of what he was refuting. His method was the more effective because he accepted vulgar misrepresentations of these ideas, in terms of popular liberty or elective monarchy, as the targets he chose to attack. Thus in the chapter he

[64]*Methodus*, pp. 173–5.
[65]*République* (1583), III, 5, p. 436.
[66]*Ibid.*, III, 4, p. 427.
[67]*Ibid.*, p. 417. Cf. *Methodus*, p. 208.
[68]*République* (1583), III, 4, p. 429. "But it is also necessary to take care lest the pretence of conscience and ill-grounded superstition may open the way to rebellion; for since the magistrate must rely upon his conscience in the difficult matter of enforcing instructions, he may make a dangerous (*sinistre*) judgment about the conscience of his prince."
[69]Another instance which at first sight suggests the contrary occurs at *République* (1583), III, 5, p. 445. "But there is no divine or human law that permits subjects to avenge injuries done them by magistrates in deed or force, as some have thought. For if a subject be allowed to take revenge for a magisterial act or use of force, the same arguments will be used to resist sovereign princes and the laws will be trodden under foot." The marginal references, however, are to civilians, and any chance of connection with the theory of magisterial resistance appears extremely remote.

directed against election (*République*, VI, 5) he wrote: "There is need to employ necessary arguments and examples to refute the opinion that several persons print for the subjects of another [prince], and by such means encourage rebellions to change well-ordered monarchies and shake heaven and earth. That kind of thing is done under the pretence of virtue, piety and justice. There are even to be found some who dare to publish books to maintain against their natural prince, who has come to the throne by legitimate succession, that it is better to have the right of choice in a monarchy."[70] The particular example he gave to support this opinion was an Oxford disputation on the relative merits of election and hereditary succession debated before Queen Elizabeth in 1566 – perhaps the prototype of more celebrated Oxford disputations on defence of king and country. Bodin's real target would appear to have been the *Francogallia*, or its vulgarisation in the second dialogue of the *Reveille-Matin*. Since the latter work was addressed to the estates, princes, nobles and people of Poland,[71] its title would fit Bodin's remarks about encouraging rebellion against foreign rulers.

Apart from discussing European precedents for the inevitable growth of factions and conspiracies associated with royal election, Bodin assailed Hotman and his imitators upon their own ground, and reviewed the course of Frankish history. He began this section of the chapter by referring to the opinion that "the kings of France were elective, and that in former times the kingdom was subject to choice, and that such was the case with the Merovingian, Carolingian and Capetian lines."[72] It was his aim to show that each of these dynasties used rules of hereditary succession. It was an impossible task for him to demonstrate the practice of primogeniture, but he did his best. The wars between the sons of Louis the Pious, he declared, were caused by the illegal grant of the better part of the kingdom to Charles the Bald, in preference to his elder stepbrothers, Lothar and Louis.[73] Since France had been paritioned between the claimants (a practice which Bodin deplored but could hardly deny),[74] the example was not a happy one. He was also obliged to admit that Louis the Pious himself had obtained his kingdom by force of arms rather than the right of succession, for Bernard of Italy was the son of Pepin, Louis's deceased elder brother, and had the better claim by primogeniture.[75] Disputed successions between uncles and nephews in Frankish history were an awkward problem for Bodin, and he

[70]*République* (1583), VI, 5, p. 973.
[71]"Ordinibus, principibus, proceribus, baronibus, nobilibus, ac populo Poloniae Eusebius Cosmopolitanus salutem ac perpetuam foelicitatem exoptat." Preface to *Dialogi ab Eusebio Philadelpho . . . compositi*. It was, of course, common practice for Huguenot writers after the massacre of St. Bartholomew to address their tracts to foreign rulers. The *Francogallia* was dedicated to the Elector Palatine.
[72]*République* (1583), VI, 5, p. 983.
[73]*Ibid.*, pp. 985–6.
[74]*Ibid.*, p. 995.
[75]*Ibid.*, p. 993.

lamely concluded that more nephews had made good their claim than had uncles.[76]

Bodin need not have followed the monarchomachs into this morass, for he concluded that the Capetians had established the sole rights of the eldest son and the exclusion of bastards.[77] It was his purpose, however, to demonstrate in universal terms, and not merely in the context of modern France, the advantages of monarchy by male primogeniture. He also argued that the maxim "the king never dies" and the form of the royal funeral ceremony indicated that the French monarchy had never been elective.[78] Further, the text of the ceremony for the coronation of Philip I in 1058 showed that both the archbishop of Reims and the pope claimed the right to appoint a king. Their claims were to be rejected, but the text did, at least, show the error of those who maintained the popular election of kings.[79] When Bodin came to discuss the advent of the Carolingians and Capetians he asserted that it was the consent of the nobility, and not of the estates, that had enabled Pepin the Short and Hugh Capet to establish their respective lines.[80]

The *Reveille-Matin* had exhibited the same distaste for gynaecocracy as did Bodin's chapter on male primogeniture and the perils of election, but in every other respect its views were clearly anathema to Bodin. In addition to its list of deposed kings, it argued that the best form of monarchy was a combination of heredity and election. Preferably the crown should remain in one family, but the best representative should be chosen, and minorities should be avoided. The Capetians were declared to be usurpers.[81] Some of these opinions were at variance with the views of the *Francogallia*, but Hotman's historic vision proved no more acceptable to the author of the *République* than did the *Reveille-Matin*.

Although the *Antitribonian* and the *Methodus* adopted identical viewpoints on the fallibility of Roman Law and the need to combine history and jurisprudence,[82] the actual history written by their authors was in most respects mutually incompatible. Each writer originated a fruitful historical myth. Bodin exalt-

---

[76]*Ibid.*, p. 994. Bodin provided a long discussion of the respective rights of uncles and nephews, concluding in favour of the latter, and mentioning the likely relevance of the issue to the succession problem of his own day. Bodin altered his opinion under the League.

Hotman discussed the issue at length in *Quaestionum illustrium liber* (2d ed. 1576, III, pp. 27–34). He concluded in favour of the uncle, but after 1584 he also changed his mind and in his works on the succession supported the claim of Henri de Navarre against his uncle, the cardinal de Bourbon (*Disputatio de controversia successionis regiae inter patruum et fratris praemortui filium*, 1585: *Consilia*, 1586: *De Iure successionis regiae in regno Francorum*, 1588: *Ad tractatum Matthaei Zampini . . . responsio*, 1588).

[77]*République* (1583), VI, 5, p. 995.

[78]*Ibid.*, p. 986. Reference to the funeral ceremony is a later addition. (*The Six Bookes*, p. 733).

[79]*République* (1583), VI, 5, pp. 984–6. The document on the coronation of Philip I had already been quoted at I, 8, p. 136.

[80]*Ibid.*, VI, 5, p. 983.

[81]*Dialogi ab Eusebio Philadelpho . . . compositi*, vol. 2, pp. 63–5.

[82]Cf. Julian H. Franklin, *Jean Bodin and the Sixteenth-Century Revolution in the Methodology of Law and History* (New York, 1963), p. 68.

ed the prowess of the Celts, and represented the Franks as Gallic colonists established east of the Rhine five centuries before Caesar.[83] Hotman glorified the Franks as the Germanic standard-bearers of liberty (although the *Francogallia* actually gave some credit to ancient Gallic institutions). Hotman's thesis that a public council, similar to the modern estates, had elected and deposed kings at will, and had divided the kingdom among them, was a wilder distortion than Bodin's. Hotman massed his citations with far greater skill (but with less objectivity) than Bodin employed in the *République*, where examples were constantly being introduced which contradicted the case they were meant to support. As already mentioned, Hotman did not intend to imply that the French monarchy should be restored to an elective form. His reference to Plutarch's remark on choosing a horse or a dog for its personal qualities rather than its breeding was merely a piece of rhetoric.[84] His stress upon Frankish election was meant to demonstrate the former sovereignty of the estates, and when he referred to the need to return to the pristine constitution, it was this he had in mind.

It was in this respect, rather than upon the issue of elective monarchy, that the *Francogallia* represented the most powerful challenge to the *République*. Accepting political change in historical terms, Bodin provided an empirical answer to Hotman's fundamentalism; yet he developed a fundamentalism of his own in rational and universal terms. Each of the two moved away from a constitutionalism to which they had once adhered in a comparable but not identical form. Traces of their former similarity remained in their writings to confuse later commentators. But Bodin's doctrine of an absolute sovereignty reposed in the French crown seems to have been enunciated in reaction to the concept of the sovereignty of the community through the estates, as implied in the works of Hotman and his fellow monarchomachs.

For all this, those sections of the *République* in which Bodin has been shown to have been following one of the purposes declared in his prefaces, and correcting the supposed errors of the Huguenot polemicists, constitute but a small proportion of the massed erudition in the book. The relationship between Bodin and the monarchomachs does not suggest that the *République* as a whole was a *livre de circonstance:* what it does suggest is that the concept of sovereignty was a *thèse de circonstance.*

[83]*Methodus*, pp. 244–51.
[84]*Francogallia*, p. 220.

6

~~~~~~

An alternative theory of popular resistance: Buchanan, Rossaeus, and Locke

Theories of jurisprudence owe much to the development of concepts of natural law and sovereignty used to justify resistance to constituted authority in the early modern period. It has long been a commonplace that there was a continuity in resistance doctrine from fifteenth-century conciliarism to the Glorious Revolution. This orthodoxy is encapsulated in Laski's phrase: "The road from Constance to 1688 is a direct one." It underlies the theme of Gierke's *Natural Law and the Theory of Society*, and it is reiterated in J. N. Figgis's Birkbeck lectures *From Gerson to Grotius*.[1] This paper suggests that there was a byway as well as a highway: not one road, but two.

The theorists of resistance held that political authority was created by the consent of the entire community and that, if it was exercised in a way contrary to the welfare of the community, it could be withdrawn. Thus the decrees of the Council of Constance declared ultimate authority in the church lay not with the pope but with the whole body of the faithful, and its exercise rested in their representative, the general council. This argument was applied to the secular state as well as to the church by such conciliar theorists of the time as Gerson, who saw the need for coercive power as the consequence of sin.[2] At the beginning of the sixteenth century the conciliarists Jacques Almain and John Mair located sovereignty in the whole body of the citizens, who empowered the ruler to act as their delegate for the common good. A tyrant who acted with contrary intent might be deprived of his authority.[3]

During the wars of religion Calvinist monarchomachs such as Beza (*De Jure Magistratuum*, 1574) and "Stephanus Junius Brutus" (*Vindiciae contra Tyrannos*, 1579), together with such a theorist of the Catholic league as Boucher (*De Justa*

---

[1]Francis Oakley, On the Road from Constance to 1688: the Political Thought of John Major and George Buchanan, *Journal of British Studies*, 2 (1962), 1–32; Quentin Skinner, *The Foundations of Modern Political Thought* (Cambridge, 1978), vol. 2, p. 123.

[2]R. W. and A. J. Carlyle, *A History of Mediaeval Political Theory in the West* (Edinburgh, 1950), vol. 4, pp. 158–64.

[3]Francis Oakley, "Almain and Major: Conciliar Theory on the Eve of the Reformation," *American Historical Review*, 70 (1964–1965), 673–90.

Henrici Tertii Abdicatione, 1589), cited conciliarist theory or precedent to justify the right of the established orders, who represented the sovereignty of the people, to lead resistance against a tyrant. In their secular aspect these "inferior magistrates" were both guardians and executors of a contract between king and people which, if voided by the ruler, allowed the people to withdraw their obedience under the direction of their natural leaders in the social hierarchy.[4] This mainstream of resistance theory considered the community as a self-sufficing Aristotelian entity, and lacked the individualist premises to speculate about a state of nature and a social contract prior to the contract of government. If man was by nature a social animal, he could not be conceived as man in any presocial condition. Further, the society of which he was a member alone enabled him to attain his potentiality, so that it was his end as well as his nature in the teleological sense of Aristotelian φυσις. By this organic imagery society was more than the aggregate of the individuals who composed it, the whole more than the sum of its parts. Finally, the doctrine of popular sovereignty was strengthened in its collectivist import by the corporative theory of the *universitas* borrowed from the glosses of canonists and civilians.[5]

In the seventeenth century the concept of popular sovereignty delineated by Protestant and Catholic monarchomachs, together with opposing doctrines of absolutist sovereignty advanced by their critics, were commented upon by Dutch and German thinkers such as Althusius, Grotius, Arnisaeus and Besoldus,[6] and then applied to English revolutionary situations where they were utlimately to be restated in an original form in Locke's *Second Treatise.* To this point little or nothing along the highroad from Constance to 1688 has suggested the sudden emergence of Locke's individualist presuppositions. With Locke organic and telological models have been replaced by mechanistic ones.

[4]As originally propounded at Magdeburg in the context of the Schmalkaldic Wars, the doctrine of the inferior magistrates was a response to religious oppression (see Robert M. Kingdon, "The First Expression of Theodore Beza's Political Ideas," *Archiv für Reformationsgeschichte,* 46 (1955), 88–100). The Huguenots, however, assimilated it to the secular as well as the religious aspects of their propaganda. Justification of resistance on religious grounds is not generally considered here, although it was, of course, a major element in French Calvinist and Leaguer theory. Among recent analyses of French sixteenth-century resistance theory are: Richard Benert, *Inferior Magistrates in Sixteenth-Century Political and Legal Thought* (University of Minnesota dissertation, 1967); Jürgen Dennert, *Beza, Brutus, Hotman: Calvinistische Monarchomachen* (Köln, 1968); Julian H. Franklin, *Constitutionalism and Resistance in the Sixteenth Century* (New York, 1969); Ralph E. Giesey, "The Monarchomach Triumvirs: Hotman, Beza and Mornay," *Bibliothèque d'Humanisme et Renaissance,* 32 (1970), 41–56; Ralph E. Giesey and J. H. M. Salmon, *"Francogallia" by François Hotman* (Cambridge, 1972); Frederic J. Baumgartner, *Radical Reactionaries: the Political Thought of the French Catholic League* (Geneva, 1975); and Skinner, *Foundations,* vol. 2.
[5]Otto von Gierke, *Political Theories of the Middle Age,* tr. F. W. Maitland (Cambridge, 1951 [1900]), pp. 64ff.; J. H. M. Salmon, *The French Religious Wars in English Political Thought* (Oxford, 1959), pp. 41–2. A recent study has criticised Gierke for his unhistorical impatience with the Aristotelian setting of early contract theory and his desire to read back into expressions of the contract of government the individualist implications of the social contract (See Harro Höpfl and Martyn P. Thompson, "The History of Contract as a Motif in Political Thought," *American Historical Review,* 84 [1979], 919–44).
[6]Salmon, *French Religious Wars,* pp. 39–57.

Natural law has been transformed into individualist natural right. A state of nature has been postulated in which men, or, at least, most men, are still moved by a sense of moral obligation. The contract of government has been subsumed by the social contract, by which men renounce their own execution of natural law in order to safeguard their basic natural rights to life, liberty and estate, and by which a majority determine the form of government. Authority to resist remains with the body of the people, and even individual resistance is allowed when natural right is endangered.[7] The idea of popular sovereignty survives in the argument (derived by way of George Lawson from Besoldus and hence indirectly from sixteenth-century resistance theory), that should government dissolve but society remain cohesive, a constituent power to set up a new government resides in the people.[8] Here lie paradoxes which perplex those who, like Rousseau, would seek to reconcile collective popular sovereignty with individual liberty, or, like Locke himself, the altruistic moral imperatives of natural law with the self-regarding demands of natural right.

It is not the purpose of this paper to present new logical solutions to these problems, but, from the historical point of view, it may help to suggest that there was an alternative line of sixteenth-century resistance theory, less defined perhaps than that of the more typical monarchomachs, and hence undeserving of the status of a main road upon the map. It is represented by George Buchanan, the Protestant Scottish humanist, and "Gulielmus Rossaeus," who was probably William Reynolds, the apostate Englishman whose Catholic extremism was called into service by the French Holy League.[9] Despite their religious polarity, they held in common two principal proto-Lockean concepts and a number of minor atypical opinions. Their two common main positions were their acceptance of a presocial state of nature, and their belief that the people really did exercise authority. With regard to the former it should be mentioned that their

[7]Few opinions about Locke are likely to escape criticism. Here I have followed Quentin Skinner (*Foundations*, vol. 2, p. 338). My own views have been heavily influenced by Peter Laslett at the time he was preparing his edition of *Locke's Two Treatises of Government* (Cambridge, 1963). For a general commentary on schools of interpretation see Charles H. Monson, "Locke and his Interpreters," *Political Studies*, 6 (1958), 120–33. See also John Dunn, *The Political Thought of John Locke*, (Cambridge, 1969), and Richard Tuck, *Natural Rights Theories, their Origin and Development* (Cambridge, 1979).

[8]This theme is elaborated by Julian H. Franklin, *John Locke and the Theory of Sovereignty* (Cambridge, 1978).

[9]On the identity of Rossaeus see Charles Labitte, *De la Démocratie chez les prédicateurs de la Ligue* (Paris, 1866, [1841]) pp. 373–7; C. H. McIlwain, *Constitutionalism and the Changing World* (New York, 1939), pp. 178–82; Salmon, *French Religious Wars*, pp. 75–6; Hermann Vahle, "Boucher und Rossaeus: zur politischen Theorie und Praxis der französischen Liga (1576–1595)," *Archiv für Kulturgeschichte*, 56 (1974), 341–2; Baumgartner, *Radical Reactionaries*, pp. 145–7. I now lean more to the opinion that the author was Rainolds (or Reynolds) because of seventeenth-century opinion to that effect. See P. R. (Robert Parsons), *A Treatise Tending to Mitigation towards Catholicke Subjectes in England* (n.p., 1607), pp. 68–9; Thomas Morton, *A Preamble unto an Incounter with P. R.* (London, 1608), p. 39; David Owen, *Herod and Pilate Reconciled* (London, 1610), p. 36 (but note confusion with Boucher); Henry Foulis, *The History of Romish Treasons and Usurpations* (London, 1671), p. 506; Edward Stillingfleet, *The Jesuits Loyalty* (London, 1677), p. 9.

Aristotelianism was mitigated by a strong dose of Ciceronian influence: as to the latter, it should not be thought that they were in any sense egalitarian, but merely that they refused to allow the sovereignty of the people to be permanently associated with any particular elitist institution.

Both Buchanan and Rossaeus were familiar with the conciliarist tradition. Buchanan was a pupil of Mair and cites the Council of Basel in his major theoretical work *De Jure Regni apud Scotos* (1579).[10] Rossaeus frequently quotes the pronouncement of the Council of Constance, and their anticipation at the Gothic Councils of Toledo, in *De Justa Reipublicae Christianae Authoritate* (1590).[11] It may well be that the radical strand of populism discernible in the two monarchomachs descends from a particular element in conciliarism itself. Both Mair and Almain were indebted to Ockham and Gerson, and relied upon Stoic and patristic ideas at least as much as they did upon Aristotle. Hence they tended to see political authority as the result of the fall, or, at least, as associated as much with the vicious as with the moral element in human nature. Almain, but not, it seems, Mair, took this attitude a stage further by anticipating Buchanan, Rossaeus and Locke, and suggesting that there had been a time when there was no social organisation and every man executed natural law as he saw fit. Further, while both conciliarists maintained that the ruler was merely the delegate of the sovereign community and could be deposed, Mair placed the power to depose in the estates as the representatives of the people, while Almain held that the whole community dethroned a tyrant king.[12]

It is true, of course, that Buchanan had been Mair's pupil, but both his humanist tastes and his religion caused him to react against his master in later years. Both men exemplified their political theory in history. Mair in his *Historia Majoris Britanniae et Scotiae* (1521), and Buchanan in his *Rerum Scoticarum Historia* (1582), discussed the circumstances in which kings had lost their crowns. The difference between the two authors is epitomised in an ironic passage in the seventh book of the latter work, where several of the depositions are described: "Although John Mair, who had a great reputation in the study of theology when I was a boy, honours the remaining acts of this king [David 1] with lavish praise, he parades in an indigestible piece of rhetoric (would that it were less true on that account!) the king's profuse largesse to the monasteries."[13] While nothing could be more alien to Buchanan than his former

---

[10]Oakley, "Major and Buchanan," p. 20.

[11]*De Justa Reipublicae Christianae in Reges Impios et Haereticos Authoritate* (Paris, 1590), 42r, 390r, 391r, 391v.

[12]Skinner, *Foundations*, vol. 2, pp. 118–23. A. J. Carlyle, *Mediaeval Political Theory*, vol. 6, pp. 241–8, also points out that Almain asserted that the form of government was a matter of popular choice and could be altered at will. Here again it is Almain, and not Mair, who anticipates Buchanan and Rossaeus. However, neither of the two monarchomachs admitted a particular debt to Almain. In his account of the ideas of Almain and Mair (note 3 above), Oakley accentuates the similarities rather than the differences between the two.

[13]*Rerum Scoticarum Historia* (Edinburgh, 1727 [1582]), p. 186.

master's Latin style and his theology, the intensity of the crisis involving the deposition of Mary Queen of Scots in 1567 moved him to rewrite the Scottish part of Mair's history, and to adapt conciliar theory to the current situation in the dialogue he also began to compose at this time, *De Jure Regni apud Scotos*.[14] In so far as he looked to history to reveal the unchanging principles of an ancient constitution, his writing assumed a specious aura of conservatism: in so far as he reshaped other men's ideas to fit the present cause, it revealed a new and radical dimension.

To refute those who would defend the queen, Buchanan thought it necessary to go back to first principles and establish the origin and purpose of society. He asks Maitland, his interlocutor in the dialogue: "Do you think that there was once a time when men lived in shelters and even in caves, lacking laws and settled abodes, and strayed about as wanderers, meeting as the mood took them, or as some [temporary] advantage or common utility brought them to- gether?"[15] When Maitland agrees and observes that it must have been the utility of providing a secure defence against enemies that put an end to this vagrant and solitary existence, Buchanan contradicts him and asserts that the pursuit of self-interest would dissolve rather than unite society. The impulse to communal living is "a certain force of nature (*quaedam naturae vis*)." While this can operate for animals as well as men, human beings alone can apprehend it rationally because it is "a light infused into our minds from heaven (*lux animis nostris divinitus infusa*)," and by it man can also "distinguish the moral from the base (*quo turpia ab honestis secerneret*)." This, says Buchanan, is what is known as *lex naturae*, and he supports his opinion with two authorities. The first is the gospel according to St. Luke (10, 27) where we are enjoined to love God *ex animo* and our neighbours as ourselves, and the second is an alleged quotation from Cicero that nothing is more pleasing to God "than the unions of men united by law which are called civil communities (*quam coetus hominum jure sociatos quae civitates appellantur*)." Maitland is finally convinced that the first formation of society is the result of divine illumination, and not man's self- perception of advantage, when Buchanan explains in organicist language that the urge to combine in such a community is so strong that its parts are united as if they were limbs to a human body.[16]

---

[14]H. R. Trevor-Roper, *George Buchanan and the Ancient Scottish Constitution*, English Historical Review, Supplement 3 (London, 1966). Note also internal textual evidence for the date of composition of *De Jure Regni*. In a passage illustrating his belief in the fixed constitution Buchanan remarks: "Istam enim potestatem Regibus nostris nunquam fuisse, praeter supplicia male administrati regni toties expetita, Joannis Ballioli calamitas ostendit: qui fere CCLX abhinc anno a nobilitate rejectus est, quod se regnumque suum Eduardi Angli imperio subjecisset: inque locum ejus Robertus Primus est suffectus. Ostendit id etiam perpetuus ille mos a primis usque temporibus continuates." *De Jure Regni apud Scotos*, p. 35. The date when Robert I replaced Balliol was 1306. "Nearly 260 years from this year" would suggest 1566, rather than 1567.

[15]*De Jure Regni*, p. 5. J. H. Burns, "The Political Ideas of George Buchanan," *Scottish Historical Review*, 30 (1951), 60–8, has noted the unreliability of available translations. I have made my own translations of both Buchanan and Rossaeus.

[16]*De Jure Regni*, pp. 6–7.

At first sight there is very little here that would seem to point to a Lockean position. Indeed, the whole passage may serve as a warning against the dangers of an anachronistic reading of Buchanan. Nonetheless, a curious tension has been created. The real Ciceronian source for Buchanan's state of nature does not contain the phrase he attributes to the master of rhetoric. The words in which presocial man is depicted echo an early passage in *De Inventione*, a youthful work about which the mature Cicero was to confess his embarrassment. In an attempt to explain the origin of eloquence Cicero speculates that men once lived as animals, scattering their seed indiscriminately and existing by physical strength and unreasoning passion. Only a great orator, says Cicero, could have assembled such creatures and changed them from wild beasts into gentle and reasoning beings.[17] Buchanan took the idea of presocial man from this passage and substituted divine illumination for the orator. Indeed, in this very section of *De Jure Regni* he explicitly scorns the idea that an orator could have had anything to do with the creation of organised society.[18] But Buchanan was equally familiar with Cicero's much more defensible argument in *De Officiis* which emphasises human rationality in calculating the utility of communal living. In common with animals man was endowed with the natural instincts of self-preservation and the desire to procreate, but he alone possessed reason, the faculty that caused men to become associated in society and to recognise mutual obligations.[19] In this way one could measure moral virtue by the extent to which it contributed to social harmony.[20] With an avowed debt to the Stoics, Cicero set out in *De Officiis* to reconcile the moral and the useful.

Thus, having slammed the front door in the face of Maitland's argument about utility, Buchanan allowed it to return by a back entrance. Human society from its beginning was infected with a sickness. The pursuit of self-interest and the exercise of the baser passions had to be curbed. A doctor was needed, and that doctor was government. Buchanan argues that the exact form the government takes does not matter so long as rulers are created by the people to provide justice. But the physician himself may be affected by the disease and may put his own pleasure before the common good. "Because the authority constituted for the public utility turns to proud domination (*quod publicae utilitate caussa fuerat constitutum imperium in superbam dominationem vertit*)," the people have to find laws to restrain the ruler to his duty.[21] In this context Buchanan cites *De Officiis* to show that laws must have been created by the people for the same reason that kings were, and that the only just law is an impartial one.[22] Cicero is Buchanan's main authority: Plato and Aristotle are declared less relevant to his purpose. The art of government proceeds through

[17]Cicero, *De Inventione*, 1.II.2.
[18]*De Jure Regni*, p. 7.
[19]Cicero, *De Officiis*, 1. IV.11–12.
[20]*Ibid.*, 1. XLIV.157–8.
[21]*De Jure Regni*, pp. 10–11.
[22]*Ibid.*, p. 12. Cicero, *De Officiis*, II.41–2.

Ciceronian prudence, and the dominant concept is Cicero's utilitarian maxim: *Populi salus suprema lex esto.*[23]

The welfare of the people is the overriding consideration, and power to make law, as well as to create and depose kings, lies in them. These were opinions that Buchanan shared with his Huguenot counterparts. but he differed from their doctrine of virtual representation. In this respect he was a more radical populist than they, and one should not pay too much attention to terms such as "the ignorant multitude (*multitudo imperita*)" and "the many-headed monster (*bellua multorum capitum*)" employed by Maitland in the dialogue.[24] Of course, Buchanan does not assume that some massed popular assembly can conceivably frame the constitutional laws needed to limit the ruler. When Maitland scoffs at the rashness and inconstancy of the mob, Buchanan replies: "I never believed that this matter (the actual framing of the laws) ought to be entrusted to the consideration of the whole people, but that, rather like our own custom, men are chosen from all the orders to go together to the king in council. From there, where the taking of counsel had been done among them, it is recommended to the judgment of the people."[25] Buchanan does not see inferior magistrates or estates as regularly exercising popular sovereignty. He mentions Roman tribunes and Spartan ephors, but only to ask why a free people, if they find such magistrates ineffective in restraining rulers, should not directly invoke their inalienable authority.[26] In some countries, Buchanan remarks, the estates meet to elect a king and make laws, but this is not a practice he favours. A simple set of laws is better than a series of legislative proposals by the estates.[27] The people are the real lawgiver, and in Scotland the ancient laws are ratified with every king at his coronation, where the ceremony symbolises the people's consent.[28]

When Maitland objects that it is absurd to expect the whole people to agree upon anything, Buchanan reveals the extent of his populism. If unanimity were expected, he argues, no law could be made nor any magistrate appointed, since there cannot be a law just enough for all nor any man devoid of critics. It is, therefore, the majority of the people who express the sovereign power, and it is this same *major pars* that must judge the tyrant. This particular term was combined by the conciliarists, and even by Marsilius of Padua, with the expression *valentior pars*, to mean the established orders in society. If, as has been asserted,[29] Buchanan intended this by *major pars*, his position would be the typical monarchomach one, where popular sovereignty resided effectively in the

[23]*De Jure Regni*, p. 18.
[24]*Ibid.*, pp. 13, 17.
[25]*Ibid.*, p. 17.
[26]*Ibid.*, p. 48.
[27]*Ibid.*, pp. 36, 23.
[28]*Ibid.*, p. 35.
[29]Oakley, "Major and Buchanan," pp. 18–19, 24–6.

estates. The full passage, however, shows that Buchanan differs fundamentally from Mair and his Huguenot adapters. Maitland demands greater precision and asks to whom the greater part transfer their power when judging a king. With that evasive irony which adds charm to the dialogue while detracting from the logical progression of its ideas, Buchanan turns the question back to his interlocutor. Maitland then denounces the baser instincts of the populace. This Buchanan will admit only for a minority. It is the many who suffer from the crimes of the tyrant: the few who benefit from tyranny and betray society by supporting it. At this point Buchanan does introduce a qualitative element in the *major pars,* but it is not one that gives added weight to the opinion of the élite. Those whose lusts abet the tyrant should not be reckoned as citizens at all. The true citizens are those "who obey the laws, who care for human society, who prefer every labour and every danger regardless of their own safety rather than growing old through immoral idleness and sloth, men whose endeavours, while unrecognised in the present, are remembered in eternity."[30] They may not be leaders, but they are reliable followers in the common cause. "And so, if the citizens are counted not in terms of their number but in terms of their worthiness, not only the better but also the greater part will stand for liberty, morality and security."[31] Here, *mutatis mutandis,* is something similar to Rousseau's explanation that to ascertain the general will one does not count heads among those whose selfish aims do not harmonise with it. Just as it is wrong to attribute a doctrine of elitist representation to Buchanan, so also is it mistaken to read into him the Lockean concept of a purely quantitative majority.[32]

It will be noted that Buchanan has evaded the issue of precisely how the people act in a constitutional crisis. In fact, the mechanism may vary, but, whatever the means, the power of the people should be expressed in the outcome. As Buchanan puts it, "I do not think it necessary to pursue by conjecture what the people is to do when I see what it has done."[33] John Balliol had been rejected by the nobility. James III had been put to death and the deed endorsed by the Scottish estates.[34] In these, and in other examples cited in *Rerum Scoticarum Historia,* Buchanan notes the variety of ways in which past tyrants had been punished. Although he refers to the conventional attributes of the tyrant (arbitrary taxation, cruelty and lust, the use of a foreign bodyguard), Buchanan defines tyranny generally as government without consent, the reign of a master over slaves, as distinct from that of a free man over free men.[35] The call to action came when the king broke the *pactio mutua* between king and

---

[30]*De Jure Regni,* p. 49.
[31]*Ibid.*
[32]Cf. J. W. Allen, *A History of Political Thought in the Sixteenth Century* (London, 1941 [1928]), p. 341.
[33]*De Jure Regni,* p. 36.
[34]*Ibid.,* pp. 35–45.
[35]*Ibid.,* p. 28.

citizens.[36] A king who acted for the dissolution of the society he was created to preserve became a public enemy. His subjects could then conduct a just war against him, and it was lawful not only for the whole people but for any private man to kill him.[37] Private resistance was not authorised by Beza and Brutus, but they did allow a usurper to be so attacked, whereas Buchanan denies permission to take private action against a usurper who rules with moderation.

Buchanan also occupies an unusual position on the role of the church towards a tyrant. It was for the secular judge to condemn him to death: the church should ensure the damnation of his soul. Yet in quoting St. Paul to the Corinthians (1.5) Buchanan seems to suggest that the faithful must hold no commerce with a criminal ruler, and hence in addition to excommunicating a heretical king, the church should at least offer counsel against a king whose crime is secular oppression.[38] In an earlier section of the dialogue Buchanan denied that Paul's injunction to obey constituted powers (Romans 13.1–2) applied to tyrants, and went on to argue that the jurisdictions of kings and bishops, although apparently distinct, overlapped in practice.[39] In this, and in many other opinions, there is a remarkably close parallel with that other exceptional monarchomach, Rossaeus.

The resemblances between the ideas of Buchanan and those of Rossaeus, and their joint differences from their respective co-religionists, might suggest that the theorist of the League had borrowed arguments from the Scottish humanist, just as Boucher unquestionably did from Beza and Brutus. Rossaeus's savage denunciation of Protestant heresy in general and of Calvinist political theory in particular does not render this supposition as unlikely as it would seem to do. Later critics of the monarchomachs could also argue that the parallelism between Calvinist and ultra-Catholic resistance theory was due less to plagiarism than to both parties having a common source in conciliarism.[40] However this may be, it is certain that Rossaeus gave a careful reading to both Buchanan's *Rerum Scoticarum Historia* and his *De Jure Regni apud Scotos*. The first is the subject of hostile comment early in Rossaeus's treatise, and the second is quoted with a measure of approval towards the end of his massive work. In the first instance Rossaeus attempts to show that Calvinists misapplied the authority that the people possessed over the ruler, and that they stirred up "the indiscriminate populace (*multitudo promiscua*)" for their own heretical ends.[41] His particular example is the deposition of Mary Queen of Scots, and

[36]*Ibid.*, p. 53. This is the only occasion in *De Jure Regni* when Buchanan used the terminology of the monarchomach contract of government.
[37]*Ibid.*
[38]*Ibid.*, p. 55.
[39]*Ibid.*, p. 41.
[40](John Maxwell) *Sacro Sancta Regum Majestas* (London, 1680 [1644]), p. 19. Cf. Salmon, *French Religious Wars*, p. 91.
[41]*De Justa Authoritate*, pp. 11r–11v.

his account of her downfall is laced with partial and misleading quotations from Buchanan's none-too-objective history. The two biases in no way cancelled each other out. To Buchanan the deposition was the just application of the sovereignty of the people. To Rossaeus it was the product of "the satanic pride and tyranny of those ministers (*satanica istorum ministorum superbia et tyrannis*)" who seized the government in defiance of the will of the majority. Rossaeus distorted Buchanan's text to make it appear that the queen was deposed for attending mass, despite the fact that she had been exempted from the law banning the Catholic rite. "I say nothing," Rossaeus continued, "about the iniquity of that decree, which they call a law, established by a few rebels against the will of most nobles and leading citizens."[42]

Rossaeus's second major reference to Buchanan occurs in the tenth chapter of *De Justa Authoritate*, where the author wishes to demonstrate two propositions: that Protestants wrongly declare any Catholic ruler who oppresses them to be a tyrant deserving death from any private citizen; and that, nonetheless, a real tyrant may lawfully be killed by an individual subject. Rossaeus could reproach Beza for defending Poltrot de Méré, the assassin of the Catholic leader François de Guise, but it was not easy to find texts from Luther, Calvin or Beza that demonstrated the first proposition. Rossaeus settled in the end for the decree of the Council of Constance that had listed the killing of sinful rulers by private men as one of Wyclif's heresies used by the Council to condemn John Huss.[43] As to the second proposition, Rossaeus had to admit the validity of some Protestant teaching on secular tyranny: "We are, therefore, unable to disprove what Protestants are wont to declaim in general against tyrants, and we do not deny that many of these things are true. So we concede what these men claim and what they preach in their books on the subject."[44] At this point Rossaeus quotes at length one of Buchanan's most eloquent denunciations of tyranny in *De Jure Regni:* "In the same way as bandits are punished who cross the frontiers of human society, those tyrants who never wished to enter the voting place must be regarded as enemies to God and men, and I think they should be treated as a species of wolf or some other kind of noxious animal rather than as men, and he who nourishes them nourishes ruin for himself and others, while he who kills them benefits not only himself but everyone together."[45] Rossaeus goes on to cite more from this passage, which he approves so strongly that he remarks it should have the force of law throughout the Christian world. He also endorses remarks about the nature of tyranny in Buchanan's history of Scotland.[46] Other references to Buchanan in *De Justa*

---

[42]*Ibid.*, p. 12v. Cf. *Rerum Scoticarum Historia*, pp. 515–16.
[43]*De Justa Authoritate*, pp. 390v–391r. On the decrees see Elie Dupin, *A New Ecclesiastical History* (London, 1699), vol. 13, pp. 120–3.
[44]*De Justa Authoritate*, p. 387v.
[45]*Ibid.*, pp. 387v–388r. Cf. *De Jure Regni*, p. 30.
[46]*De Justa Authoritate*, pp. 388r–388v. Cf. *Rerum Scoticarum Historia*, p. 171.

Authoritate convey the impression that Rossaeus was more sympathetic towards him than he was to any other Protestant writer.[47] While their views of secular resistance and tyrannicide are often extremely close,[48] it is apparent that Rossaeus is capable of taking one of Buchanan's ideas and developing it in an unexpected way.

Although published early in 1590, *De Justa Authoritate* bears a privilege dated November 10, 1589, and signed by Pierre Senault, who was one of the inner group in the revolutionary movement of the Sixteen, the registrar of the parlement, and the secretary of the new council of the League established in January 1590. There is a possibility that the populism of the treatise corresponds with the increasingly radical trend within Leaguer politics. A recent study of the political ideas of Boucher and Rossaeus within the context of the tactics of the League sees the former as manipulating the revolutionary element in Paris while disdaining its lower-class component.[49] This certainly fits in with Boucher's view of popular sovereignty as exercised by the higher orders and the estates general. It does not, however, fit Rossaeus. The latter gives no hint within the treatise of being close to the Sixteen. In fact the disguise he uses in the first edition of *De Justa Authoritate* is "G.G.R.A. Peregrinus Romanus (a Roman foreigner)," the pseudonym "Rossaeus" appearing only with the 1592 Antwerp edition. The dedication to the League's leader, the duc de Mayenne, and the concluding exhortation to accept the League's candidate for the throne, the cardinal de Bourbon, show familiarity with the general policy of the ultra-Catholic party but suggest no inside knowledge of affairs. There is no certainty, particularly if Rossaeus is William Reynolds, that the author was even in Paris for any extended period. In short, there is no reason to suppose that such radical conclusions as Rossaeus reached were the result of close association with some members of the Sixteen. These conclusions follow independently from his abstract premises, rather than constituting some kind of theoretical distillation from the practical politics of a particular group.

Just as Buchanan, in his revision of Cicero's *De Inventione*, states that it was the light of nature, and not some orator, which moved men to unite in society, so Rossaeus asserts that they abandoned their solitary existence because they were impelled by a natural force within them, *naturae lumen*. "It was not by the persuasion of eloquent men, for there were no such men among them, nor by the authority of any king, for no authority whatever existed at that point, nor, lastly, by any artificial cause such as ignorant men may devise."[50] Rossaeus is

---

[47]E.g., *De Justa Authoritate*, p. 131r, where Rossaeus cites Buchanan on the doctrinal instability of the English Calvinist, Anthony Gilby.

[48]It should be noted, however, that Rossaeus has a more complex classification of the kinds of tyranny, and his last category, the king who tries to destroy the Catholic faith, is, of course, one that Buchanan could never entertain. *Ibid.*, pp. 85r–92v.

[49]Vahle, "Boucher und Rossaeus." For a more detailed study of the Sixteen see below, pp. 235–66.

[50]*De Justa Authoritate*, p. 3v. Cf. *De Jure Regni*, p. 7 (note 18 above).

more of an Aristotelian than Buchanan, and is anxious to stress the power of the social instinct. At the same time, like Buchanan, he knew Cicero's stress upon the rationality of nature and man's apprehension of it. In order to explain the transition from the ignorant and unreasoning state of nature, Rossaeus develops the theory of divine illumination in a more sophisticated way than his Scottish counterpart. The light of nature is the gift of reason, and it is this that develops "the ingenuity and perspicacity of the human mind (*mentis humanae solertia et perspicacitas*)." As he is moved unconsciously to live in a community man suddenly becomes aware of its individual and general advantages. Nature works through both instinct and reason, and hence it can be said: "Nature induced unions and communities of men; nature made city states; nature instituted commonwealths."[51]

Rossaeus also stresses the helplessness and inadequacy of man in isolation from his fellows. A man has no natural weapons comparable to those of animals. The human infant cannot even move its lips to its mother's breast unaided. Such weakness is not merely physical: it is also mental. The mind cannot acquire knowledge without experience and training: "Although nature may introduce certain sparks of virtue and learning in us, nevertheless these intimations have to be developed by the instruction of teachers, for otherwise they would be extinguished at once in the very cradle."[52] In a subsequent passage Rossaeus explains that intimations of this kind are responsible for the beginning of society: "And so, in order to provide for the necessities of body and mind, these seeds of the virtues implanted in our minds drew dispersed and disparate men together into one place."[53] In this way instinct and rationality are in harmony, and the consequences of the social drive thenceforth become rationalised in human choice as to a form of government. The outcome is very like Buchanan's *lux animis nostris divinitus infusa*, but Rossaeus's endeavour to explain human nature in the presocial condition has raised certain issues which were to concern Locke and to which we shall return. Nor has the influence of Cicero ceased to be important, for Rossaeus concludes his account of the formation of society with a quotation from *De Amicitia* to show that friendship, an intense form of the social instinct, is the most precious thing that man possesses, and one that is not based upon self-interest.[54] Rossaeus could cite both Cicero and Aristotle without seeming contradiction.[55]

Like Locke, Rossaeus was not content to theorise about the origin of society.

---

[51]*De Justa Authoritate*, p. 4*r*.

[52]*Ibid.*, p. 2*r*.

[53]*Ibid.*, pp. 2*v*–3*r*.

[54]*Ibid.*, pp. 2*r*–2*v*. Cf. Cicero, *Laelius seu de Amicitia*, VI.22.

[55]E.g., *De Justa Authoritate*, p. 2*v* (citing Aristotle's *Politics*, I.2: "Si quis unquam alienum [a communione civili] se praebuerit – vel belluam vel deum esse"), and p. 5*r* (citing Cicero's *De Natura Deorum*, I.17: "Omnium populorum consensum ipsius naturae vocem esse"). Rossaeus could choose *De Natura Deorum* because much of it was in fact a commentary upon Aristotle's view of a rational nature.

He found exemplification for his views in the pre-history of Numidia and the tribes of ancient Germany. He quoted Ortelius on Asiatic nomads and even looked to the New World where "in our own time that same reason brought together certain Americans of the utmost west into a civil society of a superior way of life, whereas formerly they were living almost after the manner of beasts."[56] An equally exotic set of examples is provided to show that, while there is no model form of government, men universally create political authority to safeguard their welfare and security. Political practices in Calicut, Cochin China and the Moluccas are examined, together with an exhaustive list of different kinds of European governments in ancient and modern times, and of the changes effected by various peoples when the structures they had authorised failed to fulfil their purpose. Like Buchanan, Rossaeus personally preferred limited monarchy under popular control, while insisting that the gamut of institutions living and dead revealed that forms of government resulted from acts of popular will, and could be regulated or altered in similar fashion. To the question who created such variety in government, Rossaeus responds: "Certainly not God, nor nature, which is the same for all, but the will of the people themselves, their free choice and decision when they first formed their commonwealths or later reformed them."[57]

Rossaeus assumes that the institution of government was coeval with the formation of society, but, although he is explicit about the necessity for government to offset human depravity, he does not comment on the presence of the latter in the state of nature. St. Augustine, as well as St. Thomas Aquinas, are among his references, and yet he does not say directly that earthly government is the result of the Fall. At the same time he stresses the disastrous effects of "unrestrained wilfulness (*voluntas effrenata*)," "furious lust (*libido furiosa*)" and "greed (*cupiditas*)" if there were no laws and magistrates. Indeed, society would otherwise be a more dangerous place than the presocial condition: "It is much more tolerable for individuals to live in dens and lairs like wild beasts than to come together in such a way that they are exposed to violence without, in the meantime, any provision being made for its prevention."[58] Such a union would rapidly destroy itself, just as the warriors sprung from the dragon's teeth sown by Cadmus exterminated each other. It is a reasonable inference, therefore, that the state of nature is also a violent place, although there is more opportunity for mass violence when people are concentrated together. Rossaeus insists that it is a beneficent and rational nature that has driven men to society, but it is vice that obliges men to establish government when once they live in a community. Step by step, the general argument is the same as that of Buchanan.

Except in the case of military conquest, all arrangements for government and

---

[56]*De Justa Authoritate*, p. 3*v*. Cf. Laslett (ed.), *Locke's Two Treatises*, II, paras. 102, 105 (pp. 353, 355).
[57]*De Justa Authoritate*, p. 10*r*.
[58]*Ibid.*, p. 4*r*.

the control of governors anywhere in the world "emanated from the will and approbation of peoples (*hoc totum a populorum voluntate et approbatione manasse*)."[59] It follows that nothing can be more heinous than tyrants who rule against the consent of the people, flout the law, inflict violence upon the citizens, and seize their property. "Commonwealths have always dreaded them, philosophers have condemned them, and founders of the laws such as Lycurgus, Numa, Solon (the most prudent of the Romans and Greeks) have called for any citizen to kill them as public enemies, and announced great honours and rewards for doing so."[60] Here Rossaeus refers the reader to his later chapter on tyrannicide by private men, where, as we have seen, he confessed his agreement with Buchanan's *De Jure Regni*.

If Rossaeus developed his basic argument with more logic and more detailed exemplification than did Buchanan, he showed the same deliberate vagueness as the Scotsman when it came to describing the actual process whereby kings might be resisted, judged and punished. Other commentaries have dealt adequately with this aspect of Rossaeus and it is not necessary to recapitulate it here in detail.[61] Like Buchanan, he claims that the private crimes of a king may be judged by the ordinary processes of the law, and he sees the parlement fulfilling this function.[62] Like Buchanan, he refers fleetingly to a pact or contract between king and people, but it occupies no central role in this theory.[63] Like Buchanan, he attaches great importance to the coronation ceremony, for it is only when the consent of the people is signified there that the king is invested with authority.[64] Like Buchanan, he mentions particular acts by the estates, but he refuses to endow that body with the ultimate sovereignty of the people.[65] In their view that popular sovereignty is inalienable, as in their account of the origin of society, Buchanan and Rossaeus differ jointly from their fellow monarchomachs.

There are, of course, some issues where their opinions differ from each other. Rossaeus allows private men to kill the tyrant *absque titulo* on their own initiative: Buchanan refuses it if the usurper governs wisely.[66] Rossaeus re-

---

[59]*Ibid.*, p. 5*v*.

[60]*Ibid.*, pp. 10*v*–11*r*.

[61]E.g., Allen, *Political Thought in the Sixteenth Century*, pp. 350–3; Baumgartner, *Radical Reactionaries*, pp. 146–60; J. N. Figgis, *From Gerson to Grotius* (Cambridge, 1916 [1907]), pp. 182–7; Vahle, "Boucher und Rossaeus," pp. 341–9.

[62]*De Justa Authoritate*, p. 86*r*; *De Jure Regni*, p. 49.

[63]*De Justa Authoritate*, p. 41*r*; *De Jure Regni*, p. 53.

[64]*De Justa Authoritate*, pp. 31*r*–31*v*; *De Jure Regni*, p. 35.

[65]*De Justa Authoritate*, pp. 41*v*–46*v*; *De Jure Regni*, pp. 33, 45. Rossaeus puts particular stress on the sanctity of property and the role of the estates in consenting to taxation. There is an apparent inconsistency here, but Rossaeus seems not to regard consent by the estates as implying an alienation of sovereignty. In this respect the estates are treated more as a piece of constitutional machinery. Nevertheless, the passage in which he develops these views (*De Justa Authoritate*, pp. 54*r*–55*v*) discusses the need to safeguard property as one of the reasons for abandoning the state of nature.

[66]For Buchanan's views of tyrannicide, see above, notes 33–7. For Rossaeus's opinions, see above,

stricts private initiative in the tyrannicide of a legitimate sovereign, who, while not being a heretic, has acted as a secular oppressor. Here the ruler must first be pronounced a tyrant by the whole people (although the mechanism for this remains unexplained), or by the church. Buchanan seems to allow more liberty in the private judgment of such a tyrant, and, as we have seen, he allows counsel, but not action, by the church. Buchanan is no orthodox Presbyterian of the Knoxian variety, and his consideration of the heretic ruler is limited to the question of clerical excommunication. Both he and Rossaeus emphasise the importance of the relationship between bishops and kings.[67] Rossaeus, of course, allows individual action against the heretic oppressor. Buchanan denounces the tyranny of the pope in claiming power to depose kings. Rossaeus, like Boucher, grants this power, but he resembles Mair in the realisation that such an exercise of papal authority depends upon its acceptance by the body of the faithful.[68]

These differences are less striking than the similarities which distinguish them from the mainstream of resistance theory. At times, of course, they do echo opinions to be found among all the monarchomachs, such as their denial that St. Paul had prohibited all resistance in Romans 13.1–2, their restatement of the Ciceronian adage that the welfare of the people ought to be the supreme law, and their repetition of the commonplace that the king is greater than the people individually but less than they as a whole.[69] Their parroting of these shibboleths does not disguise the fact that in their populism and their account of the presocial condition of man Buchanan and Rossaeus represent a separate strand in the development of resistance doctrine. Without the advantage of Lockean hindsight, it is not surprising, however, that late sixteenth- and early seventeenth-century critics of the monarchomachs generally classified Buchanan and Rossaeus with Hotman, Beza, Brutus and Boucher. A few defenders of monarchy sensed a distinction. Adam Blackwood began his attack upon Buchanan in *Apologia pro Regibus* (1581) by associating his fellow Scot with Hotman and Brutus, but went on to notice that Buchanan had unusual views of the law of nature, which Blackwood condemned as the law of the predator and no basis for popular rights in civil society.[70] William Barclay, another Gallicized Scot who wrote on behalf of absolutism, placed Buchanan among the other seditious writers for whom he had coined the word "mon-

notes 44–6. Rossaeus's restrictions on private action against a legitimate and religiously orthodox tyrant are set out in *De Justa Authoritate*, pp. 392v–393r. Buchanan's limitation of initiative against a usurper are contained in *De Jure Regni*, pp. 28–9, 55.

[67] *De Jure Regni*, p. 41; *De Justa Authoritate*, pp. 31v–32r, 34v–35r, 36v. Rossaeus's stress upon the role of bishops is connected with his analysis of their part in the coronation of kings.

[68] *De Jure Regni*, p. 20. On Rossaeus's views of papal authority see Baumgartner, *Radical Reactionaries*, p. 156. On Mair's opinion see Oakley, "Major and Buchanan," p. 14.

[69] *De Jure Regni*, pp. 38–41, 18, 48; *De Justa Authoritate*, pp. 5v, 59r, 20r.

[70] Adam Blackwood, *Pro Regibus Apologia* (Paris, 1588 [1581]), pp. 16, 21.

[71] William Barclay, *De Regno et Regali Potestate* (Paris, 1600), pp. 6–10.

archomach," but found him more anarchic than his fellows.[71] The Anglican bishop, Thomas Morton, attacked the populism of Rossaeus and denounced Buchanan as "a schismatical demagogue."[72] Nearly all the defenders of Stuart kingship in the constitutional conflicts of the seventeenth century who mentioned Buchanan assumed that his ideas were identical with the thinking of other monarchomachs, a view popularised by Richard Bancroft in *Dangerous Positions* as early as 1593.[73] One notable exception was Peter Heylyn, the cosmographer and Anglican historian of Calvinism. Heylyn noticed that, unlike most resistance theorists, Buchanan had asserted that the people could never delegate the power to control magistrates and punish tyrants. Not surprisingly, he regarded *De Jure Regni* as one of the most subversive works ever penned.[74]

It has been the theme of this paper that the two principal views which Buchanan and Rossaeus shared, and which point towards Locke, are their acceptance of an inalienable sovereignty in the people and their adaptation of natural law theory to explain the origin of society. No direct influence can be demonstrated, for Locke never refers to either Buchanan or Rossaeus. His own views were formed in the context of English seventeenth-century political debates, and he was also influenced by those Dutch and German jurists who mediated between sixteenth-century ideas of sovereignty, natural law and resistance on the one hand and the ideological conflicts of his own age on the other. Some of these jurists distinguished between a real or communal sovereignty inhering in the whole people and an effective or personal sovereignty exercised by government. The most sophisticated balance between *majestas realis* and *majestas personalis* was defined by Besoldus. He had glossed the writings of Althusius and Arnisaeus,[75] who both accepted the idea that political authority found its sanction in some original constitutive act by the entire

---

[72]Thomas Morton, *A Preamble unto an Incounter with P.R.* (London, 1608), p. 39; *An Exact Discoverie of Romish Doctrine in the Case of Conspiracie and Rebellion* (London, 1605), pp. 9, 11, 13, 26; *The Necessity of Christian Subjection Demonstrated* (Oxford, 1643), p. 19.

[73](Richard Bancroft), *Dangerous Positions* (London, 1593), p. 15. Some examples of royalist works listing Buchanan among the French monarchomachs as having identical principles are: John Bramhall, *Serpent Salve* (1643) in *Works* (Dublin, 1676), p. 518; Henry Hammond, *Of Resisting the Lawful Magistrate upon Colour of Religion* (London, 1643), p. 23; William Dugdale, *Short View of the Late Troubles in England* (Oxford, 1681), pp. 16–19; Robert Brady, *True and Exact History of the Succession* (London, 1684), p. 355. It might also be noted that many seventeenth-century English advocates of resistance cited Buchanan in their cause without distinguishing his ideas from those of Huguenot resistance theorists. E.g., William Prynne, *Soveraigne Power of Parliaments and Kingdomes* (London, 1643), vol. 2, p. 122; John Canne, *The Golden Rule* (London, 1649), pp. 11–12; John Milton, *The Tenure of Kings and Magistrates* (London, 1649), pp. 28, 30, and *A Defence of the People of England* (London, 1692 [1650]), pp. 50, 180.

[74]Peter Heylyn, *The Stumbling Block of Disobedience* (1644), in *Historical and Miscellaneous Tracts of . . . Heylyn* (London, 1681), p. 683; *Aerius Redivivus* (Oxford, 1670), pp. 77, 194.

[75]Christophor Besoldus, *Dissertatio Politico-Juridica de Majestate in Genere* (Strasbourg, 1625), pp. 4, 5. Althusius and Arnisaeus are not, of course. the only authorities whom Besoldus juxtaposes to produce the theory of double sovereignty. Bodin, Grégoire de Toulouse, and Kirchnerus – not to mention many earlier civilians – are among his principal sources.

community. Althusius, who cited Buchanan and Rossaeus with approval,[76] leaned towards the idea that ephoral authority protected the community from abuse by its governors. Arnisaeus, who listed all the principal monarchomachs as "the sworne enemies of soveraigne majestie"[77] (to use Sir John Eliot's phrase), denied the right to interfere with the ruler's exercise of sovereignty except in extremely rare circumstances. When Besoldus defined his "double sovereignty" his ideas were adapted in their turn by George Lawson, writing in the Cromwellian interregnum. In *Politica Sacra et Civilis* (1660) Lawson asserted that the people retained the constituent power they had exercised in the first establishment of a form of government. This government could be a mixture of different elements. Should it break down by their division, the community could once more exercise its constituent power. As Julian Franklin has shown, this was the position occupied by Locke and he arrived at it by reading Lawson.[78] It was a position too radically populist to be acceptable to the main body of Whig theory, which continued to march along the highway stretching back to the conciliar movement.

The insistence by Buchanan and Rossaeus on an act of rational popular will which constituted the form of government, and could, if necessary, reform it, is an anticipation of the doctrine of constituent power because, unlike their fellow monarchomachs, they refused to allow the will of the community to be permanently delegated to a particular institutional body of inferior magistrates. The irony of this situation is that none of the seventeenth-century theorists, whose dialectical exchanges enabled the doctrine to be redefined with greater assurance, understood that Buchanan and Rossaeus were not typical monarchomachs. Like so many seventeenth-century Englishmen, Lawson himself thought that Buchanan's ideas were indistinguishable from those of the *Vindiciae contra Tyrannos*,[79] and he found no reason ever to mention Rossaeus.

When Buchanan and Rossaeus adapted Cicero's views of the origin of society, they insisted that nature, rather than reason and the calculation of utility, played the major role in the formation of society. Thereafter, by some process of divine illumination, men apprehended the rationality of natural law, and nature and reason could be used interchangeably. This argument substantially modified Aristotelian assumptions, but it did not result in the definition of a social contract into which men freely entered as a result of calculation. The

[76]Johannes Althusius, *Politica Methodice Digesta*, ed. Carl J. Friedrich (Cambridge, Mass., 1932 [1614]), pp. 138, 149, 159, 184. Note the joint invocation of Molina, Salamonius, Buchanan and Rossaeus on p. 159 to support the proposition that all authority belongs to the community in general, and that administration is entrusted to the magistrate.
[77]Heningus Arnisaeus, *De Jure Maiestatis Libri Tres* (Strasbourg, 1635 [1610]), p. 6. Cf. Sir John Eliot (translator), *De Jure Maiestatis*, ed. Grossart (London, 1882), p. 3.
[78]See above, note 8.
[79]G. Lawson, *Politica Sacra et Civilis* (London, 1660), p. 35. Lawson states that Brutus and Buchanan are wrong to imagine that "the multitude" can make and unmake kings because they possess perpetual sovereignty. In this instance he would seem to see Brutus through Buchanan, and not, as was customary, *vice versa*.

force of moral imperatives, which according to natural law tradition could operate as instinct or conscience but could also be understood rationally, remained uncertain in the presocial condition. Clearly, neither Buchanan nor Rossaeus wanted to describe this condition as entirely a state of war between all men, although Blackwood asserted that this was the logical inference to be drawn from Buchanan's account of it. Yet both monarchomachs stressed the need for government to control anti-social behaviour once the community was formed, and violence was obviously not the invention of society. The argument for the rights of the community against tyrants was dependent upon the reasons for the coming together of men in society, and this in turn upon the nature of man in the presocial condition. Each theorist tried to solve the dilemma in his own way. Buchanan insisted that the majority of men in society were guided by moral considerations, and his *major pars* excluded those whose self-interest caused them to act against the common good. Rossaeus's solution was a psychological one. He suggested that sparks of virtues and reason had been implanted in the human mind, and that once society had been formed they could be developed through experience and education.

Both the problem of natural law in the state of nature and the tentative solutions proposed by Buchanan and Rossaeus suggest parallels with Locke. To understand the historical context in which Locke composed his *Essays on the Law of Nature* in the 1660s it is necessary to examine his debts to Hooker, his reaction against Hobbes, and his modification of ideas suggested by Grotius, Pufendorf and the Cambridge Platonists.[80] None of this lies within the scope of this paper. Since our primary concern on the issues of natural law is with parallels and similarities rather than influence (for the influence of Buchanan and Rossaeus in this respect is so tenuous as to be wholly negligible), it may suffice to consider briefly how Locke posed and answered the problems encountered in an earlier age. Locke began his *Essays* by asking whether there was a natural law of morality, and he concluded that there was by following Aristotle, Aquinas and Hooker, and by reflecting on the nature of human society. He went on to state that one can accept the explanation that natural law is known by *lumen naturae* if by this we mean sense-perception guided by reason. Natural law is not inscribed in the minds of men, because innate ideas do not exist, and reason apprehends it only through sense experience. It is impossible to establish a knowledge of natural law by examining what men generally accept as moral principles because either they are based upon expediency or else are the result of abstract speculation. Natural law is not based upon self-preservation or self-interest, but is binding upon the individual as a moral obligation in which both conscience and reason concur. It is a part of man's nature which God has allowed man to know through sensation and reason.[81]

[80]W. von Leyden (ed.), *John Locke: Essays on the Law of Nature* (Oxford, 1954), pp. 36–9.
[81]*Ibid.*, analytical summary, pp. 95–106.

Renaissance and revolt

Locke carried over sections from his *Essays* to his *Second Treatise*. In particular he used his earlier arguments to demonstrate that the state of nature is not a state of war, even though some in the presocial condition do not understand the natural law and are the cause of insecurity. For this reason men decide to enter society and renounce their right to execute natural justice to a common judge.[82] However, expediency and calculation are not the only considerations. In another passage in the *Second Treatise* borrowed from the *Essays*, Locke states: "God having made Man such a Creature, that, in his own Judgment, it was not good for him to be alone, put him under strong Obligations of Necessity, Convenience, and Inclination to drive him into Society."[83] This would suggest that man's choice is far from being that of a rational free agent, and a parallel is again suggested with Rossaeus. But when Locke comes to a specific account of the beginning of society in a passage which has no counterpart in the *Essays*, he writes: "Men being, as has been said, by Nature, all free, equal and independent, no one can be put out of this Estate, and subjected to the Political Power of another without his own *consent*."[84] This is very reminiscent of Buchanan's account of a well-regulated society, where men are free and consent is the mark of the absence of tyranny. Indeed, Buchanan would seem to be more libertarian than Locke, just as Rossaeus appears to depict natural man in a less rational guise than does Locke in the previous passage. It is Rossaeus who comes to mind again when Locke, continuing to explain the origin of society, claims the purpose of men's entering into agreement with each other to be "a secure Enjoyment of their Properties." In the conclusion to this paragraph Locke explains that, once the agreement is made, it is the majority who "have a Right to act and conclude the rest."[85]

Although Lockean individualism and sensationalism have radically altered the terms of the discussion from those which applied to Buchanan and Rossaeus, the underlying similarity remains. With natural law, as with the theory of sovereignty, Buchanan and Rossaeus, and perhaps also Almain, suggest resonances with Locke's attempt to resolve the nature of political obligation in a way that does not harmonise with the tradition of Aristotelian resistance theory. Jacques Abbadie, the exiled Huguenot theorist who justified the Glorious Revolution in terms nearly as individualist as Locke's, drew attention to Buchanan's account of the state of nature to show that the establishment of society was intended to preserve certain popular rights.[86] Nearly a century later Mably went even further and remarked that Buchanan had anticipated Locke's whole theory of natural right.[87] This was an exaggerated and unhistorical judgment, but it testifies to the existence of an alternative road from Constance to 1688.

[82]Laslett (ed.), *Locke's Two Treatises*, II, paras 6, 7 and 19 (pp. 288–9, 298–9). Cf. Von Leyden (ed.), *Locke: Essays*, p. 162.
[83]Laslett (ed.), *Locke's Two Treatises*, II, para 77 (p. 336). Cf. Von Leyden (ed.), *Locke: Essays*, p. 154.
[84]Laslett (ed.), *Locke's Two Treatises*, II, para 95 (pp. 348–9).
[85]*Ibid.*
[86]Jacques Abbadie, *La Défense de la Nation Britannique* (The Hague, 1690), p. 286.
[87]L'Abbé Mably, *De la manière d'écrire l'histoire* (Paris, 1783), p. 16.

154

7

~~~~~~

Gallicanism and Anglicanism in the age of the Counter-Reformation

In the eighteenth century Gallicanism and Anglicanism offered many striking differences, particularly in terms of the social background and political attitudes of their respective episcopates.[1] In the sixteenth and early seventeenth centuries, however, the political ideologies of the two national churches showed some remarkable similarities, despite the fact that one was Catholic and the other Protestant. What initially was merely a parallel development at a time of increasing royal authority over ecclesiastical administration became, under the challenge of a resurgent papacy with universal claims, a matter of imitation, reciprocal influence, and even association.

Memories of this association still lingered in the eighteenth century. In 1706 William Wotton dedicated the last volume of his translation of Elie Dupin's Gallican-inspired *Ecclesiastical History* to Thomas Tenison, Archbishop of Canterbury and critic of the Jesuits. He was conscious of a tradition, for he noted that in 1620 Nicholas Brent had offered his English version of Paolo Sarpi's *History of the Council of Trent* to George Abbot, Tenison's predecessor during a period of intense controversy with Rome.[2] Dupin's last volume was devoted to the Counter-Reformation, particularly the discussions at Trent, the personalities of the new breed of popes, and the rise of the Jesuits and other new orders. For the events at the council and their repercussions, it drew heavily upon Sarpi's work and also upon his Gallican friends, who had collected past antipapal diatribes, resisted the reception of the Tridentine decrees, and contributed their own polemics against Rome and the Jesuit order. Anglicanism had become the leading partner in the antipapal front of this time, and Sarpi, already accepted as some sort of republican Gallican, came also to be regarded as an honorary member of the Church of England.[3]

---

[1]Norman Ravitch, *Sword and Mitre: Government and Episcopate in France and England in the Age of Aristocracy* (The Hague, 1966).
[2]Elie Dupin, *A New Ecclesiastical History of the Sixteenth Century, Volume the Second* (London, 1706), unpaginated epistle dedicatory.
[3]G. Cozzi, "Fra Paolo Sarpi, l'anglicanismo e la *Historia del Concilio Tridentino*," *Rivista storica italiana*, 63 (1956), 559–619. Another of Sarpi's works popular in England was his *History of the Inquisition*.

The events that brought together Parisian magistrates, English divines, and a freethinking Venetian member of the Servite order followed each other in rapid succession. In Elizabeth's last years the quarrel between English Catholic secular priests and the Jesuits renewed interest in the Gallican literature upon which the seculars depended, and led the French government to support their case in Rome. This debate had barely concluded when that same government allowed the Jesuits to return to France. Gallican resentment against the Jesuits simmered, while ultramontane pressure grew for the reception of the decrees of the Council of Trent. Then the occurrence of the Gunpowder Plot confirmed the worst fears of the antipapal party in France as well as in England. In 1606 the oath of allegiance to James I, imposed in the aftermath of the plot, coincided with the papal interdict against Venice and the emergence of Sarpi as the champion of the Serene Republic. From this point the controversy spread to engage the whole of Europe, with the King of England conducting the anti-Roman choir, and the former Jesuit father and now cardinal Robert Bellarmine setting the tone for those who defended the contrary position. The ideological struggle continued for more than a decade, stimulated afresh in 1610 by the assassination of Henri IV, supposedly the result of Jesuit doctrines of tyrannicide, and by a proposal in the French estates general of 1614 to enact a constitutional law depriving the pope of any right to intervene in temporal government. The relationship of Gallicanism and Anglicanism in this war of words did not spring suddenly into existence. To be understood in all its contradictory aspects it has to be seen in the perspective of the preceding age.

Gallicanism is usually explained as either ecclesiastical or political, the former describing the independence of the French Catholic church from king as well as pope, and the latter presenting an alliance of church and crown to limit papal authority. Although it was the practice of its defenders to trace the liberties of their national church back to the beginnings of Christianity in Gaul, ecclesiastical Gallicanism took coherent form only in the fifteenth century as an outgrowth of the conciliar movement. The national Council of Bourges, which drew up the Pragmatic Sanction of 1438, confirmed the decrees of the contemporary general Council of Basel, and since it maintained the superiority of councils to popes it was unwelcome at Rome. Nor was it respected by Charles VII and his successors, who failed to observe the freedom of episcopal election it affirmed. Nevertheless, the Pragmatic survived in attenuated form until it was replaced in 1516 by the Concordat of Bologna between François Ier and Leo X. The Concordat might appear as the ultimate achievement of political Gallicanism, since it gave the crown greater control of the French church and, especially, the right to nominate bishops. But there was paradox in the fact that the parlement of Paris, the court which normally served as the instrument of political Gallicanism in establishing the superiority of royal justice over ecclesiastical jurisdiction, bitterly opposed the Concordat. While it did so ostensibly on the ground that the need for papal confirmation of candidates chosen by the king would extend the pope's authority over the church, in practice the defence of the Pragmatic by the parlement seemed to endorse the spiritual rights of the national clergy.[4] This was not to be the only time when the parlement appeared to change its usual role.

There were also paradoxical elements in the theories used to justify these and later events. Ecclesiastical Gallicanism revered Jean Gerson and other conciliar writers. Gerson had taken a moderate stance on the separation of the spiritual and temporal powers. He had given the church coercive authority over spiritual offences committed by laymen, and he had avoided the issue of the pope's right to intervene in civil government. More important, Gerson had argued for the sovereignty of the community as expressed through its representatives in both church and state. Thus not only was the pope a constitutional ruler inferior to the council but the secular prince was merely the chief minister of the commonwealth. In the early sixteenth century these ideas were extended by the conciliarists John Mair and Jacques Almain. At the same time absolutist ideas of monarchy began to be expressed – or, at least, theories that the crown was limited only by its voluntary observance of divine, natural, and constitutional law. Those legists who exalted the authority of Francois Ier and listed his regalian rights often gave kingship a divine sanction. Charles de Grassaille wrote:

The king of France is in his own kingdom like a corporeal God. What the king does is not his own action, but God's. God speaks through the mouth of the king, and the king's deeds are inspired by God. The king is the minister of God on earth. The king is the delegate of God.[5]

In later years, when Gallican and ultramontane forces were locked in conflict, Gallicans applied conciliar theory to the papacy while defending an absolute monarchy by divine right, whereas papalists asserted the absolute rule of the pope over the church while viewing a king as the delegate of the community he served, and as subject to deposition both by this community and by papal fiat.

Although not mentioned in the Concordat, the pope's part of the bargain was the acquisition of annates, the proportion of a year's diocesan revenue that a new bishop had to pay to secure canonical institution. This remained an area of possible dispute in which Gallican opinion was particularly sensitive. The first major deployment of Gallican rhetoric since the confirmation of the Concordat occurred in this context. Francois Ier's *avocat-général*, Jacques Cappel,[6] stated the king's case under seventy-three heads, beginning:

First let it be assumed that to the king our sovereign lord belong the protection, guard, and conservation of the goods, franchises, liberties, tranquillity, morality, good order,

[4] R. J. Knecht, *Francis I* (Cambridge, 1982), pp. 55–65.
[5] *Regalium Franciae libri duo*, cited in Latin by Claude Collot, *L'Ecole doctrinale de droit public de Pont-à-Musson* (Paris, 1965), p. 269.
[6] On Cappel see above, pp. 55–8.

discipline, and integrity of the church, and especially the church of his own kingdom, known as the Gallican Church. This is because he is emperor in his kingdom, holding his crown immediately from God, and recognising no superior in temporal things, and also because he is the patron and principal founder of the churches of France, and holds the prerogatives, preeminences, privileges, and indults granted to his predecessors the most Christian kings, and to himself.[7]

The assertion of royal sovereignty in temporal affairs, with its denial of any superior papal right, was to be repeated in every subsequent list of Gallican liberties, and constituted the fundamental law proposed by the third estate in 1614. Its alleged corollary, the king's right to govern the church and to control clerical property and clerical discipline, presupposed a purely sacerdotal role for the spiritual power, and was usually stated in more equivocal terms than those adopted by Cappel.

After this statement of principle the rest of the Cappel memoir consisted almost entirely of historical precedents. A few, such as Justinian's punishment of heretics and criminal clerics, concerned early emperors, but the vast majority were taken from the national past and formed a kind of litany of Gallican experience. Clovis had summoned the first assembly of the clergy at Orléans in 511. Charlemagne had formulated rules for church government. His Carolingian and Capetian successors had faced the aggressive expansion of papal authority. Philippe-Auguste had laid down rules for episcopal election. Saint Louis had stemmed the tide of papal exactions with the first so-called Pragmatic Sanction. Philippe le Bel had exposed the pretensions of Boniface VIII. Charles VI had defined the Gallican liberties in legislation. The thrust of the argument was historical, or rather pseudo-historical, for change was equivalent to corruption, and the aim was to restore a pristine purity. In accordance with the climate of the age, Cappel sought to show that the liberties of the church of France, while at times overlaid by Roman aggression, constantly reverted to their independent foundation in antiquity. The Gallican Church had accepted the decrees of the earliest general councils summoned by Constantine and his successors, but it did not accept corrupting innovations applied by the papacy in later ages. The French kings, emperors in their own kingdom, had protected and revived the primitive liberties of the national church. This was the stuff of myth, and like all myths it gathered certitude in the retelling.

Gallican theory developed through confrontation, and found new intensity in the mid-century conflict between Henri II and the papacy. The new reign began amid disputes with Rome about annates, the right of the pope to appoint to vacancies caused by the death of French prelates visiting Rome, and the

---

[7]*Mémoires dressez pour le Roy tres-Chrestien et l'Eglise gallicane*, in Pierre Dupuy (ed.), *Traitez des droits et libertez de l'Eglise gallicane* (n.p., 1731), vol. 1, p. 14. Dupuy continued the collection of Gallican works begun by Pierre Pithou (see below, p. 173). Dupuy's two volumes were first published in 1639 and reissued in 1651. The eighteenth-century edition has additional material prepared by J.-L. Brunet.

inclusion of Brittany and Provence within the terms of the Concordat. Over the last of these issues the *procureur-général,* Noël Brulard, drew up a memoir to prove that the two provinces, although excluded from the Pragmatic of 1438 and hence from the Concordat, had long been associated with Gallican practice.[8] Relations with Rome became even worse when the newly elected pope, Julius III, defied the king by reconvening the Council of Trent and ignoring his alliance with Parma. In 1551 Henri II came close to repeating Henry VIII's rupture with the papacy. He had the royal council consider the appointment of a patriarch, and prepared to summon a council of the Gallican Church.[9] The schism was averted, but French bishops were prohibited by royal command from attending the assembly at Trent. During the crisis, Jean du Tillet, the registrar of the parlement, produced a historical survey of Gallican liberties based upon an unrivalled command of the archives. This was an exceptional statement of Gallican precedents, for it accepted change more dispassionately than most. Du Tillet demonstrated that procedures for the election or nomination of bishops had varied over time, and that attitudes to clerical property had also changed. The antiquarian affirmed the rights of the king in ecclesiastical administration, but he was not bound by Gallican myths, and forbore to mention Clovis and his clerical council of Orléans.[10]

A more notorious by-product of the crisis of 1550–2 was a work by Charles Dumoulin entitled *Commentaire de l'édit des petites dates.*[11] Dumoulin's reputation as one of the greatest jurists of the age was based upon his commentary on the customary law of Paris. His Gallican outburst was directed against the papal bureau for the collation of benefices known as the Datary, but he ranged widely over the temporal independence of kings and emperors against papal interference. His nationalist assumptions about the Gallican Church, together with his view of Christendom as a loosely linked ecclesiastical federation and his advocacy of the control of church property by the secular prince, made his manifesto a model for the situation in England. But the work does not seem to have been cited by later Anglican writers. Nor was it made much use of in France, except by a few Erastian historians.[12] This was probably because Dumoulin was for a time a Lutheran, and it was the practice of later ultramontane writers to accuse Gallicans within the parlement of Protestant sympathies.

[8] *Mémoires dressez par M. Maistre Noel Brulard,* in Dupuy, vol. 1, pp. 36–48.
[9] Lucien Romier, "La Crise gallicane de 1551," *Revue historique,* 108 (1911), 25–50, and 109 (1912), 27–55; Marc Venard, "Une réforme gallicane: le projet de concile nationale de 1551," *Revue historique de l'Eglise de France,* 67 (1981), 201–25. I am grateful to Frederic J. Baumgartner for allowing me to consult the typescript of his forthcoming book on the reign of Henri II on these points.
[10] *Histoire et advis . . . sur les libertés de l'Eglise gallicane,* in Dupuy, vol. 1, pp. 44–8.
[11] Jean-Louis Thireau, *Charles du Moulin, 1560–1566* (Geneva, 1980), pp. 272–347; Donald R. Kelley, "*Fides Historiae:* Charles Dumoulin and the Gallican View of History," *Traditio,* 22 (1966), 347–402.
[12] E.g. Claude Fauchet, *Traicté des libertez de l'Eglise gallicane,* in Dupuy, vol. 1, p. 85.

In 1552 the Sorbonne did in fact censure Dumoulin's *Commentaire* as containing "the heresies of the Vaudois, Wicklefists [*sic*], Hussites and Lutherans," and as reviving the doctrines of Marsilius of Padua from the fourteenth century.[13] Even the parlement, despite Dumoulin's advocacy of a royal cause and his reputation in the law, hesitated to entertain his *appel comme d'abus*, the proceeding whereby the parlement heard complaints against the misuse of spiritual jurisdiction.

Dumoulin's second contribution to Gallican theory occurred a decade later in the context of the final sessions of the Council of Trent. Although conciliar doctrine was a vital ingredient in Gallicanism, the Trent assembly was in some respects the antithesis of those of the fifteenth century. It attested the ascendancy of the pope, for it was convened, and its decrees promulgated, through papal authority. The attitude of the French government was only a little less antagonistic than it had been under Henri II. In 1562 the royal instructions to the French ambassadors to the council were thoroughly Gallican in spirit. Items 4–6 read:

Fourthly, that the decrees of the Council shall likewise not be remitted to the pope's good pleasure . . . and that pursuant to the dispositions of the ancient councils, and particularly those of Constance and Basel, he shall be obliged to pay an entire submission and obedience unto them.

Fifthly, that in matters of reformation, the fathers of the Council shall conform themselves to the discipline of the primitive church, that so the ecclesiastical state may be reduced, as near as possible, to the purity in which it was put in first.

Sixthly, that the pope shall not at all concern himself with elections or provisions of bishops, abbots, other prelates, and parish priests, nor with their administration unless in case of negligence, according to the decrees of the Holy Councils and the ancient rights and liberties of the Gallican Church.[14]

Another issue of primary concern to the French crown was, of course, the papal claim to superior jurisdiction in temporal affairs. Here Jacques Cappel and the regalian legists had insisted not only upon royal sovereignty but also upon its divine sanction. In 1561 a *cause célèbre* occurred at the Collège d'Harcourt when a student in the faculty of theology named Jean Tanquerel maintained in a debate that "the church, whose sole monarch is the pope as the vicar of Christ, holds both the spiritual and secular power and wields sway over all princes as its faithful subjects, with ability to deprive them of their kingdom and dignities should they rebel against its precepts."[15] The parlement censured this proposition as an abomination, and required the Sorbonne to subscribe to its *arrêt*. When the relationship of the spiritual and temporal powers was scheduled for debate at Trent in 1562 the French representatives refused to attend.

[13]Dupin, 2d pagination, pp. 79–81.
[14]*Ibid.*, 1st pagination, p. 203.
[15]*Arrest de la cour . . . contre Jean Tanquerel*, in Dupuy, vol. 1, pp. 50–4.

Upon this and upon the issue of whether bishops held their jurisdiction *iure divino* or by delegation from the pope the Tridentine decrees made no specific pronouncement, although they mentioned an apostolic succession of which the pope could be conceived as the dispenser. During the discussions on this matter the French bishops supported the Spanish stand that the keys had not been bestowed on Saint Peter personally but as the representative of the church. Hence Saint Peter and his successors at Rome were but the first among equals, and all bishops, like the remaining apostles, could claim to have received their sacerdotal power direct from God. Yet while the debate had proved inconclusive, the status of the episcopacy was unquestionably enhanced by the subsequent decrees, for the bishops were designated as the instrument of the reforms. It was for this reason that many French bishops came to support the reception of the decrees when the spirit of the Catholic Reformation began to be felt in France towards the end of the century. However, the parlement continued to oppose reception, even when the crown supported it, as in the reign of Henri III and the regency of Marie de Médicis. The one exception was during the time of the League.

Opposition to the Tridentine decrees was a much more equivocal criterion of Gallicanism than was opposition to the Jesuits. It was Loyola's successor as general of the order, Lainez, who had spoken at Trent against the divine right of bishops. The Jesuits were regarded with suspicion by both regular and secular clergy because they seemed to belong to both and to neither. They were particularly suspected by the magistrates because they were reputed to be the unquestioning agents of papal expansion. In 1564 Etienne Pasquier voiced such opinions before the parlement when he represented the university in a plea against the incorporation of the Jesuit college of Clermont.[16]

This was the year in which Charles Dumoulin launched his *Conseil sur le fait du Concile de Trente.* He accompanied it with a brief supporting Pasquier against the Jesuit petition to become a part of the University of Paris, together with a third tract concerning a disputed episcopal succession in Amiens. The three pieces were connected. Dumoulin saw the Jesuits as the promoters of papalism at Trent, and he used material from the Amiens case to illustrate the corrupt collation of benefices when writing against the Tridentine decrees.[17] Although he believed in absolute monarchy by divine right, Dumoulin upheld the principle of election to benefices by both clergy and laity. The Concordat of 1516 presented a clear contradiction of this principle, and Dumoulin tried to resolve the difficulty by stressing the need for royal consent. This was in fact what had been recommended by the estates general of Orléans in 1561, and it had been recognised in a reforming ordinance, although never practised. In any case, the participation of the laity seemed more Calvinist than it did Gallican. Dumoulin

[16]See below, p. 173.
[17]Dupin, 2d pagination, p. 82; Thireau, p. 343.

went even further, for he implied the absence of clerical hierarchy in the primitive church. His extremism in his consultation on Trent lost him the support of the crown, the parlement, and ecclesiastical Gallicans, despite his demonstration of the ancient independence of the French church and his denial of the legality of a council summoned and confirmed by the pope. The one hundred articles in which he set forth his findings ranged over a wide spectrum of theological opinions and historical precedents. Their general theme was the restriction of the clergy to sacerdotal functions and the close control of ecclesiastical discipline by the secular power. The *Conseil,* like the *Commentaire de l'édit des petites dates,* better suited the English situation, where the Anglican settlement was being rapidly consolidated.

While the parlement of Paris served as the agent of the French crown in the government of the church, the Tudor monarchy had recourse to parliament to break with Rome altogether, to foster Protestantism under Edward VI, to return to Catholicism under Mary, and finally to effect the Elizabethan solution. Just as there was ambiguity in the actions of the French parlement, which at times seemed to be defending the spiritual independence of the clergy against the intent of the crown, so too the triumph of the secular arm in England was clothed in language which preserved at least an appearance of a separate ecclesiastical authority. In this and other respects the Anglican settlement could not escape the contradictory legacy of Henry VIII. The letter in which the king announced to the justices of the peace his assumption of the title of Supreme Head in November 1534 declared the action to have been taken

by the deliberate advice, consultation, consent, and agreement, as well of the bishops and clergy, as by the nobles and commons temporal of this our realm assembled in our high court of parliament, and by the authority of the same . . . which thing also the same bishops and clergy particularly, in their convocations, have wholly and entirely consented.[18]

This same circular reflected another uncertainty, one that occurred also in the statutes of the Reformation Parliament and in the tracts written to justify the royal supremacy: whether the supremacy was conferred directly by God as part of the divine attributes of kingship or whether it was created by the authority of the community acting through the king in parliament.[19] What is more, the circular to the justices of the peace, while expressing the voluntarist nature of this act of sovereignty, also asserted that it merely confirmed an existing state of affairs, or, as the letter put it, "Supreme Head in earth, immediately under God, of the Church of England, as undoubtedly evermore we have been." These paradoxes descended to the Church of England under Elizabeth.

---

[18]John Strype, *Ecclesiastical Memorials* (Oxford, 1822), vol. I, part II, p. 209.
[19]J. J. Scarisbrick, *Henry VIII* (Berkeley, Calif., 1968), pp. 396–7.

Apart from its effect upon later English developments, Henry VIII's separation from Rome affected Gallicanism as precedent and warning. Henri II stepped back from the path of schism in 1551 in part because his Catholicism could not endure the religious radicalism he saw as the outcome of Henry VIII's action in contemporary England, and perhaps Julius III proved more flexible than Paul III had been because of the English example. In practice the Renaissance kings of France had nearly as much control of the national church as the Tudor monarch. There was nothing in France, of course, equivalent to Henry VIII's confiscation of monastic lands, but in the religious wars the last Valois kings forced the church to alienate clerical property, sometimes, as in the first alienation of 1563, without the prior consent of either pope or ecclesiastical assembly. After 1561 the Gallican Church paid a regular tax, the *décime*, although an assembly was necessary to confirm it at regular intervals. Tudor monarchs had a less impeded control of church revenues, and in the second year of Elizabeth's reign the statute of clerical revenues gave the queen direct authority over episcopal incomes. On the other hand, the secular control of ecclesiastical jurisdiction by the French parlement, which included a tribunal to investigate heresy under Henri II, had no judicial parallel in England, for Tudor ecclesiastical commissions, though established by statute and controlled by the crown, included bishops and took the form of courts of ecclesiastical appeal as well as spiritual instruments to enforce orthodoxy. There was no repetition of Thomas Cromwell's appointment in 1535 as vicegerent in spirituals.[20]

Whatever the practical politics of Erastian control, it was the appearance of dualism between spiritual and temporal that the Elizabeth settlement inherited from the *Ecclesia Anglicana* established by Henry VIII, and in France this found a theoretical parallel in the survival of elements of ecclesiastical Gallicanism. Having established the Church of England through parliament, Elizabeth expected to rule it by means of the ecclesiastical hierarchy. Faced with lay pressure for further reform and clerical attempts to exclude the supreme governor from doctrinal issues, the queen acted with masterly diplomacy, checking the Puritan lobby while allowing convocation to proclaim the thirty-nine articles in 1563 and parliament to confirm them in 1571. The French ambassador visited Archbishop Parker in 1564 and heard him explain the discipline of the church. According to Parker himself, the ambassador remarked that "we were in religion very nigh unto them."[21]

Elizabeth's first bishops owed their appointment to the crown and were content to regard their jurisdiction as dependent on the authority of the supreme governor. At the same time John Jewel, whose *Apology* of 1562 constituted the first major defence of the settlement, argued for apostolic succes-

---

[20]G. R. Elton, *The Tudor Constitution* (Cambridge, 1960), pp. 217–21.
[21]Claire Cross, *The Royal Supremacy in the Elizabethan Church* (London, 1969), p. 26.

sion in terms similar to those in which Gallicans interpreted the symbolism of Saint Peter's keys:

For we believe both that Christ is always present with his church, and that he neededth no vicar, . . . that the apostles, as Cyprian saith, were all of like authority, and that the rest were in the very same degree that Peter was.[22]

In this same passage Bishop Jewel affirmed the membership of the Church of England in the Catholic and universal church, much as Dumoulin had argued for national religious variants within a general body:

We do believe that there is only one church of God, and that the same is not shut up, as in time past among the Jews, into any one corner or kingdom, but is Catholic and universal, and dispersed into all the world, so that now there is no nation that may truly complain that they be excluded and can have no part with the church and people of God.

When it came to justifying Anglicanism, Jewel used precisely the same argument as the Gallicans, writing not in terms of a variant national tradition but rather in terms of fidelity to the primitive church, as contrasted with later Roman corruption:

We do prove that the sacred gospel of God and the ancient bishops, together with the primitive church, doth make for us, and that we have upon just cause both departed from these men [of Rome], and also returned now again unto the apostles and old Catholic fathers.[23]

Like the Gallicans, Jewel went on to claim that no bishop of Rome had called himself pope until the sixth century, and to trace the mounting worldly ambitions of the pontiffs from Pope Zachary's role in the replacement of Merovingians by Carolingians, through the investiture contest of the eleventh century, to the papal convocation of the Council of Trent. The pope had usurped the right to call a council, just as he had wrongfully assumed authority over bishops, "which receive commission from God touching religion."[24]

The counterpart to the other wing of Gallican theory, the stress upon a national religious tradition, was provided for Anglicanism by Matthew Parker's antiquarian history of the English church. The archbishop traced its beginnings to the mission confided to Augustine by Pope Gregory the Great. He could not draw upon Christianity in Roman Britain, as Gallicans did for pre-Frankish Gaul, because one of his principal sources was the venerable Bede, who had regarded the mission to the Saxons as a fresh start. He did, however, make use of Gallican references to the preaching of the apostle Philip and of Joseph of Arimathea, which, he said, drove out the superstitions of the Druids and

---

[22]*An Apology or Answer in Defence of the Church of England* (London, 1562), p. 10r (mispaginated as p. 8). Spelling has been modernised in quotations from English works and in their titles.
[23]*Ibid.*, p. 7r.
[24]*Ibid.*, p. 59v.

eventually crossed the Channel.[25] Parker was prepared to give Rome the credit for Augustine's new beginning, but he was nonetheless insistent on the independent privileges of the archdiocese of Canterbury and of its long line of incumbents from Augustine to himself.

The power of the supreme governor over the clerical hierarchy was put to the test by the refusal of Elizabeth's second archbishop of Canterbury, Edmund Grindal, to obey her instructions to suppress the "prophesyings." In his long letter to the queen Grindal stated:

> I say with St. Paul, "I have no power to destroy but only to edify"; and with the same apostle "I can do nothing against the truth, but for the truth." If it be your Majesty's pleasure, for this or any other cause, to remove me out of this place, I will with all humility yield thereunto and render again to your Majesty that [which] I received of the same. . . . Bear with me I beseech you, Madam, if I choose rather to offend your earthly Majesty than to offend the heavenly Majesty of God.[26]

Grindal did not dispute the queen's right to grant and withdraw jurisdiction but he would not yield to her implied claim to interpret scripture better than he. This was a classic example of the theoretical weakness of Elizabeth's position, and Grindal closed on a defiant note by likening himself to Saint Ambrose standing up for spiritual authority against Theodosius and Valentinian. Ambrose was frequently invoked in Gallican literature to show that, while the saint had defended the independence of the church in spiritual matters, he had also respected the temporal power and renounced all material means in its favour. It was in this context, too, that Jewel was to refer to him,[27] and later the role of the bishop of Milan was to become a motif in Anglican writing.

A section of the English Catholic opposition to Elizabeth and her church adopted an extreme papalism in the 1560s and early 1570s, anticipating some of the doctrines that the League was to develop in France against the monarchy and its Gallican supporters. From Louvain Thomas Harding's *Confutation* (1565) responded to Jewel with the assertion that all secular power was subordinate to the vicar of Christ, who might excommunicate and depose temporal rulers. To Harding priests held authority from God, kings from the people. From Antwerp John Rastell launched a battery of attacks upon Jewel, maintaining direct papal temporal superiority and citing Boniface VIII's notorious bull *Unam Sanctam* (*A Confutation of a Sermon*, 1564; *A Copy of a Challenge*, 1565; *A Brief Show of False Wares*, 1567). Nicholas Sanders at first denied the pope direct temporal power in *Rock of the Church* (1567), but in *De Visibili Monarchia*

[25]*De Antiquitate Britannicae ecclesiae et privilegiis ecclesiae Cantuarensis cum archiepiscopis eiusdem 70* (London, 1572), p. 3.
[26]Patrick Collinson, *Archbishop Grindal, 1519–1583: The Struggle for a Reformed Church* (Berkeley, Calif., 1979), p. 242.
[27]Jewel, *Apology*, p. 12v; *A Defence of the Apology* (London, 1567), pp. 157–8.

(1571) he combined defence of the recent bull excommunicating and deposing Elizabeth with a well-reasoned doctrine of secular resistance.[28]

The ideas of the English Catholic exiles suffered a sea-change when William Allen launched the reconversion of England in 1577. The *Apology and True Declaration* (1581), which Allen wrote to defend the English colleges at Douai and Rome, claimed that the priests trained in these seminaries would not publish the bull of excommunication, *Regnans in Excelsis,* and had not been involved in the 1579 invasion of Ireland. *A Brief Discourse* (1580) by the Jesuit Robert Parsons advised English Catholics to win toleration by loyalty to the queen and nonresistance. Since government legislation made it treason to publish the bull or to convert one of the queen's subjects to Roman Catholicism, it seemed disingenuous of William Cecil to deny in his *Execution of Justice in England* (1583) that Roman Catholics were being persecuted for their religion, and to maintain that they were traitors for adhering to a foreign potentate. Yet the queen's minister could point to the secular ambitions and material interests of the papacy. Citing the Edict of the Little Dates as an instance of the response of a Catholic monarch to papal exactions, he described how Henri II "made several strait edicts against many parts of the pope's claims in prejudice of the crown and clergy of France, retracting the authority of the court of Rome, greatly to the hindrance of the pope's former profits."[29]

Allen responded with *A True, Sincere and Modest Defence* (1584), in which he continued to assert English Catholic loyalty while maintaining the papal right to depose a heretical ruler. Since Allen was privy to plots to assassinate the queen, his position was at least as equivocal as Cecil's. A year later England was involved in open war with Spain, and the Catholic League had revived in France with the support of Philip II and Pope Sixtus V. Robert Parsons, the leading polemicist among the Catholic exiles, abandoned the pose of persecuted loyalist, and joined the theorists of the League in combining religious and secular ideas of resistance. It was at this point that Gallican and Anglican theory converged in response to the ultramontane threat.

The bull *Regnans in Excelsis* began:

He that reigneth on high, to whom is given all power in heaven and earth, has committed one holy Catholic and apostolic church, outside of which there is no salvation, to one alone upon earth, namely to Peter, the first of the apostles, and to Peter's successor, the pope of Rome, to be by him governed in fullness of power. Him alone He has made ruler over all peoples and kingdoms, to pull up, destroy, scatter, disperse, plant and build, so that he may preserve His faithful people.[30]

---

[28]For a survey of the views of these writers see Peter Holmes, *Resistance and Compromise: The Political Thought of the Elizabethan Catholics* (Cambridge, 1982), pp. 23–9.

[29]*The Execution of Justice in England by William Cecil and a True, Sincere, and Modest Defense of English Catholics by William Allen,* ed. Robert M. Kingdon (Ithaca, N.Y., 1965), p. 27.

[30]Elton, *Tudor Constitution,* p. 416.

In 1585 Sixtus V issued an equally imperious bull excommunicating and deposing the Protestant princes Navarre and Condé. The parlement of Paris had continued to defend Gallican principles in the preceding period, notably in resisting mounting pressure to receive the Tridentine decrees. In 1579 Henri III's Ordinance of Blois incorporated many of the disciplinary provisions of the decrees, but because it was a royal edict, rather than a pronouncement acknowledging papal authority, the measure was unacceptable at Rome. The last Valois king personally favoured an unqualified reception, but the magistrates continued to insist upon a saving clause to safeguard the Gallican liberties. Here the parlement was defending Gallicanism against a king who lacked the will to overrule it. In 1583 Jacques Faye d'Espesses, a *président-à-mortier* in the parlement, published his *Advertissement sur la réception et publication du Concile de Trente*, suggesting a papal conspiracy to subvert the authority of the crown and including a personal attack upon the predecessor of Sixtus, Gregory XIII.[31] When the League reformed to oppose the status of Henri de Navarre as heir presumptive to the throne, it included advocacy of the Tridentine decrees in its articles of association. Hence Sixtus's bull, *Brutum Fulmen*, brought a strong reaction from the royalist and Gallican parlement, even though Navarre was a declared Protestant.

Anglican royalism found common ground with politique and Gallican responses to the alliance of Spain, the pope, and the League. Two published replies to the bull had a ready English audience in translation: *An Answer to the Excommunication of Sixtus V*, emanating from Navarre's immediate entourage in 1585, and the more colourful *Brutish Thunderbolt or rather Feeble Fire-Flash of Pope Sixtus* by François Hotman (1586). Other tracts against the League put into English in the years 1585–9 were of Huguenot provenance, although their French versions were consciously directed towards patriotic Gallican opinion.[32] At the same time the League made capital out of Elizabeth's persecution of English Catholics and her execution of Mary Queen of Scots. Louis Dorléans, a Leaguer *parlementaire*, pretended to be one of the victims of the Protestant queen so that he might warn Frenchmen of the likely consequences if Navarre ever became king of France (*Advertissement des Catholiques anglois aux françois catholiques*, 1586).[33] A series of replies and counter-replies followed. Philippe Duplessis-Mornay, known in England as "the pope of the Huguenots," disguised himself as a Gallican Catholic to compose *A Letter written by a French Catholic Gentleman containing a Brief Answer to the Slanders of a Certain Pretended Englishman* (1589). This French propaganda became even more relevant across the Channel when the Armada was launched to execute *Regnans in Excelsis*.

[31]Victor Martin, *Le Gallicanisme et la réforme catholique: essai historique sur l'introduction en France des decrets du Concile de Trente (1563–1615)* (Paris, 1919), pp. 203–6.
[32]See J. H. M. Salmon, *The French Religious Wars in English Political Thought* (Oxford, 1959), pp. 174–7, for a list of over sixty French anti-Leaguer tracts in English during this period.
[33]See above, p. 83.

Renaissance and revolt

The most powerful counterattack to Navarre's excommunication came not from a Protestant but from Pierre de Belloy, a Catholic jurist from Toulouse. Paraphrasing the language of the parlement in matters of spiritual abuse, he entitled the first of his three royalist tracts *Moyens d'abus, entreprises et nullitez du rescrit et bulle du pape Sixte V^e*. His principal tenet was the divine right of kings, which he expressed with a clarity lacking in earlier assertions of the God-given authority of princes. "Kingdoms," he wrote, "have heaven as their sole foundation. . . . The holy scripture calls kings and princes Gods (Psalm 82) to show beyond doubt that the authority of their empire, or sovereign power, is established by, and takes its origin from, the divinity whose place they hold upon earth."[34] To Belloy the king was "the controller [*œconomé*], patron, guardian, and tutor of the church."[35] His jurisdiction extended over the clergy and their property, whereas popes, being merely human and subject to sin and error, had power neither to appoint bishops nor to tax their revenues. Although he condemned the Council of Trent as an invasion of royal jurisdiction and Gallican privilege, Belloy wrote more as a politique than as a Gallican theorist, for he had no real interest in the enforcement of doctrinal orthodoxy. His *Apologie Catholique*, known in its English version as *A Catholic Apology against the Libels of the League*, elicited a reply from Robert Bellarmine, who, embarking on his long career as the chief exponent of the indirect authority of popes over kings, held that if a ruler endangered the salvation of his subjects, the pope had a duty to intervene in temporal affairs by virtue of the higher aim pursued by the spiritual power.[36] Bellarmine expanded the theory in his *Disputationes*, which Sixtus V regarded as so inadequate a statement of his *plenitudo potestatis* that he considered placing the work upon the Index. Meanwhile Belloy went on to publish *De l'authorité du Roy*, which linked the divine right of kings with Bodin's definition of sovereignty.

The situation changed dramatically when Henri III murdered the duc de Guise and his brother, the cardinal, in December 1588. He was then excommunicated by the Sorbonne in anticipation of papal action, and the parlement of Paris, purged by the revolutionaries of its royalist members, registered what amounted to the deposition of the king by the faculty of theology.[37] The subsequent assassination of the king in August of 1589 shattered whatever unity was left in the Gallican movement after the coup d'état at Blois. It was now faced with a heretic king in Henri IV and a triumphant ultramontanism in the League. Over half the bishops supported the League, and only a handful recognised the new king.[38] A larger proportion of the robe gave their loyalty to

[34]Pierre de Belloy, *Moyens d'abus* (n.p., 1586), pp. 2–3.
[35]*Ibid.*, p. 319.
[36]*Responsio ad praecipua capita apologiae quae falso Catholica inscribitur pro successione Henrici Navarreni in regnum Francorum* (n.p., 1586), by "Franciscus Romulus."
[37]For details see below, pp. 247–9.
[38]Figures are provided in Frederic J. Baumgartner's forthcoming book *Change and Stability in the French Episcopate: The Bishops and the Wars of Religion.*

Henri IV, and at Tours the royalist counterpart of the now Leaguer parlement of Paris turned their attention to denouncing the bulls brought by nuncios accredited to the League by Sixtus V and then by Gregory XIV. The new *premier président* at Tours was Jacques Faye d'Espesses, who had led the resistance to the Tridentine decrees against Leaguer pressure for their reception at the estates general in 1588. Faye died in the royal army besieging Paris in 1590, and it was left to his brother, Charles Faye, abbé de Saint-Fuscien, to explain to a scantily attended royalist clerical assembly at Chartres in 1591 why the bulls against Henri IV and those who supported him should be proclaimed void and unjust. Two years earlier the politique abbé had been bold enough to defend Henri III against clerical censure for his "cardinalicide."[39]

A number of theoretical restatements of Gallican principles were composed at this time. One of the most extreme came from the pen of Louis Servin, *avocat-général* at Tours. Like François Hotman, Servin was a Germanophile. His *Vindiciae secundum libertatem Ecclesiae Gallicanae* praised the Franks as standard bearers of liberty and criticised the present by the virtuous standards of Frankish antiquity. Where Hotman had seen Rome as subverting the ancient constitution of Francogallia, Servin saw the original freedoms of the church in "Gallo-Francia" oppressed by papal usurpation and Spanish tyranny. Servin turned the theory of divine right into a dynastic mystique, praising the virtues of the Protestant king in the light of his descent from his remote Germanic ancestors. In this context he ridiculed the papal bulls and their justification by the Jesuits:

> Let not these new thunderbolts from the pope turn us from the right path. It is not to be conceived that bishops of Rome could have dissolved the authority of an earthly king in time past or that they can do so today. . . . It is certain that the king derives his authority from God alone, and for that reason is called King of the Franks by the Grace of God. But the Jesuits say that when kings are created they freely acknowledge the laws of the gospel, and are immediately subjected like so many sheep to the pastor, or are as parts of the body to the head, namely the president of the ecclesiastical hierarchy, and are to be judged by him and cannot make judgments against him. . . . On the contrary, the power of a king is perpetual, and greatest of all is that of the King of the Franks. Not only is the laity placed under his sway, but the clergy too, as was once the case under the Roman emperors.[40]

Like Belloy, Servin made the divine right of the ruler the first principle of Gallicanism. He marshalled the usual arguments from scripture and repeated the conventional Gallican historical precedents, adding particular stress to the

---

[39]*Discours des raisons et moyens pour lesquels MM. du clergé, assemblez en la ville de Chartres, ont declaré les bulles monitoriales décernées par Grégoire XIV contre les ecclésiastiques et autres . . . qui ont demeurez en la fidelité du roy nulles et injustes* (Tours, 1591); *Ad Tractatum de clericis praesertim episcopis in divinis, scienter et sponte, cum Henrico Valesio, post cardinalicidium responsio* (n.p., 1589).

[40]*Vindiciae secundum libertatem ecclesiae gallicanae et regii status Gallo-Francorum sub Henrici IIII Rege Francorum et Navarrae* (Tours, 1591 [1st ed. 1590]), pp. 346–7.

role of Rome in promoting the religious wars in order to abase the monarchy. An equally rhetorical piece of royalist Gallican propaganda was written by François de Clary. His *Philippiques* denounced Gregory XIV as "promoted and elevated to the Roman see by all the corrupt practices that serve Spanish ambition." "Princes," he declaimed, "have always been superintendents of clerical offices. To deny this is to resist the order established by God's prudence, both in the ancient form of the empire and in the establishment of kingdoms. For this reason Saint Ambrose knew with confidence that Jesus Christ left us this particular doctrine of the magistrate."[41]

The strident tone of Servin and Clary can be attributed to the dilemma facing Gallican royalists who served a Protestant king. It is interesting to find that some men of the robe felt impelled to write on Gallicanism in more moderate terms at this time of crisis. Two such treatises were composed by the antiquarian Claude Fauchet and the constitutionalist Guy Coquille. In his *Traicté des libertez de l'Eglise gallicane* Fauchet showed his conviction that the Gallican tradition had indeed a historical reality, but he was wary of the more extravagant myths, using phrases such as "il y a grande apparence que . . ." and "il est croyable que . . ." whenever the evidence for a particular tenet was suspect.[42] Like Fauchet, Coquille made little of the divine right of kings in his *Discours des droits ecclésiastiques*. Royalist Gallicans applied conciliar doctrine to the internal rule of the church despite their abhorrence of its secular version as used by the League to justify resistance. Coquille saw both state and church in constitutionalist terms. It was not heresy, Coquille maintained, to obey a heretic king in temporal matters, and only the estates general could decide whether the ruler's religion disqualified him from office.[43]

So strong was the Gallican mentality within the robe that it manifested itself at times even in the Leaguer parlement of Paris. The bulls of 1590 and 1591 had been registered there with the customary reservation of the Gallican liberties, although this, of course, did not prevent the royalist parlement from denouncing them in terms reminiscent of clerical anathemas. In 1592 the new pope, Clement VIII, confirmed the bulls of his predecessors and sent a brief to the League requiring the election of a Catholic king. The emergency that had moved the League to profess the doctrine of election publicly also inspired the Paris parlement to register these papal mandates unconditionally. When the royalist parlement responded, Louis Dorléans, who had become the League's

---

[41]*Philipiques [sic] contre les bulles et autres pratiques de la faction d'Espagne* (Tours, 1611 [1st ed. 1592]), pp. 1r, 20v.

[42]Dupuy included a reliable text of Fauchet's treatise in his collection (see note 7), but the editor of the eighteenth-century version added notes to restore the myth and dogma Fauchet had avoided. Where Fauchet cautiously referred to Louis IX's action to prevent the excessive payment of annates to Rome, the editor explained that this was Saint Louis's Pragmatic Sanction (vol. 1, p. 84). Where Fauchet asserted there was little or no difference between priests and bishops in the primitive church, Dupuy's editorial successor added that bishops were superior by divine right and that it was heresy to affirm the contrary (vol. 1, p. 74).

[43]Dupuy, vol. 1, p. 210.

avocat-général, justified the action of his colleagues in a speech subsequently published as *Plaidoyez des gens du roy.* This supported the indirect authority of the pope to depose temporal sovereigns and denied that the parlement's most cherished Gallican weapon, the *appel comme d'abus,* could be invoked against a papal bull. Dorléans, the apocryphal "Catholic Englishman" who had argued against Navarre's claim to the throne in terms of constitutional law, now held that the estates could elect kings and modify constitutions at will. Neither the idea of the ancient constitution nor the historically based Gallican liberties seemed relevant any longer. Yet within a few months fear of the revolutionary radicals within their own party, and the growth of a peace movement, caused a reaction among the *parlementaires* of the League. Dorléans himself headed a commission of the parlement to advise the Leaguer estates of 1593 on the reception of the Tridentine decrees. His speech to the estates recommending specific reservations was thoroughly Gallican in tone, but it did not dissuade the deputies from voting for unqualified reception.[44]

The increasing conservatism of the Leaguer magistracy culminated in the parlement's declaration of June 1593 upholding the Salic law of succession – a step that prevented the election by the estates of any Habsburg candidate. The conversion of Henri IV was a final blow to the ultramontane cause. Thereafter the bishops began to return to their allegiance to the crown, even though a large section of the clergy continued to look direct to the pope, who for two years withheld absolution from the king. In 1594, when Henri IV recovered his capital and the parlement was reunited, Antoine Hotman, brother of the author of *Francogallia* and *procureur-général* in the former Leaguer parlement, published *Traicté des droits ecclésiastiques, franchises et libertez de l'Eglise gallicane.* The pamphlet demonstrated the survival of an ecclesiastical Gallicanism in conservative Leaguer mentality. Citing Gerson, D'Ailly, and Almain, Hotman sought a middle position between papal authority and Gallican privilege. "It is good," he wrote, "to keep an honest liberty but it is dangerous to depress too much the dignity of the pope."[45] The rights of the universal bishop need not derogate from those of ordinary bishops, and, if the rights of the papacy to intervene in temporal affairs were dubious theoretically, it was nonetheless true that popes had actually wielded temporal power over Naples, Sicily, and England. But the divine right of kings was far less acceptable than that of popes. "Perhaps there are some who say," Hotman continued, "that the pope on his side ought not to have jurisdiction (*cognoissance*) over kings, and that royal sovereignty gives them the privilege of being justiciable to God alone, but this is a scabrous and thorny issue (*un passage scabreux et plein de rencontres espineuses*)."[46] To this a royalist Gallican editor of Hotman's text in later times added the note: "The Leaguer

[44]Robert Christie Gould, *Louis Dorléans and the French Catholic League* (Bryn Mawr College Ph.D. dissertation, 1975), pp. 100–35.
[45]Dupuy, vol. 1, p. 155.
[46]*Ibid.,* p. 165.

advocate plainly has difficulty in abandoning ultramontane pretensions." The refusal of the divine right of kings reveals how difficult it was for adherents of the League to accept the political Gallicanism that was reestablished and strengthened by the triumph of Henri IV, but the references to Gerson and the conciliarists indicate the paradoxical survival of an ecclesiastical Gallicanism which could blend with Catholic reformism, if not with the current resurgent papalism.

Gallicanism had shifted in emphasis when Navarre became heir to the throne. It changed again when he became king on the death of Henri III, and moved in yet another direction in the period between Henri IV's conversion and his absolution. The theory of divine right was in the ascendancy but it was necessary to propitiate Clement VIII and to reunite the disparate elements of the French church. This was the atmosphere in which Pierre Pithou composed *Le Traité des libertez de l'Eglise gallicane* (1594). Pithou, a barrister pleading at the bar of the parlement, had remained in Paris under the League, hiding his political opinions and secretly contributing to the *Satyre Ménippée*, which ridiculed the proceedings of the Leaguer estates of 1593.[47] On the return of the king, Pithou and his brother François, together with Jacques Leschassier, were associated with the restored *procureur-général* of the parlement, Jacques de la Guesle. It had been La Guesle who in 1588 had insisted to Henri III that the Tridentine decrees could not be accepted without Gallican reservations. He was a vehement defender of political Gallicanism and an exponent of divine right monarchy. When the proposition that popes had temporal power was once more offered in an academic debate in 1595, La Guesle included in the parlement's censure the statement:

As God is by nature the first king and prince, so is the king by creation and imitation God in all things here upon earth. God consists in himself alone and of himself alone, and the king depends upon God alone, who has fashioned him on the model of omnipotence.[48]

All three of La Guesle's assistants became authors of Gallican treatises, but Pierre Pithou's *Traité* was the most celebrated of them all. In eighty-three points he firmly but moderately outlined the principles of political Gallicanism. His motives were declared in his prefatory address to the king:

During the disorders and confusions occurring in this kingdom, some through malice and ambition, and others through ignorance and baseness, have either slandered or scorned, as if they were phantoms and chimeras, those sublime rights and precious palladium which our most pious ancestors have, with such care and virtue, religiously preserved for us to the present day under the title of the liberties of the Gallican Church.[49]

[47]See above, p. 84.
[48]Dupuy, vol. 1, p. 213.
[49]*Ibid.*, app. 3, p. 1.

In setting forth these liberties Pithou could hardly appear conciliatory to the Vatican. Before his death in 1596 he began the great collection of Gallican tracts subsequently published by Pierre Dupuy in 1639.[50] Pithou had once been a Protestant, and, like Dumoulin, was still so regarded in ultramontane circles.

Two of the items insisted upon by Clement VIII as conditions for absolving the king were the return of the Jesuits to France and the unqualified reception of the decrees of Trent. The Jesuits had been expelled by the parlement as abettors of the regicide late in 1594. Their trial had begun soon after Henri IV's entry into Paris on the ground that two of their members had suborned the would-be assassin, Barrière. There were echoes of the speech against the Jesuits delivered by Etienne Pasquier in the parlement thirty years earlier in the indictment launched against them by Antoine Arnauld. The hearing was scarcely an impartial one. While the judges were deliberating, the news arrived of a new attempt, by Jean Chastel, to assassinate the king. The parlement had no conclusive evidence of Jesuit involvement in regicide, but it decreed the expulsion of all members of the order as "corrupters of youth, disturbers of the public peace, and enemies of the king and state."[51] Henri IV received his absolution nevertheless, and in 1603 he kept his promise to readmit them. However, the parlement prevented him from honouring his undertaking to receive the Tridentine decrees.

In England, Protestant prejudice against the Jesuits grew out of their association with the mission for reconversion and from the assumption that they were the agents of Spain as well as of a Spanish-controlled papacy. In the years of the Armada and the League close alliance with Henri IV and exposure to the Gallican and politique literature that served his cause reinforced English fears that the Jesuit order was the most subtle and dangerous weapon employed by the national enemy. In 1594 Arnauld's speech and a new edition of Pasquier's earlier indictment appeared in English as *The Arraignment of the Whole Society of the Jesuits in France* and *The Jesuit Displayed, Containing the Original and Proceedings of the Jesuits together with the Fruits of their Doctrine.* This was also the year in which Robert Parsons issued his *Conference about the Next Succession,* and another English Jesuit, John Bridgewater, published at Trier an expanded version of *Concertatio Ecclesiae Catholicae in Anglia adversus Calvino-Papistas et Puritanos,* composed by John Fenn and the Jesuit John Gibbon a decade earlier.[52] The

[50]See note 7. Dupuy composed a long commentary on Pithou's *Traité* in which he referred to the parallel use of the terms *Ecclesia Anglicana* and *Ecclesia Gallicana* in earlier times. *Commentaire de M. Dupuy* (Paris, 1715), vol. 1, p. 7.
[51]Etienne Pasquier, *Les Recherches de la France* (Paris, 1633), p. 314. Pasquier published the third book of the *Recherches,* devoted to the Gallican Church and its relations with Rome, in 1596. Before his death in 1615 he added new chapters influenced by the continuing controversies. See below, p. 180.
[52]W. Nicholson, *The English Historical Library* (London, 1714), pp. 114–15.

last was more of a martyrology than an instrument of subversion, but Parsons's *Conference* constituted a powerful summation of radical resistance theory drawn partly from Leaguer sources. The first half of the book consisted of a general discourse on modes of monarchical succession, and here Belloy's *Apology*, with its theory of divine right dynasticism, was selected for specific refutation. The two Leaguer works to which Parsons seems indebted were *De Justa Abdicatione* by Jean Boucher and *De Justa Authoritate* by "Gulielmus Rossaeus" (William Reynolds), both written in the context of the deposition and death of Henri III and Navarre's claim to the throne.[53] The English edition of the *Conference* had nothing to say about the theory of papal deposition of kings, which was an important argument in Boucher's treatise, but two years later Parsons produced a Latin version of the second half of the *Conference*, which included a new chapter on papal authority.[54]

It was to Reynolds that Parsons seems to have looked for inspiration on secular resistance. His account of the origins of government and of its various forms, which he regarded as arbitrary human inventions, closely parallels passages in *De Justa Authoritate*.[55] Parsons saw secular authority as "ordained for the benefit of the weal public and not otherwise." Like Reynolds, he now held that the community possessed an inalienable sovereignty and the ruler merely "potestas vicaria or delegata."[56] At any point the community might choose to withdraw its commission and to alter the constitution. This sentiment was essentially that which prevailed in the League in the years 1592–3. In the last resort the theory of popular sovereignty was the solvent of the mystique of the ancient constitution.

If Anglicans and Gallicans agreed in their antipathy towards the Jesuits, their views of Calvinism were by no means identical. In France the possibility of schism from Rome remained strong until the absolution of 1595, but there was no chance whatever of religious reconciliation between royalist Catholics and the leaders of the Reformed churches. In any case, their political marriage of convenience ended with the conversion of Henri IV and the defeat of the League. It is true that there was an ecumenical trend among a few members of the high robe, such as the historian Jacques-Auguste de Thou, and also that this group was in touch with such Huguenot scholars as Isaac Casaubon, who were prepared to join Anglican and Gallican controversialists against Rome, particularly at the prompting of Paolo Sarpi.[57] Nevertheless, the opposition of

[53]See above, p. 146.
[54]Holmes, *Resistance and Compromise*, p. 152. See also Holmes's article "The Authority and Early Reception of a Conference about the Next Succession," *Historical Journal*, 23 (1980), 415–29; and Arnold Pritchard, *Catholic Loyalism in Elizabethan England* (Chapel Hill, N.C., 1978), pp. 18–21.
[55]R. Doleman (Robert Parsons), *A Conference about the Next Succession to the Crown of England* (n.p., 1594), pp. 1–13.
[56]*Ibid.*, p. 73.
[57]Irenic endeavours are discussed by Corrado Vivanti, *Lotta politica e pace religiosa in Francia fra*

the Catholic magistrates to the Huguenots is clear from the resistance they offered to the registration of the Edict of Nantes.

Calvinist theology appealed to many Anglicans, including leading prelates such as Whitgift. But if the Anglican establishment differed radically from its Gallican counterpart in this respect, it was in agreement with it on Calvinist ecclesiastical discipline. The presbytery was the enemy of the episcopate. Anti-episcopal sentiment remained a significant force in England even after the failure in 1584 and 1587 to advance the cause of Presbyterianism through parliament. Whitgift himself reacted with severity to personal attacks upon him by "Martin Marprelate" in 1588 and 1589. In response to this kind of subversion a movement appeared to recognise *iure divino* episcopacy. The idea had been supported at Trent by the French contingent accompanying the cardinal of Lorraine, but it was not revived in France until after the religious wars. In England it was taken up in a sermon delivered by Richard Bancroft in 1589.[58] The concept was then developed by Hadrian Saravia, a professor of divinity from Leyden who became an Anglican vicar and a canon of Canterbury. Saravia maintained the divine right of bishops in *De Diversis ministrorum evangelii gradibus* (1590) and defended the theory in *Defensio tractationis* (1594) against criticism from Beza in Geneva. Matthew Sutcliffe, who later became dean of Exeter, pursued it further in his *Ecclesiastical Discipline* (1591), and attacked the presbytery as a novel device in Christian church government (*De Presbyterio eiusque nova in ecclesia Christiana politeia*, 1591). It was also in this context that Thomas Bilson, soon to be bishop of Worcester and then of Winchester, produced *A Compendious Discourse proving Episcopacy to be of Divine Institution* in 1593. Bilson had criticised Catholic ideas of resistance in *True Difference between Christian Subjection and Unchristian Rebellion* in 1586, but in that work he defended the Huguenots, whom he saw as reacting against unjust persecution. Now he condemned Calvinist ecclesiastical discipline as subversive in both church and state. The same theme was developed in two works by Bancroft in 1593 (*Dangerous Positions* and *A Survey of the Pretended Holy Discipline*). While Calvinists and papalists were held to agree in separating church and state, according to Bancroft their real purpose was to assert the dominance of the spiritual arm. The divine right of bishops was employed to refute the divine right of the presbytery, but it might also suggest the independence of the episcopacy from the crown. Bancroft, who became bishop of London in 1597

Cinque e Seicento (Turin, 1963). The tendency to see Gallicanism within the robe as tolerant and enlightened is deplored by Jonathan Powis, "Gallican Liberties and the Politics of Later Sixteenth-Century France," *Historical Journal*, 26 (1983), 515–30. David Wootton considers Sarpi in this context and concludes that his religious postures were insincere: *Paolo Sarpi: Between Renaissance and Enlightenment* (Cambridge, 1983).
[58]Patrick Collinson, *The Religion of Protestants: The Church in English Society, 1559–1625* (Oxford, 1982), p. 11.

and succeeded Whitgift at Canterbury in 1604, carefully avoided this implication. The supreme governor acted mediately as the conveyor of divine election, and whatever rights of nonsacerdotal jurisdiction a bishop possessed he owed to the ruler. Further tracts in support of divine right episcopacy were published in the early years of the reign of James I and led to considerable controversy.[59]

At the same time as the theory of the divine right of bishops began to receive credence in high Anglican circles, the divine right of kings was also to be heard. "No bishop, no king" was to become the familiar aphorism of James I. In France divine right could afford a shield for both king and prelate against Rome, although little was said of the direct sanction that bishops received from heaven, perhaps because it was an ingredient in ecclesiastical Gallicanism, and the latter had been submerged by its political variant. The descending theory of regal power had, however, been a defence of the French monarchy against the doctrine of popular sovereignty as well as against the pope. The first appearance of the idea in England, apart from vague enunciations of it in the regime of Henry VIII, occurred in the translations of politique and Gallican propaganda against the League. It was sometimes reflected in Anglican writers, as in Bilson's *True Difference*, but the constitutional role of parliament was too obvious a fact to be ignored, even by those who, like Bancroft, adopted an absolutist tone in refuting Calvinist and Catholic resistance theory. It was another work by Saravia, *De imperandi Authoritate et Christiana obedientia* (1593), which first made an unequivocal case for the unlimited authority of the Tudor crown based on both divine right and Bodinian sovereignty. Following Bodin, Saravia declared England an absolute monarchy and parliament a mere advisory body. He specifically repudiated doctrines of consent, contract, and public resistance contained in the *Vindiciae contra tyrannos*, Buchanan's *De Jure Regni apud Scotos*, and the closely related Leaguer treatise by William Reynolds, *De Justa Authoritate*.[60]

The first four books of Richard Hooker's *Laws of Ecclesiastical Polity* also appeared in 1593, and it has been Hooker's book, rather than that of his friend Saravia, that has generally been credited with laying the foundation of Anglican doctrine on church and state. In their own time, however, it seems to have been Saravia, not Hooker, who received a modicum of official blessing.[61] Hooker believed that all power was ultimately ordained by God, but he rejected Saravia's version of the divine right of kings. Government was based upon the consent of the whole commonwealth, of which every Anglican was a member, just as every Englishman was a member of the national church. In the making of ecclesiastical law Hooker endorsed the authority of parliament:

---

[59] *Ibid.*, p. 12.
[60] J. P. Sommerville, "Richard Hooker, Hadrian Saravia, and the Advent of the Divine Right of Kings," *History of Political Thought*, 4 (1983), 229–45.
[61] *Ibid.*, p. 230.

The parliament of England, together with convocation annexed thereunto, is that whereupon the very essence of all government within this kingdom doth depend; it is even the body of the whole realm; it consisteth of the king and all that within the land are subject to him.[62]

The only saving clause for the role of the clergy was the phrase "convocation annexed thereunto," but this was vaguer than Henry VIII's pronouncements about the joint consent of parliament and convocation. Hooker justified his Erastian solution by reference to Aristotle: "For every politic society that being true which Aristotle saith, namely 'that the scope thereof is not simply to live, nor the duty so much to provide for the life, as for the means of living well.' "[63] In terms of Aquinas's gloss upon Aristotle, "gratia bene vivendi" entailed responsibility for spiritual welfare. Hence Hooker condemned the separation of church and state. He saw two kinds of adversaries to the royal supremacy, "one sort defending that supreme power in causes ecclesiastical throughout the world appertaineth of divine right to the bishop of Rome: another sort that the said power belongeth in every national church unto the clergy thereof assembled."[64] There was nothing in Gallicanism quite like the "judicious" Hooker. The nearest was, perhaps, Pierre Grégoire, who was also a master of ambiguity, and who had some influence upon English Catholic thought in the course of the archpriest controversy.

The debate that brought the disunity of English Catholicism into the open and presented English readers in general with fresh views of Gallican theory began with the appointment in 1598 of George Blackwell, a priest known to be under Jesuit influence, to administer the Catholic Church in England. Behind it lay a decade of acrimonious tension between secular priests and Jesuits. The lines of battle had been drawn in the detention centre at Wisbech as well as in the seminary in Rome directed by the Jesuits.[65] It was Robert Parsons, the moving force in English Catholicism after the death of Cardinal William Allen, who became the rector of the seminary, and whose *Conference about the Next Succession* became the target for attack by the seculars. A number of the secular priests had attended the University of Pont-à-Musson in Lorraine, and had there absorbed the ideas of two politique professors of law, Pierre Grégoire and William Barclay. Both were involved in a conflict between the faculty of law and the Jesuits who controlled the faculties of arts and theology at Pont-à-Musson – a conflict which became more intense when a group of Jesuits expelled from France by the parlement's *arrêt* of December 1594 found refuge there.

Grégoire had been at Toulouse with Belloy, but at this stage he showed no

---

[62] *Of the Laws of Ecclesiastical Polity* (London, 1682), book 8, p. 458.
[63] *Ibid.*, p. 439.
[64] *Ibid.*, p. 443.
[65] Pritchard, *Catholic Loyalism*, pp. 78–118.

Gallican or politique sympathies, and in fact published a plea to receive the Tridentine decrees in answer to Dumoulin's *Conseil* of 1564 (*Response au conseil de Charles des Molins,* 1583). His early works were devoted to the method or "art" of jurisprudence and to the systematising of the canon law.[66] At the time of the new influx of Jesuit fathers Grégoire turned his attention to a general study of politics, published in 1596 as *De Republica.* This encyclopaedic treatise managed to support both the ascending and the descending theories of political power. Like Hooker, he saw the origin of authority in a communal act, but in Grégoire's case it was an irrevocable transfer of sovereignty on the model of the Roman *lex regia.* At the same time the community acted as the instrument of divine will. Monarchy was the form of government most pleasing to God, and reflected the hierarchical order he had imprinted upon creation. A king was, therefore, the minister of God and the instrument of his law.[67] Grégoire was also a follower of Bodin's theory of sovereignty, but he extended its internal paradoxes so that he was both absolutist and constitutionalist. Legislative sovereignty was supreme and indivisible, but the method of administration might differ from the form of the state, and hence a monarchy could govern through aristocratic and democratic elements.[68] Moreover, the ruler could not alter fundamental laws. His power extended over the clergy as well as the laity, and he could tax the former as well as the latter. Yet the government of the church was separate from that of the state. Here Grégoire showed himself to be an admirer of Gerson ("egregius et pius vir"). The supreme authority of the universal church lay in the council, but, as Gerson had noted, its method of administration was mixed. The pope, bishops, and clergy were but men and inferior in civil matters to princes, even if the episcopal power of ordination and the sacerdotal power of the mass lay outside secular jurisdiction.[69] Grégoire managed to combine elements of both ecclesiastical and political Gallicanism, and his reliance upon Gerson was to be followed by others in the next decade.

Grégoire spoke slightingly of the League as an example of the false use of religion as a cloak to hide rebellion. Barclay's *De Regno et regali potestate* (1600) was a polemical attack upon both Leaguer and Huguenot theorists of resistance, for whom he coined the term "monarchomach." Like Belloy, he combined the theories of monarchical sovereignty and the divine right of kings. It was not Barclay's purpose in *De Regno* to rebut papalist assertions, but when he did refer to papal authority he noted that Christ had appointed Peter head of the church and had therefore chosen the monarchical form for its government.[70] In later years his posthumous *De Potestate Papae* (1609) proved to be an effective compendium of arguments against ultramontanism. Like his colleague

---

[66] On Grégoire's career see Collot, *L'Ecole doctrinale,* pp. 34–44, 55–63.

[67] *De Republica* (Lyon, 1609), pp. 37, 268.

[68] *Ibid.,* p. 113.

[69] *Ibid.,* pp. 181–2.

[70] Collot, *L'Ecole doctrinale,* p. 264.

Grégoire, he drew a line between the independence of the clergy in sacerdotal matters and their subservience to the secular prince in all other respects. Barclay was a convinced Catholic who refused James I's offer of patronage because of the attached condition that he join the Church of England. Until his last years he respected the spiritual role of the pope while advocating loyalty to the secular ruler. Hence his stance suited those English seculars who professed their obedience to the Protestant queen.

The seculars' first appeal to Rome to withdraw Blackwell's commission was rebuffed in the spring of 1599. They then referred their case to the Sorbonne, and a year later obtained a declaration that they had not acted as schismatics. Thus encouraged, they made a second appeal to the pope and it was on this occasion that they received the support of the French ambassador to the Vatican.[71] The government of Elizabeth, anxious to exploit disunity among English Catholics, also seemed to favour the appellants, who hoped to obtain toleration. Richard Bancroft, in particular, seemed to offer them a sympathetic ear. But negotiations proved fruitless, and the second decision of Clement VIII banned further contact with the Anglican establishment. In other respects the pope's brief was favourable to the appellants, for it obliged Blackwell to detach himself from Jesuit influence.

In the course of the second appeal the seculars aligned themselves with Gallican principles in a string of pamphlets, and, following the Gallican denunciations of 1594, extended the black legend of the Jesuits as sinister conspirators and murderers of kings.[72] The sentiments of the seculars expressed in print were at times scarcely less restrained than remarks in their private correspondence about "those violent and bloody spirits who continuously and unnaturally practise against their prince and country" and "those unnatural bastards that do attend to nought else but conquests and invasions."[73] The most virulent attacks came from the pen of William Watson, whose rhetoric was so extreme that his fellow appellants, Christopher Bagshaw and William Bishop, begged him to moderate his tone in the interests of their cause.[74] As the seculars were pressing their second appeal in Rome in 1602, it became known that their new protector, Henri IV, was contemplating the return of the Jesuits to France. Two Gallican tracts, *Le Franc Discours* by Antoine Arnauld and *The Jesuit's Catechism* by Etienne Pasquier, were issued to dissuade the king, and both were promptly republished in English by Watson. This occurred just after the pope's brief, and Watson took advantage of the discomfiture of the Jesuits to abuse Parsons and his colleagues in the preface to Arnauld's piece:

[71]John Bossy, "Henri IV, the Appellants and the Jesuits," *Recusant History*, 8 (1965), 80–112.
[72]Francis Edwards, *The Jesuits in England* (Tunbridge Wells, 1985), traces the origins of the legend and exonerates from political activity those members of the order working in England itself, but not those in exile on the continent.
[73]T. G. Law (ed.), *The Archpriest Controversy: Documents relating to the Dissensions of the Roman Catholic Clergy, 1597–1602* (Camden Society, 1896), vol. 2, p. XI.
[74]Pritchard, *Catholic Loyalism*, p. 156.

God preserve this realm from their Spanish designments; her Majesty from their Clem-
ents, Barrières and Ehuds of the Jesuitical inspiration; the good estate of the Catholic
Church from their frantic deformations; us poor secular priests from their malicious
practices; and you all true Catholics from the leaven of such Pharisees.[75]

Arnauld's text, discussing the supposed role of the Jesuits in the League, was
not far behind Watson's vehemence. While he paid tribute to their courage,
industry, and intelligence, he referred also to the "the deep dissembling, the
smooth hypocrisy and the secret venom which the Jesuits foster within their
breasts."[76]

Watson wrote a much longer preface, addressed to "all English Catholics
that are faithful subjects to Queen Elizabeth, our most dread Sovereign," for
his edition of *The Jesuit's Catechism*. There he referred to the writings of Grégoire, "a great lawyer and a sound Catholic," who had refuted Jesuit political
doctrine. He borrowed freely from Arnauld's tract in this preface, adding
abusive epithets and windy rhetoric:

Their minds are bloody, and altogether imbrued with the blood of the late murdered
king [Henri III]. They filled the pulpits with fire, with blood, with blasphemies, making
the people believe that God was a murderer of kings, and attributing to heaven the stroke
of a knife forged in hell.[77]

Pasquier's own text repeated material from *The Jesuit Displayed* and from the
Gallican third book of his *Recherches*. Later, in the 1606 edition of the *Recherches*, he added the new material from the *Catechism*.[78]

Watson had a keener mind than his vituperation would suggest, but even in
theoretical discussion his ardour got the better of his respect for truth. His
earlier tract, *Important Considerations* (1601), attributed the secular resistance
theory of the League to the Jesuits and associated it with the Calvinist monarchomachs. This was far from accurate, for Jesuit theorists such as Bellarmine
concentrated on the religious rather than the secular grounds of revolt, and,
apart from Mariana, they were not advocates of tyrannicide. The theories of
Boucher and Reynolds on secular resistance were not those of the Jesuits, and
in this respect Parsons's *Conference* was exceptional for his order. The *Conference* was constantly attacked by the appellants, but Parsons himself had now
dropped such ideas, and even pretended in his answers to their propaganda that
the work had been conservative in tenor.[79] Two appellant polemicists, William
Clitheroe and William Clarke, claimed that Parsons's ideas justifying revolt

[75]*Le Franc Discours, a Discourse presented of late to the French King* (n.p., 1602; English Recusant
Literature, vol. 237, 1975), unpaginated preface.
[76]*Ibid.*, p. 138.
[77]*The Jesuit's Catechism or Examination of their Doctrine* (n.p., 1602), unpaginated preface.
[78]*Recherches* (1633), p. 339, explaining the development of the book. It is clear that this section of
the *Recherches* does not live up to the praise historans have lavished upon Pasquier for his
impartiality.
[79]Holmes, *Resistance and Compromise*, p. 222.

were like those of Buchanan.[80] The observation was not so far from the mark, because Parsons does seem to have adapted Reynolds's *De Justa Authoritate*, and this work contained ideas very like Buchanan's.[81] It was not merely appellant writers who responded to Parsons's *Conference*. Anglican replies came from the pens of Matthew Sutcliffe, whose advocacy of episcopal authority has already been mentioned, and of Sir John Hayward, who was later to be associated with Sutcliffe in the foundation of Chelsea College, an institution for antipapal propaganda established by James I.[82] Sutcliffe also published refutations of Bellarmine's view of authority in the church.[83] Both he and Hayward cited Gallican and politique writers against Parsons, whom they associated with Leaguer political thought. In this way the appellants served as a bridge between Anglicans and Gallicans. A common front had emerged which was to be tested in the years that followed.

In the tensions associated with the return of the Jesuits, Gallican unity was set in doubt. The parlement, which fought hard to resist the king's edict, was at times at odds with the Sorbonne, which had censured the 1603 publication of Louis Servin's *Plaidoyers*, an extremist manifesto of political Gallicanism. A new spirit of Catholic reform was felt within the French episcopacy. At the 1605 assembly of the clergy strong pressure was mounted for the reception of the Tridentine decrees, but at the same time the divine right of the king was affirmed in the strongest possible terms by Jérôme de Villars, archbishop of Vienne. "The king," the archbishop declaimed, "holds his authority from that great God by whose eternal foresight this crown, through continual succession by blood, has been rendered the living image on earth of the eternal government he possesses in heaven."[84] Within the clergy there was a desire for compromise that could acknowledge the rights of both pope and king, and also find a place for episcopal authority. The English appellants might have suggested some precedent for this, and they had seen Pierre Grégoire as offering theoretical justification.

Grégoire was even more relevant to the problems confronting Gallicanism. He had defended both the decisions of Trent and the divine sanction accorded to kingship. Moreover, he had drawn inspiration from Gerson and had sought a *via media* in conciliarist doctrine, even if he had ended by supporting monarchical sovereignty. The compromise was not to be. Gerson was suddenly to be revived by Edmond Richer, who in 1606 edited his works, together with selec-

---

[80]*Ibid.*, p. 195.

[81]See above, pp. 144–9.

[82]Sutcliffe, *A New Challenge to N. D.* (1600) and *A Brief Reply to a Certain Odious Libel recently published by a Jesuit* (1600); Hayward, *An Answer to the First Part of a Certain Conference* (1603).

[83]*De Pontifice Romano adversus R. Bellarminum* (1600), and *De vera Christi ecclesia adversus R. Bellarminum* (1600).

[84]*Remonstrance du clergé de France,* cited by Victor Martin, *La Gallicanisme politique et le clergé de France* (Paris, 1929), p. 84.

tions from the conciliar writers Pierre d'Ailly, Jacques Almain, and John Mair.[85] But Bellarmine, scenting the dangers of revived conciliarism in the papal conflict with Venice, refuted Gerson. Richer answered with *Apologia pro Joanne Gersonio,* but the endeavour to use elements from ecclesiastical Gallicanism to establish a new harmony foundered through the intransigence of both Rome and the parlement of Paris. Such intransigence was promoted by circumstances external to France: the coincidence of the Venetian interdict and the controversy about the English oath of allegiance.

Paul V's interdict of 1606 was a response to Venetian insistence on applying civil jurisdiction to clergy accused of criminal acts, and to Venetian laws restricting ecclesiastical landholding. The Venetian ambassador in Paris had been directed to recruit Gallican support during the crisis, and it may have been Richer who supplied him with a list of conciliar and other antipapal writers suitable for publication.[86] The first outcome of this was the appearance of a tract by Gerson, translated into Italian by Sarpi, discussing the improper use of papal excommunication.[87] It was to this that Bellarmine replied with *Riposta ad un libretto di Gio. Gersone,* and Richer, at Sarpi's bidding, then embarked on his own tract and his edition of Gerson. Such printed exchanges burgeoned so rapidly that by the summer of 1607 the Parisian diarist Pierre de l'Estoile, who was in close touch with the Gallican magistrates known to Sarpi, had collected fifty-three of them.[88] Among those in this Gallican group who published tracts in defence of Venice were Jacques Leschassier, Louis Servin, and Nicolas Vignier.[89] Sarpi's contacts resulted in a continuing correspondence with Gillot, Leschassier, and De Thou, as well as with the Huguenots Groslot de l'Isle and Isaac Casaubon.[90] In later years Sarpi's letters to Casaubon are full of praise for James I in his role as the leader of the antipapal forces in the controversy about the oath of allegiance.

The Venetian crisis, like the archpriest controversy, confirmed links between Gallicans and Anglicans. What is more, it revealed extreme positions not always

[85]*Ioannis Gersonii, Doctoria et Cancellarii Parisiensis, opera . . .* (Paris, 1606). On Richer see E. Préclin, "Edmond Richer, 1559–1631. Sa vie, son oeuvre, le richérisme," *Revue d'histoire moderne,* 28 (1930), 241–69, and 29 (1930), 321–36; E. Puyol, *Edmond Richer: étude historique et critique sur la rénovation du gallicanisme au commencement du XVIIᵉ siècle* (2 vols., Paris, 1876).
[86]William J. Bouwsma, *Venice and the Defense of Republican Liberty* (Berkeley, Calif., 1968), p. 399. Bouwsma says "someone at the Sorbonne."
[87]*Trattato e resoluzione sopra la validità delle scommuniche di Giovanni Gersone,* in Giovanni Gamberin (ed.), *Istoria dell'Interdetto e altri scritti editi ed inediti,* (3 vols., Bari, 1940), vol. 2, pp. 171–84.
[88]André Martin (ed.), *Journal de L'Estoile pour le règne de Henri IV, 1601–1609* (Paris, 1958), p. 252. L'Estoile was in touch with Pierre Dupuy, Gillot, Leschassier, and Servin.
[89]Leschassier, *Consultatio Parisii cuiusdam de controversia inter sanctitem Pauli Quinti et serenissimam rempublicam Venetam* (1607); Servin, *Pro libertate status et reipublicae Venetorum Gallofranci ad Philenetum epistola* (1607); Vignier, *De Venetorum excommunicatione adversus Caesarem Baronium* (1607).
[90]Boris Ulianich (ed.), *Lettere ai gallicani* (Wiesbaden, 1961); M. D. Busnelli (ed.), *Lettere ai protestanti* (2 vols., Bari, 1931). Ulianich's introduction provides details of Sarpi's Gallican network.

evident in other contexts. Bellarmine's role reinforced the false assumption that the Jesuits were the moving force behind papal aggression. The papal champion did, indeed, seem to be passing beyond his theory of indirect power when he referred to Boniface VIII's *Unam Sanctam* to contend that both swords might be wielded by the pontiff.[91] For his part, Sarpi asserted that the spiritual arm had no enforceable powers on earth, no special rights over property, and no legal jurisdiction to punish criminous clerks. Sarpi also held that the civil power was as much a divine institution as the church, and that the state, whether republic or monarchy, had a duty to direct and supervise every aspect of human life.[92] This extremism was also to be found in Servin and Leschassier, and was expressed in their writings on the Gallican Church as well as on Venice.

Leschassier, as noted earlier, was the associate of the Pithou brothers in the office of *procureur-général* La Guesle after the fall of the League. His *Consultatio* showed how readily Gallican principles could be adapted to the Venetian conflict. His support of Venetian secular jurisdiction over the clergy was justified from the councils of Chalcedon and Antioch and the *Novella* in the *Corpus Juris Civilis*.[93] Moreover, he argued that Gallican liberties established in early Merovingian, and even in Gallo-Roman times, had then pertained to Italy also, and this enabled him to make use of the material he was simultaneously preparing for his treatise *De la liberté ancienne et canonique de l'Eglise gallicane*. In this work the historical theme assumed a force and clarity surpassing the earlier surveys of ancient Gallicanism by Du Tillet and Fauchet, which were also being set in print at this time.[94] Nor was Leschassier restrained by the need for moderation governing Pierre Pithou in his treatise of 1594. He made much more of conciliar theory than had his immediate predecessors. Three of his five concluding points were devoted to this issue, stressing the acceptability of the earliest councils of the church before the growth of papal ambitions, and affirming that "modern councils, which imposed servitude, must yield to ancient councils, which established liberty." In his fourth point he described the authority of the king over the church, describing him as "the exterior bishop" who, without possessing sacerdotal powers himself, had the duty to supervise their employment by the priesthood. His final point was to confine the divine right of bishops to a narrow interpretation of their spiritual jurisdiction, their other supposed powers being "temporal and provisional, and made for temporal human reasons."[95] Together Leschassier and Richer were defining a new balance between political and ecclesiastical Gallicanism.

---

[91]Bouwsma, *Venice*, p. 429, citing *Riposta alla riposta*.
[92]*Ibid.*, pp. 432–3.
[93]Leschassier, *Consultatio*, p. 3.
[94]Du Tillet's memoir of 1551 and Fauchet's of 1591 (see notes 10 and 12) were published in 1606 and 1608 respectively. Leschassier's *De la liberté ancienne* (1606) was also reprinted by Pierre Dupuy (vol. 1, pp. 235–40).
[95]Dupuy, vol. 1, p. 240.

While the Gallicans of the robe were applying the lessons learnt from the Venetian interdict to their own situation, a larger controversy was centred on events in England. It began when Thomas Morton, later to become a royal chaplain and then bishop of Durham, published his *Exact Discovery of Romish Doctrine in the Case of Conspiracy and Rebellion* immediately after the Gunpowder Plot. When the oath of allegiance was imposed in 1606, Morton produced *A Full Satisfaction concerning a Double Romish Iniquity*. His tactic was to damn the Jesuits in general by association with Robert Parsons, and to associate the latter with the theorists of the League, following the example of the appellants. Parsons denied connections with the plot and sought an accommodation with the king in *A Treatise tending to Mitigation towards Catholic Subjects in England* (1607). Although now maintaining English Catholic loyalty once again, Parsons did not disavow the theory of indirect papal supremacy. He compounded this mistake by a defence of Reynolds and Boucher. Morton took full advantage of this opening in further exchanges. Parsons turned to attack the king's own defence of the oath of allegiance, and was in turn addressed by James I's champion, William Barlow, bishop of Lincoln.[96]

The two principal adversaries in this ever widening ideological debate were the king and Bellarmine. The oath required English Catholics to deny papal supremacy unequivocally, and Paul V issued two briefs forbidding them to conform. When Blackwell himself disobeyed the pope, it was Bellarmine who rebuked him in an open letter. James I's *Triplici Nodo Triplex Cuneus* (1607), better known by its subtitle *An Apology for the Oath of Allegiance*, responded both to Bellarmine and to Paul V. In his answer to the king, in which he masqueraded as his own chaplain Mathaeus Tortus, Bellarmine retreated from his more exposed position over the Venetian interdict. James then came out with *A Premonition to all Most Mighty Monarchs*, using it as a preface to a new edition of the *Apology*. It was here that the king repeated the theme familiar from earlier attacks upon the Jesuits, calling the fathers "nothing but Puritan-Papists." James commented at length on the Gallican liberties, conceded the pope's primacy among the bishops without acknowledging his temporal power, and, like the Gallicans, discussed the first ecumenical councils as the cornerstone of doctrine and discipline. Even Gerson was invoked by the royal polemicist, but nothing was said to suggest the conciliarists' antipathy to theories of royal absolutism.[97] In all this James sounded very like his fellow Scot, William Barclay, who, although he refused to abandon his faith to accept the king's patronage, left *De Potestate Papae* as his testament.

One of the most penetrating summations from the antipapal camp was *Herod*

[96]Morton, *A Preamble unto an Encounter with P. R.* (1608); Barlow, *An Answer to a Catholic Englishman* (1609); etc. It is not possible to analyse here the full range of minor works in the oath of allegiance controversy. A summary is provided by C. H. McIlwain (ed.), *Political Works of James I* (Cambridge, Mass., 1918), introduction.
[97]McIlwain, *Political Works of James I*, pp. 119–27.

and Pilate Reconciled, or the Concord of Papist and Puritan (1610), by a Cambridge theologian, David Owen. This adopted a detached view of Gallican theory, and traced the subversive idea of popular sovereignty expressed by the Calvinist and Catholic monarchomachs back to Marsilius of Padua and John of Paris, rather than to the conciliarists. Robert Burhill, an Oxford divine who continued a debate with Bellarmine begun by Lancelot Andrewes, commenced with John of Paris and then looked at Mair and Almain as the progenitors of resistance theory. He traced the evolution of Gallican theory to show the interaction of its ecclesiastical and political wings, and the emergence of divine right theory as the best defence against papalism and resistance doctrine (*De Potestate regia et usurpatione papali*, 1613). Another defender of the oath of allegiance who knew his medieval precedents well was Thomas Preston, writing under the pseudonym of Roger Widdrington. Preston was an English Benedictine who revered the Pont-à-Musson school of Grégoire and Barclay.[98] The detachment shown towards Gallicanism by Owen, Burhill, and the Catholic Preston in the later stages of the controversy was perhaps due to their recognition that the role of Gallicanism had changed since the beginning of the century.

The assassination of Henri IV in 1610 produced a fierce Gallican reaction,[99] and brought more orthodox Anglican supporters of the oath of allegiance closer to French critics of the Jesuits. The parlement's burning of Mariana's *De Rege*, which included the most notorious defence of tyrannicide, symbolises the popular assumption that the Jesuits were linked to every actual and attempted murder of sovereigns since the beginnings of the League. There was nothing that Pierre Cotton, the pacific Jesuit confessor of the late king, could say to calm the storm. An anonymous French tract appeared in English as *The Hellish and Horrible Counsel used by the Jesuits in Answer of P. Cotton* (1610), and in the following year the celebrated *Anti-Cotton or Refutation of Cotton's letter for the Apologizing of the Jesuits* was noted with relish in Sarpi's letters to his Protestant friends.[100] It was at this juncture that Casaubon, having lost his royal pension by the death of his patron, moved to England and accepted James's request to answer the *Annales* of Baronio. Another learned Huguenot scholar, Pierre Dumoulin, joined the propaganda team of James I and composed a third answer to Cotton (*Father Cotton, a Jesuit, his Two and Thirty Demands and the Answer*, 1614). Huguenots became more acceptable allies for Gallicans when they became Anglicans. The sons of Casaubon and Dumoulin became Anglican clergymen and, like their fathers, received prebends from Canterbury.

Many of the strands in the complex web of Gallicanism and Anglicanism converged with the Latin and English publication of Richer's short but extremely influential leaflet in the aftermath of the regicide (*De Ecclesiastica et*

[98]Salmon, *The French Religious Wars*, p. 76.
[99]Roland Mousnier, *L'Assassinat d'Henri IV* (Paris, 1964), provides the background and discusses themes of tyrannicide.
[100]*Lettere ai protestanti*, vol. 1, pp. 144, 150; vol. 2, pp. 105, 107.

Politica Potestate, 1611; *A Treatise of Ecclesiastical and Political Power,* 1612). Through his academic brilliance and his forceful personality this "Gracchus of the Gallican Liberties" had risen from college servant to master at the Collège Cardinal-Lemoine. Elected syndic of the Sorbonne in 1608, he steered the professoriate away from the moderately ultramontane lobby who had censured Servin's *Plaidoyers* towards a Gallicanism designed by himself and Leschassier. His lucid declaration of principle was written in the context of two local controversies. The first involved, once again, the incorporation of the Jesuit Collège de Clermont as a teaching part of the university. Under the influence of the regent, Marie de Médicis, the royal council was prepared to make significant gestures to ultramontanism, and a decree authorising the measure was issued. The parlement, however, refused to confirm it until the Jesuits subscribed to four Gallican propositions designed by the *avocat-général,* Servin. The second contretemps concerned a meeting of the Dominican chapter in Pairs where the infallibility of the pope vis-à-vis that of a general council was to be debated.

Richer's intervention in these contentious issues, and his alignment with Servin and others in the parlement to block the ultramontane party, aroused the ire of the nuncio and of the regent's ecclesiastical spokesman, Cardinal Du Perron. Richer prepared his so-called *Libellus* in response to Servin's request for a statement of Gallican principles. It went far beyond the Gallican pretensions of the majority of *parlementaires;* its ecclesiastical aspects exceeded the most daring aspirations of the episcopate; and its anti-Romanism alienated Richer's colleagues within the Sorbonne. Early in 1612 the Jesuits secured incorporation by subscribing to a formula requiring loyalty to the sacred person of the king and respect for the Gallican liberties. Soon afterwards the bishops in the archdiocese of Sens censured Richer's tract, and the parlement refused to entertain his *appel comme d'abus.* Meanwhile the moderate ultramontane party in the Sorbonne rallied enough support to make Richer's position as syndic untenable. Despite his isolation, he refused to resign, and his deposition was voted by his colleagues.

The most extraordinary aspect of Richer's *Libellus* was its discordant combination of the two kinds of Gallicanism. On the one hand, Richer, a *sorbonniste par excellence,* seemed to have surrendered to the secular domination of the magistracy; on the other, he included extremist statements about the independence of the episcopate. Gerson and Grégoire were two paramount sources for his view of the government of the church, which he declared to be monarchical in form but aristocratic in the mode of its administration. Canon law was made by the infallible council of the church, and the pope's authority as chief minister in succession to Saint Peter could only be exercised under the law. The church had no authority over temporal things. The secular prince shared in its government, and was the protector of divine, natural, and canon laws, as well as their enforcer by right of the sword. The prince, through the parlement, was the ultimate judge of *appels comme d'abus,* and hence the supreme arbiter in ecclesiastical government. Beside these principles, Richer affirmed the divine right not only of the bishops but also of the lower clergy. Christ had given spiritual jurisdiction to the apostles in respect of the first and to the remaining disciples in respect of the second.[101] It was from this article that the movement known as *richérisme* was ultimately to spring. One irony of the situation in 1612 was that the episcopacy, or part of it at least, had censured Richer for upholding its own divine right. It was even more ironic that the parlement, representing a royal authority over the church the regency refused to assume, was associated with articles asserting the independence of the clergy against the civil power – an independence the clergy was unwilling to assert.

Richer's English translator, who cryptically signed himself Δ, strove valiantly to assimilate what he could of the *Libellus* to the Church of England. Beginning his prefatory remarks with the irenic observation that national churches might differ in things not vital to salvation, he noted that the king had acknowledged the church of Rome as "our mother church." Addressing "the Romish Catholics of England," the translator drew their attention to the doctrinal soundness of the Anglican establishment, beginning with James I ("a right *pater patriae*") and going on to mention the new archbishop of Canterbury, George Abbot, and his elder brother, Robert, together with Lancelot Andrewes, Richard Hooker, and James Montagu, the editor of the king's political works in 1616. Reviewing the divisions within Catholicism, the writer was perceptive enough to note that not all Jesuits followed the subversive ideas of Parsons. He followed the Gallican lead in describing the expansion of papal authority. He was cool towards Blackwell, while admitting the archpriest's loyalty as an Englishman in taking the oath of allegiance, but he wrote with warmth about the Benedictine Thomas Preston, who had turned Bellarmine's arguments for indirect papal supremacy back upon themselves. Richer he saw as a true spokesman for Gallican attitudes, and Venetian Catholics as taking a similar stand. Summarizing the articles in the *Libellus*, the translator chose to stress the divine right of the clergy:

That by the text of the scripture and doctrine of the apostles, we see directly that the authority of jurisdiction was conferred upon the apostles and disciples when Christ did send them forth: that the power of jurisdiction of inferior prelates, either bishops or curates, is immediately from God, according to the doctrine of the gospel and the apostles.

In this strange ebb and flow between the French and English churches, the idea of ecclesiastical divine right, earlier manifested in the last decade of Elizabeth's reign in England, had migrated to France and then returned, albeit through the pen of one whose ideas were not shared by less advanced Gallicans.

---

[101]This summarises the eighteen points contained in Richer's *De Ecclesiastica et Politica Potestate* (Paris, 1611).

The winds of change in France seemed to have turned against both eccle-siastical and political Gallicanism under the regency. An ultramontane trend was temporarily in the ascendancy, although Du Perron, for one, supported the divine right of kings and did not acknowledge any direct papalism. The clergy appeared to have abandoned Gallican traditions to the parlement in order to pursue Catholic reform, and the parlement as a whole had chosen not to back the new formula that had been encouraged by Leschassier and supported by Servin. It is not, therefore, surprising that it was James I and his Anglican divines who took the lead in opposing the papacy.

Gallicanism, which was, of course, to revive on several occasions later in the century, even flickered to life briefly in the closing stages of the oath of alle-giance controversy. It was Richer's friend, the magistrate Le Prêtre, who during the estates general in 1614 proposed in the third estate to enact a fundamental law safeguarding the crown against papal intervention in temporal affairs. Again it was Du Perron who spoke against the measure and saw to its suppression. There remained to political Gallicanism only the power of the parlement to block the clergy's ardent desire to have the government formally receive the Tridentine decrees without qualification. Even here Du Perron had his way. Although the council did not risk a confrontation with the magistrates by send-ing legislation on the subject to the parlement, the assembly of the clergy, meeting separately after the estates general were dismissed in 1615, voted to receive the decrees by its own authority. James I had a final word to say in the matter of this betrayal by his allies in the antipapal cause. In 1616 he published his *Remonstrance for the Right of Kings and the Independence of their Crowns*. "Of all the clergy," he wrote, "the man that hath most abandoned or set his honour to sale, the man to whom France is least obliged, is the Lord Cardinal of Per-ron."[102] It was upon this note that the ideological association of Gallicanism and Anglicanism came to an end.

It had been an association founded upon a shared antipapal interest, in which parallel experience of national tensions between church and state fostered the development of a common body of political ideas. The search for tradition was important in both Gallicanism and Anglicanism. Each national church elabo-rated a combination of myth and history that initially suited its needs but, once established, proved incapable of adaptation. Each national church drew also upon the lore of the primitive church, the ancient councils, and the Caesaro-papism of the early Christian emperors. Each contained within itself a confu-sion of political doctrine that was in part the consequence of juxtaposing the descending and ascending theories of authority, and in part the result of con-tingent circumstance. The links between Gallicanism and Anglicanism estab-lished in the age of the Counter-Reformation suggest that ideology may often fulfil its function through paradox and contradiction.

[102]McIlwain, *Political Works of James I*, p. 171.

PART III

Structures and fissures

8

~~~~~~

Venality of office and popular sedition in seventeenth-century France

It is well known that the limitations of their own environment may often conceal from generations of historians certain important features of a particular age. Yet it is difficult to believe that until quite recently two fundamental aspects of the France of Richelieu and Mazarin were generally ignored and never related to each other. In venality of office and the endemic nature of popular revolt the motive forces of seventeenth-century France have been suddenly and dramatically revealed. The connection between them has been thought to provide an interpretative key to the last centuries of the *ancien régime*, but, unfortunately, the historian of venality of office, Roland Mousnier, and the author of the first general study of the mass risings under Richelieu, Boris Porshnev, have reached antithetical conclusions as to what this connection may be.

M. Georges Pagès was the first to sense the significance of the two phenomena, but he commented on them separately. In 1932 he published an article[1] sketching possible lines of inquiry into the evolutions of the system whereby the crown had alienated direct control of bureaucratic processes to a class who held their charges as venal and hereditary property. Pagès did not regard this system as some kind of administrative excrescence, nor even as a short-sighted financial expedient, but rather as the monarchy's unconscious acquisition of a firm base in the nation. When Richelieu and Mazarin attempted to recover the crown's authority by superimposing the intendants, the venal bureaucracy was provoked into open resistance in the Fronde. Both systems survived and expanded after the crisis, but the intendants became the executors of power. Pagès suggested that in the eighteenth century the monarchy lost the support of vested interest, and that, while the intendants themselves became an oligarchy, the surviving office-holders continued a running battle with the crown which fatally weakened the *ancien régime*. In another paper,[2] published in 1937, Pagès gave an account of the rival policies of Richelieu and Marillac. He

---

[1] "La vénalité des offices dans l'ancienne France," *Revue historique,* 169 (1932), 477–95.
[2] "Autour du 'Grand Orage': Richelieu et Marillac, deux politiques," *Revue historique,* 179 (1937), 63–97.

argued that the keeper of the seals sought a solution to the problem of disorder at the expense of the Cardinal's external designs. Pagès investigated the causes of Marillac's concern, and thus revealed the importance of a continuous series of popular uprisings. While Pagès failed to explain connections between popular sedition and the system of office-holding, he pointed out that the revolts were directed against the royal fiscality, and that local authorities and provincial parlements appeared to be accomplices of the rebels.

When Pagès was writing on venality of office his pupil, Roland Mousnier, was studying the *paulette* of 1604 – the imposition of that regular annual tax upon venal office which fixed the system in its final form. The publication of M. Mousnier's magisterial work on venal institutions in 1945[3] confirmed or extended many of his predecessor's hypotheses, and dispersed the darkness obscuring the entire subject. It became clear that the practice of regarding office as property did not merely have its origins in the middle ages; it was possibly as characteristic of the medieval monarchy as it was of the later Valois and the Bourbons. Even in the fourteenth century the creation of new offices for sale had provoked tension between the crown and existing officials in the sovereign courts of the parlement, the *chambre des comptes* and the *cour des aides*.[4] In the next century, when venality was open and fully documented, it fostered contacts between gown and sword, and provided a means for ascension in the social hierarchy.[5] François Ier restricted the right to create venal offices to the crown alone, and channelled all receipts from this source to the *parties casuelles*. Henri II devised such expedients as the creation of a new range of courts, the *présidiaux*, between the provincial parlements and the *bailliages*, and the doubling of office-holders by biannual alteration. Under Henri III the market for office became saturated and the partisans were unable to dispose of blocks of offices allocated to them. At the beginning of the seventeenth century the *paulette* provided a uniform method for the inheritance of office through the right of *survivance*. Mousnier concluded that royal authority was limited by the acknowledged private ownership of administrative power in a form which could be described as a new kind of feudality.[6] Like Pagès, he argued that Richelieu and Mazarin had attempted to reconstitute direct rule; that, in reaction, the official classes had sometimes forsworn their rôle as instruments of public order, and had appeared to act in collusion with the forces of subversion.[7]

While Mousnier was developing his views on venality of office the Soviet historian, Boris Porshnev, was uncovering the extent and intensity of popular mass movements before the Fronde. His book did not appear in French until

[3]*La Vénalité des Offices sous Henri IV et Louis XIII* (Rouen, 1945).
[4]*Ibid.*, p. 9.
[5]*Ibid.*, p. 18.
[6]*Ibid.*, p. 19. Pagès had already described venal offices as a new kind of feudality: *La monarchie d'Ancien Regime en France* (Paris, 1928), p. 124.
[7]*La Vénalité des Offices*, pp. 268–9.

1963, although Russian and German versions were published in 1948 and 1954 respectively.[8] As a Marxist, he believed that class conflicts provided the motive forces in history, and he focused his attention on peasant and plebeian insurrection in seventeenth-century France with a Leninist conviction that the peasantry always led the van of revolutionary elements.[9] In the first section of the book he gave a general account of the risings of the *Croquants* and of the urban revolts in Dijon, Aix-en-Provence, Lyon, Bordeaux, Moulins and elsewhere. In both this and the second part (devoted to the *Va-nu-pieds* in Normandy) he stressed the spontaneity of the attacks launched by the labouring classes upon the agents of royal taxation. As riot and massacre multiplied into revolution, these classes, according to Porshnev, directed a class war against those who had exploited them. Where the local authorities appeared to have taken the lead in resisting the demands of the crown, as before the riots of the *Lanturelus* at Dijon in 1630, Porshnev claimed the initiative for the populace, and denied that the defence of provincial liberties had created a revolutionary situation.[10] Where the leaders of resistance were undeniably from the upper bourgeoisie, as when President Cariolis and his sons led the *Cascaveoux* at Aix in 1630, he argued that a small fraction of the middle class had exploited the revolutionary fervour of the mobs in their own interests.[11] Where a nobleman commanded a peasant army, as La Mothe de la Forêt commanded the *Croquants* of Périgord in 1637, Porshnev commented that seigneurs were seldom mentioned among rebel leaders.[12] The real directors of revolution were men like the *vigneron* Anatoir Champgenêt at Dijon,[13] the peasant general of the *Croquants*, Pierre Greleti,[14] and the clock-maker Gorin, who led the mobs in Rouen during the rising of the *Nu-pieds*.[15]

Unlike the first two parts, which were based principally upon a selection of the papers of Richelieu's chancellor, Séguier, held in Leningrad, the third part of Porshnev's book set forth a number of hypotheses intended to explain the Fronde in the light of the earlier series of agrarian and urban risings. Not only did Porshnev display great ingenuity in adapting his Marxist assumptions to the complexities of seventeenth-century French history, but he also re-interpreted Mousnier's conclusions to fit his own schema. Mousnier and Pagès, he had argued in his introduction, regarded the rôle of the bourgeoisie as one of necessary evolution.[16] Mousnier had regarded the rise of the venal office-

---

[8]*Les Soulèvements populaires en France de 1623 à 1648* (Paris, 1963); *Narodnie Vosstaniya vo Frantsii pered Frondoi, 1623–1648* (Moscow, 1948); *Die Volksaufstände in Frankreich, 1623–1648* (Berlin, 1954).
[9]Porshnev, *Soulèvements*, p. 580.
[10]*Ibid.*, p. 136.
[11]*Ibid.*, p. 144.
[12]*Ibid.*, p. 76.
[13]*Ibid.*, p. 137.
[14]*Ibid.*, pp. 85–7.
[15]*Ibid.*, pp. 370–1.
[16]*Ibid.*, pp. 37–8.

holders as the *embourgeoisement* of the monarchy. The real fate of this class, Porshnev asserted, had been its *féodalisation*.[17] The monarchy of the Bourbons was a feudal state, in the Marxist sense that it was the tool of the dominating class, the nobility. Factious contests for power within this ruling class could be averted only by the appointment of executors. At this embryonic stage in the growth of capitalism the French bourgeoisie experienced "inner contradictions" and proceeded in a way described by Porshnev as "two steps forward, one step back." A section of the middle class denied its own destiny and sought a *rapprochement* with the nobility. This was effected *politically* by the provision of a mass of venal offices, *socially* by the aspiration of the office-holders to live nobly, and *economically* by the diversion of bourgeois capital from trade and industry into the finances of the feudal state. Thus the *noblesse de robe* was detached from its bourgeois background, indoctrinated with the ethos of the *noblesse d'épée*, and assimilated to the class living on feudal rent. The office-holders became the administrative Janissaries of what Porshnev called "le régime féodalo-absolutiste."[18]

Porshnev explained that the peasantry were doubly exploited by feudal rent: in the centralised form of royal taxation and in the local form of seigneurial dues. The taxes which the lower classes paid to the crown were a disguised form of exploitation by that section of the nobility who looked to the crown for pensions. But increases in taxation reduced the ability of the peasantry to pay dues to those dependent upon seigneurial revenues. Consequent divisions within the ruling class were exacerbated by an inherent trend to particularism, by a desire to profit personally from the weakness of the crown, and by a resentment against any first minister who might appear to usurp the machinery of state.[19] In this way Porshnev accounted for the conspiracies of the nobility against Richelieu. At the same time he explained why the tensions between the two kinds of feudal rent impoverished the peasantry to the point where spontaneous revolt occurred, and why some dissident members of the nobility might temporarily support risings against taxes which undermined the seigneurial system.

Like Hegel, Porshnev credited Richelieu with an insight into the underlying historical forces of his time.[20] The Cardinal was thought to have perceived that the office-holders might exceed their rôle and threaten the dominance of the nobility. For this reason, and to increase the effectiveness of the central power, he began to reform the system by imposing the intendants. Yet venality of office had become an unfortunate necessity, and its abolition would have dissolved the alliance of nobility and magistracy, and restored to the bourgeoisie its revolutionary rôle. Consequently Richelieu tried to maintain the various forces in a

[17]*Ibid.*, p. 577.
[18]*Ibid.*, pp. 545–61.
[19]*Ibid.*, pp. 530–1.
[20]*Ibid.*, p. 562.

state of equilibrium, while allowing the full weight to fall upon the classes whose resistance would be crushed by their superiors and exploiters. Mazarin violated his predecessor's system, for the demands of foreign war obliged him to seek new revenues which the peasantry could no longer provide.[21] He turned first to the financiers, where his exactions merely threw the fiscal machine into greater chaos. He then turned on the magistracy, who responded by throwing in their lot with the popular revolutionary forces. Thus, in Porshnev's view, began the first Fronde. But the magistrates resented the plebeian initiative and feared the threat to the sanctity of property. This section of the bourgeoisie was not based upon any capitalist system of production. There was no bourgeois revolution – much less a democratic bourgeois revolution which, through proletarian participation, might have been converted into a socialist one.[22] The bourgeoisie betrayed their peasant partners, whose revolutionary impetus was to be exploited by dissident members of the nobility in the later phases of the Fronde. With such a schema Porshnev could close his book with a quotation from a classical source:

The formulae of Karl Marx give the clue to the history of the French bourgeoisie in the sixteenth and seventeenth centuries: "Nothing could further delay the victory of the French bourgeosie when it decided in 1789 to make common cause with the peasants." Our researches fully confirm this reflection.[23]

Porshnev's interests were essentially in popular revolutionary movements, and not in office-holding or the clash between the venal magistracy and the new agents of the crown, the *commissaires*. The latter elements were ingeniously woven into his argument because he was attempting a total explanation of a crisis in which the revolutionary impulses of the labouring classes were, to him, the *primum mobile*. The dissidence of the magistracy was far more apparent in the final, interpretative section of his book than it had been in the first two parts. There the stress upon the initiative of the masses, and their hostility to both seigneur and magistrate, had obliged Porshnev to depreciate sedition on the part of the nobility and the middle class. Mousnier, on the other hand, entered the field through his interest in institutional history and its social implications, and not because of a preoccupation with class conflict. In his study of venality in the seventeenth century he had commented on the increasing alienation of the office-holders from the central government. When, in his replies to Porshnev, he came directly to study popular insurrection in the period, he concluded that the revolts of the masses were incited and, at times, organised by the classes of respectability.

M. Mousnier did not publish his first riposte to Porshnev until 1958.[24] He

[21]*Ibid.*, p. 576.
[22]*Ibid.*, p. 580.
[23]*Ibid.*, p. 582.
[24]"Recherches sur les soulèvements populaires en France avant la Fronde," *Revue d'histoire moderne et contemporaine*, 4 (1958), 81–113.

rejected the use of the word "feudal" in describing the economy of France in the seventeenth century in the same general sense as it might be applied to eleventh-century France. He denied that either Pagès or himself had described the *embourgeoisement* of the monarchy. The bourgeoisie, in his view, had aided the crown to establish its authority, but the crown had subordinated all classes in the process of reconstituting the state. The monarchy was not the instrument of a landed feudal aristocracy. In its growth towards absolutism it had interposed its taxes, its justice and its armed strength between seigneur and peasant.[25] Mousnier agreed with Porshnev's stress upon the universality of the risings, and confirmed his view that the majority of risings had begun with an attack upon royal fiscal agents. While he advanced his own general theory with the reservation that all the risings had yet to be fully investigated, he offered detailed evidence to show that the peasant revolts, far from being spontaneous, were provoked by the nobility. Similarly he claimed that in the towns the bourgeoisie either incited mob action against the fiscal officials or bore responsibility for the insurrections through their denunciation of royal taxes, their failure to employ local militia and their refusal to punish the rioters.[26]

Mousnier pointed out that seigneur and peasant had a mutual interest in resisting royal taxes for the very reason that Porshnev had himself advanced – that taxation restricted peasant ability to pay dues. The seigneurs organised opposition to the taxes, provoked risings and supported and concealed the rebels. There were close communal ties between nobility, peasantry and local officials.[27] Many of the magistrates were also seigneurs, and in any case the pressures brought upon office-holders by the crown moved them to organise resistance to the *commissaires*. Animosity between social classes was far less intense than general antipathy to the new agents of the monarchy and their fiscal demands. The peasant armies did not attack châteaux unless they were owned by fiscal officers or required for tactical reasons. In some instances the nobility put their fortresses at the disposal of the rebels. Sometimes peasant movements rejected seigneurial obligations as well as royal taxes, but the nobility generally refused to answer commands to march against the peasantry. Where they did so, as at Bordeaux in 1635 and Valence in 1644, they rallied to the appeal of a great nobleman with provincial ties, such as Epernon or Lesdiguières. Municipal officials acted more frequently, especially in the exclusion of external popular elements from the towns and in protecting local property against pillage and anarchy.[28] But in general the local officials, like the nobility, were reported by the intendants to have inspired the risings or supported them by their inactivity. The opposition of the provincial parlements corresponded with the rhythm of revolt.

[25]*Ibid.*, pp. 107–10.
[26]*Ibid.*, p. 101.
[27]*Ibid.*, pp. 91–2.
[28]*Ibid.*, pp. 104–5.

Venality of office

The popular disturbances under Richelieu and Mazarin were connected with increased taxation to meet the demands of war; they were also probably associated with long-term movements in prices and with subsistence crises; and they were linked with a general crisis in government and society caused by the challenge of the crown to the holders of venal offices. This re-affirmation and development of his earlier views was expressed in a number of other papers by M. Mousnier.[29] They were restated with force and clarity in his reply to Professor Trevor-Roper's extension to western Europe of his own interpretation of the English mid-seventeenth-century crisis as a revolt of the provinces against the court and the bureaucratic apparatus of state:

> The landlords, whether gentry or royal officials or municipal magistrates, incited the peasants not to pay the *tailles* or the numerous new taxes imposed by the Government, because if the peasants paid these royal taxes they would be unable to pay their feudal dues or rents, and also because it was a lord's duty to protect his peasants; the peasants then violently drove off the bailiffs with their warrants or the agents of the tax-farmers; the Government sent *commissaires* to obtain payment; officials and gentry stirred up the peasantry; gentry joined together to help their peasants to resist; in the towns, the royal officials and the *échevins* provoked risings among the urban population to help the peasants by paralysing the movements of the royal *commissaires;* then, as happened with the *Croquants* of Villefranche-de-Rouergue in 1643 and with other movements, the peasants sent some of their men into the towns; or the royal officials made the peasants come from their *seigneuries* and make up bands or companies of insurgents, as in Paris during the Fronde, in Aix and elsewhere; or sometimes the peasants themselves seized a town. Thus in most cases we do not find a revolt of the country against an oppressive public service, but the revolt of a public service which considered itself oppressed and which dragged in its wake those social groups over which the structure of society gave it influence.[30]

Behind this insistence upon the initiative of the office-holders in the revolts, which reversed the priorities of Porshnev as neatly as it did those of Trevor-Roper, Mousnier developed his general views on the rôle of venality in the last centuries of the *ancien régime*. These views had already been suggested in the concluding part of his study of venality of office. They were to be delineated with greater firmness and precision.[31] In the years 1630–1715 the crown freed itself of administrative restraint by the systematic use of *commissaires*. The period as a whole was one of foreign wars, declining prices and economic stagnation, bad harvests, epidemics and social upheavals. The monarchy assumed dictatorial aspects in response to these pressures, and while it reduced the participation of the governed in the processes of government it also sepa-

[29]E.g., "Recherches sur les Syndicats d'officiers pendant la Fronde – Trésoriers généraux de France et Elus dans la Révolution," *XVIIᵉ Siècle*, 42 (1959), 76–117.
[30]"Trevor-Roper's 'General Crisis' – Symposium" in Trevor Aston (ed.), *Crisis in Europe 1560–1660* (London, 1965), pp. 98–9.
[31]Notably in "La participation des gouvernés à l'activité des gouvernants dans la France du XVIIᵉ et du XVIIIᵉ siècles," *Etudes suisses d'histoire générale*, 20 (1962–3), 200–29.

rated itself from the sources of wealth. Pagès had suggested the dual advance of both the intendants and venal office-holders after the crisis of the Fronde, and had placed the liquidation of the system of venality in the period of the regency after Louis XIV's death. Mousnier believed that the monarchy lost its base in the nation with the continuing expansion of Colbert's *tutelle administrative*. Not only did the royal office-holders lose their share in government, but other consultative bodies such as the provincial estates, the assembly of clergy, the universities, the municipal corporations, and the corporate guilds ceased to be effective. In the eighteenth century, with an expanding economy and a less taxing series of wars, the monarchy vacillated in uncertainty before the issue of fiscal reform. The opportunity was lost, and during the temporary economic recession of 1770–1787 the injustice and inefficiency of the fiscal machine could no longer be tolerated. Belief in a hierarchical society based upon corporate groups came to be replaced by pressure for an open-class society where individuals possessed equality before the law.

Although the social and political aspirations of the office-holding class occupied the central position in M. Mousnier's *explication d'ensemble,* he became increasingly discontented with the imprecision of the vocabulary of nineteenth-century social stratification as applied to French society in the seventeenth century. He admitted that he had himself used such sociological concepts in his book on venality, but with certain modifications.[32] He came to reject the theses of Porshnev not merely on the grounds already outlined but in terms that made further controversy impossible. Seventeenth-century society, he held, was grouped in orders and estates, identified by profession or function, distinguished by a sense of collegiality, and ranked hierarchically in relation to the patterned structure of society as a whole. He added a postscript to his edition of a selection of the Séguier papers from the Bibliothèque Nationale in answer to a new foreword to the French edition of Porshnev's work in which Porshnev refused to modify his position.[33] The debate was now on different grounds. In his recent studies of the articulation of society in the age of Richelieu and Mazarin, Mousnier abandoned the broad threefold class division popularised by Marxist thought.[34]

The differences in terminology between Mousnier and Porshnev ultimately reflect the differences between their methods. Yet both initially accepted broad sociological interpretations that provided highly generalised explanations of the last centuries of the *ancien régime.* Porshnev drew from Marxism the view that feudalism in France was eventually overthrown by an alliance of revolutionary elements in the bourgeoisie and the labouring poor. To him the seventeenth-century risings were a conflict between the labouring classes and their superi-

---

[32]*Problèmes de stratification sociale – deux cahiers de la noblesse, 1649–1651* (Paris, 1965), p. 18.
[33]*Lettres et mémoires addressés au chancelier Séguier, 1633–1649* (Paris, 1964).
[34]"Problèmes de méthode dans l'étude des structures sociales des seizième, dix-septième, dix-huitième siècles," in *Festgabe für Max Braubach* (Münster, 1964), pp. 550–64.

ors, although certain cracks within the higher strata of the feudal edifice had permitted some noble and bourgeois elements temporarily to align themselves with the rebels. Mousnier drew from the Pagès tradition in French historiography the view that the monarchy had established itself against the feudal aristocracy with the aid of bourgeois office-holders; that these office-holders themselves represented a diffusion of authority; and that the monarchy, faced with war and disorder, superseded them with agents who fostered a new autocracy. To Mousnier the disorders of the seventeenth century represented the local resistance of a variety of social groups, bound together by common interests and traditions, against the assumption of centralised, dictatorial powers. Porshnev placed the revolutionary initiative within the labouring classes; Mousnier descried it among the established leaders of local communities.

Behind these contrasts lay a surprising measure of agreement. It has already been noted that both accepted the importance and universality of popular sedition in the period, and that both agreed that the actual call to revolt was generally issued in response to the arrival of agents of the central fiscality. Porshnev and Mousnier were also agreed upon the sporadic and unco-ordinated nature of the movements. They were at one in regard to the double exploitation of the peasantry by centralised taxation and seigneurial dues. They both accepted bourgeois hesitation to employ the militia to repress municipal risings, and the participation of noblemen in peasant revolts, although they differed on the meaning and frequency of such occurrences. Their explanations of the motives for the systematic employment of *commissaires* had much in common. Similarly, in his account of the alliance between the Parisian magistracy and the mob at the beginning of the Fronde, Porshnev described the combination of dissident elements in a way which did not directly contradict Mousnier's view, although it was not particularly consistent with his own reluctance to assign a rôle of importance to provincial magistrates in the earlier risings. Both Mousnier and Porshnev made extensive use of the contemporary works of the jurist Loyseau and of Richelieu's *Testament politique*. Both relied principally upon the reports and letters addressed by intendants and local authorities to the chancellor, Séguier. The similarities mentioned were imposed by the evidence. Yet, though the inferences which each historian drew from the literary and administrative sources were not always contradictory, the general presuppositions which they brought to the problem differed as much from each other as did the prevailing ideologies of the French and Russian revolutions.

There is a touch of irony in the way the whole controversy was made possible by the archival zeal of the secretary to the Russian embassy in Paris during the French revolution, P. P. Dubrovsky. Dubrovsky acquired a large part of Séguier's correspondence, which in the course of time was installed in the Saltykov-Schedrin section of the Leningrad public library. Porshnev printed 79 of the 1,275 reports in the administrative section of this collection as an appendix to his book. In his 1964 selection from the 2,932 Séguier documents held in Paris, Mousnier published 409 such papers, and in 1966 another Soviet historian, A. D. Lublinskaya, produced an equally valuable edition of 359 further letters from the Dubrovsky archive.[35] In the Leningrad collection the reports of the intendants in the generation before the Fronde are particularly well represented for southern France. Whereas Mousnier's selection illustrated fiscal policy and popular revolts throughout the whole of France, that of Lublinskaya was restricted to Languedoc, Provence and Dauphiné – areas where the intendants were confronted with strong provincial particularism.

An unexpected twist to the controversy was provided by Lublinskaya's editorial policy. The tributes to both Porshnev and Mousnier in her introduction suggested that she was determined to ignore the dispute. In reality Lublinskaya followed Mousnier's interpretation. Where Porshnev had disingenuously printed excerpts from some of his documents, she provided the missing pieces. She professed to illustrate the same trends as Mousnier, and relied upon much of the research done by Mousnier's assistants into the social background of the intendants. It is true that the interpretative section of her introduction was devoted to the administrative functions of the chancellor and the *commissaires*, and not to the nature and causes of popular sedition. Yet her acceptance of the Mousnier thesis was clearly implied by her comment that Séguier and his predecessors opposed the representatives of the nobility on the royal council in order to promote the absolutism of the crown. She argued that the effectiveness of the chancellor's rôle increased as the powers of the intendants were widened and strengthened.[36] She observed that the problems of the intendants before the Fronde were increased by their isolation from local support, and that when the intendants were re-established after 1653 the monarchy had learnt from experience to associate them with local institutions and provide them with subordinates. But in this way the intendants themselves gradually ceased to be such effective agents of the central government, and already, by the end of the seventeenth century, dynasties of intendants had emerged.[37] The work of Lublinskaya and her associates is clear evidence of the objective and scholarly methods which it is now possible for Soviet historiography to pursue – even when modern ideological considerations are involved.

Such praise cannot be accorded to Porshnev. Despite his ingenuity, it seems as though his thesis could not accommodate all the data he used. But if he exposed himself to the charge of logical inconsistency his readiness to take all facets of the problem, including Mousnier's work, into consideration says much for the integrity of his purpose. His achievement in describing the total impact of popular revolution has been a considerable one. Moreover, he was prepared

[35] *Vnutrenniya Politika Frantsuzskogo Absolyutizma, 1633–1649* [The Internal Politics of French Absolutism, 1633–1649] (Moscow and Leningrad, 1966).
[36] *Ibid.*, p. 9.
[37] *Ibid.*, p. 12.

to modify Marxist dogma on the control of the political "superstructure" by the dominant class to the extent that he accepted a trend within the monarchy to break away from aristocratic tutelage after the Fronde. Thus his view of the "feudalisation" of a section of the bourgeoisie could be said to derive some support from the defence of privilege by the parlements in opposition to the crown during the eighteenth century. Mousnier, on the other hand, has been far less hampered by ideological considerations, and it will be obvious that his views command a greater sympathy from the writer. Nevertheless, the desire to refute Porshnev's interpretation, and to find the local nobility and officials, rather than the peasants, responsible for the uprisings, may have resulted in some over-simplification.

Just as the sociological categories of the nineteenth century provide too crude a conceptual framework for any meaningful generalisation about the social structure of seventeenth-century France, so also the political vocabulary of modern liberalism distorts the historian's vision. Mousnier has professed to the writer his discontent with the term "absolutism," as something seen in necessary contradistinction to a modern puralistic democracy.[38] In his study of the Fronde, Ernst Kossmann criticised as imprecise the description of the monarchy under Richelieu and Mazarin as either absolutist or constitutional. Nor, for that matter, was he content with assertions that the aims of the parlements were either revolutionary or reactionary. The political history of the Fronde suggests alignments differing from those explained in social terms by Mousnier and Porshnev for the earlier revolts. The provincial parlements and the masses were generally to be found in opposition to the municipalities. Nor were the motives of the urban militia necessarily those of the bourgeoisie, for the militia itself included lower-class elements. It does not seem, however, that Kossmann's denial of any logical symmetry by the substitution of the concept of the baroque state, in which dissident and unrelated elements were always in conflict, brings the general problem nearer to solution.[39]

The clear distinction drawn by Mousnier between the holders of venal office and the *commissaires* must also be questioned. The intendants, with one exception, were drawn from the *maîtres des requêtes*, who sat in the parlement and, under the chancellor's direction, provided the administrative staff for the business of the royal council. These officials owned their offices, although they did not possess any property rights in the additional posts they might be granted as *commissaires*. Thus the chancellor had full power to revoke their commissions as intendants but he did not directly control their tenure of office within the collegiate body of the *maîtres des requêtes*.[40] It would seem that Mousnier's view of the motives for the imposition of the intendants represents the historian's

---

[38]Personal discussion, August 1964.
[39]*La Fronde* (Leiden, 1954), pp. 2, 138, 65, 27.
[40]The point is discussed by Lublinskaya, *op. cit.*, pp. 10, 11.

rationalisation of the structure of power, rather than an analysis of the conscious policy of the crown. The monarchy may have undermined the security of the office-holders, but it never seriously envisaged the wholesale reformation of the system of venality. Indeed, as Mousnier himself showed in his study of venality of office, the monarchy had throughout the centuries continuously superimposed one administrative layer upon another without much consideration for the shape of the structure as a whole. The shading of the boundary lines between the *commissaires* and the actual owners of judicial and financial office makes it easier to understand the co-existence of the two after the Fronde, and the eventual assimilation of the intendancies with the general system.

Another concept where modern constitutional overtones suggest a misleading *nuance* in the attitudes of Pagès and Mousnier is their description of venality of office as providing a firm base in the nation. This appeared almost as an incidental insight in M. Charmeil's massive study of a group of holders of venal office, the *trésoriers de France*.[41] The *trésoriers*, as Mousnier has shown,[42] were responsible for organising resistance among other holders of venal office in the period of the Fronde. After the Fronde they resisted the reimposition of the *commissaires*, and Séguier accused them of "not merely rebelling against their masters and superiors but trying to stir the people and other officers to resist the orders of the king."[43] The *trésoriers*, like many other kinds of officials, held on to their venal offices largely for purposes of social prestige, although they had little useful function to perform. Their rôle in the apportionment of taxation and its local administration had been partially superseded. They identified themselves with local interests and engaged in endless wrangles with a rival group of financial officials, the *élus*, and with the *cours des aides*. Although they were often descended from administrative dynasties who had provided many of the *commissaires* of the sixteenth century, and although there were still rare instances of a *maître des requêtes* being selected from their ranks, they regarded the intendants as their principal enemies. They, and the *élus*, whose appointment was often an infringement of provincial liberties, were sometimes identified by rioting mobs as associated with the royal fiscality. But in reality they were its most bitter opponents. Thus their position, in respect of the connection between popular sedition and venality of office, was an anomalous one. Charmeil argued that their rôle demonstrated that venal office-holders, far from providing the monarchy with a base in the nation, as Pagès had believed, made "constitutional monarchy" impossible.[44]

An issue which involved so searching a review of established generalisations about the history of French society in the last centuries of the *ancien régime* naturally provoked wider comment. Victor Tapié and Robert Mandrou made

[41]Jean-Paul Charmeil, *Les Trésoriers de France à l'époque de la Fronde* (Paris, 1964).
[42]See note 29.
[43]Charmeil, *op. cit.*, p. 401.
[44]*Ibid.*, p. ix.

early and suggestive contributions to the debate. In his history of France under Louis XIII, Tapié gave one of the first French surveys of the results of Porshnev's research.[45] He also provided the first general historical work on the period which described the course and intensity of all the popular risings. He accepted the view that the movements were directed against both the royal fiscality and the rich, but he did not accept Porshnev's comparison with the Fronde. He stressed the close-knit nature of urban communities and their roots in the countryside. He held that the rural risings might best be compared with the resistance of La Vendée to the Revolution, as movements led by the nobility and encouraged by the clergy in support of traditional ways of life.[46] He also contributed a brief analysis of economic distress in the provinces, emphasising the depreciation of bad coinage, which was alone available in rural life. In 1959 Mandrou wrote a notice on the forthcoming French edition of Porshnev's book in which he expressed support for many of Porshnev's particular views, if not for his general interpretative schema.[47] He found it difficult to accept some of the criticism made against Porshnev, and he refused to attribute to the nobility a general movement of resistance to the crown. The nobility, he asserted, were simply protecting their own local interests. But his most valuable contribution was to ask in what way the risings under Richelieu differed from the *jacqueries* of other periods. He held the tradition of peasant revolt to be the fundamental element, and suggested that any explanation was faulty which lacked a psychological account of the collective memory of rural insurrection. These views were expanded in a series of lectures given by him at Pisa in 1960 and published in 1965.[48]

A further contribution to the interpretative problem of popular sedition is made by Orest Ranum.[49] Ranum points out that the higher orders in seventeenth-century France regarded the peasantry as debased and irresponsible. Seigneurial obligations were supposed to restrain their *méchanceté*, and when violence occurred the seigneurs were held culpable by the same reasoning that held the owner of a dangerous dog responsible if it slipped its leash. Local officials and seigneurs might blame the tax collectors for peasant revolt, but the intendants and the central government blamed the nobility and parlements. The seigneur who was accused of responsibility for popular revolt often joined the forces of insurrection. The reports of the intendants were believed by those administering the fiscal machine and supporting the policy of foreign war; the contrary reports were welcomed by the factions that launched the Fronde.

---

[45]*La France de Louis XIII et de Richelieu* (Paris, 1952), p. 260.
[46]*Ibid.*, p. 486. It is difficult to maintain the view that La Vendée was essentially the revolt of a close-knit rural community after Charles Tilly's *The Vendée* (Cambridge, Mass., 1964).
[47]"Les soulèvements populaires et la Société française du XVIIᵉ siècle," *Annales: Economies, sociétés, civilisations*, 14 (1959), 756–65.
[48]*Classes et luttes des classes en France au début du XVIIᵉ siècle* (Messina and Florence, 1965).
[49]*Paris in the Age of Absolutism* (New York, 1968), p. 200.

Popular violence and rioting had become an accepted part of everyday life. Attacks on tax collectors and estate managers arose spontaneously in the wake of crop failures, but the forces of repression tended to attribute rebellion to evil-minded men or to sinister conspiracy rather than to its economic causes. These views add psychological depth to some of the explanations of Pagès and Mousnier, but they make no specific connection between popular sedition and the discontents of the holders of venal office.

Early in the controversy Mousnier called for further research into the circumstances of particular risings, and expected assistance from current demographic studies of seventeenth-century France. In the latter context the comparative paucity and irregularity of registers before 1670 have led to the period being described as one of demographic darkness where the technique of family reconstruction is impossible.[50] Recent work has suggested that the first half of the seventeenth century, like the preceding century, was a time of population expansion, with movements of recession like those of an incoming tide. These recessions correspond with subsistence crises and epidemics, which are related to the urban and peasant risings. The two principal crises occurred round the years 1630 and 1650, and there were many regional variations. Correlations between increases in the price of grain and the incidence of famine and plague have been clearly established.[51] Poverty and hunger are an essential element in any discussion of causal priorities. Tensions between social groups, or between local communities and the central authority, might provide the focus of discontents, but behind them lay a fear and desperation born of starvation and disease. The lack of co-ordination between the risings, and the absence of political and even social objectives from the plans of many of the revolutionary movements, would be incomprehensible without the context of *la misère*.

Several detailed studies of particular revolts have been completed, for the most part under Mousnier's direction. The rising of the *Croquants* near Villefranche in 1643 was investigated by Mlle. Degarne in an article published in 1962.[52] In his comments upon this rising Porshnev quoted criticism by the intendant Charreton of the local governor, Noailles, for his sympathies towards the peasant forces of insurrection. Porshnev also noticed similar sympathies among the municipal officials in Villefranche and officers of the Rouergue *présidial*, and he stressed the prolonged hostility of the parlement of Bordeaux to the crown and the intendants during the rebellion. However, he asserted that resistance by the parlement was ineffective until it coincided with the spon-

---

[50]Pierre Goubert, "Recent Theories and Research in French Population between 1500 and 1700," in *Population in History: Essays in Historical Demography*, ed. D. V. Glass and D. E. C. Eversley (London, 1965), pp. 457–73.
[51]Jean Meuvret, "Demographic Crisis in France from the sixteenth to the eighteenth century," in *Population in History*, pp. 507–22.
[52]"Études sur les soulèvements provinciaux en France avant la Fronde," *XVIIe Siècle*, 56 (1962), 3–18.

taneous revolt of the peasants.[53] Mlle. Degarne emphasised the climate of disobedience encouraged by the defence of provincial liberties by the parlement of Toulouse and the *cour des aides* of Cahors. The Toulouse parlement criticised the intendants during the troubles, revoked unverified commissions and prevented the collection of extraordinary taxes. Charreton, on the other hand, claimed that the peasant revolts were surreptitiously begun by the gentry and local officials. He directly charged the magistrates and notables of Villefranche with responsibility for the disorders in the town. The revolt in Villefranche was preceded by a popular assembly to demand a reduction in the *taille,* and this moved Charreton to predict the rising. The arrival in the town of a financial official, Duperré, was followed by the incursion of a band of 1,200 armed *Croquants.* The intendant himself promised relief in taxation, and in July the governor also attempted to restore obedience by persuasion. However, in August Noailles suddenly arrested the leaders of the rebellious forces in the town – a mason, a saddler and a surgeon. The *Croquants* retorted by besieging the governor in the citadel. On the very day of the peasant incursion the *présidial* sent one of its members to invoke the support of the parlement of Toulouse. Another judge of the *présidial,* who was the father-in-law of the mayor or *juge-mage* (himself accused of responsibility for the disorders), was a wealthy landowner and seigneur, whose peasantry were among the first *Croquants* in the area. The consuls also supported the rising, one of them being at the head of the peasant forces. A few of the rural gentry were among the *Croquants,* and the majority did nothing to repress the insurrection. Behind the outbreak were general causes, such as bad harvests, epidemics and the passage of armies, but the immediate cause was the weight of the royal fiscality. All these were conclusions supporting Mousnier's thesis; but, at the same time, the conflict of evidence as to responsibility revealed the dangers of taking the reports of the intendants or the manifestos of the parlements entirely at their face value.

Conclusions similar to those of Mlle. Degarne were reached by M. Pillorget, who in 1964 published a study of the rising of the *Cascaveoux* in Aix in 1630.[54] Another paper, by M. Leguai, considered popular sedition within the *généralité* of Moulins throughout the seventeenth and eighteenth centuries but gave particular attention to the Moulins popular rising of June 1640.[55] This began with the murder of the tax collector, Jacques Puesche. The municipal authorities took no action against the rioters, and the governor, Saint-Géran, reduced the tension by pretending to remit some of the taxes. This created a schism within the revolutionary forces, and soon afterwards the prince de Condé arrived to threaten and cajole the municipal government to employ the bourgeois militia

---

[53]Porshnev, *Soulèvements,* pp. 96–9.
[54]René Pillorget, "Les 'Cascaveoux' – L'insurrection aixoise de l'automne 1630," *XVIIe Siècle,* 65 (1964), 3–30.
[55]"Les 'Emotions' et séditions populaires dans la généralité de Moulins aux XVIIe et XVIIIe siècles," *Revue d'histoire économique et sociale,* 43 (1965), 45–65.

against the rebels. The militia, however, maintained a benevolent neutrality towards the lower classes. Saint-Géran then secretly arrested the rebel leader, Rivet, and, when the local judicial authorities refused to intervene, summarily executed him. Late in August the militia finally crushed the uprising. Though the mayor and the governor disputed the credit for the victory, Condé condemned both the municipal administration for its weakness and Saint-Géran for failing to assemble the local nobility. The town was punished by the quartering of several regiments within it, and a royal pardon was not accorded until a year after the affair had ended. In his account of this rising Porshnev gave unusual prominence to the early goodwill of the bourgeois militia towards the rioters. He even remarked that the bourgeois authorities, having the same antipathy to the royal fiscality, incited the rising of the labouring poor. It was, he observed, an anticipation of the Fronde, where the bourgeoisie at first supported the revolutionary forces and then betrayed them.[56] In his own comments on the Moulins revolts Mousnier emphasised the complicity of local officials, pointing out that the governor had been obliged to imprison one of the city councillors, that the mayor was accused of abandoning the governor and that the municipal magistrates and the court of the *présidial* sympathised with the rebels.[57] Now, Leguai in his survey of risings in the town and district over two centuries has remarked that the 1640 revolt was the only one which momentarily assumed the aspects of a class war between the lower classes and the bourgeoisie. The general pillaging of bourgeois property by the rioters in July 1640 was apparently not repeated in later popular movements. The 1640 popular rising was one among several which began in Moulins as protests against taxation. Others, such as those in the last period of Louis XIV's reign, were caused by famine, and others again by the levying of recruits, the passage of troops or "accidental" brushes with the authorities.

The progress of recent research into peasant movements in seventeenth-century France has been summarised in the 1966 report prepared by Mousnier as director of the Centre de Recherches sur la civilisation de l'Europe moderne.[58] Work on the *Nu-Pieds* of 1639 has been pursued by Mlle. Foisil, on the Provençal revolts by M. Pillorget, and on the risings in Guyenne by M. Bercé. Joint research has been continued into the *Croquants* of 1636–7, the movements of 1643–4 and the Breton revolt of 1675. Not the least interesting of the techniques adopted at Mousnier's centre has been the comparative discussion of the French risings beside studies of the Russian revolts of Bolotnikov and Stenka Razin.

Further research and interpretative contributions have both deepened and widened the problem, but they have not entirely resolved it. In an analysis of the

---

[56]*Op. cit.*, pp. 192–213.
[57]Mousnier, "Recherches sur les soulèvements populaires . . . ," p. 102.
[58]"Le Centre de Recherches sur la civilisation de l'Europe moderne," *Annales de l'Université de Paris*, 1966, p. 22.

revolts of 1662, 1664–5, 1670 and 1675, Leon Bernard reached conclusions very like Porshnev's as to the spontaneity of the risings and the hostility of the lower classes to their superiors.[59] In her review of Porshnev's book and Mandrou's lectures on its themes, Menna Prestwich drew attention to the need to explain both the geographical distribution of the risings and their diminution after 1675.[60] It will be suggested that the answer to the former question is connected with the areas of peasant revolt in the wars of religion; the explanation of the second question may be found in the increasing use of the royal army to counter internal subversion in the period between the Dutch war and the war of the League of Augsburg. A part of the explanation might also be the reduction of local privileged authorities by the crown[61] and the suppression of tensions within the official class by Colbert. These were measures which must have deprived the masses of the support of the upper classes for major acts of rebellion. Nevertheless, the condition of the peasantry during the last decades of Louis XIV's reign would assuredly have produced revolts additional to those of the Cévennes if Porshnev's theory of peasant initiative were valid. Nor is it without significance that Fénelon and his fellow critics of Louis XIV's policy, and its consequences for the labouring poor, were members of the party of aristocratic reaction who condemned the Sun King's satrapy of bourgeois officials.

Beyond these problems, aspects of the general controversy remain uncertain. It can be said, at least, that three elements in the debate have been clearly established: the tensions within the ruling classes took the form of antagonism towards the *commissaires* of the central government; the demands of foreign war increased the financial burden on the lower classes and often coincided with famine and pestilence; the consequent risings of the masses further divided the upper classes and increased the monarchy's reliance on the *commissaires*. The circular relationship between these elements is revealed in a protest against military expenditure which Claude de Bullion, *surintendant des finances*, submitted to Richelieu in October 1639:

Expenditure in cash is up to at least forty millions. The *traitants* (taxfarmers) are abandoning us, and the masses will not pay either the new or the old taxes. We are now at the bottom of the pot . . . and I fear that our foreign war is degenerating into a civil war.[62]

---

[59]"French Society and Popular Uprisings under Louis XIV," *French Historical Studies*, 3 (1964), 454–74.
[60]*English Historical Review*, 81 (1966), pp. 565–72.
[61]A recent study of the suppression of municipal independence by Colbert and the subsequent direct government exploitation of town finances during the eighteenth century is by Nora Temple, "The Control and Exploitation of French Towns during the Ancien Régime," *History*, 51 (1966), 16–34.
[62]Quoted from *Lettres, instructions diplomatiques et papiers d'Etat du cardinal de Richelieu*, ed. G. d'Avenel (Paris, 1853–77), vol. 6, p. 608 by Orest A. Ranum, *Richelieu and the Councillors of Louis XIII* (Oxford, 1963), p. 145.

Further agreement is prevented by differing assumptions about the articulation of society. To Mousnier the integration of venal office-holders within local communities provided the focus for the risings; to Porshnev the exploitation of the peasantry resulted in spontaneous lower-class revolt in which a class of "feudalised" bourgeois office-holders momentarily made use of peasant initiative. Both explanations assume that French society in the seventeenth century experienced a critical change of direction which foreshadowed, if it did not predetermine, the subsequent history of the *ancien régime*. But it may be argued that a direct causal nexus is not to be established simply in terms of seventeenth-century tensions. The crisis may lie further back in time. Venality of office and popular sedition may be the product of separate chains of cause and effect which happen to intersect in the period of Richelieu and Mazarin. The roots of the problem may be sought in a period of even greater anarchy, the concluding phases of the wars of religion. Porshnev devoted some peremptory remarks at the beginning of his first chapter to the peasant revolts of the 1590s, and Mousnier observed that Professor Trevor-Roper's interpretation was far more relevant to sixteenth-century France than it was to the period of the Fronde.[63] But the popular movements in the time of the League have yet to be studied as a whole, and their relationship with their counterparts under Richelieu has yet to be established in terms more precise than those of Mandrou's collective psychology.

It may be significant that the principal areas in which popular sedition occurred under Richelieu and Mazarin were often those where the peasant armies of an earlier generation had fought indiscriminately against foreign armies and the native forces of the Guisard and politique factions. Such a revolt had occurred in Dauphiné in 1579, where peasant revolts took place in the years 1641–5. The *Va-nu-pieds* of Normandy had been preceded by the *Gauthiers*, the *Francs Museaux* and the *Lipans* in 1589–93. In Brittany the risings of 1639 and 1640 evoked the terrible memories of the campaigns of mutual extermination conducted by the nobility and peasantry in 1590–5. The *Croquants* of

---

[63]Mousnier in *Crisis in Europe*, p. 103. The theory of the economic decline of the French rural nobility in the price revolution, and the transmutation of economic discontents into political action was advanced by Henri Hauser long before Professor Trevor-Roper's enunciation of similar views in the context of seventeenth-century England. The French controversy about this issue cannot be discussed here, but among the principal works are: Pierre de Vaissière, *Gentilshommes campagnards de l'Ancienne France* (Paris, 1903), pp. 8–9, 36–7, 215–24; Henri Hauser, "Les caractères généraux de l'histoire économique de la France du milieu du XVIe siècle à la fin du XVIIIe," *Revue historique*, 173 (1934), 313–18; Paul Raveau, "La crise des prix au XVIe siècle en Poitou," *ibid.*, 162 (1929), 1–44 and 268–93; Marc Bloch, *Les caractères originaux de l' histoire rurale française*, Vol. 1 (Oslo, 1931), pp. 123–31; Fernand Braudel, *La Méditerranée et le monde méditerranéen à l'époque de Philippe II* (Paris, 1949), pp. 624–8; Henri Drouot, *Mayenne et la Bourgogne* (Paris, 1937), vol. 1, pp. 32–53; Pierre Goubert, *Beauvais et le Beauvaisis* (Paris, 1960), pp. 218–21. More recent research has tended to deny any general decline in noble fortunes. See, for example, James B. Wood, *The Nobility of the Election of Bayeux, 1463–1666: Continuity through Change* (Princeton, 1980).

1634–7 and 1643 might have recalled the pitched battles which their counterparts had fought in Guyenne, Périgord and Limousin in 1593. There is no
surviving archival material for the peasant rising during the League to parallel
the official correspondence from which the seventeenth-century revolts have
been reconstructed. But such evidence as does exist suggests that the former
were much closer to Porshnev's account of class war than were the latter.[64]
Moreover, in contrast to the blind revolts of the seventeenth century, the
peasant risings of the time of the League sometimes had some primitively
defined objectives, opposing both seigneurial dues and tithes as well as royal
taxes. Such, at least, was the conclusion of Le Roy Ladurie in his study of the
peasantry of Languedoc.[65]

There are differences, too, between the urban revolutionary movements of
the masses in the two periods. In certain towns the period of the League had
seen the establishment of revolutionary régimes based upon popular movements. Such were the reigns of Charles Casaux in Marseille and of Pierre Biord
in Arles. In Paris the mob had defeated the royal troops in the riots of May
1588. The conspiratorial group of parish *curés* and lesser officials known as the
Sixteen had subsequently held the capital in a reign of terror, purged the
parlement and attempted to initiate similar movements in other cities – all in
defiance of the aristocratic leadership of the League. During the period of the
Fronde only the Ormée in Bordeaux could claim resemblance to these earlier
urban movements. Popular revolution in the Leaguer towns, unlike most of the
urban risings in the next century, was for a time united by a coherent religious
and political cause. Moreover, these earlier movements were led by *avocats* and
procureurs who, according to one theory, were disappointed in their hopes of
obtaining venal office through the erection of barriers across the path to social
ascension.[66]

The wars of religion were succeeded by a period when social mobility was
restricted, and when rivalries within the serried ranks of office-holders, as well
as between sword and gown, came to the surface. The wars were also the cause
of vast changes in the distribution of land, and their last phase was marked by
the only demographic crisis of the century which substantially checked population growth. It would be surprising if seigneurial relationships survived this
period unchanged. It has been argued that the shift of emphasis to share-
cropping (*métayage*) in the sixteenth century, and the expropriation of the peas-

[64]E.g., *Mémoires du chanoine Jean Moreau sur les guerres de la Ligue en Bretagne*, ed. Henri Waquet
(Quimper, 1960), and J. Baudry, *La Fontenelle le Ligueur et le brigandage en Basse-Bretagne pendant
la Ligue, 1574–1602* (Nantes, 1920), where the Breton conflict between peasant armies and the
nobility is discussed in detail. One of the themes developed by Robert Mandrou is the growth of
class consciousness as a consequence of the wars of religion: *Introduction à la France moderne: essai
de psychologie historique, 1500–1640* (Paris, 1961), pp. 141–8.
[65]Emmanuel Le Roy Ladurie, *Les Paysans de Languedoc* (Paris, 1966), vol. i, pp. 393–404.
[66]Drouot, *loc. cit.*

antry in many areas as a consequence of bourgeois rural investment, amounted to some form of agricultural revolution. After the wars of religion the seigneur, whether of the old *noblesse* or the new, was less a companion in peasant misery than its partial cause.[67] Thus Olivier de Serres, writing his handbook of agriculture in 1600, seemed the heir to conflicting traditions. On the one hand he could advise:

The seigneur (*père de famille*) should love his subjects and cherish them like his children. He should support them with credits and favours when they are in need. He should, in case of necessity, protect them from the passage of troops and like occurrences, screening them from exactions and unjust charges and instances of violence, which may from time to time occur.[68]

On the other, he could write:

Neither the passage of time nor the conversion of servitude into liberty have in the least been able to extinguish the old trend to rebellion and disobedience on the part of the *gens de service*, and there is still much of it today among our hired workers, who do not wish to recognise God's grace in their being born free, or to appreciate that poverty does not deprive them of their liberty, which they have in common with the wealthiest. They are given to idleness, destruction and desertion, . . . and the civil wars (in which several of this kind have been employed) have made them all the more insolent and arrogant, because the length of time the wars have lasted has habituated them to idleness and to all kinds of vices and disorders.[69]

De Serres' first seigneur is also the nobleman or local officer depicted by Mousnier as leading his peasantry against the crown. His second seigneur is the exploiting nobleman who, as Porshnev would tell us, directly or indirectly drove his peasantry to spontaneous revolt. But in whatever guise de Serres would have him appear, he is indubitably the product of the sixteenth century.

Like the debate over the gentry and aristocracy in England, the controversy which has been reviewed here is concerned with the basic character of early modern society and government. The writer has endeavoured to trace the development of the dispute, to criticise the conceptual framework in which it has been set and to summarise the research it has promoted. It is his belief that the use of the Séguier correspondence as the central point of reference in the debate has restricted the vision of the participants more severely than have any of the ideological preconceptions they may possess. Many of the ingenious and scholarly arguments that have been advanced will become clearer when full account is taken of the impact of the wars of religion upon French social structure.

[67]Cf. Elizabeth S. Teall, "The Seigneur of Renaissance France: Advocate or Oppressor," *Journal of Modern Hist.*, 37 (1965), 131–50, and the summary given by Georges Livet, *Les Guerres de Religion* (Paris, 1962), pp. 90–7.
[68]*Le Théâtre d'Agriculture et Mesnage des Champs* (Paris, 1804), vol. 1, p. 25.
[69]*Ibid.*, p. 36.

9

Peasant revolt in Vivarais, 1575–1580

Since the beginning of the controversy between Boris Porshnev and Roland Mousnier a generation ago, studies of popular revolts and affrays have been centred in the seventeenth century. Even when they have begun by questioning Mousnier's general conclusions, nearly all these studies have ended by re-affirming them.[1] Resistance to the agents of royal taxation was the dominant motif, and local solidarity between the social orders against the centralising state was more evident than the hostility of the labouring classes towards their betters. But there has been too great a readiness to apply the seventeenth-century model to the risings of the later sixteenth century. In his popular overview of peasant revolt in both periods (and indeed beyond), Yves-Marie Bercé has taken the great Pitaud (or Pétault) revolt of 1548 as establishing a pattern which was to repeat itself continuously with one or two variations and exceptions.[2]

Two other recent surveys have modified the set image and given more attention to the peasant risings of the religious wars. In the long term Jean Jacquart finds the exploitative power of the seigneurial apparatus and the growth of peasant indebtedness to urban interests to be at least as disruptive of peasant political economy as state taxation. Distinguishing the risings of the later sixteenth century from those that followed, he attaches importance to warbands, seigneurial and church dues, and resentment of country against town as primary causes of peasant discontents. In contrast with Bercé, Jacquart stresses evidence for antiseigneurial motives in the Croquant movement of the 1590s, which he calls the most consciously revolutionary of all the revolts.[3] In a

---

[1] E.g. René Pillorget, *Les mouvements insurrectionnels de Provence entre 1596 et 1715* (Paris, 1975), pp. xlviii and 987. Pillorget's introduction gives a just summary of the positions of Mousnier and Porshnev. In this connection see also above, pp. 191–9.
[2] Yves-Marie Bercé, *Croquants et Nu-pieds: les soulèvements paysans en France du XVIᵉ au XIXᵉ siècle* (Paris, 1974). See also Bercé's magisterial *Histoire des Croquants* (2 vols., Geneva, 1974). An interpretation of the Croquant revolt of 1594–1595 that differs in some respects from Bercé's and a general account of other peasant risings in the religious wars are offered by J. H. M. Salmon, *Society in Crisis: France in the Sixteenth Century* (London, 1975), pp. 276–91.
[3] Jean Jacquart, "Immobilisme et Catastrophes, 1560–1690," *Histoire de la France rurale, tome 2* (Paris, 1975), pp. 329–53.

similar survey Emmanuel Le Roy Ladurie describes the risings of the religious wars at greater length than those under Richelieu and Mazarin and calls the rebels of the southwest in the later period "Néo-Croquants," remarking that they showed more respect for the social hierarchy than did their predecessors. Ladurie sees local peasant solidarity in the later sixteenth century as the result of self-defence against warbands, and as directed subsequently against fisc, seigneur, and *dîme*.[4]

There are elements in this revisionism that are particularly relevant to the one major peasant rising entirely ignored in the surveys provided by Bercé, Jacquart, and Ladurie: that of Vivarais in the late 1570s. At the same time there is one aspect of the Vivarais revolts that appears superficially to resemble the seventeenth-century model, for the first rebel initiatives took the form of a tax revolt. This was not, however, in any sense a matter of provincial resistance to the central state apparatus, which had at best a peripheral role to play. In fact, the society in which the peasant violence erupted was in some respects quite untypical of the time. The local history and geography of Vivarais (the modern Ardèche) had conspired to form institutions markedly different from those of the better known provinces of Renaissance France. On the eastern border, the Rhône, lay prosperous fortified towns, such as Bourg-Saint-Andéol, Viviers, Rochemaure, and Tournon, with populations not much in excess of three thousand. The steep hills blocking the artery of the Rhône valley from the interior are intersected by tributaries, the Cance, Doux, Eyrieux, and Ardèche, whose upper reaches provide lines of communication through the tangled ranges of the eastern Massif Central to Forez, Velay, and Gévaudan (the modern departments of Loire, Haute-Loire, and Lozère). Where the river gorges widen into valleys lie the towns of the hinterland: Annonay (the largest urban centre and focus of the leather industry) on the Cance; Lamastre on the Doux; Chalençon and Le Cheylard on the Eyrieux; Privas on the Ouvèze; and Aubenas (the second largest town and centre of the wool trade) on the Ardèche. The northern Cévennes, where the Loire and the Allier find their source, are crossed at right angles by an irregular linc of volcanic basalt, running from Velay to the Rhône at Rochemaure. To the south of this chain lie tilted lime-stone plateaux where villages perch on outcrops or shelter beside the streams that join the Ardèche. In the sixteenth century this was the only area of Vivarais where cereals were grown in quantity, and even here wheat grew poorly and rye predominated. As if in compensation, the lower slopes of the mountains throughout Vivarais were forested with chestnut trees, *l'arbre à pain* of the Ardèchois. In this barren territory, where each secluded valley could be a world unto itself, lived a proudly independent rural society, combining the tenacity of the Auvergnat with the optimism of the Occitain.

[4]Emmanuel Le Roy Ladurie, "Révoltes paysannes et histoire sociale," *Histoire économique et sociale de la France, tome 1, de 1450 à 1660, vol. 2 Paysannerie et Croissance* (Paris, 1977), pp. 819–58.

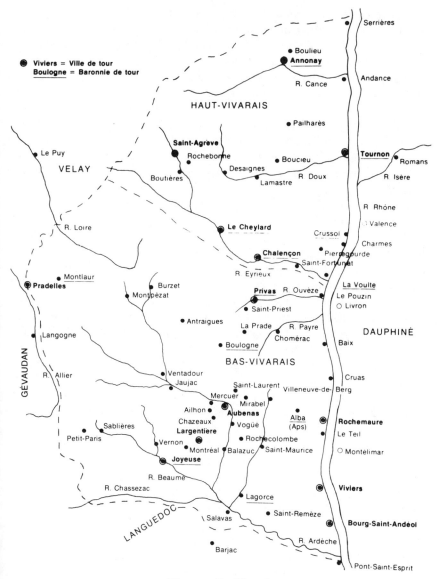

Figure 1. Le Vivarais

Among the nobility feudal relationships still had political meaning, for clientage followed the bonds of homage. In Haut-Vivarais, north of the Eyrieux, the high nobility had external links: the Tournon with Viennois, the Saint-Vallier with Valentinois, and the Crussol with Uzès. The barons of Tournon and Chalençon had not become direct vassals of the king until the final absorption of Dauphiné into the royal domain in the fifteenth century. Most of Bas-Vivarais had been under the temporal administration of the bishop of Viviers, whose overlordship had been steadily eroded by the southern barons since his acknowledgment of the royal suzerainty of Philippe le Bel. On the eve of the religious wars there were twelve *barons de tour* throughout the province, who constituted the noble order in the estates. Their *baillis*, who usually represented them in this body, were themselves noblemen of the sword. Some of the great baronial families played national rôles under the last Valois kings. Cardinal de Tournon sat on the inner council of François Ier and Henri II, while the royal mistress, Diane de Poitiers of the Saint-Vallier family, was baronne de Privas as well as duchesse de Valentinois. Under Charles IX the Crussol family was influential at court, and under Henri III the Joyeuse reached the pinnacle of royal favour. The Lévis-Ventadour of La Voulte were closely allied by marriage with the Montmorency.

The lesser nobility, ranging from a baron's *bailli* to the petty lord of a few rock-strewn acres, proliferated in the first half of the sixteenth century, recognition being a local affair with little regard for registration in the king's courts. There were sometimes ten or more petty gentry associated with a single parish. Equal division of inheritances broke up the seigneuries, many possessing several coseigneurs who disputed the distribution of peasant dues. To take a single example, the Vogüé family, who rose from relative obscurity in the fifteenth century to absorb the baronies of Montlaur, Aubenas, and Joyeuse in the eighteenth, held sole seigneurial rights in only three of their villages when the religious wars began. They were coseigneurs of Vogüé itself with the Rochemaure du Besset and the Beaumont-Brison. They had coseigneurs in four other parishes, and had only recently succeeded in renouncing homage to the seigneurs of Balazuc in respect of a fifth. They acknowledged the general overlordship of the barons de Montlaur, who had themselves thrown off the suzerainty of the bishop of Viviers. Guillaume de Vogüé, who acted as *bailli d'épée* to the seigneur of Aubenas, acted as a local peacemaker in the wars of religion. He was engaged in complex manoeuvres to free himself from his overlord and also to evict some of his coseigneurs from their joint jurisdiction. However, it was only in the next generation that the family expelled their rivals from Vogüé itself and moved from their donjon in the fortress village of Rochecolombe to the main château.[5]

In the thirteenth century the seigneurs of Vogüé had followed the general practice in Vivarais of freeing their peasantry from serfdom. There remained, nonetheless, a few parishes where servile status continued into the sixteenth century, the last known Vivarais seigneurial charter of enfranchisement being

---

[5] Jean Charay, *Vogüé sur Ardèche* (Aubenas, 1968), pp. 16–20. A general account of the nobility of Vivarais is provided by Charles du Besset, "Essai sur la noblesse vivaroise," *Revue historique, archéologique, littéraire et pittoresque du Vivarais*, 20 (1912), 217–32, 265–81, 306–19, 346–58, 413–30, 436–48.

dated 1561. Apart from feudal incidents, the obligations of free peasants towards their seigneur consisted of a labor *corvée* (one or two days in the year), a nominal cash sum, and a proportion of certain specified crops. The latter requirement varied enormously from parish to parish but seldom exceeded twenty per cent of peasant revenue and was usually much less. The church tithe was generally less than ten per cent. In the less fertile areas subsistence farming was the rule, and surplus produce was exchanged in barter rather than in coin. It was the demand for coin that made taxation seem more onerous than seigneurial dues. Each village had its own peasant hierarchy, and the practice of share cropping had not yet advanced to the point where any sizeable proportion of small tenants had been expropriated and forced to become day labourers. Especially in the mountains, the parishes were self-sufficient units with pride in their independence. The rural *communautés* were vigorous corporations, which could successfully negotiate between the rival claims of coseigneurial jurisdictions through their elected syndics and *procureurs*.[6] Violence was an accepted part of life in the hill country, and communal solidarity provided its own means of protection when the authority of the government and that of the seigneur were ineffective. This was the area where the Tuchins had terrorised the towns in the late fourteenth century and where peasant militia had resisted the brigand bands of the *routiers* in the last phases of the Hundred Years War. Most peasant communities were Catholic, especially in the western valleys of Bas-Vivarais. In the upper basins of the Doux and the Eyrieux, however, groups of Calvinist peasants existed. Lower down these rivers, and also on the Ouvèze and the Payre, many of the small towns had been early centres of Protestantism.[7]

The towns had obtained their charters in the thirteenth century, the period when the peasant communes had won theirs. Unlike many towns in other provinces, where charters had resulted from royal intervention in quarrels between nobles and bourgeois, the Vivarais towns had bought their freedom from the seigneurs. Yet the separation was not complete. In the *villes de tour*, with the exception of Bourg-Saint-Andéol, Rochemaure and those still nominally acknowledging the temporal authority of the bishop (Viviers, Pradelles, and Largentière), the *bailli d'épée* of the appropriate baron cooperated with the consuls in municipal administration. The consular corps were merchant oligarchies which sent their sons to the new humanist university of Valence across the Rhône. Some studied the law there, but there was little opportunity for a career in judicial office because the only royal courts in the province were the *cours bailliagères* of Villeneuve-de-Berg (which moved to Largentière during the Huguenot occupation in the civil wars) and Annonay (formerly at Boucieu)

---

[6]Pierre Bozon, *Histoire du peuple vivarois* (Valence, 1974), pp. 60–3, 140–2.
[7]The history of Calvinism in Vivarais is the subject of several detailed studies by Samuel Mours, notably *Le Protestantisme en Vivarais et en Velay* (Valence, 1949). See also Eugène Arnaud, *Histoire des Protestants du Vivarais et du Velay* (2 vols., Paris, 1888).

in the north. There was such an infinite variety in size and independence between the larger centres and the small *bourgs*, and between the *bourgades* and the more prosperous villages, that urban life melted into rural. It was this situation that made possible a close liaison between small-town notables and peasant communes. During the peasant revolts a deep division emerged between the rural population and the administrative circle of nobles and consuls who sat in the local estates. This was the more remarkable because the provincial governing authorities were often responsive to the needs of the lower orders, upon whom their own welfare depended.

Just as the Vivarais *cours bailliagères* were subordinate to the courts at Nîmes and Beaucaire, so the local estates were theoretically dependent on the estates of Languedoc, and the *receveur* received directions in fiscal matters from the *trésoriers* of Toulouse. In practice, however, the estates of Vivarais controlled the finances of the province, and their permanent officials often received direct communications from the royal council that enabled them to temporise with the authorities of Languedoc. The Vivarais estates, consisting of a consular representative from each of the thirteen *villes de tour* and the twelve barons or their *baillis d'épée*, had no deputies from the ecclesiastical order.[8] In normal times the estates met twice a year for a week in the house of a consul or nobleman in one of the *villes de tour*. Between sessions the administration was in the hands of the officers of the estates, the syndic, the *receveur*, and the *greffier*. These officers usually resided in the southern towns on the Rhône which were not under joint baronial control. During the civil wars some of these towns tried to preserve neutrality, refusing entry to garrisons sent by the noble factions.[9] The syndic was often in touch, of course, with noble governors of the towns and subprovinces of Upper and Lower Vivarais, but when confronted with rival contenders for these positions he usually looked to his bourgeois colleagues for advice. He also communicated with the lieutenant of the royal *bailli* and with the *juge de Vivarais*, who sat with the deputies in the estates. The wars caused the estates to split into Catholic and Protestant segments which met in emergency sessions. Even among the nobility provincial unity at times proved stronger than the call of the national parties, especially when a Catholic third party formed under Montmorency-Damville, the governor of Languedoc, in 1574. On several occasions a national truce was anticipated by Vivarais men of the sword and subsequently confirmed by the reunited estates. Nevertheless, the countryside

---

[8] In the fourteenth century the three *bailliages cévénols* of Gévaudan, Velay, and Vivarais possessed a composite representative body. In 1422 the Vivarais estates came into separate existence, thereafter sending one baron and five consular deputies as their delegation to the Languedoc estates-general. From 1434 the Vivarais clergy were no longer summoned, a phenomenon associated with the desire of the nobility to break up the secular domains of the bishop of Viviers and with the willingness of the crown to grant their demands under pressure of the war with the Burgundians and the English. See Auguste Le Sourd, *Essai sur les Etats des Vivarais depuis leurs origines* (Paris, 1926).

[9] Nicole Maufront, *Le Vivarais en pleine dissidence, 1574–1600* (Privas, 1943), p. 9.

suffered severely from local warfare and banditry after the accession of Henri III.

By the beginning of 1575 it had become clear that the horrors of war were no longer perpetrated in a spirit of religious fervour. Calvinists and Catholics had coexisted in Annonay, but when the Protestant Charles de Barjac reinforced the Huguenot garrison there with some Catholic troops under his command, it was they who began to desecrate the churches and harass the priests. Meanwhile the soldiers of Saint-Chamond, the Catholic governor of Haut-Vivarais, were pillaging the valley of the Doux to the south. The opposing Protestant captain Erard of Vernoux, a man already notorious for his banditry, followed suit by ravaging Lamastre and its environs, until his superior, Charles de Barjac, hanged him for his atrocities. Barjac freed a number of well-to-do peasants whom Erard had been torturing to exact ransom.[10] In the course of the year the Protestants seized and garrisoned twenty-six small towns and strong points in Vivarais, and the Catholics seventy-eight. Large numbers of refugees fled to the shelter of châteaux and walled towns held by their coreligionists. The captains of local warbands established themselves in the fortresses and began to live off the surrounding countryside. The local chronicler, André Lafaïsse, described 1575 as the most disastrous year the province had known: "The peasants removed tiles and beams from their houses and brought them to sell in Aubenas in order to keep alive through war and famine. The countryside was despoiled by the treachery of the soldiers of both religions. They cooperated with each other in betraying wealthy civilians, and in committing atrocities, thefts, and all kinds of evils."[11]

The Catholic segment of the estates reacted to the growing anarchy by increasing direct taxation to pay for the garrisons. This provoked the first isolated peasant rising, which took the form of a tax revolt. On August 11, 1575, the estates in session at Pradelles heard their syndic, Olivier de Leyris, report on necessary measures of repression. He described the peasant leagues to the west of Largentière as "combinations, conspiracies, and rebellions perpetrated in the said region by *plusieurs Catholiques*, who have formed a syndicate to refuse royal taxes and all others, ordinary or extraordinary, imposed on the district, and resisting with united force and display of arms the sergeants and commissioners sent to execute our instructions."[12] Leyris had obtained from the Catholic governor of Languedoc, the ex-Huguenot Jacques de Crussol, duc d'Uzès, a special commission to reinforce the *prévôt des maréchaux* against the peasants. Soon afterwards the estates heard that some garrisons had to be disbanded for

---

[10]Erard was described by his contemporary, the Annonay lawyer Achille Gamon, as "one who professed to be of the Reformed Religion but in reality lived without any faith, taking complete licence to do evil." *Les mémoires d'Achille Gamon, avocat d'Annonay-en-Vivarais, 1552–1586*, ed. J. Brun Durand (Valence, 1888), cited by Mours, *Le Protestantisme en Vivarais*, p. 98.

[11]Mours, *Le Protestantisme en Vivarais*, p. 107.

[12]Archives Départementales de l'Ardèche (hereafter A.D.A.), ms. c334/101–102.

lack of pay, but the pillage continued, and early in 1576 the deputies at Largentière encouraged a proposal for a provincial truce, intended "to call a halt to so many crimes, forays, robberies, and sackings commonly committed against the poor people, and to provide for general welfare and relief and the public peace."[13]

In February the truce became a definitive local peace treaty at La Borie de Balazuc, where Catholic and Protestant captains signed an agreement in the château of the Catholic commander in Bas-Vivarais, François de Borne de Leugières. Once again it was the situation of the common people that the signatories had in mind, for the treaty specified its purpose thus:

> To put an end to the distress, calamities, and oppressions which have occurred during the said troubles in the province of Vivarais, by means of which the inhabitants are reduced to such an extremity that they can no longer survive the exactions and expenses they endure, having nothing to live on for the rest of this year as a result of the ravaging, pillages, ransomings, and other hostile acts daily committed in the said province, even to the point where their lands remain untilled because of the violence of the war, lack of livestock, and dearth of seed.[14]

By the treaty war impositions were annulled and pillage forbidden. The Catholics recognised Crussol as governor and the Protestants Damville. The terms were ratified by members of the estates of both religions at Viviers. In May 1576 the national peace was confirmed by the deputies meeting in Leyris's house in Bourg-Saint-Andéol. This assembly also heard "the exposition and remonstrance made by the syndic and several others of the province that several parishes have risen in arms and refused to pay any kind of royal or other tax."[15] Clearly, sporadic peasant resistance was continuing despite the attitude of the provincial government.

The recommendations in favour of toleration advanced by the Vivarais and other Languedoc deputies at the ensuing national estates-general did not prevail. A new civil war followed the royal declaration against the Protestants early in 1577. For a time, however, the moderate party in Vivarais preserved the settlement of La Borie de Balazuc. Gradually the pattern of raids and sieges resumed, and by the summer the province was again involved in the general war. In the middle of June six parishes in Sablières and Petit-Paris rose in arms and massacred the garrison that was exploiting them.[16] To prevent the nobility from levying impositions on the countryside to sustain their troops, the royal commander on the Rhône, marshal Bellegarde, issued an ordinance on July 12, requiring all "seigneurs et gentilshommes" to pay their military expenses from

[13]Mours, *Le Protestantisme en Vivarais*, p. 109.
[14]*Ibid.*, p. 110.
[15]A.D.A. ms. c334/254.
[16]Maufront, *Vivarais*, p. 11.

their private resources.[17] The syndic of Vivarais also made known a plan to reduce the number of garrisons. In the Largentière region Leugières protested indignantly to both Bellegarde and Leyris, claiming that such a reduction would mean the loss of half the local strongpoints and threatening to resign his command. His postscript suggests the nature and scale of peasant reaction to the garrisons: "I have received warning that the twenty-two parishes which have rebelled are on the point of joining the Huguenot party and have massed in force. If something is not done there will be a rash of these evil beggars. I am sure that they could still be assembled for some purpose if properly handled on our part."[18]

During the following weeks the Catholic Vivarais estates discussed the dilemma at assemblies in Viviers and Bourg-Saint-Andéol. Finances were lacking to support the garrisons, but past experience suggested that if they were partially disbanded, the soldiery as well as the peasant communes might join the Protestant forces. Faced with a new ultimatum from Leugières, the estates abandoned Leyris's planned reductions, offering the pious wish that the king, rather than the province, should stand the cost. Bellegarde summed up the attitude of the governing élite towards the problem when he wrote on July 30: "The revolt of the Vivarais parishes is the beginning of popular rule [*estat populaire*], and its cause is the ruin, extortion, and oppression they have been made to suffer."[19]

Before news had reached Vivarais of the general peace of Bergerac, a local truce had been signed by Catholic and Protestant captains at Jaujac, not far to the north of the centre of the peasant risings at Sablières. Gaspard de Clastrevielle and Jean du Mas agreed to join forces to repel any external troops entering the area.[20] This was not unlike the way the peasant leagues themselves set aside religious differences to resist soldiery of any political color, and it is possible that the two commanders were acting in concert with the peasants. Although the treaty of Bergerac was recognised throughout Vivarais by late October 1577, the garrisons remained in the towns and fortresses, and the peasants continued their resistance in the southwest.

In 1578, the year when the better-known rising of the Chaperons-sans-cordon began east of the Rhône, the Vivarais estates grappled once more with the related problems of military funding and rural revolt. After some preliminary hesitation, the Catholic deputies met their Protestant counterparts in Privas and swore to uphold the peace and punish those captains who infringed it at the expense of the unprivileged. They were also united in finding a scaepgoat in

---

[17]"Le docteur Francus" (Albin Mazon), *Notes et documents historiques sur les Huguenots du Vivarais,* tome 3 (Privas, 1903), p. 33.
[18]A.D.A. ms. c1022/85.
[19]Mazon, *Notes et documents,* p. 51.
[20]*Ibid.,* pp. 39–40.

the *receveur*, Jacques Reynier, whose acquisition of his post had allegedly been followed by six years of peculation. The estates responded to the rural crisis by establishing a tribunal to inquire into wrongful impositions upon the peasantry since 1572 by local captains of both parties. They deplored the seizure of food and livestock by the soldiery, and asked for a two-year suspension of the *taille*. Jacques Froment of Rochemaure, who was shortly to succeed Reynier as *receveur*, was sent to court to present the requests of the estates directly to Henri III. Froment was to receive further instructions from the syndic after consultation with Géraud de Bézangier, the Protestant *bailli* in La Voulte of the politique Lévis-Ventadour. Neither this consultation nor the general inquiry appears to have taken place.

In October the Vivarais estates, meeting at Bourg-Saint-Andéol, received commissioners sent by the *trésoriers* of Languedoc to complain about arrears owing in taxation. A deputy of the *receveur* named Allamel explained that little or nothing could be collected because "the inhabitants of the *pays*, especially those of the so-called reformed religion and the [peasant] leagues, refuse to pay the said taxes and beat and maltreat the commissioners sent to collect the said revenues."[21] The only relief was a letter from Henri III granting delay in the repayment of debts incurred by the estates. This was a part of the royal response to the submissions of the Privas assembly. The king forbad any local impositions to be levied without his express consent. A similar letter was received by Leyris from the queen mother, who was on a mission of conciliation in Guyenne. Like Bellegarde, she suggested that the peasant leagues might spread into a general social anarchy, and she ordered their immediate dispersal.[22]

In February 1579 Catherine de Médicis signed the treaty of Nérac with the Huguenot leader, Henri de Navarre, extending the rights granted the Protestants under the peace of 1577. It was a measure designed to check the growth of anarchy throughout southern France, and nowhere was the restoration of order more necessary than in Vivarais. Rosilhes, the *bailli* of Joyeuse, wrote to Leyris to report that the parish of Vernon just to the north of the town had joined the general revolt of the peasant communes in the basins of the upper Ardèche and Beaume rivers.[23] At this moment the peasants had found a leader who seemed able to weld their isolated endeavours into a coherent movement. He had not the *panache* of Jean Serve, who had allied the artisans of Romans with the army of the Chaperons-sans-cordon, nor did he possess the political vision of the notary La Saigne, who directed the armies of the Croquants in Périgord fifteen years later. His motives, moreover, carried a strong suspicion of self-interest. His name was Jean Rouvière (or La Rouvière), and he came either from Mer-

[21]*Ibid.*, p. 49.
[22]Auguste Le Sourd, "Une lettre inédite de Catherine de Médicis, le 7 novembre, 1578," *Revue . . . du Vivarais.* 27 (1920), 195–9.
[23]Mazon, *Notes et documents*, p. 54.

cuer or Chazeaux, small *bourgades* just to the west of Aubenas. He may have
been a notary or a small merchant. In 1581 a man named Jean Rouvière of
Mercuer was commissioned by the estates of Vivarais to act as lieutenant to the
prévôt des maréchaux, responsible for preserving order in the region of the
Ardèche and its tributaries.[24] Whether this man was the peasant leader or
whether his cousin from Chazeaux fulfilled that role depends upon how the
actions of the leader during the revolt of 1579–1580 are interpreted. It seems to
have been the La Rouvière styling himself "procureur des suppliants du tiers
estat" who composed a document which is the most valuable of all these
fragmentary sources in determining the nature of the Vivarais risings.

Drawn up in February 1579, this document took the form of a petition to the
king from "the poor people of the third estate of Your Majesty's barren and
desolated countryside of Vivarais – poor, miserable, martyrised, and abandoned
men."[25] They justified this self-description with a list of atrocities inflicted
upon them by "the insolence, authority, and power of the *gentilshommes,* captains, and soldiers." Their heads had been bound with ropes and tightened
until their eyes spurted from their sockets; they had been buried alive in heaps
of manure, thrown into wells and ditches and left to die, howling like dogs; they
had been nailed in boxes without air, walled up in towers without food, and
garrotted upon trees in the depths of the mountains and forests; they had been
stretched in front of fires, their feet fricasseed in grease; their women had been
raped and those who were pregnant had been aborted; their children had been
kidnapped and ransomed, or even roasted alive before the parents. Beside such
horrors, in which neither sex nor age had been respected, their other sufferings
might seem slight. There had been burnings, sackings, ransoms, levies, *tailles,*
and tolls together with seizures of goods, grain, and livestock. In one year
impositions placed upon them first by the Catholic and then by the Protestant
garrisons had exceeded the amount of the *taille* in thirty years. Maimed, pen-
niless, and starving, they implored the king to grant them peace, justice, and
relief.

The specific requests that followed this exordium make this document even
more remarkable than the manifestos and petitions of the Pitauds and the
Croquants. Some items were directed against the troops and the seigneurs,
others against the provincial administrators. In respect of the soldiery, the
petitioners demanded a vigorous and reformed system of justice "to purge the

[24]Mazon (*Notes et documents,* p. 86) and Maufront (*Vivarais,* p. 13) support the view that the peasant
leader was La Rouvière of Mercuer. Le Sourd (*Etats,* p. 282), refusing to believe that the estates
would appoint so bitter an enemy to a responsible position, declares the leader to have been a
cousin of the *lieutenant du prévôt.* The spelling of "Rivière" in one of the associated documents
(Bibliothèque Municipale de Toulouse, ms. fr. 613/40) is evidently in error.
[25]The original manuscript of this petition, from which subsequent passages are quoted in translation, is held in Privas as A.D.A. ms. c699/8. A later incomplete copy is A.D.A. ms. 1028/53.
Another copy is in the Bibliothèque Nationale ms. fr. 16225/73–80. A printed version is provided by Mazon, *Notes et documents,* pp. 54–67.

country of this vermin" and to punish those whose crimes contravened the peace edict. A special court should be established for this purpose since the existing two were too remote and ineffective. Additional officers of the *prévôté des maréchaux* were needed to patrol the countryside, and their salaries should be guaranteed, unlike those appointed by the Vivarais estates, who failed to act because they were seldom paid. Since the syndic of the estates could not be trusted to act in the interest of the peasantry, the communes should be allowed to elect "un syndic commun du plat pays." He should assist in the prosecution of the wrongdoers and represent the rights of the "peuple orphelin" in "all public assemblies with right of entry and observation as if he were one responsible for the common expenses of the said province." This startling claim for permanent representation was more sophisticated in form than the comparable submission made by the Croquants to the Périgord estates in 1595.[26]

The petition did not criticise the seigneurial system. Its animus against the rural gentry was inspired by the use of their châteaux by the warbands. Instead of protecting the peasantry, the seigneurs who encouraged this practice had become oppressors or at best accomplices of the exploiters:

In as much as the seigneurs of the said region, together with their officers of one religion or the other, have permitted and continue to permit, with connivance and dissimulation, infinite crimes and excesses, and do maintain, shelter, defend, and sustain the murderers, robbers, rebels, and disturbers of the public peace, may it please Your Majesty to command and enjoin most expressly that they must abstain from withdrawing the above named into their houses and from giving them comfort, help, and aid; and that henceforth they must insist upon the exercise of justice in their lands and seigneuries, and install well-intentioned and learned judges and officers, who may well and worthily execute the said justice without exception of person or religion.

Should the seigneurs persist in their evil ways, the governors and the lieutenants of the *prévôt des maréchaux* should attack their strongholds and seize the criminals. If these officers needed assistance "to purge the province and give it security, they should, if need be, assemble the communes by sound of trumpet." In another article of the petition the *gentilshommes* were accused of converting church benefices into private patrimony. Priests of proper vocation should be appointed, and the *dîme* used only for their upkeep. Where Protestant seigneurs were collecting the tithe, it should be used to maintain a preacher and an *hôtel-dieu*.

Among other grievances was a novel imposition, the "bilhete," illegally extracted by governors, captains and "quelques gentilshommes" to support garrisons of towns and fortresses. Whenever peasant complaints against this practice had been directed to "their estates" (i.e. of the nobles and consuls), they had been ignored. This indication of lack of confidence in the governing orders was followed by protests against forced labour in siege operations and against

[26]Salmon, *Society in Crisis*, p. 290.

the seizure and sale of property by the soldiery. Further articles pleaded for the remission of the *taille* for ten years and the abolition of all non-customary impositions, tolls, and new offices "erected against the liberties, welfare, and utility of the said *pays*." There were charges of peculation against the fiscal officers of the estates. The accounts of the *receveur* should be inspected by impartial commissioners, and not by the syndic, *baillis*, judges, and consuls associated with the estates. Bonds raised on the yield of the *octrois* and *aides* in the reigns of François Ier and Henri II had been manipulated to the personal profit of the *receveur* and syndic, who should be imprisoned until they disgorged. Fiscal officers had collaborated with the captains of garrisons in authorising levies with collection charges three times as large as the impositions themselves. Tax rolls should be maintained by a new body of honest controllers, whose salaries should not be an additional burden on the taxpayer. Within each parish authorised taxes should be distributed by a *procureur*, a notary, and ten elected members.

There were also articles referring to problems of debt. Where the parishes had had to borrow to discharge tax arrears and to ransom prisoners, usurers had charged exorbitant interest. Where the estates had borrowed money on behalf of the provincial administration, it was the deputies who should be held responsible for repayment, and not the peasant communes, which had never been consulted. Such debts should be verified by "commissaires non suspects." The petition cited a clause in the peace edict of 1577 requiring war debts to be paid by the faction that had incurred them rather than being passed on to the community at large. During the past wars, it was argued, both parties had used the same agents and officials to raise money, and now the parties had united to shift the burden upon those who had had no part in the conflicts.

The king reviewed the petition in council, and had comments and decisions written in the margin and signed by secretary of state Villeroy under the date of March 13, 1579. It was stated that commissioners had already been sent to enforce the edict of pacification, and that the negotiations at Nérac would result in the cessation of local welfare and the punishment of lawbreakers. While the peasants could elect their syndic to aid the prosecution of criminals for a single year, nothing was said about the demand for permanent representation. The king would not agree to a new court of justice, but he ordered archers to be sent from Languedoc to support the *prévôt des maréchaux*. He forbad the sheltering of criminals by "all persons of whatever quality, *gentilshommes* and others, on pain of exemplary punishment, confiscation of their fiefs and levelling of their châteaux." He ordered the verification of debts and accounts and the investigation of suspect officials, but he refused to authorise new controllers to maintain the tax rolls. A few minor matters, such as the suppression of the unnecessary venal office of a *receveur alternatif* and the review of a new wine tax, were freely accorded. Other issues in the petition (the proper performance of religious duties, the review of good debts, and the remission of taxation) were said to be

grievances to which the king had already responded in his answer to the remonstrances of the Vivarais estates in the previous year. Henri III chose to
appear indulgent towards the Vivarais peasants, just as Henri IV was to express
sympathy for the Croquants in the 1590s.[27] The tenor of the marginal comments was designed to mollify the petitioners, and although the king did not
accept criticism of the institutional structure, he implicitly accepted some of the
charges against particular members of the higher orders. As in all peasant
revolts, the crown was seen as the ultimate authority which could grant redress
against its own officials as well as unauthorised exploiters of the common
people. The wording used in the council was deliberately intended to sustain
this illusion.

The petition and the royal reply clearly reveal that the basic cause of the
Vivarais rising was the reign of terror inflicted upon the countryside by the
warbands. The seigneurs were associated with this oppression. The geography
of Vivarais made this a more general phenomenon than it might otherwise have
been. The lines of communication ran through the mountain valleys dominated
by seigneurial châteaux or fortified *manoirs*. These strongpoints were of such
strategic significance that the gentry who controlled them could not remain
neutral. If they failed to take sides in the civil war they faced siege or eviction.
Many, of course, willingly entered the struggle because of family or feudal ties,
because of religious conviction, or simply because fighting was their vocation.
Many, like Erard, acted as bandits. The most notorious brigand captain of the
Cévennes was Mathieu de Merle, originally from Uzès, who terrorised Mende
in Gévaudan and sold it to both Navarre and Condé, the rival Huguenot
leaders. He obtained the seigneurie of Lagorce in Bas-Vivarais, and spent his
last years in the château of Salavas, where the Ibie joins the Ardèche.[28]

As opposed to brigands like Erard and Merle, and to stern but sincere
soldiers such as the Catholic Jean de Balazuc-Montréal of the Largentière area
and the Protestant Jacques de Chambaud on the Eyrieux, the moderates who
favoured peace and saw the disastrous effects of war upon the lower orders
were trapped by opposing forces. The Catholic Guillaume de Vogüé and the
Protestant *baillis* of Aubenas and La Voulte, Bérenger de la Tour and Géraud
de Bézangier, shared the apprehension of the bourgeois deputies and officials
of the estates. But, as we have seen, they believed that the only way to stop the
depredations of the garrisons (since the military situation prevented their dis-
bandment) was to pay the troops adequately, and to do this required additional
taxation that stirred the communes to further action. It was essentially the
Catholic segment of the estates that levied these taxes, and it was this situation
that moved the Catholic peasants to collaborate with the Huguenots. Leugières,
who had prevented the reduction of the garrisons, had predicted this outcome,

[27]*Ibid.*, p. 285.
[28]Le comte A. de Pontbriant, *Le capitaine Merle* (Paris, 1886), p. 125.

and there were indications of mutual sympathy in the petition itself. This sympathy was soon to become open collusion.

Finally with regard to the petition, the remarkable sophistication of the document deserves notice. It was not the product of peasant mentality, for even the suggestion of no taxation without direct and formal representation of their own order was a novelty alien to the traditional outlook of the rural parishes. An intricate knowledge and a deep suspicion of the apparatus of provincial government were evident in the articles about corruption in the offices of syndic and *receveur*, the demand for the external audit of accounts, the alleged investigation of the bonds on the *octrois* and *aides*, the suppression of supernumerary venal office, and the establishment of new courts and tax controllers. These items, together with the reference to the peace edict on the debts of the factions, and the suggestion that the governing orders in both factions were using "their estates" to pass the costs of civil war on to the lower orders, seem to reflect the attitudes of small-town bourgeois. La Rouvière exploited, and perhaps even inspired, this lack of confidence in the governing élite and their independent institutions. The development of his movement in the months following the petition supports this hypothesis.

News of the treaty of Nérac, which accorded Saint-Agrève and Baix in Vivarais to the Huguenots as additional surety towns, did not move the local warlords to disarm. The queen mother began to journey eastwards, attempting persuasion and reconciliation wherever she went. Meanwhile the syndic Leyris, having received Henri III's comments on the petition, went even further than the king in his gestures of appeasement. He recognised four *procureurs du plat pays*, and invited them to attend a meeting of the Vivarais estates at Annonay. Besides La Rouvière, these were Raymond de Saléon and two men, who were possibly notaries, named Sibleyras and Teyssier. Sibleyras seems to have come from the region of Privas and Teyssier from the upper Ardèche near Jaujac. Saléon was a Calvinist jurist and financier from the town of Saint-Fortunat on the Eyrieux and acted as *receveur* for the reformed churches of Vivarais. He was a friend of the *bailli* of La Voulte, to whom he later dedicated a compilation of royal ordinances.[29] His association with La Rouvière suggests the collaboration of Huguenot small-town notables with the peasant communes. Saint-Fortunat was in the area controlled by the Protestant captains Jacques de Chambaud and François de Barjac.

Saléon wrote to Leyris on July 27, 1579, to accept the invitation. "You know," he remarked, "that the poor people want nothing but a good peace, and if it cannot be accomplished they will be their own worst enemy. War is their ruin, as experience has taught them only too well."[30] If the edict of pacification

---

[29]Raymond de Saléon, *Sommaire abrégé des ordonnances des roys de France despuis Sainct Loys jusqu'à présent* (Lyon, 1586).
[30]Mazon, *Notes et documents*, p. 70.

were enforced, and the estates showed themselves reasonable and compassionate, Saléon believed the peasants would disarm. At the Annonay estates, which he attended in August with Teyssier and La Rouvière, La Rouvière was empowered to tour the disaffected areas to persuade the peasants to submit. He was voted funds for this purpose, together with 1086 livres in compensation for money he had advanced to the communes. The estates also named a new commission to investigate peasant allegations, consisting of the *bailli* of Tournon, the consul of Le Cheylard, and "one other such as the parishes of the *plat pays* may wish to elect." The new *receveur*, Jacques Froment, confirmed the fears of the deputies about the finances of the province, and the estates begged the king to delay demands for tax contributions.[31] Catherine de Médicis also heard of this request. In July she had visited Romans, the focus of the Dauphiné uprisings, and experienced at first hand the consequences of popular revolt. She wrote from Grenoble on August 27 to the Vivarais estates expressing hopes of reconciliation and promising to write to the *trésoriers* of Languedoc to approve the tax delay.[32]

Meanwhile the former *receveur*, Jacques Reynier, and the *juge de Vivarais*, maître Josserand, had received a commission from the *trésoriers* of Languedoc to report upon places occupied by Protestant garrisons. Reynier, already accused of corruption by the peasant leaders, tried to convince them of his good faith. Saléon responded: "Monsieur, I have received your letter, by which I understand that in the investigation you intend to pursue concerning the occupied places, you do not wish to disturb *les pauvres gens* who want to take advantage of the peace edict. They are deeply obliged to you."[33] The tenor of this correspondence suggests understanding between some Huguenot centres and the communes. This was not true, however, of the Huguenot high command in Vivarais. Jacques de Chambaud was continuing to force contributions from Catholic parishes. A month later Josserand reported that the mission had to be postponed because Chambaud was not cooperating and the valleys of the Doux and the Eyrieux were too dangerous to traverse. In fact Chambaud wrote to Reynier just at this time, saying that he had received instructions from Josserand about the towns he was authorised to hold, and that it was his intention to keep the peace so long as those of his religion were justly treated.[34] The attitude of Chambaud's brother-in-law, François de Barjac, is less clear from his correspondence. He held the strong castle of Pierregourde for the Protestant cause and was the elder brother of that Charles de Barjac who had executed the bandit Erard. Like Charles, François had strong sympathy for the

[31] Most of the *procès-verbaux* of the Vivarais estates from 1579 to 1582 are missing. These details on the Annonay assembly have been reconstructed by Le Sourd (*Etats*, p. 283) from subsequent correspondence.
[32] A.D.A. ms. c1476/17.
[33] A.D.A. ms. c1455/20.
[34] A.D.A. mss. c1455/33/35.

plight of the peasantry. In August 1578 he had written to Leyris, declaring his willingness to enforce the peace and asking the syndic to consider "le sollage-ment du pauvre peuple."[35] On the other hand, a letter Barjac sent to Reynier in November 1579 suggests that he disapproved of armed revolt by the com-munes, especially when it was manipulated by local warlords. He warned the former *receveur* that a new peasant uprising had occurred at Boutières in the mountains southwest of Saint-Agrève. In this region, according to Barjac, two Huguenot captains, Fornier of Privas and the sieur de Lachesserie, were urging the peasants not to pay taxes and promising them protection in return for tribute.[36] A year later, as it will be seen, Barjac was himself reported to be leading combined peasant forces against the garrisons that continued to oppress them.

At the beginning of October 1579 a royal decree had been issued pardoning and abolishing "leagues and associations in our province of Vivarais, whether made by the *habitans* themselves or by others of our subjects in contravention of the prohibitions contained in our edict of pacification." The peasant leagues were blamed upon "the corruption and lawlessness which the said troubles have introduced in these times of abuse, rather than any sinister intent to alienate the loyalty our subjects owe us." Included in the amnesty were "asso-ciations, convocations and illicit assemblies, carrying of arms, demonstrations, and other things done in hostile manner, as much by the *gentilshommes* and others as by the commonalty of the said *pays*." The declaration followed the spirit of the royal reply to the February petition, for it excluded from pardon those whom "interested parties may pursue by justice for robberies and assassinations."[37]

While the king's letter was being promulgated in the last week of October, La Rouvière in Aubenas was engaged in an acrimonious exchange with Froment in Largentière. The "procureur des suppliants du tiers estat de Viveroys" accused the new *receveur* of failing to pay him the sum authorised at Annonay, a sum which, it now appeared, La Rouvière had borrowed from Reynier on behalf of the peasants. Moreover, Froment had failed to provide the details of the tax accounts and debts of the province which were to have been made available to him. In the end La Rouvière received and acknowledged the necessary papers. However, he delayed the visits he was required to make to the disaffected parishes of Petit-Paris and Boutières, and he now suggested a new method of placating the peasants. Leyris should convoke three special assemblies of no-bles and consuls who had not attended the Annonay estates, and public oaths to keep the peace should be sworn to restore the confidence of the common people. These proposals were accompanied by demands to pay La Rouvière's

[35]A.D.A. ms. c1022/85.
[36]A.D.A. ms. c1455–41.
[37]Bibliothèque Municipale de Toulouse, ms. fr. 612/130. Reprinted by Mazon, *Notes et documents*, pp. 71–2.

personal expenses, despite his failure to complete the missions he had promised to undertake.[38] The suspicion arose that La Rouvière was keeping the peasants in arms for his own purposes. It is also possible that the movement had escaped from his control and that he feared personal danger from the captains who had taken a hand in its direction.

At this time Damville, the governor of Languedoc, was energetically promoting the queen mother's policy. Following a letter distributed to the Protestant nobility in October, in which he implored the Huguenots to abide by their assurances,[39] he issued a general list of all major infractions of the peace over the preceding five months in Gévaudan, Velay, Vivarais, Auvergne, and Rouergue. Among recent acts of aggression was that "at Saint-Agrève in Vivarais, where *le capitaine* Vacherolles [Chambaud], commanding there, has issued *billets* upon Catholics, forcing them to provide at least half their goods for the support of his soldiers, with similar exactions from other towns at present held and occupied contrary to the undertakings given at the conference at Nérac."[40] Among other infringements in Vivarais was the seizure of "an almost inaccessible fortress called Saint-Sauveur, belonging to the seigneur de Joyeuse, into which they [the Huguenots] have withdrawn and begun to show their intention of preying upon *le pauvre peuple* by levying contributions and making forays against them."[41] For three weeks in December 1579 a conference took place between Damville and Henri de Navarre, which resulted in a joint declaration condemning infractors of the peace and enjoining "all seigneurs, *gentilshommes*, towns, villages, and *communautés* to comply, expressly forbidding them to receive, shelter, aid, or favour any such infractors."[42]

External efforts to persuade the warlords had as little effect as the endeavours of the local peacemakers. The royal government began to consider the use of force. Guillaume de Joyeuse, the lieutenant-general in Languedoc whose Vivarais estates at Saint-Sauveur had recently been occupied, arrived on the southern border of Pont-Saint-Esprit was a small army. He wrote to Catherine de Médicis that he hoped "to set upon an infinity of robbers who are springing up hourly in Vivarais and along the banks of the Rhône."[43] At the end of November Joyeuse wrote again from Pont-Saint-Esprit:

I am going to Vivarais, where I am told that most of the people have refused to pay the *taille* to the king this year, and want none to be imposed. They speak of nothing but killing the *receveurs* and their agents when asked to pay the king's *deniers*. Those of the one religion are as much involved as those of the other, and those who have not suffered depredations from either party are the ones most to blame. There is need to act at once,

---

[38]La Rouvière's letters to Froment of October 23, 26, and 27, 1579 (A.D.A. liasse c1149) are reprinted by Le Sourd (*Etats*, pp. 570–3).
[39]Cl. Devic and J. Vaissète, *Histoire génerale de Languedoc*, vol. 12 (Toulouse, 1889), p. 1284.
[40]*Ibid.*, p. 1302.
[41]*Ibid.*, p. 1303.
[42]*Ibid.*, p. 1317.
[43]Mazon, *Notes et documents*, p. 75.

Madame, so that this fire will not spread from neighbourhood to neighbourhood. I understand, Madame, that there are some petty ruffians who call themselves syndics or deputies of the *pays*, and who pester Your Majesties with remonstrances full of frivolous requests. While awaiting a reply they persuade the people to pay nothing and promise them to obtain exemption. They seem to be able to hold the people firm in the view that they should pay nothing. Yet these fellows do not exempt themselves from being paid, for when they go off on their jaunts they have themselves so well remunerated that it is another *taille* on the people. We can better inform Your Majesties of the state of the province and what the people really need than these syndics, who are nothing but mercenary fellows, skilled only in stealing from the people.[44]

Beneath the contempt that Joyeuse expressed for the peasants and their leaders lay a sense, common among the governing élite, of the serious threat posed by the revolt. Since the organising hand of La Rouvière had touched the movement, since the support of Huguenot notables like Saléon had been accorded, and since the expedient intervention of a few local commanders had become manifest, the peasant rising had grown rapidly in militancy and cohesion. La Rouvière himself still seemed to be running with the hares and hunting with the hounds. Some conditional promises to disarm were obtained between Aubenas and Largentière, but at Jaujac the local consuls, who were in complete support of the rural communes, told the commissioners "that they had received instructions from a messenger who was travelling everywhere to carry the decision of a peasant assembly near Sablières to pay nothing."[45] In the concluding days of 1579 a letter from Froment to Leyris, who, much to the exasperation of La Rouvière, had temporarily left the province, made clear the widening alliance between the Catholic peasant leagues and the Huguenots: "The general rebellions have increased since your departure, especially since a general assembly of those of *la prétendue religion* at Privas decided to pay nothing at all."[46] Joyeuse and his army had remained inactive. The threats, concessions, and cajolings of external authorities had proved futile, and the Vivarais estates and their officials still faced intransigent warlords and fiscal ruin. The king in council at last responded to the remonstrance of the Annonay assembly, which had listed recent borrowings to support the *gens de guerre* as over one hundred thousand *écus*, by renewing the moratorium on the debts of the province. The essential problem remained, and it was agreed to follow La Rouvière's plan to hold local assemblies of notables to restore the confidence of the *plat pays*.

The legal records of the meetings held at Largentière on January 30 and February 9, 1580, have fortunately survived. They were presided over by maître Louis de Chalendar, lieutenant of the royal *bailli* of Vivarais. They were at-

---

[44]Jean Loutchitsky, *Documents inédits pour servir à l'histoire de la Réforme et de la Ligue* (Kiev, 1875), pp. 152–3.
[45]Le Sourd (*Etats*, p. 285), citing the commissioners' report dated November 4, 1579 (A.D.A. liasse c1149).
[46]Mazon, *Notes et documents*, p. 77. This letter also contains an account of the massacre by Merle of the priests of Mende as they were celebrating mass on Christmas eve.

tended, in the first instance, by "seigneurs ecclésiastiques et de la noblesse," and in the second, by representatives of the towns as well as clergy and nobility. La Rouvière appeared with other *procureurs* on behalf of the communes to declare that, if peace were restored, the peasants would resume payment of *taille, dîme,* and seigneurial dues. Then, according to the *procès-verbaux:*

The said assembly, promised, swore, and protested all fidelity to his said Majesty to observe and keep, as they always have done, friendship and favour to the said third estate, and to risk their own lives and goods for the safeguarding of the said edicts and the conservation of the said *pays;* and all together, as much from one party as the other, they swore to keep and observe inviolably all of the above on the Holy Gospels of God, held between the hands of maître Louis Larchier, *curé* and bishop's judge [*official*] of the said Largentière, one after another and then all together. Thus did they perform this act.[47]

The proceedings of the second meeting were considerably longer and involved a recitation of all acts contravening the peace edicts. This assembly also agreed that, in view of the inadequacy of the forces of law and order to deal with bandits (*voleurs*), a special militia would be established in each district under command of a designated seigneur. This provision seems to reflect the desire expressed in an article of the petition of February 1579 for peasant armed forces to be used under official direction against their oppressors. The author of this second document had an unexpected taste for humanist embellishment. He commented on military ethics by referring to "the saying of an ancient captain of Sampuda *neque amicos parat neque inimicos tollit* [that he neither provided for his friends nor ruined his foes], which has to be taken in conjunction with a law of Solon declaring those who remain neutral in time of trouble to be enemies." He even spoke of the official oath-taking in terms of Roman honour, citing the opinion of Polybius who, "even if he were a Greek, compared his countrymen unfavourably with the Romans, saying that if a Greek should borrow a hundred crowns, it was mandatory to have ten notaries and twenty seals, and even this paraphernalia could not prevent his breaking faith." At the foot of this bizarre record of the proceedings appear the names of vicars, consuls, and noblemen. There is also the signature: "La Rouvière, procureur des supplians du tiers estat de Viverois."[48]

The assemblies and their oaths may have mollified the peasants, but they did not cause the garrisons to disband. Barjac, who had expressed his concern to Leyris at the plight of the peasants and had later criticised the manipulation of the parishes by certain captains in his own party, now decided to apply the proposal about using peasant militia against lawbreakers in his own fashion. He led the forces of the *plat pays,* combined with his own Calvinist following, against the Catholic garrison in Crussol, just to the east of his base in Pier-

[47]Bibliothèque Municipale de Toulouse, ms. fr. 613/40.
[48]*Ibid.,* ms. fr. 613/41.

regourde. Antoine Guérin, a magistrate in the troubled city of Romans, reported the attack as follows: "The lords of Pierregourde and Saint-Cierge, with a great number of men of both religions, have begun a campaign to have broken, as they put it, all taxes and impositions on the people, and also to force the evacuation of all garrisons from the towns and châteaux. To start with they put the castle of Crussol to the torch yesterday."[49] There is bias in this report from Guérin, who was shortly to acclaim the bloody coup that overthrew the popular rule of Jean Serve in Romans during the Mardi Gras carnival.[50] It is true that in the course of the rising of the Chaperons-sans-cordon in Dauphiné the Catholic authorities had enlisted the peasant army to destroy a nest of Protestant bandits in Châteaudouble. But it is unlikely that Barjac was pursuing a similar policy in his own self-interest. In the light of his earlier declarations it is probable that Barjac, far from extending the tax revolt, was personally putting a forcible end to the oppression that had first provoked it.

La Rouvière maintained his organisation for several months, while the last peasant army in Dauphiné was being hunted down and destroyed at Moirans. Although it has been suggested that the risings on either side of the Rhône were coordinated, there is no evidence to support such a hypothesis. Unlike the Chaperons-sans-cordon, the Vivarais rebels were not defeated in battle: they simply faded away. Brigandage continued to be a greater problem in the province in 1580 than the official hostilities of the brief war in that year. La Rouvière called two further meetings of the peasant leagues in May at Chomérac and Ailhon which were also attended by some members of the higher orders. Protestants were in a majority at Ailhon, while at Chomérac there were radical proposals to resist forcible military recruitment and taxation levied without consent.[51] It may be that the purpose of these meetings was to secure wider peasant approval of the earlier peace assemblies at Largentière. In any event, no subsequent documents attest to the continuation of the movement. If La Rouvière, the *procureur* for the peasant communes, was also the man who was appointed lieutenant to the *prévôt des maréchaux* in 1581, it may be that he made his peace with the provincial estates and their officers, and accepted his new post in reward for persuading the leagues to dissolve.

Signs of a growing reaction in government circles accompanied the last phase of the leagues. The king sent a personal letter to Jean de Balazuc-Montréal complaining that the royal remission of a part of the tax arrears and the decree

[49]J. Roman, "La Guerre des paysans en Dauphiné," *Bulletin de la Société d'Archéologie et de Statistique de la Drôme*, 11 (1877), 24.
[50]For recent accounts see L. Scott Van Doren, "Revolt and Reaction in the City of Romans, Dauphiné, 1579–1580," *Sixteenth Century Journal*, 15 (1974), 71–100, and E. Le Roy Ladurie, *Le Carnaval de Romans* (Paris, 1979).
[51]Interpretations of the Chomérac and Ailhon meetings differ (Le Sourd, *Etats*, p. 287; Maufront, *Vivarais*, p. 14; Mazon, *Notes et documents*, p. 103). However, the manuscript record of proceedings at Chomérac (Bibliothèque Municipale de Toulouse, ms. fr. 613/23) shows them to be a form of reconciliation between nobles, towns, and peasant representatives.

on the moratorium for debts were being wilfully misinterpreted in Vivarais as a far more extensive set of concessions.[52] Damville reported persistent banditry and an unwillingness to vote taxes throughout Languedoc. He condemned suggestions from an assembly in Nîmes for changes in administrative boundaries as part of a trend to seek dangerous novelties: "They cannot restrain themselves from advertising what they take to be liberty, and desire a licentious authority to be placed in the hands of the people, who are attracted by [the example of] the leagues of Dauphiné and by the outbreak of the same in Vivarais."[53]

A final contemporary comment appears in a letter written on May 28, 1580, by Guillaume de Chalendar de la Motte, the syndic-general of Languedoc and a former syndic of Vivarais. He bitterly reproached Leyris, his successor, for: "allowing your rights to be usurped by some mean fellow called Rouvière, who styles himself *procureur* and syndic of the third estate, and has disturbed everything in the province by convoking assemblies on his private initiative to arrange matters prejudicial to the king's service."[54] Leyris did not deserve this. He had acted in a disinterested and moderate manner, only to become the target of opprobrium from both peasant spokesmen and his own colleagues within the Vivarais estates. He understood better than anyone the chain of cause and effect that led social hostilities to be superimposed on the political and religious ones of the civil war. The predatory behaviour of the warbands, the increased taxation, and the refusal of payments of any kind by the peasant leagues formed a vicious circle that destroyed the confidence of the lower orders in local institutions and the men who directed them. The syndic could find no way to break the circle, and a few months later he was to die; some said of the plague and others of the cares of his office.

There were to be further peasant risings in the mountains of western Vivarais in 1594. These spread through Gévaudan and Velay from the Croquant revolts to the west of the Massif Central. The Vivarais rebels of this generation were called Croquants too, unlike their predecessors of the 1570s, who received no sobriquet and have remained unnoticed by all save a few local archivists. The fragmentary nature of the sources and the fact that many of the documents provide the comments of those unsympathetic to peasant attitudes make it difficult to reconstitute motives and events with entire confidence. Several broad trends emerge, however, which can be related to the generalisations about sixteenth-century peasant revolts offered by Bercé, Jacquart, and Ladurie.

In the first place it is clear that the self-contained nature of administration in

---

[52]Mazon, *Notes et documents*, p. 95.
[53]Loutchitsky, *Documents*, p. 141.
[54]A.D.A. ms. c1456/20.

Vivarais contradicts any argument about the provocation of the risings by the intrusion of the agents of the central state. Bercé may be correct about the 1548 Pitaud revolt being the harbinger of the seventeenth-century popular rebellions, but during the religious wars elements other than the expansion of the state apparatus have more significance. Vivarais represents an extreme instance, not of local solidarity against the fisc, but of the fragmentation of an independent administrative élite. It is the political breakdown of a regional system that engenders the social pressures so clearly stated in the petition of February 1579. None of the evidence, except for the clause in the petition concerning seigneurial justice, suggests that long-term economic exploitation by the seigneurs was an important factor in the risings. Jacquart's interpretation in this respect does not seem to apply to Vivarais, where the solidarity and relative independence of the mountain peasant communes would have given greater prominence to such a cause. It is true, of course, that the debts of the peasant *communautés* constituted a significant problem, but these were debts arising from the situation of the civil wars. Nor is Jacquart's stress upon hostility between town and country supported by evidence from the Vivarais revolts. On the contrary, the small towns, especially those under Protestant domination, made common cause with the Catholic peasantry.

The emphasis placed by Jacquart and Ladurie on peasant resistance to garrisons and warbands fits conditions in Vivarais better than any other element in their schemata. If objections to local taxation seem to have sparked the initial revolts, they were to tax increments for the support of the garrisons, and as we have seen, refusal to pay intensified the direct exploitation of the peasants by the soldiery. The association of the local gentry with the garrisons gave the risings their antiseigneurial tone. It seems to have been only as a result of peasant identification of the *gentilshommes* with the military exploiters that the popular movement came to refuse payment of dues. There was no programme to restructure rural society. Revolutionary proposals for a measure of representation and consent may have had social overtones, but they were political in motivation and probably inspired by small-town notables.

When the peasants rose against the garrisons and the seigneurs they associated with them, they were acting out a kind of spontaneous judicial process against those whom they saw as murderers, robbers, and infractors of royal peace edicts. Since the system of order and justice had broken down, they took the matter of punishment into their own hands before appealing to the king to sanction their endeavour. Royal indulgence could go only so far in this respect, and those who directed the peasants drew back when they saw the inevitable repercussions of their policy. If men like La Rouvière were moved by personal resentment against the oligarchy of the local estates and their officers, they were ultimately prepared to come to terms with the existing system. It was not, however, easy to arrest a movement in which the trust of the common people in their superiors had been undermined. For this reason the extraordinary Largentière ceremonies of oath-taking by the higher orders were invested with such symbolic significance. It can be said, then, that although social antagonisms played a major part in the Vivarais risings, they were largely the poduct of political circumstances that escaped the control of the local governing élite.

~~~~~~

10

The Paris Sixteen, 1584–1594: the social analysis of a revolutionary movement

The movement known as the Sixteen occupies a special place in the series of popular uprisings that occurred in France during the later phases of the religious wars and in the seventeenth century. This is because it was truly revolutionary in the sense that it embodied conscious social antagonisms – a characteristic less easily identified in the antifiscal risings during Richelieu's régime.[1] Studies of the later risings, undertaken by Roland Mousnier and his colleagues in response to the work of the Soviet historian Boris Porshnev, have been prefaced by salutary warnings against the anachronistic use of nineteenth-century models of class conflict in the context of the preindustrial *société des ordres*.[2] But some elements within the Sixteen were nonetheless revolutionary because they appealed to the collective social hostilities existing in their own day: indeed, Mousnier himself has argued that the movement intended to transform society into a dictatorial democracy directed by an élite of religious zealots.[3]

The most superficial acquaintance with contemporary sixteenth-century opinion reveals an awareness of social conflict. Observers with a reputation for dispassionate judgment, such as Jacques-Auguste de Thou and Etienne Pasquier, denounced the Sixteen as the criminal dregs of society, who had usurped the authority properly exercised by their social superiors, and created anarchy.[4] The diarist Pierre de l'Estoile, whose bias against every aspect of the Catholic League is patent, concluded his account of the popular installation of a revolu-

---

[1] Robert Mandrou, *Classes et luttes de classes en France au début du XVIIe siècle* (Messina and Florence, 1965), p. 17.

[2] The views of Mousnier, Porshnev, and others are discussed at length above, pp. 191–210.

[3] Roland Mousnier, *Les hiérarchies sociales de 1450 à nos jours* (Paris, 1969), pp. 46–54.

[4] "Après s'être donné un gouverneur à leur dévotion, ils avoient mis à la tête des seize quartiers de Paris seize personnes tirées de la lie du peuple, tous gens ruinés ou qui avoient sujet d'appréhender la rigueur de la justice" (J.-A. de Thou, *Histoire universelle, depuis 1543 jusqu'en 1607* [London, 1743], 10:511). "On dit aussi que les Seze, des plus seditieux de Paris, gens de basse condition, y ont empieté toute authorité et puissance, que l'on appelle le Conseil des Seze. C'est une vraye anarchie–" (Estienne Pasquier, *Lettres historiques pour les années 1556–1594*, ed. D. Thickett [Geneva, 1966], p. 396).

Renaissance and revolt

tionary commune in the Paris Hôtel de Ville after the barricades of May 1588 with the remark: "In the place of men of honour and repute exercising authority in the city, tradespeople [*petits mercadans*] were appointed and a rag-tag of Leaguer n'er-do-wells."[5] On the other hand, the most authentic statement from the radical wing of the Sixteeen, *Le Dialogue d'entre le Maheustre et le Manant*, threw back the challenge to the upper classes, and especially to the *noblesse de race*, who, the Manant maintained, made war in their own interest and exploited their social inferiors while defaming the Sixteen and the curés of Paris, the defenders of the people.[6] There were many indictments of the nobility in the later stages of the religious wars,[7] but only the extremists of the Sixteen suggested an ultimate remedy for the class the Manant called "cette sangsue de noblesse" which had exploited "la sueur et sang du pauvre peuple."[8] What the Manant proposed was to abolish the hereditary basis of the aristocracy.[9]

In the light of modern interest in the popular uprisings of the period, it is surprising that no one has hitherto identified the members of the movement within their social milieu, or examined their shifting role in Parisian government and society throughout the whole decade 1584–94. This is not to say that the Catholic League has lacked historians, especially in the nineteenth century, when interpretations of the Sixteen reflected the preconceptions of the age. To Michelet the Sixteen were part of a sinister Catholic conspiracy intent upon the subversion of individual freedom and the national interest; to Capefigue they represented an archetypal alliance between popular democracy and the Catholic clergy; to Robiquet, who terminated his detailed study of the Parisian League with the assassination of Henri III, the movement was merely the instrument of Rome, Spain, and the aristocratic house of Guise.[10] As with Madelin on the Fronde, there was a general tendency to draw analogies with

[5]Pierre de l'Estoile, *Mémoires-Journaux* (Paris, 1888), 3:167. L'Estoile at first entered the word *artisans*, instead of *petits mercadans*, and then replaced it.
[6]"Et au contraire la Noblesse a receu et englouty tout ce qui a esté levé, et la Noblesse a ce proverbe commun, qu'il faut que le Manant paye tout, et se moquent du pauvre peuple, des Prédicateurs, et des Seize, qui le soustiennent, appellans les Prédicateurs seditieux, et les Seize, les appellent brouillons, voleurs, larrons, gens de néant, et autres infinies calomnies." (*Dialogue d'entre le Maheustre et le Manant contenant les raisons de leurs debats et questions en ses [sic] présens troubles au Royaume de France* [n.p., 1593], p. 246). For further information on the provenance and authorship of the *Dialogue*, see Appendix. On the *Dialogue* as satire, see above, pp. 92–4.
[7]See Davis Bitton, *The French Nobility in Crisis, 1560–1640* (Stanford, Calif., 1969), pp. 76–91.
[8]*Dialogue d'entre le Maheustre et le Manant*, p. 141.
[9]*Ibid.*, p. 252.
[10]Jules Michelet, *Histoire de France: La Ligue et Henri IV* (Paris, n.d.), 2:1508–11; J.-B.-H. Capefigue, *Histoire de la Réforme, de la Ligue et du règne de Henri IV* (Paris, 1834), 8:410–13; Paul Robiquet, *Paris et la Ligue sous le règne de Henri III* (Paris, 1886), pp. 577–81. Translations of these passages will be found in *The French Wars of Religion*, ed. J. H. M. Salmon (Boston, Mass., 1967).

the Revolution of 1789 that produced more heat than light.[11] More recent studies have subordinated the role of the Sixteen to ultranational forces, or have condemned them by comparing their support of Spain with Nazi collaboration.[12] The most percipient of modern historians of the League, Henri Drouot, confined his attention to Mayenne's political association with Burgundy and to the elements of social conflict within that province, and offered no more than a number of slight but stimulating parallels with the Parisian Leaguers.[13]

In general there have been two barriers to an understanding of the Sixteen: neglect and misapprehension of sources, on the one hand, and the tendency to treat the composition of the movement as static, on the other. It is a bizarre circumstance that one of the primary sources, *Le Dialogue d'entre le Maheustre et le Manant*, has sometimes been read by historians who have used later editions of the work as the antithesis of what it was intended to be; for the original *Dialogue*, first published in December 1593, was immediately converted into a piece of politique propaganda by the skilful revisions of a royalist writer, and it is this version that has almost invariably been consulted.[14] Even those aware of the deception have failed to make a critical study of the striking differences between the versions and to examine the actual situation of the Sixteen when the first *Dialogue* was composed. Apart from this confusion, little account has been taken of the unpublished sections of the anonymous history of the League written soon after the event by someone connected with the Sixteen.[15] Most important of all, the registers of the Hôtel de Ville have never been used to study the unexplored power struggles within the Parisian League in the period

---

[11]There are, of course, many superficial similarities among the Parisian crowd scenes of May 1588, August 1648, and July 1789, and indeed, among the interventions of the populace on other occasions in each of these revolutionary crises. But even when there is a conscious endeavour on the part of the participants in one situation to recall the events of another, such parallels can be misleading. Cardinal de Retz, for instance, recorded that part of the crowd during the barricades of August 26–27, 1648 bore emblems associated with the League of 1589, but there was nothing within Retz's popular following to compare with the organisation of the Sixteen (Retz, *Mémoires*, ed. Maurice Allem [Paris, 1956], p. 101).

[12]De Lamar Jensen, *Diplomacy and Dogmatism: Bernadino de Mendoza and the French Catholic League* (Cambridge, Mass., 1964); André Moreuil, *Résistance et Collaboration sous Henri IV* (Paris, 1960). Cf. A. A. Lozinsky, "La Ligue et la diplomatie espagnole," *Annales E. S. C.* 23 (1968), 173–7.

[13]Henri Drouot, *Mayenne et la Bourgogne: Etude sur la Ligue (1587–1596)* (2 vols., Paris, 1937). Since the initial publication of this essay two full-scale studies of the Sixteen have appeared. See above, pp. 19–20.

[14]See Appendix.

[15]MSS Fr. 23295, 23296, Bibliothèque Nationale, Paris. The work traces the history of the League until the surrender of Paris in March 1594. The first volume of the manuscript, covering the years 1574–89, was edited by Charles Valois and published as *Histoire de la Ligue: Oeuvre inédite d'un contemporain* (Paris, 1914). The second, unpublished volume is critical of the aristocratic leader of the League, Mayenne, and sympathetic to the Sixteen. As Valois explains in his introduction, the manuscript was copied in the seventeenth century at the Oratoire, where at least four descendants of the Sixteen were inmates.

1589–94.[16] It is these registers, taken in conjunction with better-known sources, that have made possible the social analysis of the Sixteen presented here. Some 200 members of the faction have been identified in the preparatory research for this paper, for there never were, as it is often said, precisely sixteen members of the party. The movement took its name from the revolutionary committees established in the sixteen *quartiers* of Paris in January 1589.

The social analysis of this whole group is not a static one but marches in train with political events. In common with most long-drawn-out revolutionary situations, the decade in question witnessed a series of violent shifts in the structure of power, in the course of which one group of former radicals would take on a conservative aspect and be replaced within the revolutionary movement by a more extreme section. To accept the royalist propaganda of the time at its face value, and to label the entire leadership of the Sixteen as members of the lower classes, is a common and fundamental error: to assume that the Sixteen represented a dissident section of the upper classes, and that the triumph of the League in Paris involved merely the replacement of one part of the establishment by another, is a more venial, but still mistaken, conclusion.[17]

The Sixteen were drawn from all sections of the variety of social groups – each with its collective loyalties and vested interests – that participated in the administration of Paris under the last Valois kings. Officially the government of the city was shared between the sovereign court of the *parlement*, the royal officers of the *prévôté* and its tribunal at the Châtelet, and the *bureau* of the Hôtel de Ville. The *bureau* consisted of the mayor or *prévôt des marchands* and four *échevins*, joined by the *conseillers de ville* in formal sessions. The latter, who held their offices for life and passed them on to their heirs, were often magistrates of the sovereign courts, and it was not infrequent for the *prévôt des marchands* to be elected from their ranks. A few of the wealthier merchants were also city fathers, and such individuals were closely linked with the magistracy by marriage and the venal offices they purchased for their sons. There were occasions when deputies from the sovereign courts, including the *chambre des comptes* and the *cour des aides*, and also from the religious communities, participated in special assemblies of the Hôtel de Ville and joined committees charged with preparing remonstrances against the king's attempts to tax the city or to tamper with the *rentes* (the government bonds guaranteed by the municipality). The general assembly, which elected a new *prévôt des marchands* every second year and replaced two *échevins* annually, consisted of the full *bureau*, together with the sixteen *quarteniers* and two bourgeois from each *quartier*, who were certified to be either office-holders or *marchands non mécaniques*. The *quarteniers*, who, like the *conseillers de ville*, had established the right of *survivance* for

---

[16]These sources are ignored, for example, by François Léger, *La fin de la Ligue (1589–1593)* (Paris, 1944). However, Peter Ascoli, who read a draft of this paper, has informed me that he made use of these sources in preparing a dissertation at the University of California, Berkeley.

[17]See Orest Ranum, *Paris in the Age of Absolutism* (New York, 1968), p. 36.

their heirs, were the chief administrative officers of the *quartiers* and their subdivisions, in turn controlled by *cinquanteniers* and *dizainiers*. Eight local notables in each *quartier*, including the two or three *cinquanteniers*, chose four from their number as possible delegates to the general assembly, and two of these, selected by lot, possessed the power to vote.

Within the magistracy the *conseillers* yielded precedence to those agents of the royal council, the *maîtres des requêtes*, and they to the *présidents* of the sovereign courts. The *conseillers* were the superiors of the *avocats*, who envied the status of the *robins* and were known corporatively as the *barreau*. Associated with them in the same corporation but inferior in social prestige were the *procureurs*, who were the approximate equivalent of solicitors. Lower down the scale were the notaries, whose corporation in the parlement and the Châtelet was familiarly termed the *basoche*. Associated with these lesser men of the law were the minor officials of the courts and the *commissaires-enquêteurs* (detectives) and sergeants at the Châtelet. In matters of public order these officers were supplemented by detachments from the three municipal companies (*les Trois Nombres*) of the archers, arquebusiers, and arbalestriers as well as the royal watch (*le Guet*). The militia were a poorly disciplined body, with each company based upon a *dizaine* under the command of a captain who was elected according to the rolls maintained by *quarteniers* and *dizainiers*. In each *quartier* the companies were grouped together under a colonel elected by the subordinate officers. The militia officers were usually *gens de robe*, and owed a dual allegiance to the Hôtel de Ville and the governor of Paris, appointed by the king. In an age of violence the junior militia officers themselves were often the source of disorder. In 1575 the captains joined dissident students from the university to begin a riot against the Italian tax farmers operating within the royal fiscality. Five or six officers were arrested, and one was executed as an example to the rest.[18] In 1585 the king replaced the elected militia officers with senior magistrates, but these did not succeed in keeping the militia loyal to the crown in the crises of the League.

As a revolutionary movement, the Sixteen profited from the general disaffection of Paris in the reign of Henri III. The excesses and prodigality of the royal court, coupled with alternate displays of bluster and weakness on the part of the king, united all social classes within the city against him. Religion and finance were the underlying sources of this opposition. The city had revealed the intensity of its hatred for Protestantism in the great massacre of 1572. In the years of the League the curés of Paris openly criticised the court from the pulpit and inflamed popular passions against a ruler who, for all his bouts of penitential piety, earned the reputation of *un fauteur des hérétiques*. On the material side, the king's frequent demands for subsidies from the municipality led to remonstrances in which the fiscal policies of the crown were vigorously assailed. In March 1582, and again a year later, the king's agents seized funds in the

[18]Robiquet, pp. 12–13.

municipal treasury.[19] In April 1587 the money intended to pay the *rentiers* their due was intercepted,[20] while less arbitrary postponements of the interest on the *rentes* were the subject of continual protest. The clergy, who had undertaken to provide the necessary funding to the Hôtel de Ville, defaulted from time to time and caused the municipality to seek injunctions from the parlement. Yet the onus for this was placed upon the government and the upper clergy, and the deputies of the religious communities were associated with the municipal *bureau* in criticisms of the episcopacy.[21] Attempts to seek direct contributions from the existing office-holders provoked lively opposition, and proposals to sell new offices, such as those of inspectors of customs and trades created in 1581 and 1586, encountered the combined resistance of the parlement and Hôtel de Ville.[22] The *avocats* successfully invoked the protection of the *robins* when the crown tried to force them to declare their fees in 1579,[23] and the *procureurs* threatened to strike in 1586 when the king sought to apply an edict declaring them office-holders and as such subject to a confirmatory tax. The intervention of the parlement forced the revocation of the latter edict.[24] In the following year the magistrates warned the king that they would refuse to sit unless the crown met the demands of the Hôtel de Ville for the satisfaction of the *rentiers*.[25]

Lacking the ability to carry through the reforms of Saint-Germain-en-Laye, which were intended to balance the budget and gradually to eliminate venality of office,[26] the crown pursued piecemeal fiscal expedients that alienated the governing classes of Paris. The king had lost the support of the joint oligarchy of magistrates and merchants who ruled the city, and he had done so in circumstances where a religious cause united them with the lower classes. There were some extremists to whom the protests of the Hôtel de Ville and the sovereign courts appeared insincere and ineffectual. This was the situation which enabled the Sixteen to embark upon their conspiracy, and it explains why some of their number were drawn from the most respectable circles in the city.

Although the Catholic League was a strictly aristocratic association when it was first formed under the patronage of the house of Guise in 1576,[27] there

---

[19]*Ibid.*, pp. 145, 151.
[20]*Ibid.*, p. 269.
[21]*Ibid.*, pp. 121–5.
[22]*Ibid.*, pp. 137–8, 239.
[23]Gaston Zeller, *Les Institutions de la France au XVIe siècle* (Paris, 1948), p. 209.
[24]Robiquet, pp. 239–41.
[25]*Ibid.*, p. 270.
[26]See Aline Karcher, "L'Assemblée des Notables de Saint-Germain-en-Laye (1583)," *Bibliothèque de l'Ecole des Chartes* 114 (1956), 115–62.
[27]The articles of the League of 1576 described its membership as "princes, seigneurs, et gentilshommes catholiques," and provided no place for the initiative of the third estate. Municipal authorities were mentioned only insofar as they might be secretly summoned by sympathetic governors to furnish men and materials (Palma Cayet, *Chronologie novenaire* [1608], *Mémoires relatifs à l'histoire de France*, ed. Claude-Bernard Petitot [Paris, 1832], 38:254–7).

were, even then, a number of active sympathisers among the Parisian upper classes. Their organiser was Jean de la Bruyère, who was later slightingly described by critics of the Sixteen as an apothecary, but who was in fact a wealthy merchant and supplier to the Hôtel de Ville.[28] His son, Mathias de la Bruyère, held an influential post as *lieutenant-particulier*, the deputy of the chief judicial officer in the *prévôté*, the *lieutenant-civil*. The younger La Bruyère's zeal was manifested in 1577, when he reported the unwillingness of certain *parlementaires* to sign the articles of the League.[29] At this time the senior *gens de robe* had little sympathy for the League, but there were certain notable exceptions. Among them was Etienne de Neuilly, a *conseiller* from the parlement of Brittany who became *président* at the *cour des aides* in Paris and served as *prévôt des marchands* for two terms from 1582 to 1586. Neuilly took the lead in the resistance offered by the Hôtel de Ville to the financial demands of the crown in this period. An older and better-connected family of magistrates which supported the League from the beginning was that of Pierre Hennequin, *président à mortier*.[30] Antoine Hennequin was a *président des requêtes* and *conseiller de ville;* René Hennequin was a *maître des requêtes;* and Aymar Hennequin was bishop of Rennes. All these notables played a prominent part in the League, but only one member of the family, Jean Hennequin de Manoeuvre, a *trésorier de France*, can with certainty be said to have joined the Sixteen. The two La Bruyères and Neuilly were also among the early conspirators.

Late in 1584, when the League of Guisard princes was reestablished to prevent the recognition of the Protestant Henri de Navarre as heir to the throne, the secret society of the Sixteen was formed independently in Paris. Apart from the *Dialogue d'entre le Maheustre et le Manant*, the principal source for the early activities of the plotters is the judicially recorded evidence of Nicolas Poulain,[31] a *lieutenant* in the *prévôté*, who joined the group soon after its establishment and acted as a royalist spy. The anonymous *Histoire de la Ligue* carefully avoids mentioning the names of the conspirators, although it provides additional details of their organisation. The information about the Sixteen given twenty years later by Palma Cayet in his *Chronologie novenaire* is mainly derived from *Le Maheustre et le Manant*. There is no evidence to prove that the group was established by the Guises, although, of course, Henri de Guise, his brother Mayenne, and his cousins the duke and the chevalier d'Aumale were anxious to cooperate with it and, if possible, to manipulate and exploit it. The fact that Guise appointed three members of his clientèle among the *noblesse* (Mayneville,

[28]*Histoire de la Ligue*, p. 19.
[29]*Ibid.*, p. 42.
[30]*Registres des délibérations du bureau de la ville de Paris*, vol. 8, *1576–1586*, ed. Paul Guérin (Paris, 1902). p. 126.
[31]*Dialogue d'entre le Maheustre et le Manant*, pp. 92–103; *Le Procès verbal du nommé Nicolas Poulain, Mémoires relatifs à l'histoire de France*, ed. Claude-Bernard Petitot (Paris, 1825), 45:411–45.

Cornard, and Beauregard) to act as liaison officers testifies to the independence of the movement.

According to the Manant, the founder of the Parisian conspiracy was Charles Hotman, sieur de la Rocheblond, who is described as a receiver for the episcopal revenues of Paris. Hotman was a member of an influential family of the robe. Like his cousin Antoine, who was later *avocat-général* in the parlement under the League, he was a magistrate in the *chambre des comptes*. One of his nephews, Philippe, was a judge at the Châtelet and an *échevin* of the city; another, Daniel, was among the founders of the Oratoire. His best-known cousin was the Huguenot author of the *Francogallia*. Charles Hotman consulted the two curés notorious for their criticism of the royal court, Jean Boucher and Jean Prévost. He also talked with Mathieu Launoy, a canon from Soissons, who was known for his attempts to provoke the duke of Savoy to destroy Geneva, and who was also an acquaintance of Henri de Guise.[32] On their advice Hotman formed a secret council, among whose first members were two other *maîtres des comptes*, La Chapelle-Marteau, who was Neuilly's son-in-law, and Acarie, whose widow in later life was to become the celebrated Sainte Marie de l'Incarnation. Three financial officials were among the founders: the *trésorier* Jean Hennequin; Nicolas Roland, a *général des monnaies;* and his brother Jean (also known as Martin) Roland, an *élu* who was arrested for his public criticism of the king at an assembly of the Hôtel de Ville.[33] There was also a wealthy merchant (Compans), three *avocats* (Dorléans, Caumont, and Minager), two *procureurs* (Bussy le Clerc and Crucé), two additional members of the lower clergy (Pelletier and Guincestre), a *commissaire* (Louchart), and a notary (La Morlière). A nobleman from Auvergne named d'Effiat, whose family was to gain prominence under Richelieu, is also shown on the Manant's list of the first conspirators, but he soon withdrew when he learned the objectives of the group.

The Manant lists the formal aims of the Sixteen as the preservation of the Catholic religion, the defeat and expulsion of heresy, and the reformation of "the vices, impiety, injustices, and evils that afflicted all orders of society in France."[34] He explains how Paris was divided into five sectors, in each of which La Chapelle-Marteau, Compans, Le Clerc, Crucé, and Louchart formed their own cell. These five men, together with Hotman, formed an executive committee and met in company with four of the other leading conspirators as a governing council.[35] Poulain explains how he arranged the purchase of arms and how recruitment was undertaken.[36] *Commissaire* de Bar and sergeant Michelet were deputed to engage the boatmen and the labourers on the wharves; Crucé was to

---

[32]*Histoire de la Ligue*, pp. 107–8.
[33]Robiquet, pp. 273–4. Robiquet is mistaken, however, in assuming that Nicolas, rather than Jean Roland, was arrested.
[34]*Dialogue d'entre le Maheustre et la Manant*, pp. 99–100.
[35]*The Histoire de la Ligue* (p. 125) claims that the governing council initially had eight members and that later there were twelve.
[36]Poulain, *Procèz verbal*, pp. 414–16.

marshal the students at the university; the tinker Poccart and the butcher Gilbert were to organise the Paris butchers; and Louchart was to work among the men of the horse markets. Others were instructed to seek supporters within their own professions. The Châtelet, like the *chambre des comptes* and the *barreau* and the *basoche* of the parlement, provided a strong contingent. Apart from Poulain, five early leaders of the Sixteen at the Châtelet were Cruce, La Bruyère, Louchart, Michelet, and the *avocat* Ameline, who toured the northern cities to establish similar groups. Hotman died in 1587, and La Chapelle-Marteau replaced him in the revolutionary leadership. The strength of the movement at this time was shown by the 700 or 800 mourners who attended the funeral of the founder.[37]

If d'Effiat and Guise's liaison officers are excluded, the names of forty-eight members of the Sixteen during the early, clandestine phase of the movement may be ascertained from the accounts of Poulain and the Manant. In most instances the status and profession of these conspirators may be verified or ascertained from the registers of the Hôtel de Ville, where in later years (when they played an active part in the militia and the municipal assemblies) their names and occupations frequently recur.[38] These members of the Sixteen may be divided into the following groups:[39]

1. Clergy — 5
2. Magistrates of the sovereign courts — 6
3. Merchants of wealth and status — 5
4. Middle-echelon officers of justice and finance — 5
5. *Avocats and procureurs* — 10

[37]*Histoire de la Ligue*, pp. 123–4.
[38]*Registres des délibérations du bureau de la ville de Paris* (Paris, 1902), vol. 9, *1586–1590*, ed. François Bonnardot; vol. 10, *1590–1594*, ed. Guérin.
[39]These categories, which are also employed in subsequent analyses, involve some necessary oversimplification. Despite the legal situation regarding precedence, wealthy merchants without royal office are placed high upon the list because of the prestige they enjoyed at the Hôtel de Ville. Among the middle-echelon officers are ranked the *trésoriers*, *élus*, and *lieutenants*. Among the minor functionaries are some, such as Senault, *greffier* of the parlement, whose offices bore considerable esteem. Those shown as "status undetermined" are unlikely to include persons who might be listed within the first three categories, although they could include persons known as *bourgeois* who were in fact living as *rentiers*. Two of those whose professions cannot be identified on this list (Joisel and Courcelles) were captains of militia. The third (Le Turq) is described by L'Estoile (6:102 [n. 5 above]) as a debauched and impious acquaintance of La Chapelle-Marteau. Other names within the categories given are: (1) Boucher, Guincestre, Launoy, Pelletier, Prévost; (2) Acarie, Hotman, La Chapelle-Marteau, Le Maître, Neuilly, Tronson; (3) Béguin, Bray, Hébert, Jean de la Bruyère, Pigneron; (4) Jean Hennequin, Mathias de la Bruyère, Poulain, the two Rolands; (5) Ameline, Caumont, Cruce, Dorléans, Drouart, Emmonnot, Fontanon, Le Clerc, Michel, Mignager; (6) Bar, Choulier, Haste, Laistre, La Morlière, Le Leu, Louchart, Michelet, Noblet, Santeuil, Senault; (7) Gilbert, Poccart. Twenty-six of these names are given by Poulain and thirty-one by the Manant. Only ten are common to both lists, a circumstance that reflects the secrecy with which the movement was organised and suggests that the combined list is very far from being complete. A few errors in identification may have been caused by the appearance of several persons under the same name in the registers, but wherever possible additional evidence of identity has been used in such instances.

6. Minor functionaries   11
7. Artisans and shopkeepers   2
8. Status undetermined   3

The list shows the Sixteen to have been widely representative of the middle classes, with particular strength among the middle and lower ranks of the legal profession.

The respectability of the leading conspirators suggests that they shared the social attitudes of the established classes. Indeed, the Manant emphasises that merchants such as Compans and Costeblanche were members of Old Parisian bourgeois families. He described Hotman as of "noble, good, ancient, and reputable family" and claims that he organised the Sixteen because of his despair at "the general distress, the ambition of the great, the corruption of justice, the insolence of the people, and, above all, the ruin of the Catholic, apostolic, and Roman religion."[40] While the Sixteen set out to mobilise popular discontent, they displayed both contempt and fear for the masses as an instrument of insurrection. Poulain reported that the conspirators were concerned lest the *menu peuple* should spoil their plans for an uprising by premature riot and pillage.[41] It was also the intent of the Guises to exploit the masses for their own political ends. During a stay in Paris in the spring of 1586, the duc de Guise deliberately cultivated the favour of the artisans, and in the following year, when Mayenne obliged the *prévôt des marchands* to order the release of La Morlière (one of the Sixteen arrested for his open defiance of the crown), a scheme was proposed for the boatmen to set siege to the mayor's house.[42] The duc d'Aumale and his brother, the chevalier, were ready to lead troops into the city to support a popular rising, and the chevalier was so intimate with the revolutionary circle that he later demanded the title of "the seventeenth Sixteen."[43]

However, the good relations between the Sixteen and the Guisard princes before the murder of Henri de Guise in December 1588 represented no more than a marriage of convenience. Guise did not control the Parisian movement and expressed his disapproval of the armed defiance which the Sixteen offered to royal officials, and his disquiet at their plans to ambush the king.[44] The plotters displayed a certain distrust of the *noblesse de race*. The instructions with which Ameline was provided were intended to create a league of revolutionary communes independent of the aristocracy, and this was, indeed, what was attempted, although with little success. Ameline's instructions provided for the establishment of cells similar to the Sixteen in Paris. In the event of Henri III's death they called for the mobilisation of armed forces and the election of the

[40]*Dialogue d'entre le Maheustre et le Manant,* pp. 88, 93.
[41]Poulain, *Procèz verbal,* p. 419.
[42]L'Estoile, 2:327; Poulain, *Procèz verbal,* pp. 420–1.
[43]*Ibid.,* p. 419; L'Estoile, 5:71.
[44]Poulain, *Procèz verbal,* p. 429.

cardinal de Bourbon, Navarre's uncle, by the estates general. The command of these forces might be offered to the nobility, provided that precautions were taken against their possible defection.[45] Yet it is clear that the leaders of the Sixteen did not at this time envisage any fundamental social changes, and, given their own background, this is not surprising. They sought the support of the established classes wherever they could find it, and Ameline's papers suggested the recruitment in provincial centers of "men of property and quality, clerics, gentry, officers of justice, and prosperous bourgeois of good reputation, so that our movement may be composed of more men of substance from the three orders."[46]

At the barricades of May 12 and 13, 1588 the revolutionary plans of the Sixteen were finally put into effect. Despite the orders of the king, Guise had come to Paris as the result of a message from the Sixteen carried by their emissary, the *avocat* François Brigard. The duke, however, prudently took no hand in the direction of the revolt. It was Oudin Crucé who commanded the university students and erected the first barricades in the place Maubert, and François Pigenat, with other doctors from the Sorbonne, who led a contingent of armed monks and priests.[47] Guise's role was restricted to the rescue of the king's Swiss troops from the fury of the mob. L'Estoile testified to the fervour with which all ranks of society welcomed the uprising.[48] The militia defected to the Sixteen or remained inactive. The king fled from his capital, and the Bastille and other strongpoints surrendered. The *prévôt des marchands* was arrested, and the *échevins* (although two of them supported the League)[49] left the city or remained at home. The duc de Guise presided at two general assemblies at the Hôtel de Ville packed by the Sixteen and their adherents. After a little manoeuvring, La Chapelle-Marteau became *prévôt des marchands*, while Compans, Costeblanche, Robert Desprez, and Nicolas Roland were elected as *échevins*, and François Brigard was appointed *procureur du roi* to the municipal government.[50] Of the new *bureau*, only Desprez, a wealthy merchant like Compans and Costeblanche, cannot positively be identified as a member of the Sixteen, but his enthusiasm for the League was undoubted.[51]

The triumph of the Sixteen at the barricades was so complete that for a time their organisation was swamped by new adherents. They were transformed

---

[45]Cayet (n. 27 above), 38:328.

[46]*Ibid.*, p. 327.

[47]Robiquet, pp. 327, 346.

[48]L'Estoile, 3:139: "L'artizan quitte ses outils, le marchant ses traffiques, l'Université ses livres, les procureurs leur sacs, les avocats leurs cornettes, les présidens et les conseillers mesmes mettent la main aux halebardes."

[49]One of these two Leaguer *échevins*, the *avocat* Saintyon, left a detailed account of the barricades: *Histoire très véritable de ce qui est advenu en ceste Ville de Paris, depuis le VII May 1588 jusques au dernier jour de Juin ensuivant audit an*, in *Satyre Ménippée*, 3 vols. (Ratisbon, 1726), 3:39–64.

[50]*Registres des délibérations du bureau*, 9:118–22. The entry gives no list of those present, merely describing the assembly as "faicte de grand nombre de notables Bourgeois."

[51]*Ibid.*, 10:2.

from a clandestine to a pseudoconstitutional status through their capture of the Paris municipality. The extent of their success ultimately brought about their downfall, for the unity of Parisian society, in face of royal misgovernment, a threat to religion, and the introduction of foreign troops into the city, diminished as the circumstances changed. Social divisions within the Sixteen began to appear. Four of the six leaders elected by the Sixteen to the *bureau de ville* in May 1588 were in 1593 to be declared traitors by the author of the *Dialogue d'entre le Maheustre at le Manant.* As to the two others, Compans had died in September 1590, and Costeblanche had been evicted from his colonelcy of militia by the Sixteen in May 1591.

Revolutionary *élan* was not lacking, however, in the immediate aftermath of the rising. The new commune justified itself in terms of popular suffrage. Their predecessors were declared to have been deprived of office "for being disliked and hated by the people."[52] An address was sent to the king denouncing those of his advisers who had persuaded him to leave the city. They were held to be persons "who feared the just indignation of the people against them. – For the future [this manifesto continued] we beg Your Majesty to allow the inhabitants of the city to elect, with liberty and by the customary forms, their *échevins* and magistrates. For, when the said magistrates are elected by the people, this is the true means of keeping the populace in unity and tranquillity."[53] The letter went on to demand the abolition of municipal venal office, especially in the capacities of *conseiller de ville* and *quartenier,* and required the free biennial election of every official. Other aspects of the programme of the Sixteen were manifest in a series of letters to other towns from the Hôtel de Ville, requesting mutual aid. Here it was the financial and judicial agents of the crown who were the target: "The entire people have been gnawed to the very bone in order to fatten a small number of such men, who still know neither satiation nor surfeit."[54]

The new *bureau de ville* proceeded to purge the militia, replacing thirteen colonels appointed by the king and leaving two sympathetic to the Sixteen and one, *président* Blancmesnil, who was to be arrested the following year.[55] The

[52]*Ibid.*, 9:119.
[53]*Ibid.*, p. 134. This letter was signed by the cardinal de Bourbon, La Chapelle-Marteau, Roland, Compans, and Costeblanche, but not by Desprez. See *Mémoires . . . de Nevers* (Paris, 1665), pp. 733–41.
[54]*Registres des délibérations du bureau,* 9:140 (to Rouen, Troyes, and Sens). See *Mémoires de la Ligue* (Amsterdam, 1758), 2:339–40.
[55]*Registres des délibérations du bureau,* 9:129, 180–1. Among the reasons announced for the purge were the age and incapacity of the former colonels, their preoccupation with "other more important matters and public offices of justice and finance," and the fact that they performed their duties so carelessly that the people would no longer obey them. The last list of the former colonels is given in the registers for May 12, 1588 (*ibid.*, p. 117), and the next complete list is not to be found until a year later (*ibid.*, p. 357). The two colonels on the old list supporting the Sixteen were *conseiller* Du Four of the parlement and Boursier, listed simply as "bourgeois." The latter was probably a member of the Sixteen, for the group's purge of *président* Brisson in 1591 was plotted in his house. In general the history of the subsequent social divisions within the Sixteen may be followed from the political alignment of the militia colonels.

new commanders were all men of substance, merchant oligarchs and *robins*, and they included La Chapelle-Marteau's father, Grandrue, and five members of the Sixteen (Compans, Costeblanche, Neuilly, Pigneron, and Tronson).[56] Junior officers were also replaced, and the new captains soon proved their worth with a demonstration at the Palais de Justice to intimidate the parlement. The Sixteen also played a prominent part in the Paris preparations for the meeting of the estates general at Blois in October 1588. Among the chosen deputies were La Chapelle-Marteau (who acted as the spokesman for the third estate at Blois), Neuilly, Compans, Costeblanche, and Dorléans, together with the two curés from the Sixteen, Julien Pelletier and Jacques Cueilly, who were among the delegates for the clergy.[57]

In December the king's murder of Guise and his brother, the cardinal, was accompanied by the arrest of the leading Parisian deputies. Amid the violent and fanatical reaction of the capital to the royal coup, the Sixteen ruled without check to their power. They arranged the popular election of the duc d'Aumale as governor of Paris and of two of their number, Drouart and Crucé, together with a sympathiser, the merchant and former *intendant des finances* Bordeaux, as temporary replacements on the *bureau de ville* for the imprisoned La Chapelle-Marteau, Compans, and Costeblanche.[58] The younger La Bruyère had already been made *lieutenant-civil* at the Châtelet, and the control of the *prévôté* by the Sixteen was completed by the subsequent appointment of La Morlière as *lieu-tenant-criminel* and the registrar Oudineau as *grand prévôt*. On January 16, 1589 Bussy le Clerc, Louchart, Senault, La Morlière, and Olivier (all members of the Sixteen) purged the main source of opposition to their rule, the parlement. Twenty-two magistrates were arrested, many of whom subsequently bought their liberty. The executive members of the court were replaced, the cautious Barnabé Brisson becoming *premier président* and the *avocats* Dorléans and Le Maître, *avocats-généraux*. Le Maître's father, the *président*, had earlier left the Sixteen.

The Sixteen then turned their attention to the appointment of a substitute general government, empowering a "Council of Forty" through a municipal assembly.[59] The list was drawn up by Pierre Senault, one of the original members of the Sixteen who was registrar of the parlement and now became registrar of the council. It included nine members of the first estate, of whom

---

[56]Grandrue is said to have supplied Guise with a cuirass during the barricades, and it was in Pigneron's house that Crucé and the captains of the University met to concert their resistance at that time (Robiquet, pp. 329, 335). Tronson, a *maître des requêtes*, was the brother-in-law of L'Estoile.

[57]*Ibid.*, pp. 431–2. The documents concerning the election of the deputies and the confirmation of the *cahiers* are missing from the registers.

[58]*Registres des délibérations du bureau*, 9:227–8. The Manant describes Bordeaux as a merchant (*Dialogue d'entre le Maheustre et le Manant*, p. 117), and the registers entitle him "receveur et payeur de Messieurs des Comptes." The family was also established in the parlement, where one member was a *consellier* and another an *avocat*.

[59]*Registres des délibérations du bureau*, 9:289.

six were members of the Sixteen and a seventh, bishop Guillaume Rose of Senlis, was closely identified with them; seven *noblesse de race*, all officers in the army of the League; and twenty-four representatives of the third estate, of whom eight had been members of the initial conspiracy of the Sixteen. It is significant that nearly all of the representatives of the third estate on the council were notables, twelve of them being magistrates of the sovereign courts.[60] Moreover, the ordinance establishing the council allowed for further members from the parlement, the episcopacy, the *bureau de ville*, and provincial towns.[61] In any event, when Mayenne arrived in Paris on February 12, he made the council more conservative still by the nomination of members of his own entourage, including the Villeroys and two representatives of the Hennequin family.[62] Thereafter it was known as the "Council General of the Union." After nine months of operation Mayenne, who had no wish to share his authority as lieutenant-general with the body that had given it to him, quietly discontinued the general council and used his own council of state instead.

Between the barricades and Mayenne's arrival the influence of the Sixteen also triumphed throughout the Parisian clergy. François Pigenat dispossessed Legeay from the curé of Saint-Nicolas-des-Champs, and another Sixteen preacher, Guincestre, replaced Pierre Chauveau as curé of Saint-Gervais. On January 7, 1589 the preachers of the Sixteen overcame royalist resistance in the Sorbonne, and, without awaiting papal action, deposed Henri III.[63] It was at this time that Jean Boucher and the pseudonymous "Rossaeus" began the composition of their respective treatises justifying the deposition, although neither of these massive works appeared until after the assassination of the king in August.[64] Using the Council of Forty as a cover, Aumale and the temporary *bureau de ville* began to issue instructions and exhortations to other towns, and among these circulars was included the Sorbonne's statement that "Frenchmen can take up arms, raise money, and band together for the Catholic, apostolic, and Roman religion against a king who has violated the public faith in the assembly of the estates."[65]

[60]The initial lists provided by the Manant (*Dialogue*, p. 143) and Cayet (39:47) are not identical for the third estate. The Manant omits Gobelin and Lescaut (or Sescaut), who are shown on Cayet's list, but Cayet omits Crucé, whose name is given by the Manant. The eight original members of the Sixteen who were members of the council for the third estate are Neuilly (although he was still held by the king), Acarie, Bray, La Bruyère, Fontanon, Drouart, Halvequin, Crucé, and Senault.

[61]Robiquet, p. 528.

[62]*Ibid.* See *Dialogue d'entre le Maheustre et le Manant*, p. 145. The two Hennequins were Aymar, bishop of Rennes, and René, sieur de Sermoise.

[63]Those who promoted the declaration in the Sorbonne were: Guillaume Rose, bishop of Senlis; Aubry, Boucher, Hamilton, Prévost, and Pigenat (all curés); Bernard (a Feuillant); Feu-Ardent (a Cordelier); and Commolet (a Jesuit). All were members or fervent supporters of the Sixteen. See Robiquet, p. 501.

[64]Boucher, *De justa Henrici Tertii abdicatione e Francorum regno, libri quator* (1589); Rossaeus, *De justa reipublicae Christianae in reges impios et haereticos authoritate* (1590). On the identity of Rossaeus as William Reynolds and the theme of his treatise see above, pp. 138, 144–50.

[65]*Registres des délibérations du bureau*, 9:273.

The Paris Sixteen

After the murders at Blois the Sixteen not only established control of all the superior institutions of government in Paris but also strengthened their organisation in the *quartiers*. In each of the sixteen sections of the city a committee of public safety of nine persons was created with a member of the inner group at its head.[66] These committees appear to have superseded or supervised the work of the *quarteniers*, several of whom had been replaced in the aftermath of the barricades.[67] The committees seem to have chosen the delegates to extraordinary assemblies of the Hôtel de Ville. They instituted a reign of terror against suspected *politiques* and acted with the clergy and the officers of the militia in collecting revenue. These committees and the Council of Forty were the two innovations introduced by the Sixteen at either end of the governmental scale. For the most part, the Sixteen merely took over the existing institutions and failed to carry through their proposed reforms. The venal offices within the municipality remained. The right of *survivance* continued for the registrar of the city, as it did for the *quarteniers* and the *conseillers de ville*.[68] It is true that the *quarteniers* were controlled for a time by the committees of the Sixteen, and that the city fathers attended the special municipal assemblies in very irregular fashion;[69] nonetheless, the survival of traditional offices and institutions, reflecting the corporate structure of the Parisian bourgeoisie, provided a strong conservative influence. Although the new municipal government paid far more attention to the relief of the lower classes than its predecessor had done, and although the new *bureau* justified itself in populist terms, the old social attitudes remained. When Nicolas Roland informed an assembly at the Hôtel de Ville of a plan to set the poor to work on the fortifications, he explained that relief and defence were not the only reasons for the measure: the major purpose was "to prevent riots by the *menu peuple*, who, while they remain idle and in necessity, are likely to stir up mutinies."[70] With the arrival of Mayenne, the socially conservative elements in the Sixteen and their supporters within the magistracy began to assert themselves, and the more radical members of the group began to resist the influence of their superiors through the organisation they had created in the *quartiers*.

At the beginning of August 1589 Paris was saved from the advancing armies of Henri III and Navarre by the knife of Jacques Clément. Two weeks later, when fervent acclamation of the act of regicide had hardly subsided, the radical elements in the Sixteen were locked in an electoral battle with Mayenne's supporters over the replacement of two of the *échevins*. For the five preceding

[66]These committees were recognised by Mayenne at the assembly of February 16, 1589 (*ibid.*, p. 296).

[67]*Ibid.*, pp. 144, 182 (note).

[68]See various meetings of the *bureau de ville* to authorise *survivance* in particular cases, as described in the registers (*ibid.*, 9:449, 515; 10:72, 279).

[69]Between the barricades and the end of 1590, an average of eleven *conseillers de ville* attended those assemblies and meetings of the *bureau de ville* where the names are listed in the registers.

[70]*Registres des délibérations du bureau*, 9:219.

249

extraordinary assemblies in this year the registers of the Hôtel de Ville do not list the names of the bourgeois deputies. They indicate, however, that it was the practice to summon four representatives from each *quartier*, except for the election of Bordeaux, Crucé, and Drouart, when six had been called.[71] The August 1589 election was the first regular assembly since the barricades, but it did not follow the prescribed form. A total of 128 bourgeois delegates, or eight per *quartier*, appeared, and of these forty-seven may be positively identified from the radical group.[72] At the same time large deputations attended from the sovereign courts, although their members possessed no electoral franchise in this capacity. Moreover, all twenty-six *conseillers de ville* were present – the only occasion under the rule of the League when a full roll of city fathers was recorded. The prisoners of Blois had been released some months before and had resumed their duties at the *bureau*, but it seems clear that the lower orders in the Sixteen wished to inject a more radical note in the leadership, and that Mayenne frustrated them. The registers break off without indicating the outcome, and in subsequent documents the full existing *bureau* survives unchanged. The diarist Pierre Fayet records that Mayenne was so angered by the display of faction that he issued an ordinance changing electoral procedures.[73] There is no record of such an edict, but two years later complaints were voiced against novel forms introduced by the Sixteen at electoral assemblies.[74] There were five later extraordinary assemblies during the remainder of 1589, and at four of them, where the registers provide an incomplete list of the bourgeois deputies, the junior ranks of the Sixteen were substantially represented.[75] La Chapelle-Marteau apparently tried to recover the confidence of the radicals, for in October he helped Bussy le Clerc and Louchart free one of their number, sergeant Du Gué, who had been arrested for assaulting *conseiller* Favier of the parlement.[76]

Favier, an alleged politique, was one among many victims of the terrorism of the Sixteen during the autumn of 1589 and in the following winter.[77] In November *président* Blancmesnil was imprisoned by the Sixteen. The parlement responded to the killings and beatings of less august citizens by insisting upon the provision of warrants and due process of law, and at least one captain of militia and former leader on the barricades was executed for murder.[78] During the summer of 1590 the city experienced the horrors of famine and siege, but

[71]*Ibid.*, pp. 227, 288, 295, 308, 402.
[72]*Ibid.*, pp. 425–32.
[73]*Journal historique de Pierre Fayet sur les troubles de la Ligue*, ed. Victor Luzarche (Tours, 1852), p. 99.
[74]*Registres des délibérations du bureau*, 10:150.
[75]*Ibid.*, 9:434–6, 446, 454–6, 495–6. From eight to twelve of the more notorious members of the Sixteen are shown among the partial lists of bourgeois deputies at each of these assemblies.
[76]Fayet, pp. 88–9.
[77]L'Estoile, 5:8, 10, 14.
[78]*Ibid.*, p. 10.

the crisis did not heal the rift between the Sixteen and the magistracy. On May 4, ten days before the motley ranks of the ecclesiastical orders passed in martial order before the legate, cardinal Gaetano, a rumor spread that Bussy le Clerc had been arrested for defending Hamilton, the most militant of the curés, against the accusations of the archbishop of Lyon, a moderate Leaguer and critic of the Sixteen. Barricades were erected, and one of Bussy's soldiers threatened to assassinate Midorge, a *conseiller* in the parlement and colonel of the *quartier* of Saint-Antoine, unless his captain was released. On the following day Midorge resigned his command, but this did not save him from the mob, who pursued him and threw him into the Seine.[79] Popular passions were heightened throughout that long summer, but the exhortations of the preachers proved no substitute for bread, and many of the Sixteen died of starvation and plague during and after the siege.[80]

Throughout 1590 members of the Sixteen continued to appear at extraordinary assemblies at the Hôtel de Ville, but these occasions appear to have been dominated by their former leaders within the Parisian oligarchy and by the deputations of the sovereign courts.[81] The customary election was not held in August because of the siege, and in September the invasion of Parma's Spanish army from the Netherlands obliged Henri IV to lift the blockade. In the following month Mayenne visited Paris and used his influence to promote the election of an even more conservative *bureau de ville*.[82] The new *prévôt des marchands*, Charles Boucher, sieur d'Orsay et de Dampierre, was a *maître des requêtes*, who had been made *président* of the court of the *grand conseil* and had been appointed to the Council of the Union by Mayenne as one of the additional and conservative members. Soon after his election Boucher transferred his office of *conseiller de ville* to one of his brothers, whence it was later passed to another brother.[83] He was a cousin of the curé Jean Boucher, and, while he was unsympathetic to the Sixteen, he was chosen by Mayenne as a firm opponent of Navarre. The three new *échevins*, Brethe, Langlois, and Poncher, held similar

[79]Fayet, pp. 88–9.
[80]Including Senault's brother-in-law, the *procureur* Michel; his father-inlaw, Hugues Lemasson (called by L'Estoile "le père des seize"); the merchant Compans; the *avocats* Saintyon, Fontanon, and Cocquin; the *commissaire* Bar; and the notaries Bureau and Haste. L'Estoile is mistaken (5:28) in listing the death of the curé François Pigenat: it was his brother, the Jesuit provincial Odet Pigenat (also identified with the Sixteen), who died.
[81]Names of members of the Sixteen appear as attending all three of the six general assemblies of 1590 where the bourgeois deputies are listed (*Registres des délibérations du bureau*, 9:602; 10:72, 79).
[82]According to the registers (*ibid.*, 10:60), Mayenne paid a short visit to Paris on September 18, and the *bureau* sent Brigard to him a week later with a request to authorise the election. Fayet (p. 99) states that Mayenne personally supervised the election of October 17, and that he chose not to insist upon the new procedure he had ordained after the electoral battle of the previous year (see n. 73 above). Whatever the form that was followed, some of the Sixteen entered a protest, which was referred to during the elections of 1591 (*Registres des délibérations du bureau*, 10:149).
[83]*Ibid.*, pp. 83, 243.

political opinions, and the fourth, Robert Desprez, was the former *échevin* and associate whom the Sixteen now recognised as their enemy.

Mayenne's personal intervention may well have been a response to the demands presented by a deputation from the Sixteen which waited upon him in September in the camp near Corbeil, where he had effected a junction with the duke of Parma. These demands included the reestablishment of the Council of Union, the waging of war *à outrance*, the expulsion of those in Mayenne's retinue who had no regard for the complaints of the lower classes, and the creation of a committee to investigate the loyalties of the Parisian magistracy. The close liaison between the Sixteen and the Spanish enabled them to speak with some confidence, but they received no satisfaction from Mayenne. They were prevented from seeing Parma and they were mocked by the nobles and high *gens de robe* in Mayenne's entourage. Their requests apparently did not include a demand for the convening of the estates general to choose a successor as king to the late cardinal de Bourbon, who had died four months earlier. According to Palma Cayet, Mayenne's council of state believed that the Sixteen intended to abolish the monarchy and to create a republic.[84]

The essential problem for Mayenne was to maintain the spirit of resistance to Henri IV while preserving the traditional political and social structure. Although the Sixteen were his most fervent agents in the former regard, their opposition to the Parisian magistracy, and the growth of radical social attitudes among them in the course of this contest, compromised their usefulness. Moreover, their association with the Spanish interest, upon which Mayenne was becoming increasingly, but unwillingly, dependent, made them dangerous allies. The magistracy was torn between its natural inclination to legitimacy and its Catholic abhorrence of a heretic sovereign.[85] Since its adherence to traditional forms made it a suspect force to both religious zealots and the ambitions of the Guisard aristocracy, it could not be trusted with too great a measure of independence, and its enemies among the lower classes of Paris provided the natural counterweight. To the Sixteen it appeared as though the La Chapelle-

---

[84]Cayet, 40:130. Cayet's account of the deputation is largely based upon that of the Manant (*Dialogue*, pp. 175–80), who is silent, however, on the issue of antimonarchical opinion among the Sixteen. Cayet states that the deputation was composed of Jean Boucher, Bernard the Feuillant, Le Gresle, Crucé, and Borderel-Rosny. The Manant adds to this list the names of Le Tellier, Saintyon the younger, Jablier, Thinot, and Lescossier.

[85]The dilemma was neatly illustrated by the Leaguer *avocat-général* Louis Dorléans, a moderate member of the Sixteen who later disavowed the extremists. In his pamphlets Dorléans used many historical examples, and openly adapted François Hotman's *Francogallia* to suit his purpose. The laws of succession were not denied, but they took second place to the yet more fundamental law that prescribed the religion of the king. Dorléans repeated the instances of Merovingian and Carolingian deposition recited by Hotman, and argued that, if these kings had been dethroned for debauchery, treachery, and oppression, there was an even greater need to depose, or exclude from the succession, a king who was a heretic (*Response des vrays Catholiques François à l'avertissement des Catholiques Anglois* [n. p., 1588], p. 232). Later, when extremist opinion within the League urged the frank acceptance of an elective monarchy, the parlement remained the defender of tradition and the Salic Law. See above, pp. 170–1.

Marteaus, the Costeblanches, the Neuillys, and the Rolands who had led them before the barricades preferred their ties of interest and of family status to the necessity to suppress traitors among the high *gens de robe*. Their disenchantment with the Parisian oligarchy was reinforced by the earlier suspicions within their movement that the *noblesse de race* had abandoned political principles and social obligations.

Faced with the combination of Mayenne and his new *bureau de ville* in the autumn of 1590, the Sixteen rejected their former leaders among the upper classes and used their local organisations to challenge the magistrates and city oligarchs. With the possible exception of Passart, a merchant and colonel of militia, none of the heads of the committees of nine belonged to the establishment.[86] Five of them were *avocats* or *procureurs* and six were petty officials. Several had moved up the scale of administrative status under the League. The registrar Oudineau had become *grand-prévôt*, the notary La Morlière had been appointed *lieutenant-criminel*, and Mathias la Bruyère had moved from the post of *lieutenant-particulier* to that of *lieutenant-civil*. In addition, Bussy le Clerc had become governor of the Bastille; Senault, secretary to the council; and the *drapier* Messier, an *intendant de police*. Such advancement as members of the group received in no way diminished their revolutionary zeal. They now recognised the high magistracy as the immediate obstacle to their cause, and in the course of that struggle throughout 1591 they used every weapon at their disposal to break the authority of the ruling class.

At the beginning of the year the Sixteen renewed their demand to Mayenne to establish a tribunal to investigate the loyalties of those whom they suspected. Receiving no satisfaction, they displayed their independence by sending a letter to the pope.[87] Mayenne may have seen a need to bring pressure against the moderates, for in April a wave of proscriptions and arrests began, directed particularly against the *chambre des comptes*.[88] The *maître des comptes* Acarie may have had a hand in this. He was the only one of the magistrates belonging to the early movement to continue to support them unreservedly, but he was no longer among the leaders of the Sixteen. As yet extreme measures were not used against suspects within the magistracy, although Oudineau directed the summary execution of more humble traitors.[89] It was at this time that Bussy le Clerc arrested his cousin and former confederate, François Brigard, the *procureur du roi* for the city appointed after the barricades. The parlement proved unwilling to press charges of attempting to communicate with the enemy, and took advan-

[86]The Maheustre (*Dialogue d'entre le Maheustre et le Manant*, p. 131) lists the leaders of the sixteen committees at this point as La Bruyère, Crucé, Bussy le Clerc, Louchart, La Morlière, Senault, Bar, Drouart, Halvequin, Emonnot, Jablier, Messier, Passart, Oudineau, Le Tellier, and Morin.
[87]MS Fr. 23296, pp. 394–8, Bibliothèque Nationale; Cayet, 40:178–81. The signatories for the clergy associated with the Sixteen were Génébrard, Boucher, Aubry, and Launoy. La Bruyère, Crucé, and Senault were the lay signatories.
[88]L'Estoile, 5:80–1.
[89]*Ibid.*, p. 91.

tage of a conflict of jurisdiction to leave the case unanswered while Brigard remained in prison for over six months.[90] Meanwhile the Sixteen turned their attention to the militia and succeeded in replacing the discredited colonel Costeblanche with Machault, a *conseiller* in the parlement sympathetic to their cause.[91] One of their members, lieutenant Josset, unsuccessfully challenged colonel Daubray, a *conseiller de ville* and former *prévôt des marchands* who became their foremost critic.[92]

In May and June municipal assemblies met to compose the *cahier* and select the deputies for a meeting of the estates general, which Mayenne had reluctantly agreed to convoke and which was expected to choose a king from the various candidates available to the League.[93] Many of the radicals sat on the commission concerned with the *cahier*, but the deputies named were Charles Boucher, Neuilly, Dorléans, and Nicolas Roland.[94] The Sixteen then attempted to capture the Hôtel de Ville, and on August 16, they confronted the city fathers in the electoral assembly. Acting as the radical spokesman, the *avocat* Oliver Besançon submitted that the intended manner of replacing two *échevins* was irregular, and that the *quarteniers*, some of whom had earlier been arrested as persons of doubtful loyalty, had nominated certain representatives without consulting the local electors. Besançon was not himself a deputy and was ruled out of order by the *prévôt des marchands*, who referred to Mayenne's anger at similar attempts to disturb the assembly in the previous year. The municipal government had anticipated the attack and had restored authority to the *quarteniers*. Only two bourgeois deputies per *quartier* were present, and, although several of the radical Sixteen were among them, they were easily outvoted by the conservative majority. Desprez and Langlois, the two retiring *échevins*, were returned for a further term.[95]

The Sixteen refused to accept this defeat. In the succeeding week Mathias de la Bruyère presented a petition in terms similar to Besançon's, and Senault signed an order on behalf of Mayenne's council requiring a new election. Desprez and Langlois were obliged to resign, and the *quarteniers* were forced to convene the local notables to choose the deputies. The new assembly that met

[90]*Ibid.*, p. 93; *Registres des délibérations du bureau*, 10:188–9 (note). According to the *Histoire de la Ligue*, Brigard and others were arrested by order of Mayenne's council of state, which at first accepted the Sixteen's demand for a special tribunal and appointed Neuilly and Cromé as prosecutors. Later the case was referred to the parlement (MS Fr. 23296, p. 463, Bibliothèque Nationale).

[91]L'Estoile, 5:198.

[92]*Registres des délibérations du bureau*, 10:136.

[93]The Sixteen were themselves divided on this issue. François Pigenat, whose tract *L'Aveuglement et grande considération des politiques, dicts Maheustres* (Paris, 1592) was typical of the theocratic populism of the Sixteen clergy, preferred the son of the duke of Lorraine. Most of the Sixteen seem to have favoured Philip II of Spain or his daughter, and some may for a time have supported the son of Henri de Guise.

[94]*Registres des délibérations du bureau*, 10:122–3, 130–1.

[95]*Ibid.*, pp. 147–51.

on August 26 contained only eight of the thirty-two representatives who had appeared ten days before. However, the Sixteen still lacked the majority that would outweigh the conservative vote of the *conseillers de ville*. They managed to secure the reading of a submission by *commissaire* Louchart that accused the conservative lobby of disloyalty and nepotism and demanded a voice vote in place of the usual ballot. These tactics were partially successful, for, although the voting procedure was unchanged, two conservative candidates (one of them a cousin of Charles Boucher) were discredited. Even if they were members of the establishment, the two new *échevins*, Denis le Moyne of the *chambre des comptes,* and Antoine Hotman, were less unacceptable to the radicals than those indicated by Louchart.[96] Nonetheless, the attempt to work within existing institutions had failed, and the Sixteen turned back to the path of violence.

Several alleged royalists were murdered by the Sixteen in September and October, but their principal victim escaped them.[97] *Premier président* Brisson ordered the release and expulsion from the city of François Brigard, but the Sixteen were not mollified by the appointment of one of their number, the *procureur* Morin, to succeed him as *procureur du roi.*[98] Another member of the group, Louis (also known as François) Morin de Cromé, a radical magistrate in the *grand conseil* and the probable author of the *Dialogue d'entre le Maheustre et le Manant,* had printed the charges against Brigard and used soldiers from Cruce's militia company to prevent the seizure of the press by the officers of the parlement.[99] Cromé had a personal vendetta against Brisson, who had prosecuted his father for peculation as a *trésorier de l'épargne* in 1566.[100] In the first two weeks of November the Sixteen held a number of meetings, at which they appointed a committee of ten to plan a coup against the parlement and to take control of the city's finances by making one of their number receiver of the revenues. They succeeded in effecting the arrest and summary execution of Brisson and two other magistrates.[101]

---

[96]*Ibid.,* pp. 153–9. The votes of the Sixteen and their supporters probably went to the *avocat* Le Gresle and the goldsmith and colonel of militia, Turquet, who had aligned himself with the radicals. Desprez and Langlois were absent, and there were fourteen *conseillers de ville* and fifteen *quarteniers* in attendance. Each elector named two candidates on his ballot, and a total of 128 votes were recorded on this occasion. Of the four leading candidates, Le Moyne received fifty-seven votes; Hotman, twenty-five; Turquet, eighteen; and Le Gresle, thirteen. Thus the Sixteen commanded about a quarter of the total vote.

[97]Fayet, pp. 105, 107.

[98]*Ibid.,* pp. 187–90.

[99]Cayet, 40:364. On Cromé and the *Dialogue* see Appendix, p. 265, and above, pp. 92–4.

[100]See Paul Gambier, *Au Temps des Guerres de Religion: le président Brisson, Ligueur (1531–1591)* (Paris, 1957), p. 106.

[101]Details of the conspiracy are provided by Cayet (40:364–78) and L'Estoile (5:112–26). The more accurate Cayet lists the Committee of Ten as Saintyon, Le Gresle, Du Bois, Ameline, Louchart, Thuaut, Borderel-Rosny, Durideau, Rainsant, and Besançon. L'Estoile omits the first three names, adds Acarie and Le Goix, and lists Borderel-Rosny as two persons. The latter was the man intended by the Sixteen to become receiver for the city. His name occurs in the city registers on several occasions, but his profession is never given. Cayet explains how others joined

This outrage terrified the magistracy and the Hôtel de Ville. Belin, the governor of the city appointed by Mayenne, was without authority. Bussy le Clerc threatened the *prévôt des marchands* and forced the *bureau de ville* to sign articles acknowledging the guilt of the victims. Charles Boucher was also obliged to accompany Louchart on a visit to the executive officers of the parlement to request the assembly of the court. The magistrates refused to meet, and the *prévôt* and *échevins* had the humiliating task of calling upon selected *conseillers* to ask them personally to attend the Palais de Justice. This, too, produced no response. Louchart and another conspirator named Soly[102] demanded that the council of state establish a *chambre ardente* to dispose of heretics and traitors. The demand included the names of most of the *avocats* and *procureurs* among the Sixteen as the staff of the tribunal. A counterproposal from the council that the new court should include a number of judges from the parlement delayed this attempt to legalise the authority of the revolutionaries. Many of their own, more moderate members were alienated by the plot. Dorléans, the *avocat-général*, ordered Louchart out of his house when he came to request the convocation of the parlement.[103] Oudineau, who was thought to have passed a warning to Brisson, was temporarily expelled from the movement.[104] The tailor La Rue resigned from the Sixteen, and colonel Passart became known thereafter as a principal enemy of his former associates. Jean Boucher and Pierre Senault had no wish to be implicated in the murders and spent the day when the arrests were made at Vincennes. Nor did they join the seventeen extremists who wrote to Philip II at this time imploring further Spanish aid.[105]

Mayenne arrived in Paris on November 28. He temporised for a few days while he summed up the situation and used La Chapelle-Marteau to negotiate with Bussy le Clerc for the surrender of the Bastille. During this delay the Sixteen were sufficiently encouraged to ask the lieutenant-general for immunity in respect of their coup, and renewed their demand for a *chambre de justice* under their own control. Mayenne could dissimulate no longer. He had already ensured that the Spanish garrison in Paris would not support the radicals, and

---

the committee, and how Bussy le Clerc and Hamilton became its directors and the *procureur* Lochon, its secretary. The *Histoire de la Ligue* (MS Fr. 23296, p. 465, Bibliothèque Nationale) provides few details of the plot but states that the Sixteen had prepared a list of twenty-seven persons for summary execution.

[102] The Soly who was a member of the Sixteen does not appear to be identical with *conseiller* Soly of the parlement, who was, however, a supporter of the radical cause and a member of the Council of Forty. The former is shown to have been deprived of his captaincy of militia by Mayenne in the aftermath of the plot (see n. 108 below). He is perhaps identical with Michel Soly, described in the registers as one of Roland's lieutenants. Fayet (see n. 103) describes him as a merchant.

[103] These details, which are not to be found in other sources, are given by Fayet (pp. 112–141). L'Estoile asserts that it was Boucher who provided the list for the *chambre ardente*, and that upon its rejection by the council of state he submitted a second list, containing forty-four members of the magistracy (5:128–9). Fayet's name appears on both L'Estoile's lists.

[104] *Dialogue d'entre le Maheustre et le Manant*, p. 189.

[105] L'Estoile, 5:120, 135–6.

he proceeded to hang four of them (Ameline, Anroux, Emonnot, and Louchart) in the presence of Boucher and Senault, and to arrest another six. Launoy, Cromé, and the *avocat* Cochéry, who had prosecuted Brisson at his mock trial, were among those who fled from Paris. Bussy le Clerc and Crucé were expelled from the city, and the *procureur* Parset, a brother-in-law of Emonnot who had acted as registrar in Cochéry's interrogation of Brisson, was questioned and released.[106] Mayenne did not pursue the clerical members of the Sixteen, although Hamilton, the curé of Saint-Cosme, had taken a major part in the murders. Within the parlement he made *présidents* of the younger Le Maître, Neuilly, and Hacqueville, upon all of whom he felt he could rely for continuing opposition to Henri IV, and appointed Antoine Hotman second *avocat-général* in place of Le Maître. This caused a vacancy on the *bureau de ville*, and on December 18 Langlois, one of the two *échevins* defeated by the Sixteen after the assembly of August 16, was elected to fill Hotman's place.[107] An oath of loyalty was imposed on the militia officers, and those among them who were members of the Sixteen were dismissed.[108] The oath was then administered to the bourgeois in the *quartiers* by the surviving colonels and captains.[109] The attitude of the Hôtel de Ville toward the Sixteen was made clear in the letters sent to other Leaguer towns to rehabilitate the memory of the murdered magistrates and to denounce the conspirators, "who, under the usual pretext of discovering treason, had sought to make odious the names of the aforesaid departed, and to conceal their own inhumanities, and to stir up sedition and general revolt against all the magistrates."[110]

The inner group of the Sixteen who had planned and executed the coup against the parlement and signed the letter to Spain were about equal in number to the known conspirators before the barricades. The forty-six names mentioned by the sources in the former respects may be analysed as follows:[111]

---

[106]Fayet, pp. 115–19; Cayet, 40:385–5. The best account of Mayenne's purge is provided in the *Histoire de la Ligue* (MS Fr. 23296, pp. 466–74, Bibliothèque Nationale). The author declared (p. 460) that the ruin of the League and the ultimate surrender of Paris were the outcome of these events, and exculpated the plotters by claiming that Mayenne had earlier resolved to prevent the election of anyone save himself as king, and to destroy the Sixteen (p. 464).
[107]*Registres des délibérations du bureau*, 10:207–9.
[108]Ibid., p. 198. The officers dismissed were captains Montjol, Thuaut, Godard, Thomas, Josset, Rainsant, Le Normant, Nicolas, Soly, Dupuys, Saintyon, Courcelles, Cochéry, Gontier, and Crucé.
[109]*Ibid.*, p. 205.
[110]*Ibid.*, p. 198.
[111]Names within these categories are: (1) Boucher, Génébrard*, Hamilton*, Launoy*, Martin*, Pelletier, Sanguin*; (2) Acarie*, Cromé*; (3) Boursier, Cappel*, Turquet*; (4) La Bruyère*, La Morlière, Le Goix; (5) Ameline*, Besançon, Bussy le Clerc, Cochéry, Crucé,*, Drouart, Dubois, Durisdeau, Emonnot, Gourlin, Le Gresle, Lochon, Mongeot, Minager*, Morin*, Parset, Rainsant*, Saintyon; (6) Anroux, Borderel-Rosny, Choulier, Le Normant, Louchart*, Senault, Soly*, Thuaut; (7) Poteau (junk dealer), Régis (candlemaker), Renault (cooper), Thierri (printer); (8) La Mothe. Asterisked names indicate signatories of the letter to Spain.

1. Clergy   7
2. Magistrates   2
3. Merchants of wealth and status   3
4. Middle-echelon officers of justice and finance   3
5. *Avocats* and *procureurs*   18
6. Minor functionaries   8
7. Shopkeepers   4
8. Status undetermined.   1

The social balance has shifted noticeably since the period 1584–8. Magistrates, merchants, and senior officers of justice and finance are less important, and the *avocats* and *procureurs* dominate the movement. Whereas those members of the upper classes in the second, third, and fourth categories composed 34 percent of the leadership in May 1588, they were a mere 17 percent in November 1591. On the other hand, the *avocats* and *procureurs*, who had made up 21 percent of the revolutionary élite before the barricades, composed 39 percent of the group who effected the coup against the parlement. It may be that the frustrations experienced during the later phases of the religious wars by this ambitious, articulate, and well-educated group within the legal profession are part of the general explanation for the revolutionary rôle that some of them fulfilled.[112] Yet conviction played as large a part as the hunger for office in the motivation of individual *avocats*. Louis Dorléans displayed a legalistic and socially conservative attitude in his pamphlets before he became *avocat-général* in the parlement of the League. In contrast, Jean Caumont published a fiery tract denouncing the nobility as early as 1585 – eight years before the march of events persuaded Cromé to launch his assault upon the upper classes through the mouth of the Manant.[113] Radical social convictions as well as religious zeal inspired both Caumont and Cromé, and the same revolutionary fervour is to be found in certain individuals within the lower clergy, who in 1591 played a greater part in the leadership of the movement as well as sustaining it with their pulpit propaganda. Nor should the importance of the minor functionaries be overlooked. If it were possible to compile a complete list of the radical wing of the League at this point, it is likely that the sergeants, ushers, clerks, and process servers would form the most substantial group.[114] If the *chaire* and the *barreau* provided the ideologues, the men of the *basoche* were the street activists and assassins. Artisans and shopkeepers are generally absent from the inner circle, and, while the movement claimed to speak for the lower classes, it was far from being directed by them.

In the spring of 1592 the triumphant *bureau de ville* and the parlement began

---

[112]Drouot (n. 13 above), 1:52–3. Drouot suggests that in Paris, as in Dijon, the monopoly of high venal office by established families of *gens de robe* checked the advance of qualified *avocats*.
[113]Jean de Caumont, *De la vertu de noblesse* (Paris, 1585).
[114]In the first list submitted for the proposed court of inquisition in the immediate aftermath of Brisson's murder, eight such persons are named as minor functionaries. Only one of them, the *huissier* Choulier, is also included in the analysis given in n. 111 (L'Estoile, 5:128).

to hunt down those lesser agents of the Sixteen whose terrorism and violence had previously gone unpunished.[115] Those of the more respectable members of the group who had escaped Mayenne's purge were more fortunate. Bishop Rose of Senlis, together with Jean Boucher and Génébrard, the prior of Saint-Denis-de-la-Chartre who was created archbishop of Aix by the League, sought to reconcile the factions. A number of meetings were arranged in which Acarie, Le Gresle, Borderel-Rosny, and Senault represented the Sixteen, and three colonels of militia, L'Huillier, Marchand, and Pigneron (the former associate of Crucé in the barricades), expressed the opinions of the conservatives.[116] The radical curés continued to support the popular cause, Boucher defending Louchart as a martyr. The so-called politiques or *maheustres* (a term of opprobrium used by the Sixteen) were organised by Daubray, who had the support of the militia in his *quartier* and on one occasion called them to arms when a rumour spread that the Sixteen had begun a massacre.[117] The growth of politique and anti-Spanish opinion inevitably promoted a desire for peace and negotiation with Henri IV. In January the *bureau de ville*, as if to reassure Mayenne that his support against the Sixteen would be repaid by their continued loyalty, had issued a declaration against "the heretic Henri de Bourbon, so-called King of Navarre."[118] By October the *chambre des comptes*, with the exception of Acarie, L'Huillier, and two other magistrates, had voted in favour of treating with the enemy, and the representatives of the high guilds, the six *métiers*, had presented a petition at the Hôtel de Ville for the holding of an assembly to express the needs of the city. Discussions proceeded in the *dizaines* at meetings formally convened for the purpose, and their spokesmen began to press for peace negotiations on the assumption that Henri IV would accept conversion. Mayenne returned hurriedly to Paris on October 24 to check the peace movement with the promise that he would convoke the long-deferred estates general.[119]

The lieutenant-general had postponed the August municipal elections, but the *bureau de ville* had been so concerned with traditional forms that an assembly had met to extend the authority of the existing officers on a provisional basis. The debates that had accompanied these proceedings revealed a desire to insist upon a method that would ensure the selection of bourgeois deputies from the established classes.[120] In November the election finally took place, and the letters of convocation used the ancient formula to require the attendance of "bons et notables bourgeois et marchans non mécaniques." As it turned out, the majority of deputies were members of the magistracy. L'Huillier's opportunist stand against the peace proposals in the *chambre des comptes* had won him

[115]*Ibid.*, pp. 162, 165, 169.
[116]Cayet, 40:147.
[117]L'Estoile, 5:197.
[118]*Registres des délibérations du bureau*, 10:219.
[119]*Ibid.*, pp. 303–6; Fayet, pp. 124–9. Fayet's account at this point provides a number of details missing from the registers.
[120]*Registres des délibérations du bureau*, 10:285–90.

Mayenne's favour, and he succeeded in displacing Charles Boucher as *prévôt des marchands*. Mayenne was less happy with the voting for the *échevins*. He discarded the candidates at the top of the list and selected two with fewer votes. One of these was a cloth merchant named Neret, of moderate opinions; the other, an *avocat* named Pichonnat, who had replaced Etienne Pasquier as *avocat-général* of the *chamber des comptes*, was a member of the Sixteen.[121] In preferring his own judgment to the views of the electors, Mayenne was following a practice employed from time to time by Henri III and his predecessors. He had asserted the traditional authority of the crown to check the drift of the magistracy towards the legitimate king. While all his instincts favoured the defence of the upper classes, Mayenne was prepared to restore a measure of influence to the enemies of the established order so that he might thereby stiffen the resolution of the moderates. Mayenne's politics, as the Maheustre and the Manant stated clearly enough, were those of a pragmatist.

In January 1593 a municipal assembly confirmed those deputies to the estates general who had been chosen with the support of the Sixteen eighteen months before and had since been recognised as traitors to the radical cause. The wheel had turned even further, for Charles Boucher, Dorléans, Neuilly, and Roland had themselves been displaced by more conservative patricians, and the assembly went on to add to the delegation men such as Daubray and Le Maître, who had long been the avowed enemies of the Sixteen.[122] As the estates general began to meet in Paris, some of those discredited members of the Sixteen who had fled in December 1591 came quietly back to the city. According to L'Estoile, Cromé was recognised and would have been arrested, had it not been for Mayenne's protection. Rainsant entered Paris with some of Mayenne's officers, but such was his notoriety that he had to escape for the second time. The *commissaire* Le Normant returned after promising Mayenne not to conspire against him, but the *avocat* Mongeot and others of the Sixteen suspected this bargain and started rumours against Le Normant which reached Mayenne's ears.[123] Even the less compromised among the group were denounced by those who had once supported them. Passart insulted Senault and canon Sanguin, and Le Maître publicly reproved La Bruyère.[124] The Sixteen bitterly opposed the opening of discussions with the royalist representatives at Suresnes in April 1593, and in June they petitioned the divided estates general to proceed with the election of a king.[125] But they no longer commanded the support of popular opinion. The butchers threatened Jean Boucher for preach-

---

[121]*Ibid.*, pp. 309–13.
[122]*Ibid.*, pp. 328–31.
[123]L'Estoile, 5:204, 206–7, 224; 6:17–18. Le Normant was declared a traitor in the *Dialogue d'entre le Maheustre et le Manant* (p. 196).
[124]L'Estoile, 5:231; 6:33.
[125]*Ibid.*, p. 23; Cayet, 40:285–93; see also a manuscript containing an account of the 1593 estates general, MS Fr. 16265, p. 55r, Bibliothèque Nationale.

ing against the politiques, and some of the curés themselves began to waver. Guincestre even agreed to participate in Henri IV's instruction in the Catholic faith, while those of his colleagues who persisted in their opposition to the Bourbon, whether converted or not, were still divided as to their own candidate for the crown. Boucher favoured the endeavour of the Spanish to promote the claims of the infanta at the estates, but Aubry, the curé of Saint-André, supported Mayenne.[126] Some of the Sixteen resorted to isolated acts of terrorism, but their cause was lost.[127] When the parlement opted for the maintenance of the Salic Law, there were only six of the magistrates who opposed the measure.[128] If this small minority once more found itself supporting the same political aim as the Sixteen, it was not because of any rapprochement between them but simply because they followed Mayenne's lead.

The estates were prorogued without reaching any solution to the impasse facing the League. Mayenne had of necessity to turn once more to the Sixteen to maintain the spirit of resistance in the capital. He was not prepared, however, to break with established institutions, and although he now saw, as clearly as did the Sixteen, that the parlement was the major threat to his cause, he refused the advice of Neuilly and three of his other supporters among the magistrates to suspend that body.[129] Once again the Sixteen were themselves divided by internal faction. Some were prepared to accept Mayenne's direction, and others recognised in him the mixture of social conservatism and political ambition that betrayed the hopes they had reposed in the estates. As a gesture to the radicals, Mayenne had obliged colonels Daubray, Marchand, and Passart to leave Paris in December, but he had no intention of allowing a major shift in the balance of power at the Hôtel de Ville. When the *Dialogue d'entre le Maheustre et le Manant* appeared at this time, Mayenne suppressed the piece, arrested the printers, and sponsored the publication of a tract refuting its criticisms of his policies. He continued to balance faction against faction. Despite the ban of the parlement, the Sixteen were permitted to assemble at will in the early months of 1594. There were harangues by Senault and Jean Boucher and talk of a popular rising, but the lower classes only wanted peace, and the militia remained under the control of the conservatives.[130] When Henri IV entered Paris on March 22, Hamilton tried momentarily to put his revolutionary principles into action in the streets, but no one answered his call.

A few of the minor accomplices in the murder of Brisson were executed in the months that followed. Although the king's policy was one of clemency, a list was published of some 120 persons who were required to leave the city. The list was a roll call of the radical party over the years. Since it contained some who

---

[126]Labitte, p. 246. See also n. 93 above.
[127]MS Fr. 16265, pp. 149v–50v, 155r, Bibliothèque Nationale.
[128]The six were Beaufort, Bordeaux, Hacqueville, Here, Machault, and Neuilly (L'Estoile, 6:41).
[129]*Ibid.*, p. 124. The three others were Hacqueville, Fleuri, and Du Four.
[130]*Ibid.*, pp. 138–85.

were expelled because of their continuing support for Mayenne, rather than their past or present association with the Sixteen, the list served more as a history of the movement than as an indication of its remaining strength. The list may be divided into the categories used for the earlier analyses:[131]

1. Clergy (including one bishop, Guillaume Rose)   13
2. Magistrates   7
3. Merchants of wealth and status   4
4. Middle-echelon officers of justice and finance   8
5. *Avocats* and *procureurs*   19
6. Minor functionaries   29
7. Artisans and shopkeepers   17
8. Status undetermined   22

Doubtless a considerable number of other petty officials, shopkeepers, and artisans not represented here still gave their loyalty to the Sixteen, but the movement had exploited the urban masses rather than being solidly based within them. After it had emerged from its clandestine phase at the barricades, it had itself been exploited by a segment of the upper classes. Religious enthusiasm had served to conceal the tensions within the leadership until the election of the new *bureau de ville* in October 1590. In 1591 the extremists within the lower strata of the church and the law had tried to seize power. Dispersed by Mayenne after their brief moment of triumph, those survivors who were prepared to come to terms with the leader of the League lent themselves to his complex system of balance between the factions. Their extremism rose in proportion to the peace movement, but Mayenne never again permitted them to escape his control. The Parisian upper classes had almost entirely deserted them. Referring to the situation in the late summer of 1593, the Maheustre of the *Dialogue* estimated those in the establishment who were still sympathetic to

---

[131]This list was collected by L'Estoile (6:334–6) and also appears separately published (*Satyre Ménippée* [n. 49 above], 2:518–21). An accompanying instruction requires the *quarteniers* to expel those named in their *quartier* for an unspecified period. Only fourteen *quartiers* are shown, and the group of twelve persons named at the beginning of the list presumably were domiciled in the two missing *quartiers*. The list contains professions beside many names, and where these are not given they have often been ascertained from the registers. Some of the names are garbled (e.g., Tuant for Thuaut), and in one or two instances no name is given at all, the entry reading "un apoticaire" or "un espicier jambe de bois" (actually Charles du Sur). Sometimes a person proscribed is listed merely by his relationship to a member of the Sixteen (e.g., "Oudineau et son frère," "Robiot et son gendre"). In one instance the same person appears to be listed twice. Beside Boiset (actually Boisel) occurs the entry "et son fils." Boisel's son was captain Du Ruble, who is shown below after "La Bruyère le père." Wherever possible further identification has been sought, but the analysis is likely to contain a few errors. When one adds all the names of the identified past and present members of the Sixteen who had died or left Paris before the surrender, or who remained in the capital and were not proscribed, the relative proportions of the various categories are not substantially changed. However, the social balance within the leadership changed from phase to phase, as shown above in n. 111.

the Sixteen as five magistrates of the parlement, four *conseillers de ville,* five colonels of militia, and three *quarteniers.*[132] Since he was probably considering the same persons more than once under the first three categories, this support was minimal indeed.

The *Dialogue d'entre le Maheustre et le Manant* spoke with the authentic voice of that part of the Sixteen which survived every phase in increasing isolation until in the end it found itself entirely divorced from the traditional power structure. The Manant sadly retraced the history of the Sixteen, recalling the golden days when the revolutionary commune had ruled "with the consent of the people, with a common voice, and in accordance with the freedom of ancient times."[133] The Sixteen, said the Manant, had sought "religion without simony, justice without abuse, and a populace without disobedience."[134] In all these aims their intentions had been frustrated by the great. Mayenne had destroyed the original Council of the Union because it was based upon popular suffrage. He had postponed the estates general and prevented their desire to elect a king because they would not choose him or his son. Leaguer and royalist aristocracy alike had exploited the poor and continued the war in their own interest, and the magistracy and officials of the League and the crown had treated with heretics and grown fat upon the spoils of venality. Only the simple faith of the common people remained untainted in a sea of corruption, and it was to God that the people must turn in their despair.

But the Manant who voiced this lament was not the impoverished peasant that the frontispiece to the doctored royalist version of the *Dialogue* depicted: nor was he the respectable artisan described in the phrase so often employed by the *bureau de ville* – the *bons bourgeois, habitans et manans* of Paris. The author of the *Dialogue* was an intelligent and radically minded member of the legal classes, and his desire to pull down the great and to destroy the hereditary aristocracy was the product of the failure and isolation of the last remnant of the Sixteen. This remnant spoke in the name of the people, but it lacked a truly popular base, and it is misleading to define its aims in terms of modern participatory democracy. The civil wars had been fought for so long that the complex corporate structure of society was being replaced in the minds of the defeated and destitute with a society polarised between the oppressors and the oppressed. The Tard-Avisés of Périgord and the Croquants of Limousin banded together against the gentry and officials in 1594 under impulsions of this kind. They did not rationalise their action with the sophistications used by the author of the *Dialogue,* who preached class war but had no proletariat to man his barricades.

---

[132]*Dialogue d'entre le Maheustre et le Manant,* p. 181.
[133]*Ibid.,* p. 110.
[134]*Ibid.,* p. 123.

APPENDIX: A NOTE ON THE *DIALOGUE D'ENTRE LE MAHEUSTRE ET LE MANANT* AND ITS VARIANTS

The *Dialogue d'entre le Maheustre et le Manant* is perhaps the most fascinating, and certainly the most misunderstood, polemic in all the voluminous literature of the French Catholic League. The version in which it is generally known is that published as a tailpiece to the three-volume eighteenth-century editions of the *Satyre Ménippée* (Ratisbon, 1709, 1711, 1714, 1726), but this is the text of a royalist adaptation of the original work. The frontispiece of the second royalist edition of 1594 depicts a mounted and heavily armed knight confronting an impoverished peasant, and distorts the image of the two roles presented in the original *Dialogue*, where the Manant was a respectable Parisian artisan and the Maheustre more of a diplomat than a soldier. The word *maheustre* or *maheutre*, a Leaguer term of abuse for a *politique*, is probably derived from the name of the padding with which court favourites enhanced their anatomy, rather than from the German *meister*.

The original author endowed the *Dialogue* with a lively dramatic tension, from the initial "Qui vive" that sets the scene to the Manant's final despairing cry that God will provide for His people by the agency of the papacy and Spain, even if the French aristocracy and upper classes have betrayed them. The Maheustre is no passive foil for the Manant's pleading, and it is through the Maheustre that the author launches his attack upon Mayenne and the nobility and high officials of the League. The royalist editor (perhaps Pierre Pithou) sustained the literary qualities of the *Dialogue* and even quickened its pace by breaking up some of the longer speeches of the Manant with new and more effective ripostes by the Maheustre. He altered the rhythm and order of the Manant's part, but he allowed most of the latter's ideas to stand unchanged. He could afford to do so because they were of so radical a nature in the original that simply to repeat them seemed effective satire of the attitudes of the Sixteen. Moreover, the editor so strengthened the Maheustre's part that he offered a persuasive defence of the Bourbon cause in addition to exposing the divisions within the League. Passages in the original text where the Maheustre had admitted doubt of the sincerity of Henri IV's conversion, and professed that he might consider joining the League, were carefully excised ([1593], pp. 159–60; 2d royalist ed. [1594], pp. 87r–87v). Where the original Maheustre states that, if the king had not been to mass, the nobility, who had deposed other kings in the past, might have dethroned him, the new Maheustre supports divine right and the Salic Law ([1593], pp. 47–8: 2d royalist ed. [1594], p. 29v). Where the Maheustre of 1593 allows the Manant to expound the doctrine that the king-dom is elective and not hereditary, his *alter ego* of 1594 fiercely interrupts to denounce such talk as political heresy ([1593], p. 15; 2d royalist ed. [1594], p. 9r).

So much of the original was retained that it seems likely that the royalist editor hoped to deceive contemporary readers, and to induce them to read royalist justification under the impression that they were reading the notorious original. If this was his aim, he succeeded, at least with later generations of historians. The confusion caused by the royalist version of the *Dialogue* is evident in Lenient (*La Satire en France, ou la littérature militant au XVIᵉ siècle* [Paris, 1886], 2:98–107), who describes the ideas of the Manant with some measure of accuracy but misrepresents the Maheustre. In his short analysis of the work Henri Hauser declares that "it is almost impossible to unravel the author's own ideas" (*Les Sources de l'histoire de France – XVIᵉ siècle* [Paris, 1912], 4:171). The confusion is at its worst in those modern writers who, on the basis of the doctored text, assume the work was originally composed by a politique supporter of Henri IV. Thus J. W. Allen (*A History of Political Thought in the Sixteenth Century* [London, 1941], p. 348) remarks: "Though writing from the point of view of a Politique, the author does justice to his opponent and actually appreciates his point of view." However, in his brief discussion of the *Dialogue*, Georges Weill (*Les Théories sur le pouvoir royal en France pendant les Guerres de Religion* [Paris, 1891], p. 261) shows awareness of the true situation.

The *Dialogue* was composed about September 1593, as may be established by the remark in the text ([1593], p. 213) that it had been eight months since the estates general assembled in Paris in January 1593. The circumstances of its December publication and of Mayenne's persecution of the printers are described by L'Estoile (*Mémoires-Journaux* [Paris, 1888], 6:110–13). L'Estoile recounts how after the arrest of the printers, Rolin Thierri and Lyon Cavelat, the preachers of the Sixteen defended them from the pulpit. The extreme rarity of the original version can be explained by the hunting down and destruction of copies ordered by Mayenne. L'Estoile himself claims to have resold the copy which found its way to Henri IV at Saint-Denis, and upon which the royalist version was doubtless based.

Three members of the Sixteen have been credited with authorship of the work. The case in favour of Oudin Crucé rests upon L'Estoile's report that he had been seen at the printer's, and had arranged for the binding of the pamphlet. However, L'Estoile himself favours Cromé as the author, an opinion supported by Palma Cayet. The third candidate, Nicolas Roland, is suggested by Labitte (*La Démocratie chez les prédicateurs de la Ligue* [Paris, 1886], p. 152) and Lenient (2:97), but it will be abundantly clear from the account of Roland's defection from the radical group given above that he could not have been the author. Indeed, Roland may be the author of the refutation sponsored by Mayenne (*Censure d'un livret n'agueres imprimé à Paris en forme de Dialogue soubs les noms du Manant et du Maheutre, entreparleurs* [Paris, 1594]; Bibliothèque Nationale reference 8° Lb35.510).

The full title of the original *Dialogue* reads: *Dialogue d'entre le Maheustre et le Manant contenant les raisons de leurs debats et questions en ses présens troubles au Royaume de France* (Bibliothèque Nationale Rés. Lb35.509, 288 pp. in 8°). Two editions of the royalist version appeared in 1594 (Bibliothèque Nationale Lb 35:509 A and B, pagination on recto only, pp. 123 and 158 in 8°). A third edition of the royalist version appeared in 1595 (Bibliothèque Nationale Lb35.509 C, pagination on recto only, 201 pp. in 12°). There are no substantial variations among these three royalist editions, and their title is identical with that of the 1593 original, except that the word *ses* is corrected to *ces*. The 1599 edition of the *Satyre Ménippée* included a section entitled *Abrégé des Estats etc*, which consisted largely of an adaptation and abridgement of some sixty pages of the royalist version of the *Dialogue*. The Maheustre and the Manant disappear as the two controversialists in this text. It provides factual information from the *Dialogue* on the origins of the Sixteen, the capture of the Hôtel de Ville after the barricades, the constitutional arrangements made by the Sixteen after the murder of Henri de Guise, the murder of Brisson, and Mayenne's revenge against the Sixteen. The wording of the *Dialogue* on these matters is followed quite closely, except that the Manant's phrases implying justification of the Sixteen are replaced by neutral or condemnatory expressions (*Satyre Ménippée de la vertu du Catholicon d'Espagne* [n.p., 1599]; Bibliothèque Nationale 12° Rés. Lb35.454, pagination on recto only, leaves 131–45 mispaginated as 121–35; the *Abrégé des Estats etc* occurs at 127r–145r; pp. 127v–140r roughly correspond to pp. 92–148 of the 1593 *Dialogue* and pp. 50v–80v of the second royalist edition of 1594). As already stated, it is the full royalist version, and not this partial abridgement, that was printed with the *Satyre Ménippée* in the eighteenth century.

In 1596 the author of the original 1593 *Dialogue* wrote a sequel (*Continuation du dialogue d'entre le Maheustre et le Manant, de ce qui est passé en France entre les deux partiz, tant de celuy de l'union des Catholiques que de celuy du roy de Navarre, et la response à la censure faicte contre le premier dialogue*), but no copy has been seen since the nineteenth century (J.-C. Brunet, *Manuel du libraire et de l'amateur de livres* [Paris, 1842–4], 2:72). To complicate matters further, there is a direct royalist reply to the original *Dialogue* written in burlesque verse and collected by L'Estoile under the title *Les entreparoles du Manant-de-ligué et du Maheutre* (L'Estoile, 4:300–4). For details of a modern edition of the *Dialogue*, published since the first appearance of this study, see above, p. 19.

11

The Audijos revolt: provincial liberties and institutional rivalries under Louis XIV

I. CAUSES OF THE REVOLT

Although the Audijos uprising of 1664–7 is mentioned briefly in recent surveys of peasant discontents,[1] and although it has been the focus of a massive collection of published documents,[2] its most interesting aspect has not been studied. The revolt coincided with the early years of Colbert's administration, a period of centralising *étatisme*, and it affected a number of small territories in the Pyrenees whose privileges and local institutions displayed considerable vitality. In the course of the rising these institutions did not always co-operate in defence of provincial immunities, but neither did governors and intendants always work together in their endeavours to assert the royal will. It is upon this clash of interests, especially in Béarn, rather than upon the details of the insurrection itself, that this paper is focused.

The revolt was led by a petty gentleman of Chalosse, Bernard d'Audijos,[3]

---

[1]Pierre Goubert, *La vie quotidienne des paysans français au XVIIᵉ siècle* (Paris, 1982), p. 285; Daniel Borzeix, René Pautal and Jacques Serbat, *Révoltes populaires en Occitanie* (Paris, 1982), pp. 239–41.
[2]Armand Communay, ed., *Audijos: La Gabelle en Gascogne: documents inédits* (Archives historiques de la Gascogne, fascicules 24–5, 1893–4). Fifty-nine letters from the intendant Pellot to Colbert about the revolt were also published by G. B. Depping, *Correspondance administrative sous le règne de Louis XIV* (Paris, 1852), vol. 3, pp. 68–123. Apart from official correspondence, the three contemporary accounts of the revolt have also been published. The first was composed in about 1672 by Louis de Froidour, an official in the administration of the Waters and Forests (Jean Bourdette, ed., *Mémoire du pays et des états de Bigorre* [Paris/Tarbes, 1892], pp. 35–40); the second is a diary kept during the revolt by Henry de Laborde-Péboué in the village of Doazit, close to its original centre (*Relation véritable de choses les plus mémorables passées en la Basse-Guienne*, published by Bernard-Augustin de Chabannes, baron de Cauna, in *Armorial des Landes et partie du Béarn* [Paris/Bordeaux, 1869], vol. 3, pp. 455–573); the third is a memoir by the lieutenant of the sénéchal of Bigorre, Germain d'Antin (J. Carsalade du Pont, ed., *Petits Mémoires* [Paris, 1884]).
[3]The paternal grandfather of Audijos was a merchant. His father was an official who had been ennobled and who was related to a group of seigneurial officers managing the estates of the provincial governor, Antoine de Gramont. His mother came from a distinguished family of the sword, Talazac-Bahus. His three brothers had military careers. One of his sisters married an apothecary and the other two married notaries. Everything that is known about Audijos (or Daudeyos, or Audigeos) is in the biography by Colonel Michel Ferron, *Un cadet de Gascogne: Bernard Daudeyos, 1638–1677* (Extrait du *Bulletin de la Société de Borda*, Auch, 1962). The author depicts Audijos as "le défenseur des droits de la Gascogne" (p. 405), and denies the contrary tradition that he was more of a brigand than a hero.

who had served as a youth in a royal regiment at the end of the Fronde, when Henri de Baylens, marquis de Poyanne and lieutenant-general in Béarn and Navarre, had opposed Condé's German commander, Balthazar, in Gascony. Poyanne and other nobles of the sword were accused by the intendant of inaction or complicity during the guerrilla war waged by Audijos. In this, and in other respects, the revolt followed an established seventeenth-century pattern.[4] It was provoked by the attempt of the central government to strengthen or assert its fiscal powers; it attracted the sympathy and sometimes the support of local society as a whole; and it was fought by peasantry whose villages suffered from the reprisals of the king's dragons.

The particular arm of the fisc against which Audijos led his band was the gabelle, or salt tax. The Pyrenean lands of Labourd, Navarre, Soule, Béarn and Bigorre were *pays francs,* that is outside the areas in which salt was a royal monopoly administered by tax-farmers and their agents controlling the storage depots or *greniers.* To the north the towns along the river Adour and its tributaries (Bayonne, Dax, Tartas, Mont-de-Marsan, Saint-Sever and Aire) were also outside the gabelle, being in *pays rédimés,* or lands where exemption from the salt tax had been purchased. Their position, however, was much less strong, and both Richelieu and Mazarin had attempted to impose *bureaux de perception,* to which local revolts were the response (Bayonne, 1641; Dax, 1645). In 1655 bureaux were announced once more for all the towns mentioned except Bayonne. Apart from Aire, the municipal governments concerned bought off the government: in Aire a sporadic resistance culminated in the disappearance of the commandant of the bureau. In the *pays francs* salt cost about a third of its price in the *pays rédimés,* and a sixth to a tenth of its price in the *pays de gabelle.* Smugglers profited from this situation by bringing salt from Spain, or from the Béarnais salt fountain of Salies, into the higher-priced areas. The administrators of the gabelle in Bordeaux sent patrols of the so-called *gardes du convoi* to intercept the trains of *faux sauniers,* killing their baggage animals or sinking their boats. As the salt trains were accompanied by armed guards, numerous clashes occurred. Something more than this, however, was needed to provoke the Audijos rising.

In 1661 the regiment in which Audijos served was disbanded, and he returned to the village in which he had been born, Coudures. This was also the year in which Mazarin died and a more celebrated Gascon, d'Artagnan,[5] ar-

---

[4]For a summary of the different patterns of popular revolt and of modern interpretations see above, pp. 191–212.

[5]The identity of the real d'Artagnan and his friends, about whom Courtilz de Sandras and Alexandre Dumas constructed their fictions, provides a cross-section of the Gascon nobility who served the king as soldiers outside their province and at home criticised the *gabeleurs* from the representative estates. The bourgeois father of the Tréville who, like d'Artagnan, was captain of the musketeers, moved from Oloron to buy the seigneurie of Troisvilles in Soule. D'Artagnan came from the family of Batz-Castelmore near Fezensac, and in 1665 the intendant Pellot protested to Colbert about some of his lands being declared exempt from the taille and hence noble

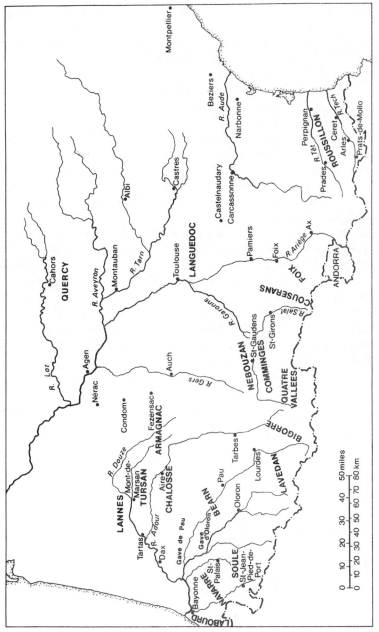

Figure 2. Provinces of the Pyrenees

rested the superintendent of the finances, Nicolas Foucquet, thus inaugurating the administrative regime of his rival, Colbert. Among Colbert's earliest acts was the revival of schemes to increase the yield of the gabelle, even though his orders to this effect seemed to contradict the assurances to respect local immunities that the king had given in the summer of 1660, when he returned through Gascony from the Spanish frontier with his new queen, Maria Theresa. In January 1662 Colbert signed a new lease with the tax-farmer, Gervaizot of Bordeaux, tightening and increasing a host of duties upon wines and foodstuffs passing through all the ports of the west from La Rochelle to Saint-Jean-de-Luz, and through their hinterlands. Clauses 71–7 of this agreement banned traffic in salt into and through the *pays rédimés*, established bureaux at Dax, Tartas and Mont-de-Marsan, and authorised patrols in the valleys of the Adour and its tributaries, even including the *gaves* flowing through the *pays francs* in the foothills of the Pyrenees.[6] Early in 1664 Claude Pellot took up his duties as intendant in Bordeaux and Montauban. He was a client of Colbert, to whom he was related by marriage, and for whom he had played an important part in the downfall of Foucquet.[7] His father, a *trésorier de France* and mayor of Lyon, had been a client of Richelieu's brother, the archbishop of Lyon. It was Claude Pellot who had to enforce the new regulations, and he who had to deal with the revolt they occasioned.

Pellot had early experience of the office-owning provincial judiciary in the context of peasant revolts, for the chancellor, Séguier, his first patron, had him appointed to the parlement of Rouen in the aftermath of the rising of the Nu-Pieds. Pellot was subsequently a master of requests and then intendant in Grenoble, where he feuded with the parlement of Dauphiné. Despite pressure from the magistrates, he insisted upon the execution of a pregnant woman condemned for a crime of which, according to the parlement, she was innocent. Thereafter he lived up to the reputation he had acquired as "l'impitoyable."[8] He served next as intendant in French-occupied Catalonia, then in Poitou and Limousin. In 1663 he came to know the people of the Pyrenees when sent to Foix to inquire into false nobles in the area. Before assuming his new position in Guienne Pellot was briefed by Colbert on the problems Gervaizot's lease had

(Communay, *Documents*, p. 155). The real Aramis was Henri d'Aramitz, a member of the lowest section of Béarnais nobility known as *abbés laïques*, and his estate lay in the valley of the Vert, south-west of Oloron. The original Athos was Adrien de Sillèque d'Athos, the son of a royal musketeer, from a village near Sauveterre on the Gave d'Oloron. Porthos was probably based on Jean de Portau, who left the musketeers to assume his father's office as secretary to the estates of Béarn. The father, Isaac de Portau, was also a magistrate in the parlement at Pau. See J.-B.-E. de Jaurgain, *Troisvilles, d'Artagnan et les Trois Mousquetaires* (Paris, n.d. [1910]).
[6] Communay, *Documents*, pp. 82–7.
[7] It was Pellot who secured the papers of Foucquet's secretary, Pellisson. Pellot married the daughter of Nicolas Le Camus, a controller of finance, and his mother-in-law was thus Marie Colbert, Colbert's aunt. E. O'Reilley, *Mémoires sur la vie publique et privée de Claude Pellot* (Paris/Rouen, 1881), vol. 1, pp. 268 and 15.
[8] *Ibid.*, pp. 194–202.

encountered. In the face of new opposition organised in Bayonne the royal council had decided to establish the bureaux in smaller towns and to confiscate the Béarnais salt spring at Salies. In March 1664 the pattern of Pellot's reports to Colbert was established when he described a deputation from the estates of Béarn, who asserted an ancient communal title to the salt fountain and claimed that provincial privilege dispensed them from recognising any external justiciar save the king. It would be impolitic, Pellot suggested, for the council to reverse its decision on Salies, since such weakness would encourage a great many difficulties and exceptions to proper procedure on the part of Béarn.[9]

In April the new bureau at Hagetmau was attacked and its officials put to flight by the local inhabitants. This small town lay within a barony in the possession of a great nobleman at the court of Louis XIV, the marshal-duke Antoine III de Gramont, who happened to be the absentee governor of Béarn and Navarre as well as of the town of Bayonne. The family of Gramont had occupied the château of Bidache for six centuries, and revealed its pride with its Béarnais motto *Soy lo que soy* (I am what I am). Gascons did not forget that the marshal-duke's grandmother, Corisande d'Andoins, had been the mistress of their beloved king, Henri de Navarre. The estates of Navarre and Béarn and the council of Bayonne voted generous subsidies to their governor, for the Gramonts were secure in local affections and a power within the land. Antoine II was remembered for his confrontations with the parlement at Pau and his troubled private life. Antoine III had a more regular domestic history, being married to a niece of Richelieu, and a better military reputation than his father. Antoine III's brother, the comte de Toulongeon, was sénéchal in Bigorre and, from 1667, governor in Soule and lieutenant in Navarre. In the fourth generation Armand de Gramont, who became governor of Béarn in 1668, repeated the confrontational politics and private scandals associated with his grandfather, Antoine II. Antoine III, however, used his influence at court with subtlety and discretion.

Despite Pellot's vehement demands, reprisals for the incident at Hagetmau were held off by the diplomacy of the marshal-duke until late in the summer, when companies of dragoons were quartered among the communities of Chalosse. It was then that the name of Audijos began to be heard as the leader of the revolt. His small band of *invisibles* struck against Gervaizot's agents and their guards rather than the soldiers. His greatest success was the ambushing of Boiset, the commandant of the convoy, in October 1664.[10] Audijos operated in wooded, broken country where he could strike swiftly and disappear, relying upon local society to provide him with shelter and supplies and to conceal his movements. As pressure from the dragoons increased Audijos led his band, which seldom numbered more than forty men, across the border into the refuge of Béarn.

[9]Communay, *Documents*, p. 110.
[10]*Ibid.*, pp. 111–12, 116–40; Laborde-Péboué, *Relation véritable*, pp. 539–47.

The intendant responded with a policy of merciless repression. Writing to Colbert about the use of the dragoons, he stated: "We must assuredly wear down (*lasser*) this *pays*, and completely humble (*mortifier*) it, so that we can put an end to the support it gives the rebels and cause them to be seen as the source of its misfortune."[11] Pellot himself visited Chalosse with two judges and two executioners. This grim tribunal left rotting on gibbets the dismembered bodies of those few of Audijos's followers it could catch, and sent those suspected of sheltering them to the galleys. The diarist of Doazit, who recorded all this before himself taking refuge in Béarn, interlarded his narrative with lamentations such as "O! la grande misère!" "I pray the good Lord," he wrote, "that it please Him to appease His anger, for I think all these disasters are the result of our sins."[12] Gramont obtained a royal order for the troops to be withdrawn from his own house and lands at Hagetmau, and early in 1665 Pellot reluctantly complied with this command.[13] Other towns were less fortunate. Audijos was now continuing his raids from bases in Béarn. The king ordered the marquis de Saint-Luc, the grandson of Henri III's favourite and the royal lieutenant-general in Basse-Guienne, to march into Béarn and Bigorre. Audijos retired to the mountain valleys of Lavedan. Provincial liberties were now at stake.

II. LOCAL INSTITUTIONS

Colbert deserved his reputation as a ruthless and efficient bureaucrat who sought order and uniformity and saw government in terms of obedience, not participation. Yet while his administration posed a greater threat to provincial immunities than any before him, he had to accommodate himself to the means and methods at his disposal. One factor that restrained him was the system of influence and clientage by which he and others exercised power. Hence in September 1663 he wrote to Hotman de Fontenay, an intendant who, like Pellot, was closely tied by marriage into Colbert's personal system of patronage:

Monsieur le comte de Saint-Aignan has given us to understand that the inhabitants of Loches are so poor that it would be just to give them relief, in terms both of the taille and the salt tax. As he is one of my particular friends, I should be obliged to you if you would help me put his request into effect; but in this kind of thing equity and justice ought always to prevail over every other consideration.[14]

Here Saint-Aignan was playing the protective role that Gramont fulfilled in respect of Gascony, and Colbert was clever enough to know that, having made a concession, one might as well dress up the appropriate order with high-sound-

---

[11]Communay, *Documents*, pp. 130–1.
[12]Laborde-Péboué, *Relation véritable*, p. 540.
[13]Communay, *Documents*, p. 147.
[14]Depping, *Correspondance*, vol. 3, pp. 49–50. Hotman married Marie Colbert's sister.

ing words of principle. Moreover, "equity and justice," which, certainly, were unusual words in the Colbertian canon, could mean conformity with the king's needs as well as with the subject's liberties. Another cause of restraint was the familiar lesson that too brutal a display of authority could provoke an opposition that rendered the end it sought unprofitable. Such was the attempt in May 1661, while Foucquet was still superintendent, to ignore the estates of Boulonnais by imposing taxes without consultation. The outcome had been a fierce local revolt in the following year. This example may have been in Colbert's mind when he dealt cautiously with the initial opposition to the Gascon salt clauses in Gervaizot's lease.

In contrast, the attitude of Pellot was one of arrogant intransigence towards those over whom he held authority and obsequiousness to his masters in the king's council. He remained respectful towards Antoine de Gramont, although their interests were in conflict during the revolt of Audijos. It was once thought that seventeenth-century intendants invariably worked to undermine the authority of provincial governors, but more recently it has been held that they co-operated.[15] Both were representatives of the king and both could exercise power in administrative and financial as well as military matters. However, an important element in the relations between an intendant and a provincial governor was the existence of representative bodies. Colbert, and intendants like Pellot and Hotman, saw the estates as obstructive and desired their abolition,[16] but governors with their roots in the provinces they governed could have a very different view. Thus the estates of Béarn and Navarre looked to Gramont and were defended by him against the intendant. Similarly Poyanne, as lieutenant-general in Béarn and acting governor in Gramont's absence, found himself aligned with local interests. Pellot was extremely critical of Poyanne, who, outside Béarn, was also governor of the towns of Dax and Saint-Sever and sénéchal of Lannes. But if Gramont and Poyanne were at odds with the intendant, François d'Epinay, marquis de Saint-Luc and lieutenant-general of Basse-Guienne, collaborated effectively with him, especially in military matters concerning the revolt. There were no estates to complicate relations between Pellot and Saint-Luc, for the lieutenant-general was based in Bordeaux.

The estates general of Guienne had not met for a century, and in the Adour valley taxes had been assessed by royal *élus* since the early years of Louis XIII's reign. In this area there were still memories of the assemblies of the *sénéchaussées*, and a part of the opposition in Bayonne to the new plans for the gabelle in 1663 took the form of an attempt to convoke four such assemblies

---

[15]Roland Mousnier, *Les Institutions de la France sous la monarchie absolue* (Paris, 1974–80), vol. 2, p. 462. R. R. Harding, *Anatomy of a Power Elite: the Provincial Governors of Early Modern France* (New Haven, 1978), passim. On the intendants see Richard Bonney, *Political Change in France under Richelieu and Mazarin, 1624–1661* (Oxford, 1978), and G. Livet, "Royal Administration in a Frontier Province: the Intendancy of Alsace under Louis XIV," in Ragnhild Hatton, ed., *Louis XIV and Absolutism* (Columbus, Ohio, 1976), pp. 177–96.
[16]J. Russell Major, *Representative Government in Early Modern France* (New Haven, 1980), p. 632.

together as regional estates.[17] In May 1665 Pellot was asked if the defunct assembly of Lannes might meet, but he insisted that there be no criticism of the bureaux and no support for Audijos. These were terms the bishop of Aire, and the deputies he had assembled to make the request, could not accept.[18] In contrast with these dead or moribund representative institutions, those in the Pyrenean lands which had once been ruled by the house of Foix-Navarre showed varying degrees of vitality.[19] In the west the estates of the Basque provinces, Labourd, Navarre and Soule, met regularly and controlled their own taxation. In Navarre the bishops of Bayonne and Dax presided in the upper house, alternating according to whether the assembly met at Saint-Jean-Pied-de-Port or at Saint-Palais, which were in their respective dioceses. A handful of clergy sat with those of the hundred or more eligible nobles who cared to attend, but voted separately. The third estate, whose vote was recognised as paramount on financial issues, consisted of twenty-eight delegates representing five towns and seven valleys or rural communities.

In the larger estates of Béarn clergy and nobility not only sat but voted together in the upper house. Eligible to attend were two bishops, three abbots, sixteen barons and a host of lesser gentry divided into *cavers* (knights), *domengers* (squires) and lay abbots. A memoir on the estates drawn up in 1698 calculated that there were 540 nobles with right of entry through possession of a fief, but the register of the estates during the Audijos crisis reveals between forty and fifty names present at each session.[20] The lower house had a comparable attendance in this period, representing forty-two towns and communities for each of whom, following a reform in 1657, the *jurats* (or municipal councillors) selected one or more deputies. The estates of Bigorre sat in three houses and were convoked by the sénéchal. There were eight clergy in the first estate, eleven barons and seventy-four gentlemen in the second, and deputies from the seven towns and the seven mountain valleys of Lavedan in the third. To the east of Bigorre the territories of Quatre Vallées, Nebouzan, Comminges, Couserans and Foix had succeeded in retaining their representative institutions and in remaining independent of Languedoc and its estates to the north. Except for the first, these petty estates felt themselves under threat of extinction. Like the estates of Labourd, Soule and Navarre, they do not appear to have played any significant part in the Audijos rising, but all were concerned about their privileged position regarding taxes and especially their freedom from the gabelle. A petition from the estates of Nebouzan assembled at Saint-Gaudens in 1669

[17]Communay, *Documents*, p. 107.
[18]*Ibid.*, p. 196.
[19]An excellent summary of these estates is provided by J. Russell Major (*Representative Government*, pp. 123–35). Since this section of his survey does not cover the reign of Louis XIV, additional details in the summary that follows are drawn from Depping, *Correspondance*, vol. 1, pp. 603–21 (*Etats du Béarn et les petits pays de Pyrénées*).
[20]*Ibid.*, p. 603: Archives Départementales Pyrénées Atlantiques (hereafter ADPA), ms. C727 (*Délibérations des Etats de Béarn, 1664–65*).

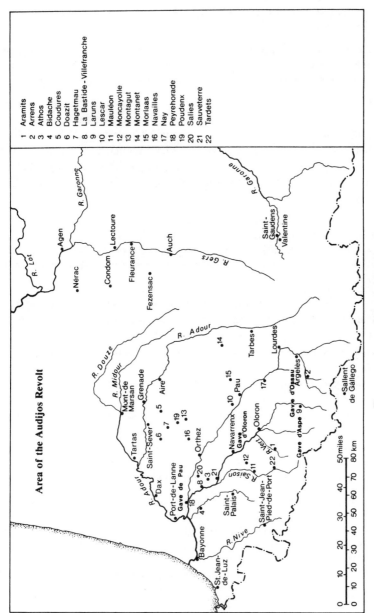

Figure 3. Area of the Audijos revolt

Area of the Audijos Revolt

1	Aramits
2	Arrens
3	Athos
4	Bidache
5	Coudures
6	Doazit
7	Hagetmau
8	La Bastide - Villefranche
9	Laruns
10	Lescar
11	Mauléon
12	Moncayolle
13	Montagut
14	Montanet
15	Morlaas
16	Navailles
17	Nay
18	Peyrehorade
19	Poudenx
20	Salies
21	Sauveterre
22	Tardets

constitutes a typical example. Their land was so poor, they pleaded, that no cereals would grow and they had to depend upon meat, and hence upon salt. The petition concluded:

The said estates send deputies to His Majesty to offer their most humble remonstrances, and, placing at his feet the titles of their privileges, they beg him to have the goodness to allow their continued enjoyment, and particularly for liberty in the use of the salt.[21]

In the early 1660s Colbert was engaged in protracted negotiations to extract more money from the larger *pays d'états*. The Pyrenean estates were a similar source of vexation and there is little doubt that Colbert would have abolished them if he could. A month after the fall of Foucquet, Hotman de Fontenay wrote to Colbert from Montauban deploring the fact that Saint-Luc had given the estates of Comminges permission to meet at Valentines, near Saint-Gaudens:

So it is not just in Comminges but in all other particular territories – at least the ones that pay tailles – that it is absolutely vital to stop the holding of estates, which have no other objective but to allege the poverty of the people and procure some indirect advantage to those participating. Such has been my experience of all estates convoked over the past three years.[22]

In 1673 the bishop of Comminges reminded Colbert that Pellot had suppressed the taxatory powers of the estates of Comminges and Quercy, and in 1681 Colbert himself again considered abolishing the estates of Bigorre, remarking that such bodies served not only to pillage the people but to encourage sedition.[23]

The policy of destroying the Pyrenean estates was so well known in 1663 that the bishop of Tarbes, president of the estates of Bigorre, boldly warned Colbert of the consequences. It was not unusual for a bishop to serve in such a capacity, and the bishop of Lescar traditionally was president of the estates of Béarn. Claude Malier du Houssay could write of secular administration with assurance since he had been an intendant of finance before taking the vows that enabled him to become bishop of Tarbes. He did not mince words with Colbert:

First, I would say to you that this poor country is under my care (*tutelle*) and protection, and that these endeavours to oppress it and deprive it of its privileges, to force it to live under the laws of other peoples, are strongly repugnant to the dual paternity I bear towards it, that is, as its bishop and as its temporal leader and president of these little estates. By the duty that is attached to my cross I would have you, sir, consider freely that the king's service may one day receive some harm from the suppression of these estates, and of those of Foix and of all the other countries that border the Pyrenees and enjoy their privileges from time immemorial.[24]

[21] Depping, *Correspondance*, vol. 1, p. 621.
[22] *Ibid.*, p. 619.
[23] *Ibid.*, p. 622; Major, *Representative Government*, p. 632.
[24] Depping, *Correspondance*, vol. 1, p. 612.

The bishop even dared to suggest that to destroy the estates would be to provoke civil war. The people of Béarn, he warned, were profoundly disturbed by the threat to their constitution. Moreover, Bigorre, Nebouzan and other estates had voted more subsidies over the past century than the king could ever have extracted by direct taxation. "It is better from time to time," he concluded, "to have them bear willingly their share of the burdens of the state than it is to degrade them and drive them to a despair entailing such evil consequences."[25]

Each of these representative bodies had one or two syndics, a secretary and a treasurer. In Navarre and Béarn these permanent officials could call a kind of skeleton meeting of the estates, known respectively as *jointes de Navarre* and *abrégés*. In Béarn, Jean du Haut de Salies, the president bishop of Lescar, and the syndic, Bernard de Poudenx, used the *abrégé* to protest against Pellot's actions. Poudenx was a member of the high nobility, a friend of Poyanne, and, like the lieutenant-general, a landowner in both Béarn and Chalosse. Pellot tried to block the opposition of Poudenx by having the king issue him a special warrant to hunt down Audijos. Later, he was to accuse the syndic of being an accomplice of the rebel leader.

The estates were favoured by two general circumstances: the existence of ancient charters of liberties or *fors*, and the fact that the strongest institutions of self-government existed among the communities within the high valleys that guarded the Spanish border. The mountain men were strongly represented in the estates of Béarn and Bigorre. Each valley had its own assembly and its syndics, and the valleys of the three tributaries of the Gave d'Oloron, the Vert (or Barétous, "barred to all"), the Aspe and the Ossau, possessed *fors* as ancient as any in Béarn. In Bigorre, the seven valleys of Lavedan were similarly organised, each constituting a little world of its own.[26] Further to the east, the assembly of Quatre Vallées owed allegiance to no one save the king. The legends of Henri de Navarre were treasured among them, and in the nineteenth century Michelet recorded in his journal the stories still told about this most popular of kings.[27] In Béarn the valleys claimed a special relationship with the house of Gramont, sending the governor linen from the Ossau valley and cheese from the Aspe.

Proud of their privileges, the mountain people preferred smuggling to politics and generally kept on good terms with their Spanish counterparts. Holding the keys of the mountain passes, they resented lowland interference from either side of the border. In 1654 the men of Lavedan successfully repulsed an armed force under Saint-Luc, sent to enforce tax collection. In 1660, when agents

---

[25]*Ibid.*, p. 614.

[26]Jean Bourdette, *Le Labéda ou Lavendan: Récits* (Argelès, 1890), and *Annales des Sept Vallées du Labéda* (4 volumes, Argelès, 1898–9).

[27]Jules Michelet, *Journal*, ed. Paul Viallenix (Paris, 1959), vol. 1, p. 191. The story is told that the Béarnais scored a point against Louis XIV when they were constrained to erect a statue of the Sun King, engraving upon its pedestal: "Voici le petit-fils de notre grand Henri." P. Tucoo-Chala, *Histoire du Béarn* (Paris, 1962), p. 73.

sent by the parlement of Pau entered the seven valleys to investigate alleged crimes, they were "attacked by brigands, wounded and put to flight."[28] In 1661 the curé of Moncayolle, north-east of Mauléon in Soule, who bore the bizarre soubriquet of "Matelas," raised an army of several thousand mountain men against the threat of tax-gatherers.[29] While the nobility played little part in the high valleys, the clergy frequently assembled and led the armed peasantry there. The bishop of Tarbes declared that he could not control the priests of Lavedan. The force that gathered to support Audijos was led by the archpriest of Juncalas, and two of Audijos's principal agents were the curés of Arrens and Marsous.[30]

Louis de Froidour, the official of the Waters and Forests who knew the Pyrenees well, described the hatred of the mountaineers for the gabelle and the manner in which Audijos persuaded them to accept him as their "liberator." Froidour had no high opinion of their personal traits, calling them "brutal, treacherous, cruel, and nourished among murders and assassinations." They were, he wrote, "a kind of men with no more reason than bears." The women were "sullen, black and ugly enough to inspire fear"; the men "gross, rustic and boastful." They lived underground with their domestic animals for half the year in dwellings full of the smoke of green wood, and emerged like foxes from their lairs.[31] These were the people whose voice carried a particular kind of authority within the estates, and among whom Audijos found refuge.

If the central government had to handle the mountain communities with care, it had also to respect, or at least appear to respect, the *fors* of Béarn. In 1617, when the royal council proposed to integrate Béarn into France, the estates adopted a resolution stating:

Inasmuch as the *for* . . . is the fundamental and contractual law between the sovereign and the inhabitants of the said *pays*, his subjects, the sovereign having sworn to observe the *for* at his accession; and inasmuch as it follows from the said *for* that the said *pays* is a sovereign seigneurie, distinct and separate from any other sovereignty and kingdom, and that the said inhabitants, who at the beginning governed themselves by their *fors* and customs, have elected their seigneurs to preserve the latter, without being able to alter, correct or reform them without consent of the estates of the said *pays*; therefore his said Majesty cannot, saving his respect, unite the said *pays souverain* to the said kingdom of France without consent of the said estates except by destroying the principal mark and basis of their said *fors* and liberties . . .[32]

When Louis XIII enforced his will at the head of an army in 1620, he also swore to observe the *fors* which he had just infringed, thus posing an essential contradiction that was never resolved.

[28]Borzeix et al., *Révoltes populaires*, p. 231.
[29]Louis Puech, *Histoire de la Gascogne* (Auch, 1914), p. 385; Communay, *Documents*, p. 287.
[30]Communay, *Documents*, p. 162.
[31]Froidour, *Mémoire de Bigorre*, pp. 35–8, 72, 82–3, 115–16.
[32]Pierre Tucoo-Chala, *La vicomté de Béarn et le problème de sa souveraineté, des origines à 1620* (Bordeaux, 1961), p. 197.

The *fors* were as much collections of custom and ancient laws as they were statements of special immunity. Codification by Henri II d'Albret in the sixteenth century had not altered their medieval character. The preamble for the general *for* of the vicomté, for example, gave a cautionary tale of a knight from Bigorre who was elected seigneur of Béarn for a year and put to death by an assembly at Pau for failing to preserve the custom.[33] Besides the general *for* and the particular ones of the three valleys, there were charters of enfranchisement for the towns of Morlaas and Oloron dating from the late eleventh century. Concessions from the medieval vicomtes of Béarn, judgements from the old baronial court (*cour majour*), and loose feudal contracts had come to be regarded in the seventeenth century as guarantees of liberty and statements of protection against arbitrary rule. What they actually said was less important than their supposed intent, and it was this that was echoed in every remonstrance by the estates at each constitutional crisis. In 1640, for instance, a protest against the levying of impositions by the intendant spoke of "the just plaints and griefs which the deputies of the estates receive and suffer against their laws, *fors*, customs and regulations."[34]

Apart from intensifying the friction between the intendancy on the one hand and the estates together with the governorship and royal lieutenancy on the other, the Audijos revolt affected the relations of the parlement at Pau with all these instruments of government. In 1620 Louis XIII united the old chancery of the kingdom of Navarre with the judicial high court (*conseil souverain*) of Béarn to form the so-called parlement of Navarre. Its jurisdiction extended over Navarre, Béarn, Soule and the *prévôté* of Dax. This area of competence differed from the jurisdictions of the financial courts. The *chambre des comptes* at Nérac had been reunited with its Béarnais equivalent at Pau in 1624, but the *cour des aides* at Montauban and the parlement at Toulouse also had authority within some Pyrenean territories. Ecclesiastical dioceses overlapped *pays d'états* and *pays d'élections*. The relationship between the military rights of the governor or lieutenant in Basse-Guienne and their counterparts in the Pyrenean towns and provinces was often undefined, and the intendancy in the *généralités* of Basse-Guienne and Montauban was only saved from confusion because Pellot served as intendant in both. Such a mosaic of overlapping authorities was normal in this period, and it ensured that officials spent as much time extending or defending one jurisdiction against another as they did in providing for the needs of government and society. The parlement of Navarre was second to none in its capacity to feud with its rivals.

There were twenty-nine magistrates in the court at Pau, owning their offices

[33]Gustave Bascle de Lagreze, *Essai sur la langue et la littérature du Béarn* (Bordeaux, 1856), p. 14. A full text is provided by Mazure and Hatoulet, *Fors de Béarn: législation inédite du XIᵉ au XIIIᵉ siècle, avec traduction* (Pau, n.d.). For commentary see Louis La Caze, *Les libertés provinciales en Béarn* (Paris, 1865), and Léon Cadier, *Les Etats de Béarn* (Paris, 1888).
[34]ADPA ms. C869 (reprinted in the introduction by the archivist Paul Raymond to *Inventaire-Sommaire des Archives Départementales antérieures à 1790 series C et D* [Paris, 1865], vol. 3, p. 14).

as property and jealous of their prerogatives and their perquisites.[35] Like their counterparts in the parlement of Guienne at Bordeaux, most of the judges had no love for representative institutions. They frowned upon their colleagues serving as deputies in the third estates, but a few magistrates played a distinguished role there. Isaac de Portau, the secretary of the estates, was also a *conseiller* in the parlement.[36] The two bodies skirmished over the defence of the *fors*, the administration of the Waters and Forests, and the protection of the Salies salt fountain. The parlement had its *règlements* published by the *sénéchaussée* courts, and claimed that any recommendations from the estates, even when approved by the governor, were invalid until registered by the parlement. Navarre tamely submitted its *cahiers* for registration, but the estates of Béarn denied the *parlementaire* claim.

The short history of the parlement of Navarre was marked by clashes with the governor and the lieutenant-general. Unlike most provincial governors, the governor of Béarn had a council which could quash the *arrêts* of the parlement and issue decrees of its own. In these conflicts a family of the robe, the Lavie, proved as colourful and as headstrong as its opponents in the house of Gramont. Bernard de Lavie, the son of a *président* in the parlement of Bordeaux, exchanged his office there for that of *premier président* at the head of the parlement of Pau. He was a hot-tempered man who, on one occasion in 1637, responded to an insult from a colleague by striking him during a full session of the court.[37] Three years later the parlement's secret register recorded a confrontation between Lavie and Antoine II de Gramont.[38] Before the Fronde the government sometimes appointed a special intendant of Béarn and Navarre, and Lavie objected to the selection of his colleague, president Jean de Gassion, to this post. Gassion was the intendant who tried to levy the impositions for the support of troops already mentioned, and who provoked the remonstrances of the estates.[39] Faced with an alliance of estates and parlement, Gassion invoked the support of the governor. Gramont arrived in Pau with an armed guard, broke the parlement's *arrêt* denying Gassion's competence, and threatened to lodge his soldiers in the houses of the magistrates. At the town of Nay, where the parlement's ban against Gassion had been posted, Gramont, according to Lavie's report on the matter, tore up the *arrêt* and said to his carabiniers: "The parlement has nothing but words. I have what it takes (*j'ay des effets*). Here! Use this to load your muskets."[40] Lavie obtained assurances of the parlement's jurisdiction from the royal council, but Gassion's commission remained in force

---

[35]See in general Pierre Delmas, *Du parlement de Navarre et ses origines* (Pau, 1898).
[36]See note 5 above.
[37]ADPA ms. B4538[x], fol. 4r–8v. This, the "secret" register of the parlement, has 73 sheets beginning at one end of the volume, and 78 sheets inverted and beginning from the other end. References to the former are marked[x].
[38]ADPA ms. B4538, fol. 14r–16r.
[39]See above at note 34.
[40]ADPA ms. B4538, fol. 14v.

until 1646. In December 1640 the temporary alliance of estates and parlement broke up when the magistrates tried to stop the deputies voting the governor's gratuity. This time Gramont tore up the parlement's *arrêt* in the hôtel de ville in Pau, in front of the assembled estates and to the sound of trumpets.[41]

Thibaud de Lavie, the son of Bernard, served as *avocat-général* in the parlement of Bordeaux. He was briefly suspended from office and indicted by a colleague for seducing a cousin, marrying her off when pregnant to someone else, and murdering her father. The charges were declared groundless, but the prosecutor, Lavie's rival, was subsequently to win the post of *premier président* at Bordeaux which Lavie coveted. Lavie incurred the wrath of the governor of Guienne, the duc d'Epernon, in 1649 when he led opposition to a tax upon wine. Epernon called him "evil-minded and double-faced."[42] In the Fronde Thibaud de Lavie acted as a deputy to the parlement of Paris in the joint *parlementaire* campaign against Mazarin, and then worked strenuously for the interests of the cardinal-minister. In 1655 he assumed his father's office in Pau. Six years later he became involved in a conflict with the marquis de Poyanne that revealed at once the pride and the pettiness of the robe. The judges would not allow their colleagues in the *chambre des comptes* to sit upon benches near their own in the church where the magistracy worshipped. The *chambre* obtained an order from the royal council to accord them parity, which the parlement refused to obey. Poyanne, who was called upon to execute the order, had the support of the bishop of Lescar, president of the estates, in the installation of the benches. He had a dilatory usher from the parlement roughed up by his men and told a protesting judge that he knew how to deal with rebels, for he was "l'homme du roi."[43] The parlement attended services in another church, and sent an account of the affair to the king, asking for protection against further violence. Lavie defended the parlement in the interminable correspondence that ensued. With these disputes behind him, he was to play a decisive role in repressing the Audijos revolt.

III. CONSEQUENCES OF THE REVOLT

The peasant army assembled by the archpriest of Juncalas at the prompting of Audijos moved from Lavedan down the Gave de Pau towards Lourdes in February 1665. According to four independent sources it consisted of some 6000 men, all determined to exterminate the *gabeleurs*.[44] Heavy snow was

---

[41]Delmas, *Parlement de Navarre*, p. 297.

[42]Théophile Bazot, *Le parlement de Bordeaux et l'avocat-général Thibaud de Lavie* (Bordeaux, 1869), p. 15.

[43]ADPA ms. B4538ˣ, fol. 38r. The affair of the benches occupies fol. 36r–52r.

[44]This is the estimate of Germain d'Antin, Froidour (*Mémoire . . . de Bigorre*, p. 36), the bishop of Tarbes, and Saint-Luc himself. Letters on the Lavedan rising by the latter two men, together

falling when their advance guard approached the city crying "Vive le Roi et Audijos!" No major fighting occurred. Lourdes was already occupied by six companies of dragoons, and negotiations took place until, in early March, Saint-Luc and Pellot arrived with further troops, making a force of 2700. Despite Pellot's urging, Saint-Luc would not march into the valleys in the winter weather without reconnaissance. During this stalemate Gramont's brother, the comte de Toulongeon, worked out an agreement with the peasant leaders. As sénéchal of Bigorre he alone had the trust of the mountaineers, but that was nearly forfeited when Pellot broke the terms and arrested some of the Lavedan deputies, intending to make an example of them. Toulongeon angrily obliged the intendant to release his intended victims and the agreement held. Saint-Luc was able to lead his army on a token march to Argelès and back while the peasant army dispersed. Saint-Luc reported to Colbert that the mountain people were basically loyal and that he had had advice of their refusal of money and arms offered by a Spanish agent, Miguel Joan. On the other hand, Pellot wrote criticising Saint-Luc's weakness and Toulongeon's obstinacy, and regretting that the opportunity to seize and execute the leaders of the valley communities had been let slip. It was Saint-Luc's advice that Colbert and the king followed, for a royal pardon for the men of Lavedan was proclaimed in April. By this time Audijos was long gone, having slipped away to Nay and Lescar in Béarn and recommenced his raids into Chalosse.

There was as much sympathy for Audijos in the town of Bayonne as there was in the high valleys and the rural *plat pays*. A popular song about him could be heard in the streets and had to be banned by the municipal council.[45] His agents organised a revolutionary group among the artisans, but, according to a confession later extracted from one of them, Audijos refused to authorise a revolt in the town when he visited the area. The local merchant oligarchy feared disorder but strenuously resisted Colbert's plan for the gabelle and his scheme to divert to the king's revenues a proportion of the customs dues which the municipality levied under its charter. It maintained its own lobbyist at the royal court and relied upon the intercession of the town governor, Gramont. Thus it proved a considerable embarrassment to the hôtel de ville when a crowd rescued a group of suspects being escorted to prison, and the city authorities had to rescue the guards themselves by pretending they had in turn been arrested. The city pulled every string within its networks of patronage and sent further deputations to protest its loyalty in face of the threat of exemplary punishment demanded by Pellot. It proved impossible to prevent the occupation of the two citadels in the town, but further repression was avoided by rounding up those

with Pellot's reports and an extract from d'Antin's *Petits Mémoires*, are printed by Communay (*Documents*, pp. 160–78).

[45] Communay, *Documents*, p. 211. It was described as "une ordonnance portant deffiances à toutes sortes de personnes de crier par la ville 'vive Daudijos', et de chanter sa chanson."

dissidents who had not fled the city and executing two of them. The intendant busied himself with a scheme to reform the municipal constitution to exclude all popular participation, but it came to nothing.

Pellot's report on the disturbance in Bayonne also expressed the need to chastise further the people of Chalosse, and once more demanded the confiscation of the Salies salt fountain, without which, he contended, Béarn would have to be permanently ringed by guard posts.[46] The intendant again visited the upper Adour valley, where Audijos was still active. He reported that the entire gentry of the area supported the revolt, including the bishop of Aire, whom he described as a troublemaker. Pellot began to punish local notables, razing châteaux where Audijos had been sheltered, quartering troops upon the royal lieutenant of Saint-Sever, Louis de Barry, baron de Batz, and hanging the royal *prévôt* there, Pierre de Borrit, who was said to have entertained the rebel leader.[47] In June 1665 Audijos fought an indecisive battle in the woods near Hagetmau. Then he withdrew to Orthez in Béarn, where Poyanne and the one officer who pursued Audijos with energy, Lieutenant Nogent, failed to apprehend him. In July Audijos was surrounded in a house at La Bastide-Villefranche on the Béarnais border, but he made a daring escape, leaving his wounded second-in-command to be executed. By this time a German officer with long experience in the king's service, Graf von Podewiltz, had been placed in general command of the dragoons, who traversed Béarn at will.[48] Audijos ascended the Ossau valley and escaped to Spain. He was taken in by the man who had offered Spanish support for the peasant army of Lavedan, Miguel Joan. Joan was constantly in touch with his friends in the valleys from his house at Sallent, a few miles south of the border.

From April 1665 the *abrégé* of the estates began to receive a series of complaints against harassment of village communities in north Béarn by the guards of the convoy and against orders served on Béarnais citizens to appear before Pellot's tribunal.[49] In one instance a gentleman of Montagut, who protested against the invasion of his house and the molesting of his daughter, had been seized and taken to Saint-Sever. A notary who began legal proceedings for the violation of Béarnais jurisdiction was himself arrested on orders from Pellot. Groups of people from Montaner and Navailles, villages in Béarn where Audijos had found refuge, were arbitrarily taken to prison in Chalosse. On the suggestion of the bishop of Lescar, the *abrégé* made a strong appeal to Poyanne and Gramont. The parlement also began to protest, Lavie writing to both Pellot and Colbert on the violation of the *fors*. Pellot started to issue his agents with writs of *pareatis*, applying to one jurisdiction an ordinance that had been regis-

[46]*Ibid.*, p. 206.
[47]*Ibid.*, pp. 179, 196, 216; Laborde-Péboué, *Relation véritable*, p. 550.
[48]Communay, *Documents*, pp. 259, 263.
[49]ADPA ms. C724 (*Breve de las assemblades des seigneurs deputats labrege des estats, 1659–1670*).

tered in another. Perhaps through the intervention of Gramont, Pellot briefly changed tack. In May he released the prisoners from Navailles and Montaner and ordered his officers to show more respect for legal formalities.[50]

The parlement was placed in a difficult position in its defence of the *fors*. It resented the traditional claims of the estates to be the guardian of provincial immunities, but it could not afford to flout an enraged public opinion by failing to support the *abrégé* on this issue. At the same time its own primary role was as guardian of law and order, and Audijos had been branded by the king as an outlaw, and a price put on his head. Pellot was at first sceptical of the parlement's ability to act against the rebels. He told Colbert that the seditious knew they had little to fear from the magistrates, that the prisoners taken by the latter were simple wretches whose indictment was merely a face-saving device, and that the parlement's real interest was to obstruct those who served the king.[51] However, Lavie saw an opportunity to humiliate his rival, the vicomte de Poudenx, syndic of the estates. As mentioned earlier, Poudenx had been placed in a dilemma by a royal commission ordering him to act against Audijos. Lavie complained about the syndic's failure to submit his warrant for registration by the parlement, and did not hide his view that, in any case, Poudenx was inadequate for the task. Representing himself as the rightful executor of the law, Lavie wrote late in July 1665 to one of the *jurats* of Oloron, regretting that the local authorities were obeying Poudenx instead of himself.[52] At this moment Pellot was reporting to Colbert that, while the syndic was making some show of executing his commission, he was really to blame for allowing Audijos to escape via the Ossau. Poudenx wrote to Colbert to justify himself and to complain that Lavie was subverting the authority with which the king had empowered him: "Monseigneur, I most humbly beg you to be persuaded . . . of the sincerity of my intentions, and kindly make this clear to the king, whatever care the *premier président* of Navarre takes to have them interpreted in a bad light."[53]

Pellot derived some wry amusement from this battle between the leading officials of the two bodies he regarded as inimical to his own authority, but he had to admit that Lavie was acting effectively against Audijos. Early in August he told Colbert that the first president had taken over from Poyanne and Poudenx the main role of suppressing the rebel movement in Béarn: "He has had decrees issued by the parlement to run headlong (*courir sus*) against Audijos and his accomplices. He has commanded the militia to arrest them in the passes: he has had two of them captured."[54] At the same time Pellot had had too much experience of friction between intendants and parlements to expect the magistrates of Pau to become his willing agents. The parlement jealously

[50]Ferron, *Daudeyos*, pp. 484–5.
[51]Communay, *Documents*, p. 248.
[52]*Ibid.*, pp. 286–7.
[53]*Ibid.*, p. 278.
[54]*Ibid.*, p. 284.

defended its own jurisdiction, maintaining, despite the fact that it was not a purely Béarnais institution, that under the *fors* a man of Béarn must be judged by his countrymen and not by an external tribunal. Pellot assumed that any criminal act connected with Audijos, wherever it had been perpetrated, must be dealt with by his personal court, and he was angered not only by Lavie's insistence upon trying Béarnais suspects but also by his refusal to send them to the intendant for interrogation.

The first president condescendingly offered Pellot the opportunity to attend the trial in Pau of the suspects he had arrested. In the letter to Colbert in which he made this proposal he remarked that he had already suggested to Pellot's understudy in Montauban, the *subdélégué* Carratan, that the latter could interrogate the prisoners on Béarnais territory, and also that he had made arrangements with Podewiltz for them to be escorted to the border where they might be confronted with suspects held by Pellot and Carratan to the north. Had the bishop of Lescar known of this plan, he would hardly have approved of Lavie's tacit acknowledgement of the presence of the dragoons in Béarn, which he held to be also contrary to the *fors*. The intendant was angered by the discovery that not only had the parlement at Pau refused to release the prisoners to him, but it had declared the instructions for interrogation issued by Carratan to be *ultra vires* in Béarn. For his part, Poudenx, who seems to have settled his differences with Lavie, wrote apologetically to Saint-Luc to say that he would be delighted to hand over the prisoners to Pellot, were it not for an undertaking he had given to the first president.[55]

Pellot continued to demand jurisdiction in Béarn, repeating his earlier assertion that the parlement's obstinacy was sponsored by its desire to defend local communities in the province. He now proposed a new invasion of the *fors*, suggesting that those villages in Béarn which had sheltered Audijos should be forced to pay *amendes* which could contribute to the cost of the troops. At the end of August the central government upheld the jurisdictional rights of the parlement of Navarre, but ordered the prisoners to be made available to Pellot for questioning. This was less of a compromise than it seemed, for the *amendes* were also authorised. The intendant once more began to praise Lavie's zeal, and in due course reported the cruel fate of those judged both by him in Chalosse and by Lavie in Béarn. The first president had in fact realised his ambition to assume a role beyond his judicial capacity. Late in September he went to Saint-Sever to consult with Pellot and Podewiltz about the future conduct of the campaign of repression.[56]

While the intendant and the first president vied with each other in the ferocity of their punishments, the *abrégé* protested vigorously against Carratan's orders that representatives from Béarnais communities should be sent to him

---

[55]*Ibid.*, pp. 294–6, 299, 300–1.
[56]*Ibid.*, pp. 312–13, 317, 320–1, 330–1, 338.

for general interrogation. Lavie had used the indignation of the estates as a lever in his letter to Colbert on this subject. When the estates suggested a joint commission to defend the *fors*, Lavie, sensing perhaps that many of his own colleagues did not approve of his co-operation with the intendant, offered no objections. It was at this time, early September 1665, that the bishop of Lescar sent to Colbert an eloquent protest outlining the three ways in which the immunities of Béarn had been abrogated: the external interrogations, the denial of Béarnais justice, and the sending of troops into the province without verification of their commissions by the parlement. The bishop stated that he was to head a deputation including members of the nobility and the third estate. "I understand," he went on, "that the parlement will send its own delegates, since we find ourselves in the same boat, and the novelties that have given rise to my deputation have wounded the jurisdiction of the parlement no less than they have violated the privileges of the province."[57] Reminding the king that he and his predecessors had sworn to preserve the *fors* of Béarn by a special oath, he declared:

With this buckler this province has always defended itself against all kinds of novelties and extraordinary charges, and kings have been so touched by the most humble remonstrances made to their majesties upon this subject that, on every occasion when they have been presented, our privileges have been preserved to this very day, this province never having been unworthy of the contract (*engagement*) under which our princes have been very willing to agree to maintain the said privileges.[58]

These words echoed the past resolutions and remonstrances of the estates of Béarn, and, if they were more emphatic than some earlier protests, their daring in this respect was born of the realisation that the crisis in constitutional relationships provoked by the Audijos rising was more severe than any since the years 1617–20. They must have seemed an affront to a king as conscious of his dignity as Louis XIV, and yet they were answered with benevolent platitudes, assuring continued respect for the *fors* and appreciation of the loyalty of the people of Béarn. Such was the magic of the crown that these empty formulae were much valued, despite the fact that by the time they were received seventeen Béarnais communities faced *amendes* amounting to 49,000 livres. The full estates met at Sauveterre on 24 November 1665, when the bishop of Lescar proposed that the province as a whole should bear the charges. The issue was long debated. Although his view carried much weight in the upper house, the argument of the third estate prevailed, namely, that if the estates accepted responsibility for the levies, they would endorse the very violation of the *fors* against which the bishop had protested.[59]

The Audijos revolt seemed to have run its course. No new troops entered

[57]*Ibid*, p. 326.
[58]*Ibid.*, p. 327.
[59]ADPA ms. C727, fol. 200r–207r.

Béarn after August 1665, and the occupation was much milder than its counterpart in Chalosse. Inspired by a gratuity from the town of Orthez, Podewiltz
maintained good discipline and even received the formal thanks of the estates.[60] A detachment under Lieutenant Nogent twice tried unsuccessfully to
cross the frontier to seize Audijos in Sallent. Pellot discovered more and more
about the rebel organisation as the dual inducements of torture and reward had
their effect upon the followers of Audijos. The extent of the conspiracy in
Bayonne was revealed, and a leading citizen, Jacques Lalande de Luc, was
exiled by *lettre de cachet*. Convinced that Gramont's officers in Hagetmau had
incited the original sedition, the intendant asked Colbert for permission to
prosecute. His unwonted caution in this instance was prompted by fear of
Gramont's influence, and the governor did in fact ensure that Pellot received
no answer to his request. The intendant also received no reply to his demand
for authority to proceed against Poudenx, who, according to one of Pellot's
victims, had had three meetings with Audijos after the murder of Boiset.
Poyanne, too, was the subject of accusations, but Pellot contented himself with
branding the lieutenant-general's lack of action as "une grande et blasmable
négligence," stimulated by his desire to block the establishment of the bureaux.[61]

In November 1665 Podewiltz's troops were withdrawn, leaving garrisons only
in Bayonne, Dax, Lourdes and Saint-Jean-Pied-de-Port. The king issued a
general amnesty in the following month, excepting only Audijos and ten of his
followers. Pellot's tribunals ceased to operate in 1666, for the parlement of
Bordeaux sent one of its judges to preside over the trial of those excluded from
the amnesty and those who committed subsequent attacks on the guards of the
convoy. There continued to be a few incidents of the latter kind,[62] but the
authorities seemed determined to maintain that the revolt was over. During the
summer of 1666 the royal council decided on several contentious issues affect-
ing Bayonne. These were all resolved in the city's favour, for once again it was
Gramont's advice, and not Pellot's, that was accepted. Bayonne kept its old
constitution; it was not obliged to build a new gate in the town walls for the
convenience of the royal garrison;[63] and Lalande de Luc was allowed to return
from exile. Colbert gave early warning of these decisions to Pellot, so that he
might swallow his pride and hypocritically pretend that he had obtained for
Bayonne concessions which in fact he had bitterly opposed.[64]

The terms of the December amnesty suggested that the king's grace had

[60]Ferron, *Daudeyos*, p. 511.
[61]Communay, *Documents*, pp. 340–1.
[62]*Ibid.*, p. 365; J. Fr. d'Estalenx, *Un adversaire du rebelle Audijos* (Dax, 1938). The author of the
latter work describes an affray between one of his ancestors and Audijos in January 1666.
[63]The relatively trivial matter of the gate involved expensive deputations, a vast correspondence,
and the attention of several ministers individually and in council. Communay, *Documents*, pp. 359,
368, 370–5 etc.
[64]*Ibid.*, p. 392.

been extended to a society which had been guilty of sedition as a whole. For Pellot this was probably not far from the truth, but neither the Bayonne council nor the estates of Béarn would accept so sweeping a condemnation.[65] The momentary co-operation between estates and parlement that had enabled joint discussion in defence of the *fors* in the previous September collapsed when it became known that the parlement had registered the amnesty in March 1666 without questioning its implications. This matter preoccupied the estates meeting in Oloron in June. Hostility between the two institutions again began to grow, exploding in an unprecedented clash two years later.

A few more leading members of Audijos's band were caught in the second half of 1666. One revealed under torture that Audijos himself had been living in secret near his home town of Coudures since December 1665.[66] The leader's part in the occasional attacks on the convoy after that date was not clearly established, nor were his subsequent hiding places in France ever known. There were sufficient incidents, however, and enough official fear of a new revolt, for the soldiers to be sent back into Chalosse for the period March–September 1667. At some point Audijos recrossed the Pyrenees into Spain. From time to time he was rumoured to be in the valleys, and in January 1675 it was said that he was at the head of 500 men in Lavedan. In July that year he was granted a royal pardon, and in September he appeared before the parlement of Bordeaux, kneeling with leg irons and bared head, to make his *amende*.[67] This was merely pantomime, for Audijos had also been given a brevet to command a regiment recruited from his followers. In 1677 he died leading his regiment on campaign in Sicily.

Other Pyrenean revolts against the agents of the gabelle flared up in this period. From July 1668 to April 1669 the salt-smuggling Miquelets defied an attempt to impose the gabelle in the upper valleys of the two rivers of Roussillon, the Tech and the Têt. The problem was very like that presented by Audijos. The intendant Maqueron wrote to Colbert: "Although there seemed at first to be only two or three of these rogues, all the peoples of the mountain [the Canigou] have the same aversion as they for the guards of the gabelle."[68] This revolt also shows that Lavie's desire to take command of the forces of repression was felt by others of the robe. In the newly acquired province of Roussillon a judicial *conseil souverain* had been established. Its president and two judges led an armed column into the valleys, only to be ambushed and forced back in disorder. At the other extremity of the Pyrenees an armed revolt occurred in Labourd during the first three months of 1671. There is no evidence of the participation of Audijos in this rising, although it has been speculated that he was in touch with Jacques Roure, the leader of a major rebellion in

[65]*Ibid.*, pp. 368–9; Ferron, *Daudeyos*, pp. 512–14.
[66]Communay, *Documents*, p. 401.
[67]*Ibid.*, pp. 421, 423–4.
[68]Depping, *Correspondance*, vol. I, p. 179.

Vivarais in 1670. Roure was arrested at Saint-Jean-Pied-de-Port when attempting to reach Spain.[69]

New personalities emerged in Guienne and Béarn in the aftermath of the active period of the Audijos movement. The marquis de Poyanne had responded to criticism and taken a positive part in the repression in Saint-Sever, Dax and Lannes in 1666. He had been mentioned by Pellot as someone who could negotiate with Audijos when the intendant had proposed that the rebel leader be pardoned on condition that he went to America. Pellot praised him in his dispatches on several occasions at this time.[70] Poyanne died in 1667, to be succeeded by his son. In the following year the marshal-duke handed over the governorship of Béarn to his own son, Armand de Gramont, comte de Guiche. He had hoped that Toulongeon would exercise a moderating influence on Guiche, but Toulongeon showed a spirit just as autocratic as his nephew's when in 1672 he waged a campaign as sénéchal of Bigorre against the powers assumed by the president of the estates, the bishop of Tarbes.[71] Pellot himself was reassigned and removed from the ranks of intendants. Among his successes were the crushing of the revolt, the establishment of the bureaux on the Adour to stop the salt-smuggling, and the breaking of the Béarnais *fors* by the dispatch of dragoons and the levying of *amendes*. Among his failures were his plans to remodel the government of Bayonne, to exert his judicial power in Béarn, to confiscate the Salies salt fountain,[72] and to impose the gabelle itself in the *pays rédimés*. In these matters Gramont's influence combined with local resistance had proved too strong for him. At the beginning of 1669 Pellot was appointed *premier président* of the parlement of Rouen, and replaced by a more equitable intendant, Daguesseau. Finally, the marquis de Saint-Luc, who had earned the respect of all parties in armed revolt and constitutional conflict, died in April 1670.

IV. POSTSCRIPT

The appearance of the new governor in Pau to open the estates in August 1668 began a new conflict that serves as a postscript to the rivalry of parlement and estates evident in the course of the Audijos rising. The parallel rivalry between governor or lieutenant-general on the one hand and intendant on the other was not a feature of the events that followed. In the eyes of both governor and estates, the parlement was tainted by its co-operation with the intendant. Now, when the governor set out deliberately to humiliate the court and its first president, the estates, remembering the role of the magistrates in the affair of

[69]Borziex et al., *Révoltes populaires*, p. 249; Communay, *Documents*, pp. 417–19.
[70]*Ibid.*, pp. 393, 400, 415.
[71]Depping, *Correspondance*, vol. 1, p. xxiii.
[72]The salt fountain was eventually appropriated by the crown in 1681.

the amnesty, took advantage of the occasion to denounce the parlement as the great Judas, the ultimate betrayer of provincial liberties.

Religious tensions played little or no part in the Audijos revolt; but they were a habitual part of Béarnais life. Lavie shared Pellot's desire to act vigorously against the Huguenots, despite their rights under Richelieu's settlement of the problem in 1629 and the continued renewal of the Edict of Nantes by the crown. Many Protestants sat in the estates. Perhaps half the population of Pau were Huguenots, and a majority of the *avocats* pleading before the Catholic judges of the parlement were also of the reformed faith. The advent of Louis XIV to personal rule was accompanied by a "strict" interpretation of the edict of toleration. In April 1668 a royal edict suppressed more than half of the forty-three authorised places of Protestant worship in Béarn. While this suited the Catholic temper of the parlement,[73] the judges bitterly resented a clause that removed cognisance of religious disputes from the court and bestowed it upon the governor's personal council. At the opening of the 1668 estates Guiche, despite his father's warnings, had wilfully slighted Lavie on every ceremonial occasion, and the first president had responded with subtle insults against the governor's pomp and circumstance.[74] The dispute over the edict concerning the Protestants was embittered by this personal animosity. Three times the parlement was ordered to register the royal edict and three times it refused. A few weeks after the opening of the estates it submitted to a fourth demand, and in revenge disallowed *règlements* from the estates approved by Guiche on the king's behalf. This was the context in which the estates composed a declaration stating:

The parlement has destroyed almost all the ancient liberties of the *pays*, and, although it is one of the newest parlements in the kingdom, it knows as expertly as the older courts every means of exhausting the purse of pleaders and of rendering such litigation eternal.[75]

Behind this piece of polemic was not only the layman's detestation for the proliferation of the robe and the civil suits that choked the courts: it also expressed resentment at the supposed betrayal of the *fors* by a new institution that had dared to challenge the rôle of the venerable estates. The parlement, whose establishment had accompanied the union with France under Louis XIII, served as scapegoat. The intendant was silent; the governor was secure in

[73]The catholicity of the bench in Pau can be ascertained from *Notes secrètes sur le personnel de tous les parlements et cours des comptes du royaume envoyées par les intendants des provinces à Colbert sur sa demande vers la fin de l'an 1663* in Depping, *Correspondance*, vol. 2, pp. 114–16.
[74]André Poumarède, *Un conflit de prestige et d'autorité à Paus sous Louis XIV: le gouverneur, Armand de Gramont, comte de Guiche, contre le premier président du parlement de Navarre, Thibaud de Lavie* (Melun, 1966), pp. 7–10.
[75]Léon Cadier, *Documents inédits* (Pau, 1918), pp. 132–4, cited by Poumarède, *Conflit de prestige*, p. 21.

the affections of the estates; and the king was placated by the voting of a subsidy.[76]

Not content with this victory, Armand de Gramont had his council quash the parlement's condemnation of a pastor who had insulted the Catholic clergy. He even issued an order denying Lavie the courtesy title of Monseigneur. Lavie appealed to the royal council against *l'autoritarisme* of the governor, who, he said, was trying to emulate the king in pomp and power. He contended that Guiche had revived the troublesome ambitions of the estates, and converted his own council into a tribunal whose jurisdiction exceeded that of the parlement. The authority of a governor, he asserted, was confined to military matters. Responsibility for *la police générale* should rest not with the governor, but with the parlement. This argument revealed the full extent of *parlementaire* ambition. Supported by submissions to the royal council by deputies of the estates of Béarn, Guiche sent his response in May 1670. He claimed it was his duty to keep order and, of necessity, he had to quarrel with those who sought to profit from the troubles they created. He spoke not just with his own voice but through "a general harmony composed of all the communities of the province." Lavie was accused of cruelty and injustice, and the court over which he presided was said to be tainted with corruption.[77]

Antoine de Gramont praised his son's letter. As the intermediary at court for the institutions of Béarn he also felt obliged to use his influence to obtain for Lavie an interview with the king which he knew in advance would be unproductive. In this he was doing no more than continuing the methods that had proved so successful in defending local interests in Gascony against Pellot. In contrast to his father and his son, the marshal-duke preferred to outflank his opponents by subtle manoeuvres rather than assaulting them in a frontal attack. Politics, he knew, was the constant adjustment of interests, the public good a harmonising of private aspiration. Influence and clientage were the real means of exercising power, the institutions of state a facade to facilitate their internal operation. These attitudes pervaded the highest circles at the court of Louis XIV. However the king might posture as an absolute sovereign, and whatever he might write in his *Mémoires for the Instruction of the Dauphin* on the need to keep to the letter of one's promises when dealing with provincial bodies,[78] he governed by compromises and hollow phrases. It was not so much rule by command as manipulation.

The decision of the royal council on 15 September 1670 in the dispute between Guiche and Lavie demonstrated these truths. The governor could keep his ceremonial pomp. The parlement's rights vis-à-vis the estates would

---

[76]*Ibid.*
[77]These exchanges are contained in Bibliothèque Nationale ms. fonds français 4108, and are summarised by Poumarède, *Conflit de prestige*, pp. 23–8.
[78]Major, *Representative Government*, pp. 631–2.

be maintained, but it was for the governor to report abuses. The jurisdiction of the governor's council over cases arising from the edict of toleration would continue, at least temporarily, but the governor should act in association with the intendant in reaching verdicts.[79] This ruling also happened to involve all the bases of institutional authority that had been in play in the course of the Audijos revolt. Reactions to the revolt had taken the form of a continuous jostling between instruments of government (and, more particularly, the men who represented them) in a situation where the powers of one intermingled and overlapped with those of others. In the heyday of Louis XIV's centralising absolutism the results had been surprising. The extension of the fisc had been successfully resisted despite a massive display of military force and arbitrary judicial procedures; independent local bodies had remained intact; and an audacious rebel had become the commander of a royal regiment. Even absolutism, it seems, was obliged to govern through consent.

[79]Poumarède, *Conflit de prestige,* p. 29.

Index

Index

Index

Maqueron (intendant), 288
Marchand (Paris militia colonel), 259, 261
Marguerite d'Angoulême, 75
Mariana, Juan de, 180, 185
Maria Theresa, Queen, 270
Marie de Médicis, 12, 68, 100, 105, 107, 112, 113, 115, 186
Marillac, Michel de, 191–2
Marot, Clément, 75
Marseille, 209
Marsilius of Padua, 142, 185
Marsous, 278
"Martin Marprelate," 175
Marxism, 3–7, 23, 192–5
Mary Queen of Scots, 140, 144–5, 167
Mary Tudor, 162
Masson, Papire, 126
Matelas (curé of Moncayolle), 278
Matharel, Antoine, 126, 130
Maurice of Nassau, 100, 103, 112, 113, 114
Maxwell, John, 144
Mayenne, Charles, duc de, 89, 91, 92, 146, 265
  governor of Burgundy, 237
  lieutenant general of the League, 77, 248
  satirical criticism of, 86–7, 93
  and Sixteen, 78, 241, 244, 249–57, 259–62, 266
Mayneville, seigneur de, 241
Mazarin, Jules, cardinal de, 18, 20, 191, 195, 201, 208, 281
Mazières, 106
Medici, Lorenzo, II, de', 62
Meinecke, Friedrich, 9, 98–9, 103, 108, 116
Mende, 224
Menippean satire, 12, 46, 50–1, 75–6, 84–94, 95, 97
Menippus of Gadara, 75, 85
mentalité, 5–7
Mercuer, 221
Merle, Mathieu de, 224
Messier, Jean, 253
métayage, 209–10
Mettam, Roger, 22
Michel, Jean, 251
Michelet, Georges, 242, 243
Michelet, Jules, 5, 17, 99, 236, 277
Midorge, Jean, 251
Milhaud, 106
Milton, John, 151
Minager, Olivier, 242, 257
Miquelets, *see* popular revolts
mixed government, 38, 124, 129–31
Molina, Luis, 152
Mongeot, Jean de, 257, 260
Monluc, Blaise de, 99

Montagu, James, 187
Montagut, 283
Montaigne, Michel de, 14, 29, 45, 47–9, 50, 51, 52, 53, 64, 65, 97
Montaner, 283–4
Montauban, 106, 270, 276, 279
Mont-de-Marsan, 268, 270
Montesquieu, Charles de Secondat, baron de, 2, 14, 54
Montjol (Paris militia captain), 257
Montmorency, Henri II, duc de, 106
Montpellier, 104–5
Montpensier, Catherine, duchesse de, 83, 86
Montpensier, François, duc de, 66
More, Sir Thomas, 33, 75
Morin, Guillaume, 253, 255, 257
Morlaas, 279
Mornay, Philippe Duplessis, 40, 67, 119, 136, 144, 167
Morril, J. S., 21
Mortaigne, 56
Morton, Thomas, 138, 151, 184
Motin, Pierre, 97
Moulins, 193, 205–6
Mousnier, Roland, 20, 191–2, 195–9, 206, 208, 210, 211, 235
Muret, Marc-Antoine, 36, 37, 43–4, 48, 52, 62, 65

Nantes, edict of, 70, 71, 175, 290
natural law theory, 138, 140–1, 146–7, 150, 152–4
Navailles, 283–4
Navarre, 268, 271, 279
Nay, 280, 282
neostoicism, *see* stoicism
Nérac, treaty of, 220, 223, 225, 228
Néret, Denis, 260
Nero, 38, 44, 79
Neufville, Simon de, 33
Neuilly, Etienne de, 241, 247, 248, 254, 257, 260, 261
Nevers, Charles de Gonzague, duc de, 114
Nevers, Louis de Gonzague, duc de, 42
Nicolas, Jean, 257
Nîmes, 106, 232
Nizzoli, Mario, 37, 43
Noailles (governor of Rouergue), 204–5
Nogent, Lieutenant, 283, 287
Normandy, 208
Numa Pompilius, 149

oath of allegiance controversy, 16, 70, 156, 184–5
Ockham, William of, 139
Oestreich, Gerhard, 13

Index